Alastair
Sawday's

Special Places
to Stay

British
Hotels & Inns

"Sawday's promises to provide
more than just a bed for the night"

The Guardian

INSPECTED & SELECTED
by **Sawday's**
SPECIAL PLACES

Alastair
Sawday's

Special Places

Pubs & Inns
of England & Wales

"Sawday's ... champions the local,
the personal and the authentic"

The Guardian

INSPECTED & SELECTED
by **Sawday's**
SPECIAL PLACES

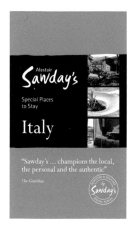

Alastair
Sawday's

Special Places
to Stay

Italy

"Sawday's ... champions the local,
the personal and the authentic"

The Guardian

INSPECTED & SELECTED
by **Sawday's**
SPECIAL PLACES

Alastair
Sawday's

Special Places
to Stay

Dog-friendly
Breaks in Britain

Foreword by
Adam Henson

INSPECTED & SELECTED
by **Sawday's**
SPECIAL PLACES

Alastair
Sawday's

Twenty-first edition
Copyright © 2016
Alastair Sawday Publishing Co. Ltd
Published in September 2016
ISBN-13: 978-1-906136-78-9

Alastair Sawday Publishing Co. Ltd,
Merchants House, Wapping Road,
Bristol BS1 4RW, UK
Tel: +44 (0)117 204 7810
Email: info@sawdays.co.uk
Web: www.sawdays.co.uk

The Globe Pequot Press,
P. O. Box 480, Guilford,
Connecticut 06437, USA
Tel: +1 203 458 4500
Email: info@globepequot.com
Web: www.globepequot.com

Series Editor Alastair Sawday
Editor Wendy Ogden
Assistant to Editor Lianka Varga
Senior Picture Editor Alec Studerus
Production Coordinators Lianka Varga,
Sarah Frost Mellor
Writing Wendy Ogden, Jo Boissevain,
Nicola Crosse
Inspections Mandy Barnes, Sue Birtwistle,
Sarah Bray, Sophie Gore Browne,
Emma Bullard, Nicola Crosse,
Peter Evans, Julie Franklin,
Catherine Gledhill, Donald Greig,
Becca Harris, Auriol Marson,
Wendy Ogden, Abbe Opher
*Thanks also to others who did an inspection
or write-up or two.*
Marketing & PR
0117 204 7801
marketing@sawdays.co.uk

*We have made every effort to ensure the accuracy
of the information in this book at the time
of going to press. However, we cannot accept
any responsibility for any loss, injury or
inconvenience resulting from the use of information
contained therein.*

Production: Pagebypage Co Ltd
Maps: Maidenhead Cartographic Services
Printing: Pureprint, Uckfield
UK distribution: The Travel Alliance, Bath
dmcentee@morriscontentalliance.com

Cover photo credits.
Front 1. Well Farm, entry 173 2. Bay House, entry 48 3. Dunhill Barn, entry 186

Back: 1. Trewornan Manor, entry 32 2. Hillview Cottage, entry 358 3. The Dovecote at Greenaway, entry 404

Spine: Archerton, entry 113

Alastair Sawday's

Special Places to Stay

British
Bed & Breakfast

4   Contents

taste and subjective opinion. We find great places and then tell the truth about them which is why our guests trust us. We're not very much interested in the 'creeping boutique' world of the 'luxury' B&B – although some of our Special Places are undoubtedly luxurious. Rather we like to champion those places where the owners have let their own personality and character be stamped right through them like a stick of Brighton rock and who then open their doors for open-minded folk to join in the fun. Usually guests leave feeling like friends.

We therefore especially cherish our B&B owners: you'll find lovers of people, guardians of our beautiful countryside, supporters of local industry, farmers, artists, cooks and gardeners. They are a richly talented lot and we have them in Italy, Ireland, Portugal, Spain and France too – a wonderful community of like-minded, generous people who share one great quality: they love having others in their houses. For travellers this is a priceless gift, and we urge you to accept it.

If you had told me years ago that the demand for B&B might rise by more than 10%, I would have doubted your sanity. But a damn has burst: countless more people are staying in others' houses now. These are exciting times for a company that has been 'gathering' Special houses and Special people for over 20 years.

In the hubbub and hullabaloo we remain a calm voice of discrimination, interesting

We have vast and tiny houses, ancient and modern, plush and Spartan. Many are beautiful; all are fascinating. We are happy that many of our owners enjoy Sawday guests so much that they are still Sawday owners after over 20 years. They, and their places, are a treat in store if you haven't yet tried them.

Alastair Sawday

It's simple. There are no rules, no boxes to tick. We choose places that we like and are fiercely subjective in our choices. We also recognise that one person's idea of special is not necessarily someone else's so there is a huge variety of places, and prices, in the book. Those who are familiar with our *Special Places* series know that we look for comfort, originality, authenticity, and reject the insincere, the anonymous and the banal. The way guests are treated comes as high on our list as the setting, the architecture, the atmosphere and the food.

Inspections

We visit every place in the guide to get a feel for how both house and owner tick. We don't take a clipboard and we don't have a list of what is acceptable and what is not. Instead, we chat for an hour or so with the owner and look round. It's all very informal, but it gives us an excellent idea of who would enjoy staying there. If the visit happens to be the last of the day, we may stay the night. Once in the book properties are sometimes re-inspected, to keep things fresh and accurate.

Feedback

In between inspections we rely on feedback from our army of readers, as well as from staff members who are encouraged to visit properties across the series. This feedback is invaluable to us and we always follow up on comments. So do tell us whether your stay has been a joy or not, if the atmosphere was great

or stuffy, the owners cheery or bored. The accuracy of the book depends on what you, and our inspectors, tell us. A lot of the new entries in each edition are recommended by our readers, so keep telling us about new places you've discovered too. Please email us at info@sawdays.co.uk to tell us about your discoveries.

However, please do not tell us if the bedside light was broken, or the shower head was scummy. Tell the owner, immediately, and get them to do something about it. Most owners are more than happy to correct problems and

Photo: Yew Tree House, entry 198

will bend over backwards to help. Far better than bottling it up and then writing to us a week later!

Subscriptions

Owners pay to appear in this guide. Their fee goes towards the high costs of inspecting, developing our website and producing an all-colour book. We only include places that we like and find special for one reason or another, so it is not possible for anyone to buy their way onto these pages. Nor is it possible for the owner to write their own description. We will say if the bedrooms are small, or if a main road is near. We do our best to avoid misleading people.

Disclaimer

We make no claims to pure objectivity in choosing these places. They are here simply because we like them. Our opinions and tastes are ours alone and this book is a statement of them; we hope you will share them. We have done our utmost to get our facts right but apologise unreservedly for any mistakes that may have crept in.

You should know that we don't check such things as fire regulations, swimming pool security or any other laws with which owners of properties receiving paying guests should comply. This is the responsibility of the owners.

Photo above: Westbrook Court, entry 203
Photo right: Seabreeze, entry 489

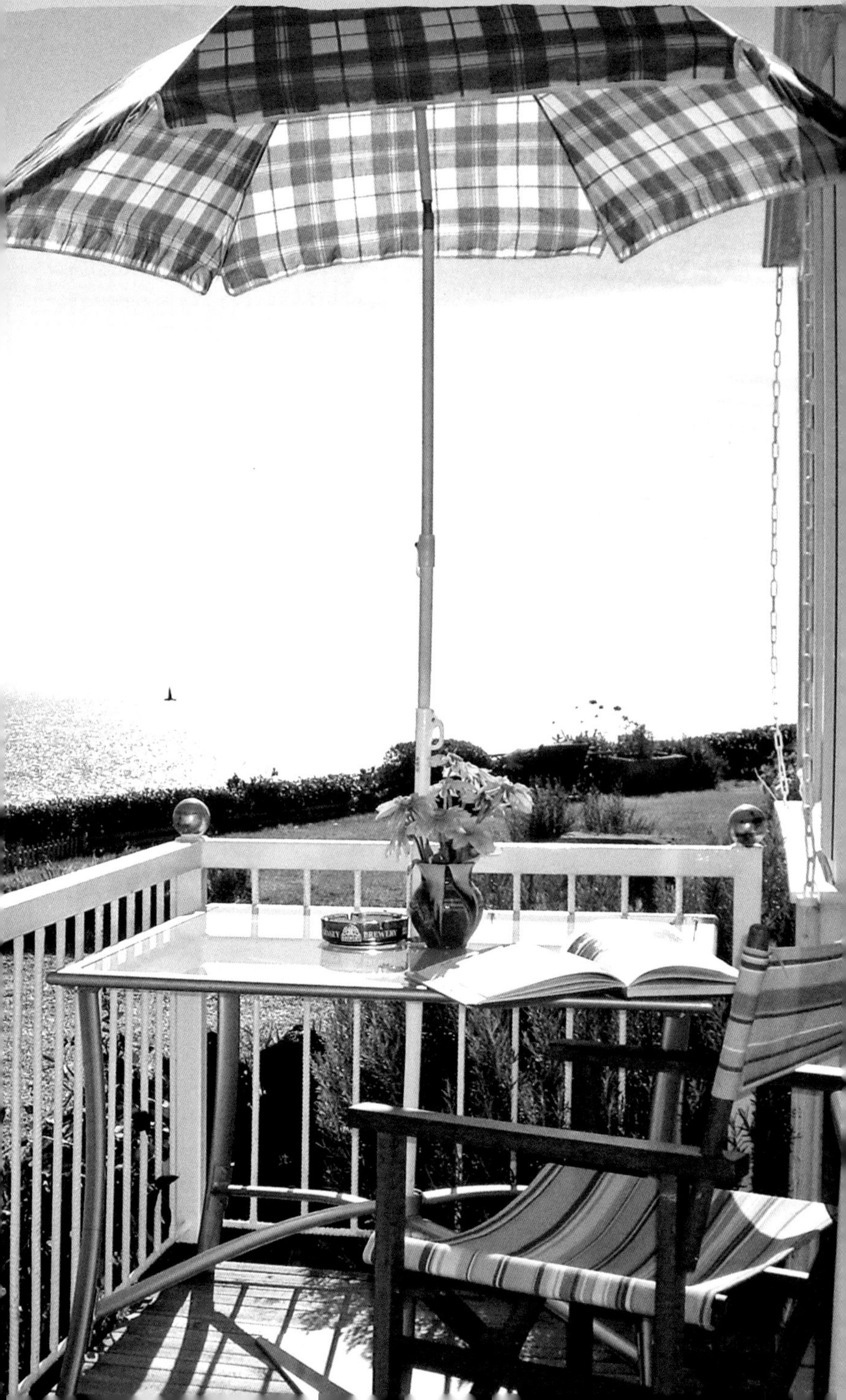

Maps

Each property is flagged with its entry number on the maps at the front. These maps are a great starting point for planning your trip, but please don't use them as anything other than a general guide – use a decent road map for real navigation. Most places will send you detailed instructions once you have booked your stay.

Symbols

Below each entry you will see some symbols, which are explained at the very back of the book. They are based on the information given to us by the owners. However, things do change: bikes may be under repair or a new pool may have been put in. Please use the symbols as a guide rather than an absolute statement of fact and double-check anything that is important to you – owners occasionally bend their own rules, so it's worth asking if you may take your child or dog even if they don't have the symbol.

Finding the right place for you

All these places are special in one way or another. All have been visited and then written about honestly so that you can take what you like and leave the rest. Those of you who swear by Sawday's books trust our write-ups precisely because we don't have a blanket standard; we include places simply because we like them. But we all have different priorities, so do read the descriptions carefully and pick out the places where you will be comfortable. If something is particularly important to you then do check when you book: a simple question or two can avoid misunderstandings.

Children – The ᵀ symbol shows places which are happy to accept children of all ages. This does not mean that they will necessarily have cots, high chairs, etc. If an owner welcomes children but only those above a certain age, we have put these details at the end of their write-up. These houses do not have the child symbol, but even these folk may accept your younger child if you are the only guests. Many who say no to children do so not because they don't like them but because they may have a steep stair, an unfenced pond or they find balancing the needs of mixed age groups too challenging.

Pets – Our 🐕 symbol shows places which are happy to accept pets. Do let the owners know when booking that you'd like to bring your pet – particularly if it is not the usual dog! Be realistic about your pet – if it is nervous or excitable or doesn't like the company of other dogs, people, chickens, children, then say so.

Owners' pets – The 🐈 symbol is given when the owners have their own pet on the premises. It may not be a cat! But it is there to warn you that you may be greeted by a dog, serenaded by a parrot, or indeed sat upon by a cat.

Quick reference indices
At the back of the book you'll find a number of quick reference indices that will help you choose the place that is just right for you.

In this edition you'll find listings of properties where:
• at least one bedroom or bathroom is accessible for wheelchair users
• children of all ages are welcome. Cots, highchairs etc are not necessarily available
• credit cards are accepted
• there are vegetarian meal options (arrange in advance)
• guests' pets are welcome

Types of places

Some houses have rooms in annexes or stables, barns or garden 'wings', some of which feel part of the house, some of which don't. If you have a strong preference for being in the throng or for being apart, check those details. Consider your surroundings when you are packing: large, ancient country houses may be cooler than you are used to; city places and working farms may be noisy at times; and that peacock or cockerel we mention may disturb you. Light sleepers should pack ear plugs, and take a dressing gown if there's a separate bathroom (though these are sometimes provided).

Some owners give you a front door key so you may come and go as you please; others like to have the house empty between, say, 10am and 4pm.

Rooms

Bedrooms – We tell you if a room is a double, twin/double (i.e. with zip and link beds), suite (with a sitting area), family or single. Most owners are flexible and can juggle beds or bedrooms; talk to them about what you need before you book. Staying in a B&B will not be like staying in a hotel; it is rare to be given your own room key and your bed will not necessarily be made during your stay, or your room cleaned. Make sure you are clear about the room that you have booked, its views, bathroom and beds, etc.

Bathrooms – Most bedrooms in this book have an en suite bath or shower room; we only mention bathroom details when they do not. So, you may get a 'separate' bathroom (yours alone but not en suite) or a shared bathroom. Under certain entries we mention that two rooms share a bathroom and are 'let to same party only'. Please do not assume this means you must be a group of friends to apply; it simply means that if you book one of these rooms you will not be sharing a bathroom with strangers. If these things are important to you, please check when booking. Bath/shower means a bath with shower over; bath and shower means there is a separate shower unit.

Sitting rooms – Most B&B owners offer guests the family sitting room to share, or they provide a sitting room specially for guests, but do not assume that every bedroom or sitting room has a TV.

Meals

Unless we say otherwise, a full cooked breakfast is included. Some owners – particularly in London – will give you a good continental breakfast instead. Often you will feast on local sausage and bacon, eggs from resident hens, homemade breads and jams. In some you may have organic yogurts and beautifully presented fruit compotes. Some owners are fairly unbending about breakfast times, others are happy to just wait until you want it, or even bring it to you in bed.

Apart from breakfast, no meals should be expected unless you have arranged them in advance. Although we don't say so

on each entry – the repetition a few hundred times would be tedious – all owners who provide packed lunch, lunch or dinner need ADVANCE NOTICE. And they want to get things right for you so, when booking, please discuss your diet and meal times. Meal prices are quoted per person, and dinner is often a social occasion shared with your hosts and other guests.

Do eat in if you can – this book is teeming with good cooks. And how much more relaxing after a day out to have to move no further than the dining room for an excellent dinner, and to eat and drink knowing there's only a flight of stairs between you and your bed. Very few of our houses are licensed, but most are happy for you to bring your own drink.

Photo above: Cuil an Duin, entry 533
Photo right: Kilbury Manor, entry 94

If you do decide to head out for supper, you can find recommendations of our favourite pubs on our *Special Places to Eat and Drink* microsite, see: www.sawdays.co.uk/pubs. If a B&B has a pub nearby, you can see this on their page on our website, too.

Prices and minimum stays

Each entry gives a price PER ROOM for two people. We also include prices for single rooms, and let you know if there will be any extra to pay, should you choose to loll in a double bed on your own.

The price range for each B&B covers a one-night stay in the cheapest room in low season to the most expensive in high season. Some owners charge more at certain times (during regattas or festivals, for example) and some charge less for stays of more than one night. Some owners ask for a two-night minimum stay and we mention this where possible. Most of our houses could fill many times over on peak weekends and during the summer; book early, especially if you have specific needs.

Booking and cancellation

You may not receive a reply to your booking enquiry immediately; B&Bs are not hotels and the owners may be away. When you speak to the owner double-check the price you will pay for B&B and for any meals.

Requests for deposits vary; some are non-refundable, especially in our London

homes, and some owners may charge you for the whole of the booked stay in advance. Some cancellation policies are more stringent than others. It is also worth noting that some owners will take the money directly from your credit/debit card without contacting you to discuss it. Ask them to explain their cancellation policy clearly before booking to avoid a nasty surprise.

Payment

Most of our owners take cash and UK cheques with a cheque card. Some take credit cards; if they do we have given them the appropriate symbol. Check that your particular credit card is acceptable.

Tipping

Owners do not expect tips. If you have been treated with extraordinary kindness, write to them, or leave a small gift. Please tell us, too – we love to hear, and we do note all feedback.

Arrivals and departures

Say roughly what time you will arrive (normally after 4pm), as most hosts like to welcome you personally. Be on time if you have booked dinner; if, despite best efforts, you are delayed, phone to give warning.

Closed

When given in months this means the whole of the month stated.

Alastair Sawday's

'More than a bed
for the night…'

Britain
France
Ireland
Italy
Portugal
Spain

www.sawdays.co.uk

Self-Catering | B&B | Hotel | Pub | Treehouses, Cabins, Yurts & More

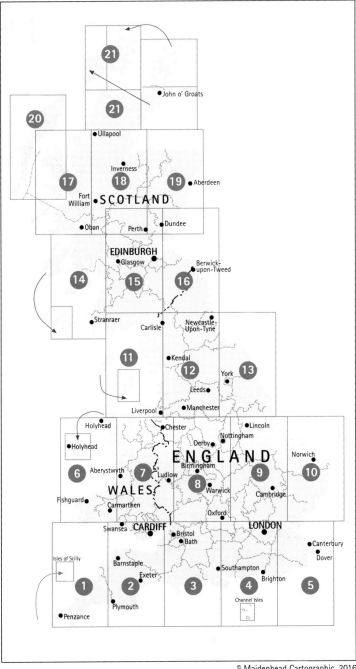

© Maidenhead Cartographic, 2016

6

Bed & Breakfast location

0   10   20   30 kilometres
0   10   20 miles

St. Govan's
Head

Lundy

Hartland Pt.
Hartland   Clovelly

Bude   Stratton

Poundstock

Boscastle
Tintagel   25

Port
Isaac   27
26   32   Bodmin
Padstow   28   Moor
33   Wadebridge
30   31   29
St. Columb   Bodmin   Liskeard
Major   CORNWALL
Newquay   55
34   A392   Lostwithiel
St. Austell
St. Agnes   54
Looe
Fowey   Polperro
37   Redruth   Truro   Mevagissey
St. Ives   35   53
51
38   36   Hayle   52
Penzance   43
St. Just   Marazion   Penryn   St. Mawes
41   42   44   50   Falmouth
40   49
39   Helston   47
45
46

Lizard
48
Lizard Pt.

Land's End

© Maidenhead Cartographic, 2016

Map 2

19

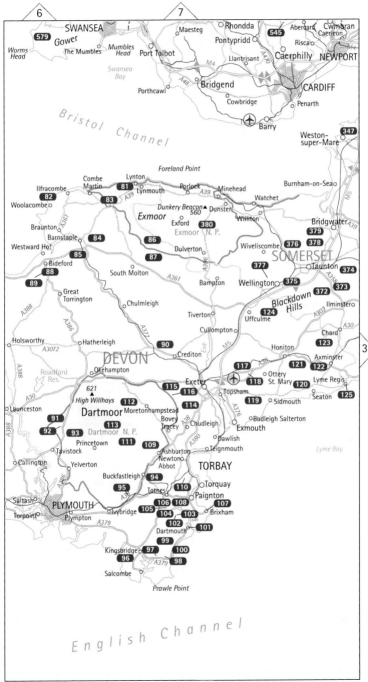

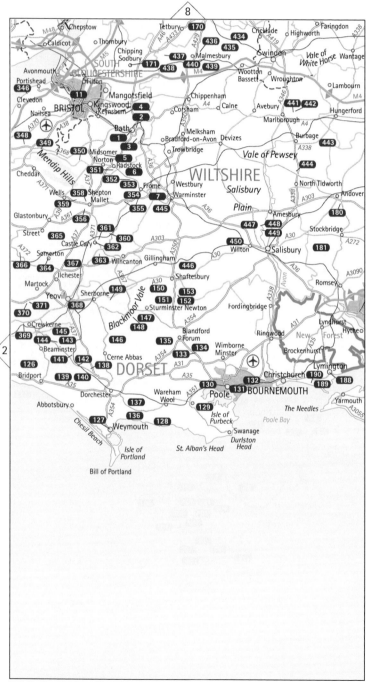

© Maidenhead Cartographic, 2016

Map 4

21

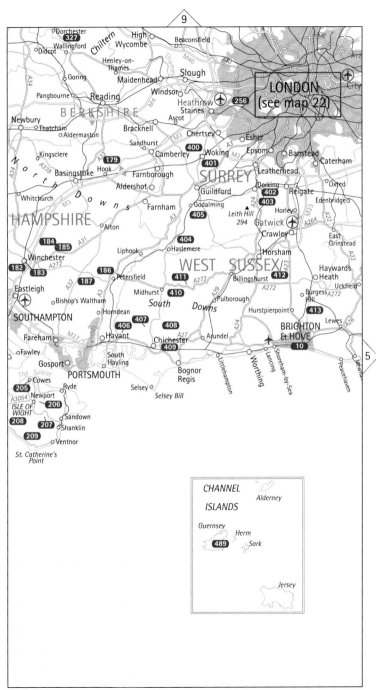

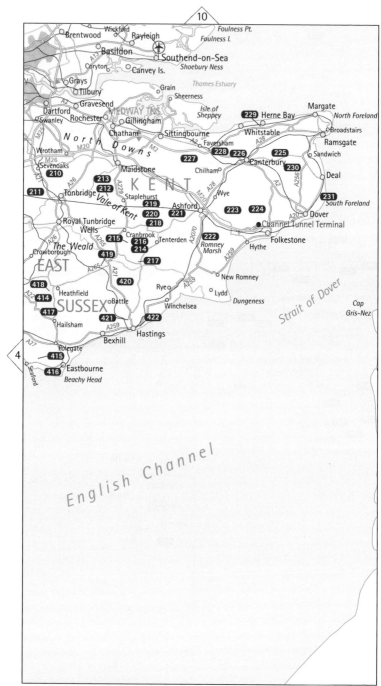

Map 6

23

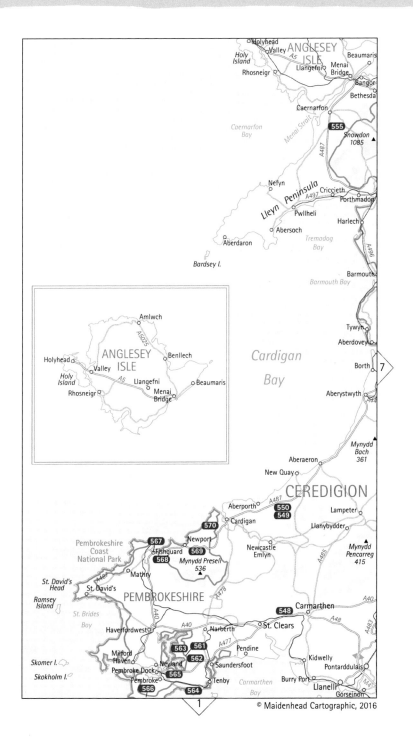

© Maidenhead Cartographic, 2016

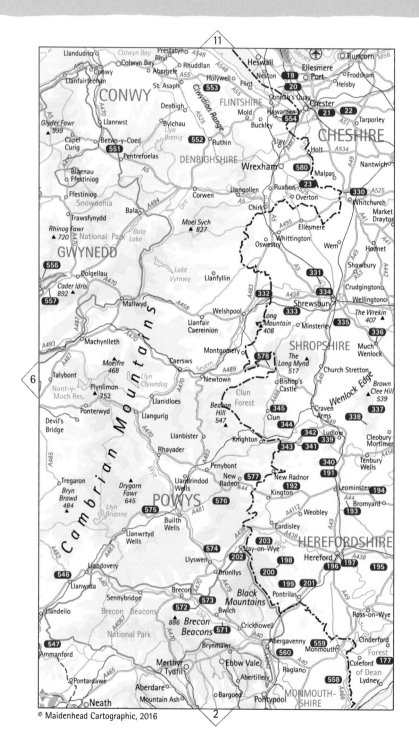

© Maidenhead Cartographic, 2016

Map 8

25

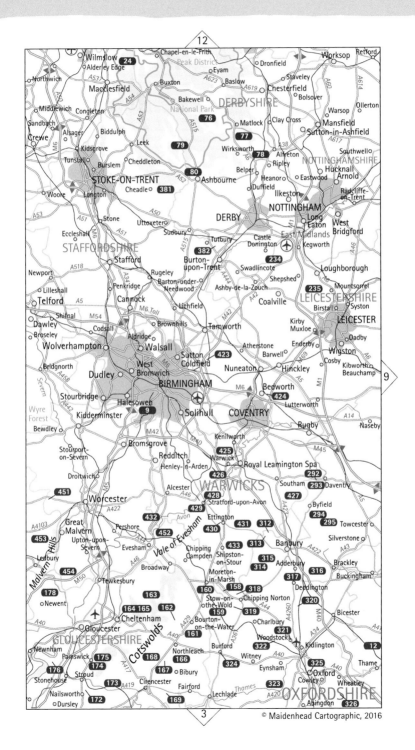

© Maidenhead Cartographic, 2016

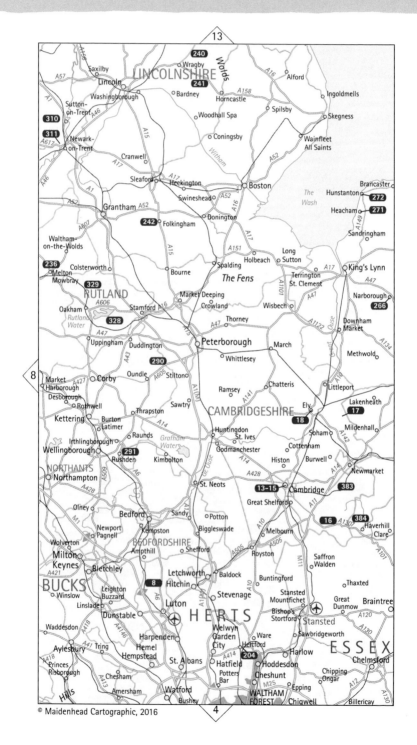

Map 10

27

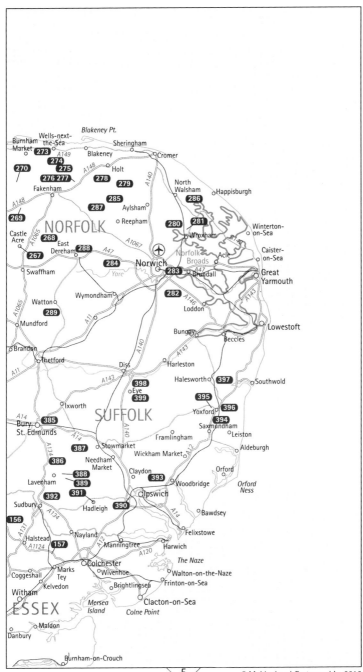

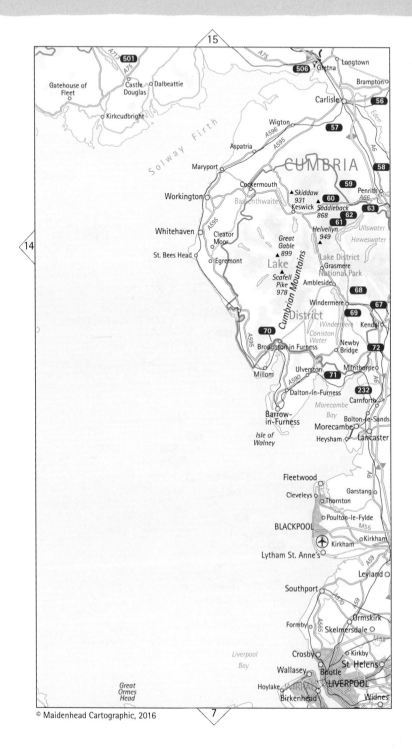

15

14

7

Map 12

29

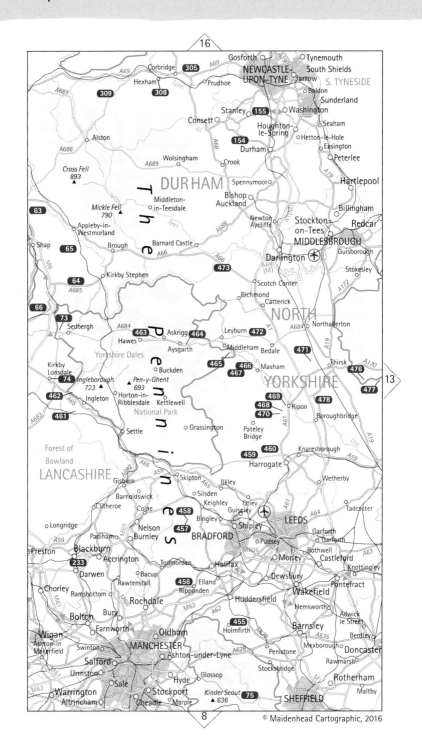

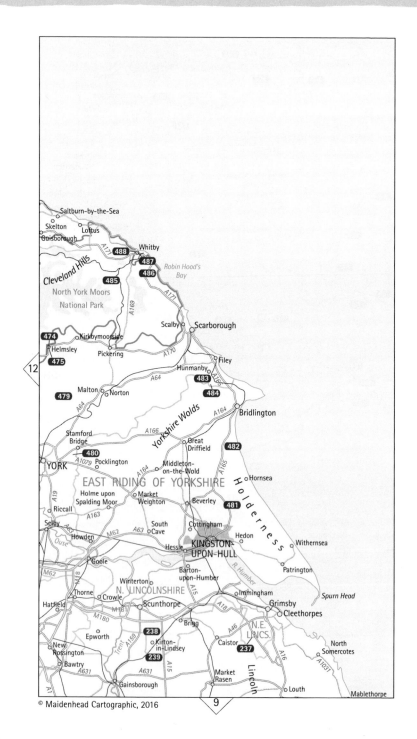

Map 14

31

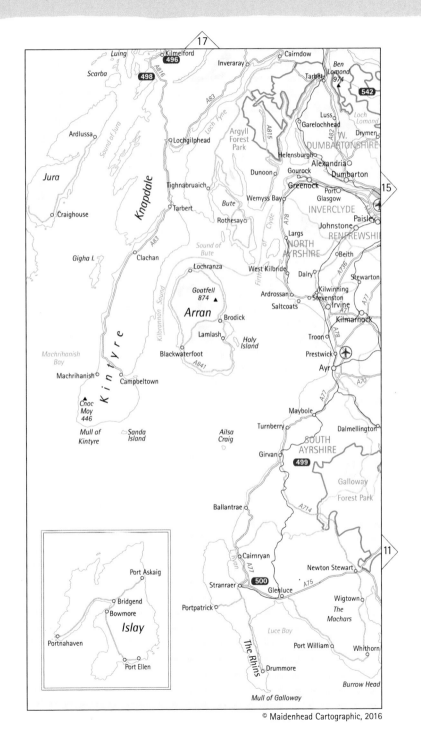

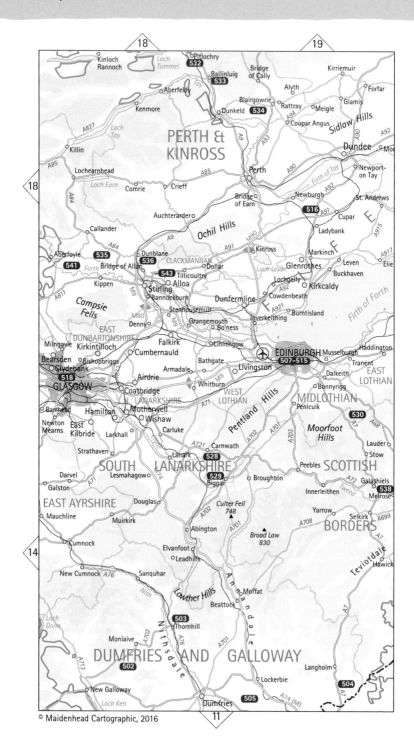

© Maidenhead Cartographic, 2016

Map 16

33

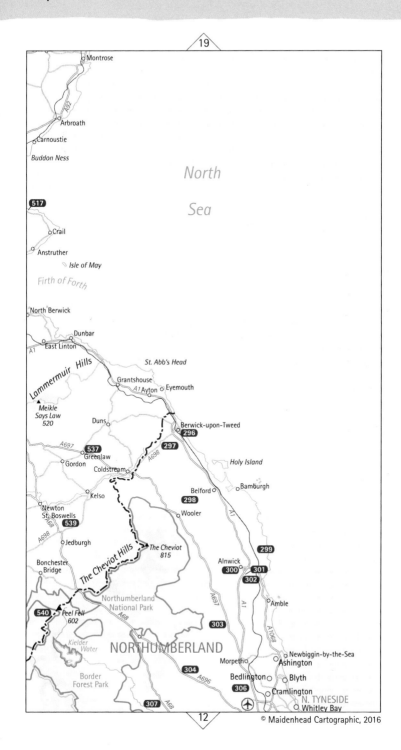

19

Montrose

A92

Arbroath

Carnoustie

Buddon Ness

517

North

Sea

Crail

Anstruther

Isle of May

Firth of Forth

North Berwick

Dunbar

A1

East Linton

Lammermuir Hills

St. Abb's Head

Grantshouse

A1 Ayton Eyemouth

Meikle Says Law 520

Duns

Berwick-upon-Tweed

296

A697

537

Greenlaw

297

Gordon

A698

Coldstream

Holy Island

Kelso

Belford Bamburgh

298

Newton St. Boswells

539

Wooler

A698

Jedburgh

The Cheviot Hills

The Cheviot 815

A1

Bonchester Bridge

299

Alnwick

300

301

540

Peel Fell 602

Northumberland National Park

302

A697

A1

Amble

A68

303

A1068

Kielder Water

NORTHUMBERLAND

Newbiggin-by-the-Sea

Border Forest Park

Morpeth Ashington

304

A696

Bedlington Blyth

306

Cramlington

307

A68

N. TYNESIDE

Whitley Bay

12

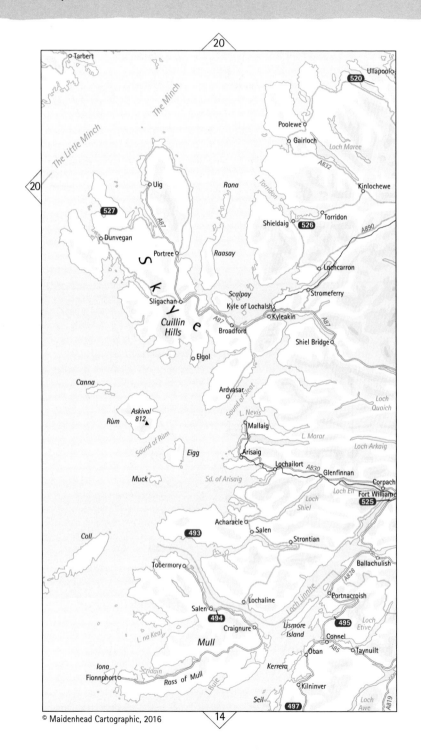

Map 18

35

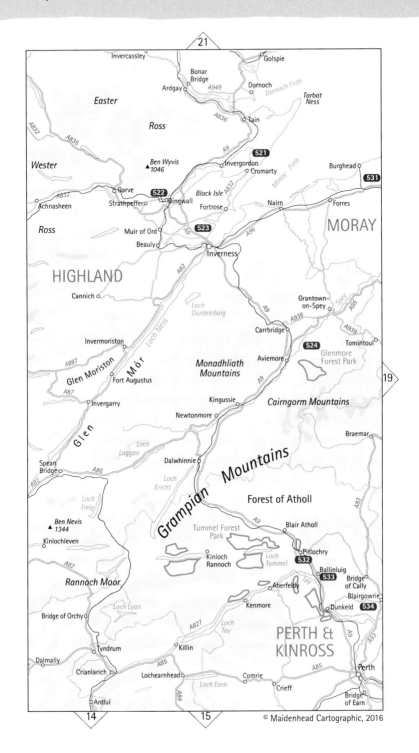

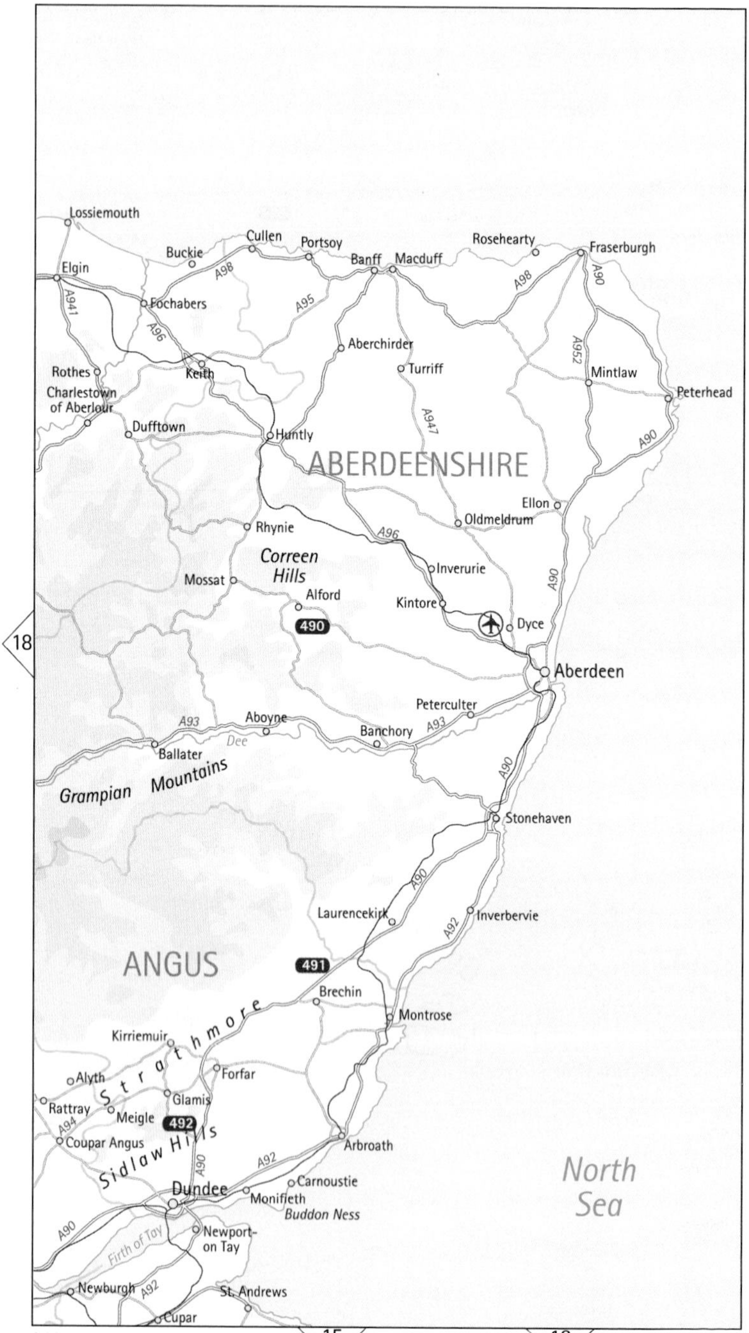

Lossiemouth
Elgin
Buckie
Cullen
Portsoy
Banff
Macduff
Rosehearty
Fraserburgh
Fochabers
Aberchirder
Turriff
Mintlaw
Peterhead
Rothes
Keith
Charlestown
of Aberlour
Dufftown
Huntly

ABERDEENSHIRE

Rhynie
Oldmeldrum
Ellon
Correen Hills
Mossat
Alford
Inverurie
Kintore
Dyce
490
Aberdeen
Peterculter
Aboyne
Banchory
Ballater
Dee
Grampian Mountains
Stonehaven

ANGUS
Laurencekirk
Inverbervie
491
Brechin
Montrose
Kirriemuir
Strathmore
Alyth
Forfar
Rattray
Glamis
Meigle
492
Coupar Angus
Sidlaw Hills
Arbroath
Dundee
Carnoustie
Monifieth
Buddon Ness
Newport-on Tay
Firth of Tay
Newburgh
St. Andrews
Cupar

North Sea

18

15   16

Map 20

37

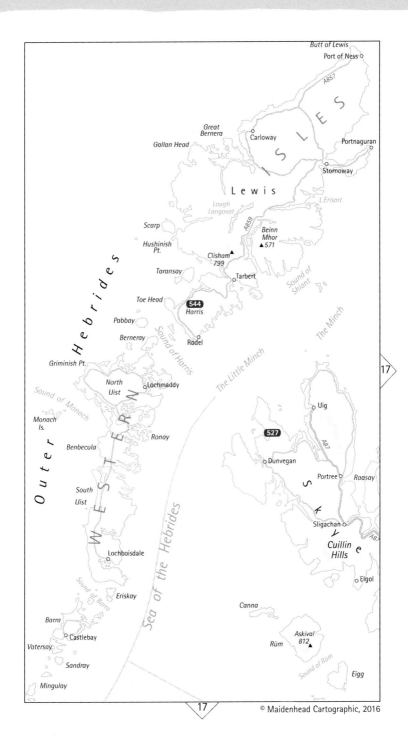

Butt of Lewis
Port of Ness
A857
ISLES
Great
Bernera
Carloway
Gallan Head
Portnaguran
Stornoway
Lewis
Lough
Langavat
L.Erisort
A859
Scarp
Beinn
Mhor
▲571
Hushinish
Pt.
Clisham
799
Taransay
Tarbert
Sound of
Shiant
Toe Head
544
Harris
Pabbay
The Minch
Berneray
Sound of Harris
Rodel
Griminish Pt.
The Little Minch
17
North
Uist
Lochmaddy
Uig
Sound of Monoch
Monach
Is.
Ronay
527
A87
Benbecula
Dunvegan
Portree
Raasay
South
Uist
Sligachan
Cuillin
Hills
A87
Lochboisdale
Sea of the Hebrides
Eriskay
Canna
Elgol
Barra
Castlebay
Askival
812 ▲
Vatersay
Rùm
Sandray
Sound of Rùm
Eigg
Mingulay

Hebrides

Outer

WESTERN

Skye

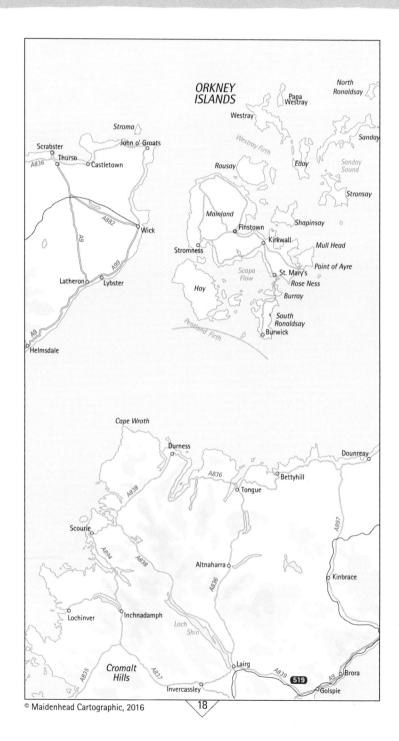

Map 22   39

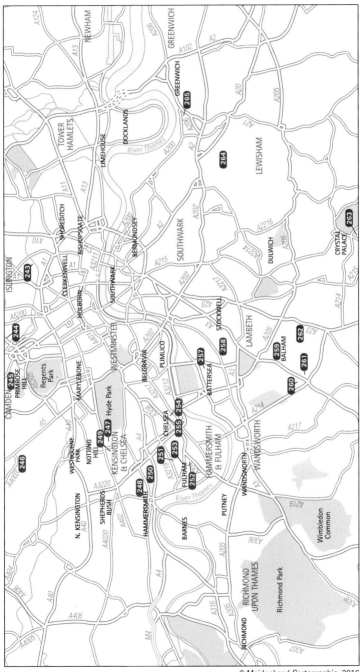

England

Photo: Ansford Park Cottage,
entry 361

Bath & N.E. Somerset

Pitt House

You couldn't be closer to the centre, nor on a calmer street. This Grade I-listed, seven-storey house, once home to William Pitt the Younger, is now inhabited by a warm, creative couple with a wry sense of humour. Inside: Georgian splendour matched by 21st-century eccentricity. Find sanded floorboards, walls of pure white, dazzling marble busts, a cow hide rug, a tumble of classical and oriental styles… collectors of antiques will keel over in a state of bliss. Bedrooms (up four flights of stairs) are only marginally less exotic, and share a fabulous bathroom and sitting room. Breakfast is the finest of continental. Outstanding.

Rooms	2 doubles sharing bath/shower (separate shower): £90–£110. Singles £75–£80.
Meals	Continental breakfast. Pubs/restaurants 2-minute walk.
Closed	Rarely.

	David & Sarah Bridgwater
	Pitt House,
	15 Johnstone Street,
	Bath, BA2 4DH
Tel	+44 (0)1225 471580
Mobile	+44 (0)7710 124376
Email	david.j.bridgwater@btinternet.com

Entry 1   Map 3

Bath & N.E. Somerset

Sir Walter Elliot's House

Utterly wonderful hosts at this Grade I-listed house. On one of Bath's finest Regency terraces, it has been so beautifully restored that the BBC filmed it for *Persuasion*; Jane Austen Society members often stay. Up several stairs are bedrooms flooded with light, two with views over Sydney Gardens, one with a bathroom in marquina marble, cherrywood and ebony. Have breakfast in the convivial family kitchen, or in the plant-filled conservatory. For the adventurous, Mechthild will serve an Austrian alternative – cold meats and cheeses, fresh rye breads and homemade cakes. Herrlich!

Minimum stay: 2 nights at weekends.

Rooms	3 twin/doubles: £125–£180. Singles £100–£130.
Meals	Pub/restaurant 300 yds.
Closed	Rarely.

	Julian Self
	Sir Walter Elliot's House,
	95 Sydney Place, Bath, BA2 6NE
Tel	+44 (0)1225 469435
Mobile	+44 (0)7737 793772
Email	visitus@sirwalterelliotshouse.co.uk
Web	www.sirwalterelliotshouse.co.uk

Entry 2   Map 3

Bath & N.E. Somerset

De Montalt Wood

Deep valley views, acres of gardens and woodland to roam, pretty places to sit and muse... all just a couple of miles from Bath. Charles and Ann's Victorian house is a smart family home with a comfortable country feel. Airy bedrooms have big beds with fine linen, a sofa, TV, and garden vistas; bathrooms are luxurious with rain showers and scented things. You breakfast in the elegant dining room: a full English, smoked salmon and scrambled eggs, fruits on the sideboard, lashings of coffee. There are lovely walks with good pubs on the way, bluebells fill the woods in spring and Bath brims with history, spa and good restaurants.

Minimum stay: 2 nights at weekends & in high season.

Rooms	1 double; 1 double with separate bath: £140-£160. Singles £70-£75.
Meals	Pubs/restaurants 5-minute drive.
Closed	Christmas & New Year.

	Charles & Ann Kent
	De Montalt Wood,
	Summer Lane, Combe Down,
	Bath, BA2 7EU
Tel	+44 (0)1225 840411
Email	bookings@demontaltwood.co.uk
Web	www.demontaltwood.co.uk

Entry 3 Map 3

Bath & N.E. Somerset

The Power House

On top of Bath's highest hill lies Rikki's Bauhaus-inspired home, its glass walls making the most of a magical spot and a sensational view; on a clear day you can see the Welsh hills. In the vast open-plan living space — homely, inviting, inspiring — are treasures from a lifetime of travels: ancient Tuareg camel sacks, kitsch Art Deco pots, gorgeous Persian chests. Bedrooms in the house are airy, with doors onto a huge balcony; the snug, colourful studio room has a wood-burner and little kitchen. Rikki is an incredible chef and uses the finest ingredients from Bath's farmers' market, ten minutes away. Breakfasts are superb — good coffee too.

Self-catering available in the studio.

Rooms	1 double: £100-£120. 1 single: £70. 1 studio for 2 with kitchen: £100-£120. 2 further small doubles available, sharing bathrooms.
Meals	Dinner £25. Pubs/restaurants 3-minute drive.
Closed	Rarely.

	Rikki Howard
	The Power House,
	Brockham End, Lansdown,
	Bath, BA1 9BY
Tel	+44 (0)1225 446308
Email	rikkijacout@aol.com

Entry 4 Map 3

Bath & N.E. Somerset

Pitfour House

Georgian gentility in a village near Bath. This is where the rector would live in an Austen novel: it's handsome, respectable, and the feel extends inside, where convivial hosts Frances (a keen cook) and Martin (keen gardener) put you at ease in their elegant home. The creamy guest sitting room gleams with period furniture, the dining room is panelled and parqueted, fresh flowers abound. The two bedrooms – one with en suite shower, one with a private bath – are compact but detailed with antiques. Take tea in the neat walled garden, admire the vegetable patch, then taste the spoils in one of Frances's fine suppers.

Minimum stay: 2 nights.

Rooms	1 twin/double; 1 twin/double with separate bath: £98-£100. Singles £78-£80.
Meals	Dinner, 2-3 courses, £30-£38. Supper: £25. Restaurant 1.5 miles.
Closed	Rarely.

Frances Hardman
Pitfour House,
High Street, Timsbury,
Bath, BA2 0HT
Tel +44 (0)1761 479554
Email pitfourhouse@btinternet.com
Web www.pitfourhouse.co.uk

Entry 5 Map 3

Bath & N.E. Somerset

Hollytree Cottage

Meandering lanes lead to this 16th-century cottage, with roses round the door, a grandfather clock in the hall and an air of genteel tranquillity. The cottage charm has been updated with Regency mahogany and sumptuous sofas. The bedrooms have views over undulating countryside; pretty bathrooms have oils and lotions. On sunny days breakfast is in the lovely garden room looking onto a colourful ornamental patio, sloping lawns, a pond, flowering shrubs and trees. A place to come for absolute peace, birdsong and walks; the joys of elegant Bath are 20 minutes away and Julia knows the area well; let her help plan your trips.

There are a few house rules for bringing pets & no dog-feeding in bedrooms. Please check on booking.

Rooms	1 double, 1 twin, 1 four-poster: £85-£95. Singles £70-£75. Dogs £10 per night per dog.
Meals	Pub/restaurant 0.5 miles.
Closed	Rarely.

Julia Naismith
Hollytree Cottage,
Laverton, Bath, BA2 7QZ
Tel +44 (0)1373 830786
Mobile +44 (0)7564 196703
Email jnaismith@toucansurf.com
Web www.hollytreecottagebath.co.uk

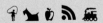

Entry 6 Map 3

Bath & N.E. Somerset

Reeves Barn

Drive under the willow to find a prettily converted studio barn, a gorgeous shepherd's hut and an away-from-it-all feel. The studio comes with limed beams, a romantic bedroom, a simple wet room with scented oils, and a mini kitchen cleverly tucked into a cupboard. Or choose to sleep under the stars in the snug and woody shepherd's hut. Artist Barbette leaves a bottle of prosecco in the fridge, and you can order dinner for your arrival; a breakfast hamper is left for you too – wake and eat when you want! Sit in the sun by pots of flowers, curl up by a wood-burner, enjoy the rustic vibe in the hut. Bath, Wells and Babington House are close by.

Rooms	Studio – 1 double with sitting room & kitchenette: £100-£115. 1 shepherd's hut for 2: £83. Extra bed/sofabed available £10 per person per night.
Meals	Dinner, 3 courses for studio guests, £35. Dinner, 2 courses & bottle of prosecco for shepherd's hut guests, £65 for 2.
Closed	Rarely.

Barbette Saunders
Reeves Barn,
17 Whitbourne Springs, Corsley,
Warminster, BA12 7RF

Tel	+44 (0)1373 832106
Mobile	+44 (0)7796 687806
Email	barbettesaunders@gmail.com

Entry 7   Map 3

Bedfordshire

Harlington Manor

Charles II may have stayed, and his bedroom has changed little… Off a busy street yet an ancient dream of a manor house, David's home is a dramatic trove of antiques, art, rich colour, grand piano, rose carvings, gorgeous bedrooms – be swept along by his enthusiasm and generosity, marvel at the attention to detail. Breakfast is served in the magnificent Tudor dining room at one long table: continental with compotes and yogurt, home-baking, tea in heirloom china. David's a good cook, and dinner with the family might include a harpsichord recital. A pretty garden, guided local tours… hop on a train from St Pancras and arrive in time for drinks.

Public transport 2-minute walk.

Rooms	2 doubles; 1 double with separate bathroom: £80-£95.
Meals	Continental breakfast at weekdays, cooked breakfast at weekends. Dinner, 2-3 courses, £20-£25. Restaurants 2-minute walk.
Closed	Rarely.

David Blakeman
Harlington Manor,
Westoning Road,
Harlington, LU5 6PB

Mobile	+44 (0)7788 742209
Email	blakeman.david1@gmail.com

Entry 8   Map 9

Birmingham

Woodbrooke Quaker Study Centre

A pleasure to find ten tranquil acres (woodlands, lawns, lake and walled garden) so close to the centre of Birmingham – run by such special people. This impressive Georgian mansion was donated by George Cadbury to the Quakers in 1903, as a place for study and contemplation. And so it remains. There are corridors aplenty and public rooms big and small: a library, a silent room, a lovely new garden lounge, and a dining hall where organic buffet meals feature fruit and veg from the grounds. Bedrooms, spread over several buildings, are carpeted, comfortable, light and airy, and most have en suite showers. Welcoming, nurturing, historic.

Rooms	7 doubles, 7 twins (most rooms are en suite): £66-£73. 45 singles (most rooms are en suite): £47-£53.
Meals	Lunch & dinner £11. Pubs/restaurants 15-minute walk.
Closed	Christmas & Boxing Day.

Marc Harbourne-Bessant
Woodbrooke Quaker Study Centre,
1046 Bristol Road,
Selly Oak, B29 6LJ

Tel	+44 (0)121 472 5171
Email	enquiries@woodbrooke.org.uk
Web	www.woodbrooke.org.uk

Entry 9   Map 8

Brighton & Hove

The Art House Hove

Peaceful, close to the sea and in the heart of popular Hove, this Victorian villa is a friendly town treat. Bedrooms on the top floor are furnished in an eclectic style, mixing antique finds with quirky light-fittings; art books, flowers, splashes of colour and brand new marble and mosaic bathrooms complete the picture. Dexter and Liz give you a breakfast feast: muesli, fruit salad, patisseries fresh from the bakery that morning, eggs, smoked salmon, hash browns. Liz runs mosaic courses and her wonderful work decorates the house. Dozens of cafés and bistros are on the doorstep; Brighton is a 15-minute amble along the promenade.

Minimum stay: 2 nights.

Rooms	2 doubles: £105-£135.
Meals	Pubs/restaurants 0.5 miles.
Closed	Rarely.

Dexter Tiranti
The Art House Hove,
27 Wilbury Road,
Hove, BN3 3PB

Tel	+44 (0)1273 775350
Email	enquiries@thearthousehove.co.uk
Web	www.thearthousehove.co.uk

Entry 10   Map 4

Bristol

9 Princes Buildings

A super city base with comfortable beds, charming owners and, without a doubt, the best views in Clifton. You're a hop from the elegant Suspension Bridge, restaurants, shops and pubs of the village and a ferry to whisk you to town or the station; yet all is quiet and the garden is large and leafy. You walk in to a big square hall; the drawing room has a peaceful feel and a veranda for the views. Bedrooms are sunny and traditional: one downstairs overlooks the garden, the top floor double is furnished more simply. Simon and Joanna give you a good, leisurely breakfast too: local sausages and bacon, homemade jams and marmalade.

Rooms	2 doubles, 1 twin/double; 1 twin/double with separate bath: £95-£125. Singles £65-£75.
Meals	Pub/restaurant 100 yds.
Closed	Rarely.

Simon & Joanna Fuller
9 Princes Buildings,
Clifton, BS8 4LB

Tel	+44 (0)117 973 4615
Email	info@9pb.co.uk
Web	www.9princesbuildings.co.uk

Entry 11   Map 3

Buckinghamshire

Long Crendon Manor

Masses of history and oodles of character at this timbered listed house with high chimneys, dating from 1187... no wonder film companies are keen to get through the arched entrance and into the courtyard! The vast dining room is a dramatic setting for breakfast: sausages from Sue's pigs, home-baked bread, plum and mulberry jam from the gardens. Windows on both sides bring light into the fire-warmed drawing room with leather sofas, gleaming furniture, family bits and bobs, pictures galore. Sleep soundly in comfortable, country-house style bedrooms (one with gorgeous yellow panelling). Peaceful.

Rooms	1 double, 1 four-poster, 1 double with extra twin in dressing room: £100-£200. Singles £80-£100.
Meals	Supper £30. Pubs/restaurants 3-minute walk.
Closed	Occasionally.

Sue Soar
Long Crendon Manor,
Frogmore Lane, Long Crendon,
Aylesbury, HP18 9DZ

Tel	+44 (0)1844 201647
Email	sue.soar@longcrendonmanor.co.uk
Web	www.longcrendonmanor.co.uk

Entry 12   Map 8

Cambridgeshire

Cambridge University

Buses, bicycles and punting on the Cam: huge fun when you're in the heart of it all. Enter the Great Gate Tower of Christ's College to be wooed by tranquil, beautiful quadrangle gardens, breakfasts beneath portraits of hallowed masters, and a serene chapel. At smaller Sidney Sussex – 1598-old with additions – you can play tennis in gorgeous gardens, picnic on perfect lawns and start the day with rare-breed sausages. Churchill has a great gym, Downing has Quentin Blake paintings on the walls, St Catharine's has a candlelit chapel. Bedrooms (some shared showers) and lounges are functional; well-informed porters are your first port of call.

Rooms spread across 13 colleges.

Rooms	60 doubles, 206 twins: £75-£128. 804 singles: £46-£79. 3 apartments for 2-3: £85-£150.
Meals	Breakfast included. Some colleges offer dinner from £7. See website for details.
Closed	Mid-January to mid-March, May/June, October/November; Christmas. A few rooms available throughout year.

	University Rooms Cambridge University, Cambridge
Web	www.universityrooms.com/ en/city/cambridge/home

Entry 13   Map 9

Cambridgeshire

Duke House

Opposite Christ's Pieces, one of the city's oldest green spaces, and right in the centre: perfect! This house has been refurbished from top to toe and all is gleaming and generous. Settle into the guest sitting room (chandelier, Regency style furniture, calm colours) and sleep soundly under Irish goose down in beautiful bedrooms all named after dukes; top-floor's Cambridge suite has a romantic balcony. The lovely breakfast room has separate tables with fabric-backed chairs overlooking a little plant-filled courtyard; Liz serves an excellent organic and homemade spread. Shops, botanical garden, restaurants... a happy stroll.

Minimum stay: 2 nights at weekends. Children over 10 welcome.

Rooms	4 doubles: £120-£150. 1 suite for 2 (extra sofabed available): £160-£195. Singles £115-£160.
Meals	Pubs/restaurants 5-minute walk.
Closed	Rarely.

	Liz Cameron Duke House, 1 Victoria Street, Cambridge, CB1 1JP
Tel	+44 (0)1223 314773
Email	info@dukehousecambridge.co.uk
Web	www.dukehousecambridge.co.uk

Entry 14   Map 9

Cambridgeshire

5 Chapel Street

Exemplary! Where: in a lovely, comfortable, refurbed Georgian house 20 minutes' walk from Cambridge centre. How: with warmth, pleasure, intelligence and local knowledge. Bedrooms have good quality mattresses, bedding and towels. Characterful pieces too – antique brass bed, freestanding bath, oriental rugs on polished floors – with flowers and garden views. The breakfasts are delicious, largely organic and local: fresh fruit salad, kedgeree with smoked Norfolk haddock, home baking (three types of bread; gluten free, no problem). If you'd like to swing a cat book the biggest room; borrow vintage bikes and thoroughly enjoy your break.

Minimum stay: 2 nights. Children over 11 welcome.

Rooms	2 doubles, 1 twin: £100-£130. Singles £90-£120.
Meals	Pubs/restaurants 5-minute walk.
Closed	Rarely.

Christine Ulyyan
5 Chapel Street,
Cambridge, CB4 1DY
Tel   +44 (0)1223 514856
Email christine.ulyyan@gmail.com
Web   www.5chapelstreet.com

Entry 15   Map 9

Cambridgeshire

Springfield House

The former school house hugs the bend of a river, its French windows opening to delightful rambling gardens with scented roses… and a yew garden, and a mulberry tree that provides fruit for breakfast. It's an elegant home reminiscent of another age, with fascinating history on the walls and big comfortable bedrooms for guests; one is reached by narrow stairs and has steps out to the garden. The conservatory, draped with a huge mimosa, is an exceptional spot for summer breakfasts, and the breakfasts are rather delicious. Good value and peaceful, yet close to Cambridge, of which Judith is a fund of knowledge.

Rooms	2 doubles; 1 twin/double with separate bath: £70-£90. Singles £55-£70. Extra bed/sofabed available £15-£20 per person per night.
Meals	Pubs 150 yds.
Closed	Rarely.

Judith Rossiter
Springfield House,
14-16 Horn Lane, Linton, CB21 4HT
Tel   +44 (0)1223 891383
Email springfieldhouselinton@gmail.com
Web   www.springfieldhouselinton.com

Entry 16   Map 9

Cambridgeshire

The Old Vicarage

Tug the bell pull and step inside a 19th-century parsonage with a labyrinth of rooms. Homemade flapjack and chocolates await, peaceful bedrooms are countrified and classy with stylish bathrooms – one a lovely en suite. Original artwork peppers every wall and is mostly for sale online. Take breakfast overlooking a big mature garden and brace yourself for a wonderful full English. Cats, dogs and chickens roam freely and if you're lucky you'll spot a proud peacock or muntjac deer within the trees. Explore Cambridge, walk Wicken Fen with its Konik ponies and birdlife, then stroll to one of the locals.

Rooms	1 twin/double; 1 double with separate bath: £90-£100. Singles £55-£60.
Meals	Pubs in village.
Closed	Christmas & New Year.

Gill Pedersen
The Old Vicarage,
7 Church Street, Isleham,
Ely, CB7 5RX

Tel	+44 (0)1638 780095
Email	bookings@old-vicarage-isleham.com
Web	www.oldvicarageisleham.co.uk

Entry 17   Map 9

Cambridgeshire

Peacocks B&B

Above their delightful riverside tearoom in the heart of Ely, George and Rachel have created two suites. Each bedroom has its own sitting room stocked with books and squashy sofas. Brewery House has a fireplace and river views; Cottage is cosy and pretty with flowery wallpaper. Both have goose down duvets and tea trays. Enjoy breakfast by the Aga: perhaps savoury crumpets, omelette or delicious Croque Madame. Browse the nearby antique centre, visit the cathedral, stroll out for dinner or explore Cambridge and the Fens; but make sure to leave time for tea – there are 70 kinds! The Peacocks are friendly and funny – lovely hosts.

Rooms	1 suite for 2; 1 suite for 2 with separate bathroom & wc: £125-£150.
Meals	Pubs/restaurants 3-minute walk. Tearoom closed Monday & Tuesday.
Closed	Rarely.

Rachel Peacock
Peacocks B&B,
65 Waterside,
Ely, CB7 4AU

Mobile	+44 (0)7900 666161
Email	peacockbookings65@gmail.com
Web	www.peacockstearoom.co.uk

Entry 18   Map 9

Cheshire

Goss Moor

Crunch up the gravelled drive to the big white house, a beautifully run family home. Bedrooms are light, bright and decorated in creams and blues; bathrooms are spotless and warm. Be cosseted by fluffy bathrobes, biscuits or flapjack, decanters of sherry – all is comfortable and inviting. After a day's exploring the Wirral and Liverpool, historic Chester and the wilds of north Wales – a short drive all – return to a kind welcome from Sarah. Expect a generous and delicious breakfast by the sunny bay window; in the summer, you are free to enjoy the garden and pool (not always heated!).

Rooms	1 twin/double; 1 double with separate bath: £80-£85. Singles £50-£55.
Meals	Occasional dinner with wine, £25. Pub/restaurant 2 miles.
Closed	Rarely.

Chris & Sarah White
Goss Moor,
Mill Lane, Willaston,
Neston, CH64 1RG
Tel   +44 (0)151 327 4000
Mobile   +44 (0)7771 510068
Email   sarahcmwhite@aol.com
Web   www.gossmoor.co.uk

Entry 19   Map 7

Cheshire

Trustwood

Small and pretty and wrapped in beautiful country, Trustwood stands in peaceful gardens with National Trust woods at the end of the lane. Outside, sweetpeas flourish to the front, while lawns run down behind to a copse where bluebells thrive in spring. Inside, warm, fresh, contemporary interiors are just the ticket: super bedrooms, fabulous bathrooms, and a wood-burner and sofas in the sitting room. Free-range hens provide eggs for delicious breakfasts, Lin accounts for the lovely scones. As for the Wirral, much more beautiful than you probably imagine; coastal walks, botanic gardens and the spectacular Dee estuary all wait.

Rooms	2 doubles: £75. Singles £50.
Meals	Restaurants 2 miles.
Closed	Occasionally.

Lin & Peter Friend
Trustwood,
Vicarage Lane, Burton,
Neston, CH64 5TJ
Tel   +44 (0)151 336 7118
Mobile   +44 (0)7550 012462
Email   lin@trustwood.freeserve.co.uk
Web   www.trustwood.freeserve.co.uk

Entry 20   Map 7

Cheshire

Cotton Farm

Only a four-mile hop from Roman Chester and its 900-year-old cathedral is this sprawling, red-brick farmhouse. Elegant chickens peck in hedges, ponies graze, lambs frisk and cats doze. The farm, run by conservationists Nigel and Clare, is under the Countryside Stewardship Scheme – there are wildflower meadows, summer swallows and 250 acres to roam. Farmhouse bedrooms are large, stylish and cosy with lovely fabrics, robes, a decanter of sherry and huge bath towels, but best of all is the relaxed family atmosphere. Breakfasts, with homemade bread, are delicious and beautifully presented.

Children over 10 welcome.

Rooms	2 doubles, 1 twin: £90. Singles £70.
Meals	Pub 1.5 miles.
Closed	Rarely.

Clare & Nigel Hill
Cotton Farm,
Cotton Edmunds, Chester, CH3 7PG

Tel	+44 (0)1244 336616
Mobile	+44 (0)7840 682042
Email	echill@btinternet.com
Web	www.cottonfarm.co.uk

Entry 21   Map 7

Cheshire

Rock Farm

The Tomkinsons' enthusiasm for their family home is infectious and it's a treat to stay in this untrumpeted part of the country with its rolling greenery and grand walking. Make yourself at home (with homemade cake) among the family paintings in the large, light and comfortable drawing room, with a roaring wood-burner on chilly days. Breakfasts 'fit for the Ritz' are served here: local farm shop bacon and sausages, fresh eggs from the hens, buttery croissants. Sleep like a log in pretty, serene bedrooms with exposed beams and slanting ceilings; the bathroom is warm and roomy. You can walk to a great pub and Chester is 8 miles. Super.

Parking & travel cot available.

Rooms	1 double, 1 twin sharing bath (let to same party only): £80-£90. Singles £55-£65.
Meals	Restaurants within half a mile.
Closed	Rarely.

Penelope Tomkinson
Rock Farm,
Willington,
Tarporley, CW6 0NA

Tel	+44 (0)1829 752326
Mobile	+44 (0)7925 296258
Email	penelope.tomkinson@live.co.uk

Entry 22   Map 7

Cheshire

Mulsford Cottage

Delicious! Not just the food (Kate's a pro chef) but the sweet whitewashed cottage with its sunny conservatory and vintage interiors, and the green Cheshire countryside that bubble-wraps the place in rural peace. Chat – and laugh – the evening away over Kate's superb dinners, lounge by the fire, then sleep deeply in comfy bedrooms: cane beds, a bright red chair, a vintage desk. The double has a roll top bath, the twin a tiny shower-with-a-view. Wake for local bacon, sausages and honey and just-laid bantam eggs. Walk the 34-mile Sandstone Trail to Shropshire; Wales starts just past the hammock, at the bottom of the bird-filled garden.

Rooms	1 double; 1 twin with separate bath/shower: £90. Singles £65.
Meals	Dinner from £18. Pub 1.5 miles.
Closed	Rarely.

Kate Dewhurst
Mulsford Cottage,
Mulsford, Sarn,
Malpas, SY14 7LP
Tel   +44 (0)1948 770414
Email katedewhurst@hotmail.com
Web   www.mulsfordcottage.co.uk

Entry 23   Map 7

Cheshire

Harrop Fold Farm

Artists, foodies and walkers adore this antique-filled farmhouse with soul-lifting views. On the edge of the Peak District, the oldest building on the farm dates from 1694 (Bonnie Prince Charlie visited here). The B&B part has a warm peaceful breakfast room, a stone-flagged sitting room, a spectacular studio. Fresh flowers, antique beds, fine fabrics, hot water bottles with chic covers, bathrooms with fluffy robes: you get the best. Gregarious Sue and daughter Leah hold art and cookery courses so the breakfast too is outstanding. Bedrooms have stupendous views – and flat-screen TVs and DVDs just in case the weather spoils!

Rooms	2 doubles: £100. 1 suite for 2, 1 suite for 4: £100–£175. Singles from £75.
Meals	Wine bar, restaurant & pub 1.9 miles.
Closed	Rarely.

Sue Stevenson
Harrop Fold Farm,
Rainow,
Macclesfield, SK10 5UU
Tel   +44 (0)1625 560085
Email stay@harropfoldfarm.co.uk
Web   www.harropfoldfarm.co.uk

Entry 24   Map 8

Cornwall

Cornwall

The Old Parsonage

A spellbinding coastline, secret coves, spectacular walks. All this and a supremely comfortable Georgian rectory with pretty gardens. Morag and Margaret are relaxed and welcoming hosts. Superb pitch pine floors and original woodwork add warmth and a fresh glow, the big engaging bedrooms (one on the ground floor) have a quirky, upbeat mix of furniture and furnishings, and the bathrooms are pampering. Breakfasts are wonderful: savoury mushrooms, Cornish oak-roasted mackerel, French toast with bacon… In front of the house the land slopes away to the Atlantic, just a five-minute walk across a SSSI. A peaceful retreat.

Minimum stay: 2 nights. Over 12s welcome.

The Corn Mill

This restored mill in a quiet Cornish valley is a relaxed and friendly home. Step inside and find a country cottage medley of flowers and family furniture, antique rugs and interesting market finds. Artist Suzie has her studio in a folly in the pretty garden; ducks and geese wander in the orchard. Cosy bedrooms have flowery fabrics, warm blankets and good cotton; bathrooms are simple and fresh with fluffy towels. Breakfast well in the farmhouse kitchen on a locally sourced spread and bread fresh from the Rayburn. Exceptional coastal walking, music festivals, great beaches and Port Isaac are all nearby.

Rooms	5 twin/doubles: £102–£130.
	Singles from £75.
Meals	Packed lunch £5.95.
	Pub/restaurant 600 yds.
Closed	November – March.

Rooms	1 double: £90–£120.
	1 family room for 4: £90–£120.
Meals	Pub/restaurant 2 miles.
Closed	Christmas & New Year.

Morag Reeve & Margaret Pickering
The Old Parsonage,
Forrabury, Boscastle, PL35 0DJ

Tel	+44 (0)1840 250339
Mobile	+44 (0)7890 531677
Email	morag@old-parsonage.com
Web	www.old-parsonage.com

Susan Bishop
The Corn Mill,
Port Isaac Road,
Trelill,
Bodmin, PL30 3HZ

Tel	+44 (0)1208 851079
Email	jemandsuzie@icloud.com

Entry 25   Map 1

Entry 26   Map 1

Cornwall

Tremoren

Views stretch sleepily over the Cornish countryside. You might feel inclined to do nothing more than wander the lovely garden or snooze by the pool, but the surfing beaches, Camel Trail and Eden Project are so close. The stone and slate former farmhouse is smartly done. Bedrooms come with soft colours, pretty china, crisp linen, a comfortable bathroom; the downstairs double has its own separate sitting room; upstairs has a sumptuous sofa in the room. For summer, there's a flower-filled terrace, perfect for a pre-dinner drink. Lanie, bubbly and engaging, runs her own catering company – bread from the wood-fired oven, delicious dinners!

Rooms	1 double, 1 double with sitting room: £90–£100.
Meals	Dinner, 4 courses, £26. Inns 0.5 miles.
Closed	Rarely.

Philip & Lanie Calvert
Tremoren,
St Kew,
Bodmin, PL30 3HA

Tel   +44 (0)1208 841790
Email   la.calvert@btinternet.com
Web   www.tremoren.co.uk

Cornwall

Higher Lank Farm

Families rejoice: come if you have a child under seven! Bring older siblings too. Celtic crosses in the garden and original panelling hint at the 500-year history of this friendly, busy farmhouse. Bedrooms have comfy beds, toys and large TVs; soaps are handmade; eco-friendly too with biomass energy and local real nappies. Nursery teas begin at 5pm, grown-up suppers are later and Lucy will cheerfully babysit while you slink off to the pub. Farm-themed playgrounds are safe and fun, there are piglets, lambs, goats, chicks, eggs to collect, pony and trap rides, a sand barn for little ones and cream teas in the garden. Lovely atmosphere.

Minimum stay: 3 nights, 5 nights in high season.

Rooms	3 family rooms for 4: £110–£160 Singles by arrangement.
Meals	Supper £23. Nursery tea £7. Pub 1.5 miles.
Closed	November – Easter.

Lucy Finnemore
Higher Lank Farm,
St Breward,
Bodmin, PL30 4NB

Tel   +44 (0)1208 850716
Email   lucyfin@higherlankfarm.co.uk
Web   www.higherlankfarm.co.uk

Cornwall

Cabilla Manor

Instant seduction as you enter the old manor house out on the moor... It's a home that is brimful of interest and colour, with a treasure round every corner. Find rich exotic rugs and cushions, artefacts from around the world, Louella's sumptuous hand-stencilled quilts, huge beds, coir carpets, vases of garden flowers. There are heaps of interesting books too, many of them Robin's (a writer and explorer), and a lofty conservatory for friendly meals overlooking a semi-wild garden – with tennis and elegant lawns. The views are heavenly, the generous hosts wonderful and the final mile of the approach thrillingly wild.

Dogs very welcome by arrangement, but not in the house: outhouse dog room available.

Rooms	1 double; 1 double with separate bath & shower; 1 double, 1 twin sharing bath & shower (let to same party only): £100. Singles £50.
Meals	Dinner, 3 courses with wine, £35. Pub 4 miles. Restaurant 8-10 miles.
Closed	Christmas.

Robin & Louella Hanbury-Tenison
Cabilla Manor,
Mount, Bodmin, PL30 4DW

Tel	+44 (0)1208 821224
Mobile	+44 (0)7770 664218
Email	louella@cabilla.co.uk
Web	www.cabilla.co.uk

Entry 29 Map 1

Cornwall

Costislost

You have independence in the 19th-century Cornish stone lodge attached to Nick and Jane's country house. Step in to a colourful eclectic mix of old and new with books, art, kilims and classic elegance. Big bedrooms have stylish iron four-posters topped with feather duvets. Breakfast (and dinner in autumn and winter) are served in the dining hall, at a long table that can seat up to 18; Nick and Jane have a hotels/catering history and meals are local, organic, delicious and convivial. There's a yoga/meditation room, a large south-facing garden sweeps down to woods and farmland, the south coast is in easy reach and there are walks galore.

Rooms	4 doubles: £100-£140.
Meals	Dinner (autumn & winter only) from £25. Pubs/restaurants 3 miles.
Closed	Rarely.

Nick Meacham & Jane Parker
Costislost,
Washaway,
Bodmin, PL30 3AP

Tel	+44 (0)1208 840031
Email	stay@costislosthouse.co.uk
Web	www.costislosthouse.co.uk

Entry 30 Map 1

Cornwall

Menkee

From this handsome Georgian farmhouse there are long views towards the sea; you're 20 minutes away from the coastal path and wild surf but you may not want to budge. Gage and Liz are deliciously unstuffy and look after you well: newspapers and a weather forecast appear with a scrumptious breakfast, your gorgeously comfortable bed is turned down in the evening and walkers can be dropped off and collected. The elegant house is filled with beautiful things, gleaming furniture, fresh flowers, roaring fires and pretty fabrics – all you have to do is slacken your pace and wind down.

Minimum stay: Two nights in high season. Charging points for electric cars available.

Rooms	1 double, 1 twin: £80–£90. Singles from £40.
Meals	Pub/restaurant 3 miles.
Closed	Rarely.

Gage & Liz Williams
Menkee,
St Mabyn, Wadebridge, PL30 3DD
Tel   +44 (0)1208 841378
Mobile   +44 (0)7999 549935
Email   gagewillms@aol.com
Web   www.cornwall-online.co.uk/menkee/

Entry 31   Map 1

Cornwall

Trewornan Manor

Drive through the white gate and listed pillars to a house that began in 1211. You'll fall in love the moment you arrive, and your hosts' enthusiasm is infectious. Guests are spoiled in off-beat boutique style in one beautiful, sprawling wing: dining and lounging downstairs, and four bedrooms up. It is sumptuous and gorgeous but definitely not swanky and the attention to detail is delightful: hot water bottles, sweeties, cookies, natural toiletries, bikes and food that tastes as gorgeous as it looks. Lose yourself in 25 acres of woods, water meadows and historic gardens – or sally forth, to Padstow and Rock.

Rooms	4 twin/doubles: £120–£190. Singles £100–£170.
Meals	Pubs/restaurants 1 mile.
Closed	Rarely.

Paul & Lesley Stapleton
Trewornan Manor,
St Minver,
Wadebridge, PL27 6EX
Tel   +44 (0)1208 812359
Email   enquiries@trewornanmanor.co.uk
Web   www.trewornanmanor.co.uk

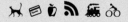

Entry 32   Map 1

Cornwall

Molesworth Manor

It's a splendid old place, big enough to swallow hordes of people, peppered with art and interesting antiques. There are palms and a play area in the garden, two charming drawing rooms with an honesty bar and open fires for cosy nights, a carved staircase leading to bedrooms that vary in style and size – His Lordship's at the front, the Maid's in the eaves – and bathrooms that are lovely and pampering. The whiff of homemade muffins and a delicious breakfast lures you downstairs in the morning, Padstow and its food delights will keep you happy when you venture out. A superb bolthole run by Geoff and Jessica, youthful and fun.

Rooms	7 doubles, 1 twin/double; 1 twin with separate shower room: £91-£131. Singles by arrangement.
Meals	Pubs/restaurants 2 miles.
Closed	November – January. Open off-season by arrangement for larger parties.

Geoff French & Jessica Clarke
Molesworth Manor,
Little Petherick,
Padstow, PL27 7QT
Tel   +44 (0)1841 540292
Email   molesworthmanor@aol.com
Web   www.molesworthmanor.co.uk

Entry 33   Map 1

Cornwall

Myrtle Cottage

A proper cottage – beautifully kept, low-ceilinged and light – in a traditional Cornish village with a good foodie pub. Rooms, with distant sea views, are invitingly cosy: uneven white walls, prettily quilted beds, pale-carpeted or varnished creaking boards, flowers fresh from the garden. Sue does great breakfasts: homemade bread, muffins and preserves, local eggs and bacon, in the dining room, the sun room, or out on the patio. There are games and toys for tots and maps for walkers to borrow. You're a 15-minute stroll from the South West Coast Path so near many outstanding beaches; Porth Joke's a favourite. Lovely.

Minimum stay: 2 nights at weekends.

Rooms	1 double; 1 twin with separate bath: £80-£90. Singles £60-£65.
Meals	Pub/restaurants 0.5 miles.
Closed	Rarely.

Sue Stevens
Myrtle Cottage,
Trevail, Cubert, Newquay, TR8 5HP
Tel   +44 (0)1637 830460
Mobile   +44 (0)7763 101076
Email   enquiries@myrtletrevail.co.uk
Web   www.myrtletrevail.co.uk

Entry 34   Map 1

Cornwall

House at Gwinear

An island of calm, this grand old rambling house sits in bird-filled acres but is only a short drive from St Ives. The Halls are devoted to the encouragement of the arts and crafts which is reflected in their lifestyle. Find shabby chic with loads of character and no stuffiness – fresh flowers on the breakfast table, a piano in the corner, rugs on polished floors, masses of books. In a separate wing is your cosy bedroom and sitting room, with a fine view of the church from the bath. The large lawned gardens are there for bare-footed solace, and you can have breakfast in the Italianate courtyard on sunny days.

Rooms	1 twin/double with separate bath & sitting room: £80-£90.
Meals	Supper, 2 courses with wine, £25. Pub 1.5 miles.
Closed	Rarely.

Charles & Diana Hall
House at Gwinear,
Gwinear,
St Ives, TR27 5JZ

Tel	+44 (0)1736 850444
Email	charleshall@btinternet.com

Entry 35   Map 1

Cornwall

Penquite

A doll's house of a B&B in a constellation of Cornwall's best attractions, set in a quiet village overlooking the Hayle estuary and bird reserve. A doctor's house from 1908, it oozes Arts and Crafts with chunky stone walls, sloping roof, winding stairs and polished oak enhanced by Stephanie's ceramics. There's a snug, bay-windowed sitting room; a private suite of cute bedrooms in the eaves; a mature garden of lofty pines, palms and summer house; a generous continental spread on the terrace or light-filled dining room. Stroll to pubs and deli, or past a golf course to the coastal path and St Ives Bay views.

Rooms	1 double: £85-£90. 1 family room for 5 (1 triple, 1 single with extra z-bed): £85-£130. Singles £85.
Meals	Continental breakfast. Restaurant 2-minute walk.
Closed	Rarely.

Stephanie Pace
Penquite,
Vicarage Lane, Lelant,
St Ives, TR26 3EA

Tel	+44 (0)1736 755002
Email	stephaniepace@hotmail.com
Web	www.penquite-seasidesuite-cornwall.com

Entry 36   Map 1

Cornwall

11 Sea View Terrace

In a smart row of Edwardian villas, with stunning harbour and sea views, is a delectable retreat. Sleek, softy coloured interiors are light and gentle on the eye – an Italian circular glass table here, a painted seascape there. Bedrooms are perfect with crisp linen and vistas of whirling gulls from private terraces; bathrooms are state of the art. Rejoice in softly boiled eggs with anchovy and chive-butter soldiers for breakfast – or continental in bed if you prefer. Grahame looks after you impeccably and design aficionados will be happy.

Over 12s welcome.

Rooms	3 suites for 2: £100-£135. Singles from £75.
Meals	Dinner, with wine, from £25 (groups only). Packed lunch from £15. Pubs/restaurants 5-minute walk.
Closed	Rarely.

Grahame Wheelband
11 Sea View Terrace,
St Ives, TR26 2DH

Tel   +44 (0)1736 798440
Mobile   +44 (0)7973 953616
Email   info@11stives.co.uk
Web   www.11stives.co.uk

Entry 37   Map 1

Cornwall

Keigwin Farmhouse

Off the glorious coast road to St Ives, in two walled acres overlooking the sea, is a very old farmhouse lived in by Gilly. Walk to the beach at Portheras Cove, dine well at Gurnard's Head, return to little whitewash-and-pine bedrooms with views that make you want to get out your paints, and a big shared bathroom with a massive old bath, fresh with organic cotton towels. A treat: Gilly's scones on arrival, eggs from her hens, stacks of books above the stairs and an arty feel – wide floorboards, creamy colours, family pieces, sculptures, ceramics, glass. A relaxed, delightful – and musical instrument-friendly – B&B.

Rooms	2 doubles sharing bathroom (let to same party only): £75-£80. 1 single sharing bathroom (let to same party only): £40.
Meals	Pubs/restaurants 3 miles.
Closed	Rarely.

Gilly Wyatt-Smith
Keigwin Farmhouse,
Keigwin, Morvah, St Just,
Penzance, TR19 7TS

Tel   +44 (0)1736 786425
Email   sleep@keigwinfarmhouse.co.uk
Web   www.keigwinfarmhouse.co.uk

Entry 38   Map 1

Cornwall

Cove Cottage

Down a long lane to a rose-clad cottage in the most balmy part of Cornwall... peace in a private cove. Your own door leads up steps to a gorgeous suite with luxurious linen on an antique four-poster, art, sofas... and a flowery balcony with spectacular views of the sea and subtropical gardens. Settle in happily to the sound of the waves. Sue is friendly and serves a great breakfast in the garden room: home-laid eggs, homemade jams and their own honey. The Penwith peninsula hums with gardens, galleries and stunning sandy beaches; Minack Theatre and Lamorna are close. Arrive to a salad supper chosen from a small but special menu. Paradise!

Minimum stay: 3 nights in high season.

Rooms	1 suite for 2: £140-£145.
Meals	Salad suppers from £12.50 available on the night of arrival. Pub/restaurant 3 miles.
Closed	November – February.

Sue White
Cove Cottage,
St Loy, St Buryan,
Penzance, TR19 6DH

Tel	+44 (0)1736 810010
Email	thewhites@covecottagestloy.co.uk
Web	www.covecottagestloy.co.uk

Entry 39   Map 1

Cornwall

The Hideaway

A tucked away little gem in the garden. Your Hideaway is behind Julie and Howard's terraced house in the heart of this popular fishing village – it has its own gate, and a small courtyard full of sun and colourful pots. Step inside to an inviting living space with a table by the window, books, TV and a very comfy bed; the big bathroom is sparkling. Friendly hosts bring over breakfast with homemade jams: full English, or compote and croissants perhaps – there's a fridge and kettle for independence. Teeming with things to do: galleries and cafés, Minack theatre, St Michael's Mount, arty St Ives... and a stream of stunning beaches.

Dedicated parking just up the road.

Rooms	1 suite for 2: £90.
Meals	Pubs/restaurants 2-minute walk.
Closed	Rarely.

Julie & Howard Whitt
The Hideaway,
Pengarth, Commercial Road,
Mousehole, TR19 6QG

Tel	+44 (0)1736 731252
Email	thehideawaymousehole@gmail.com
Web	www.thehideawaymousehole.com

Entry 40   Map 1

Cornwall

Venton Vean

Everything at Venton Vean is tip-top. Immensely helpful owners Philippa and David moved from London with their family and have transformed a dilapidated Victorian house into a supremely cool and elegant B&B. Moody colours, mid-century design classics and interesting reclamation finds make for a stunning and eclectic interior. Food is a passion – expect freshly ground coffee in your room and some of the most tantalising breakfasts around: Mexican, Spanish, even a good old full English will have you dashing down in the morning. Arty Penzance is a joy as is the craggy-coved beauty all around.

Minimum stay: 2 nights.

Rooms	4 doubles: £71–£97.
	1 family room for 4: £110–£140.
	Singles £70–£85.
Meals	Dinner, 3 courses, from £20.
	Packed lunch from £5.
	Cream tea £4.
Closed	Rarely.

	Philippa McKnight
	Venton Vean,
	Trewithen Road,
	Penzance, TR18 4LS
Tel	+44 (0)1736 351294
Email	info@ventonvean.co.uk
Web	www.ventonvean.co.uk

Entry 41   Map 1

Cornwall

Ednovean Farm

There's a terrace for each fabulous bedroom (one truly private) with views to the wild blue yonder and St Michael's Mount Bay, an enchanting outlook that changes with the passage of the day. Come for peace, space and the best of eclectic fabrics and colours, pretty lamps, Christine's sculptures, fluffy bathrobes and handmade soaps. The beamed open-plan sitting/dining area is an absorbing mix of exotic, rustic and elegant; have full breakfast here (last orders nine o'clock) or continental in your room. A footpath through the field leads to the village; walk to glorious Prussia Cove and Cudden Point, or head west to Marazion.

Rooms	2 doubles, 1 four-poster: £100–£130.
Meals	Pub 5-minute walk.
Closed	Rarely.

	Christine & Charles Taylor
	Ednovean Farm,
	Perranuthnoe,
	Penzance, TR20 9LZ
Tel	+44 (0)1736 711883
Email	info@ednoveanfarm.co.uk
Web	www.ednoveanfarm.co.uk

Entry 42   Map 1

Cornwall

Edyn at Rose Cottage

Unusual B&B for lovers of the great outdoors. You have utter privacy (away from the owners' cottage) in your hut on wheels with a veranda warmed by a wood-burner and underfloor heating inside. Views are leafy and there's a stream at the bottom of the garden – perfect for cooling your champagne. It's a short walk to shower and loo, you can toast homemade marshmallows over the fire pit and friendly owners are on hand for local advice. A delicious breakfast arrives by wheel barrow! Explore St Ives, picnic on both coasts or just stay put – as the stars come out, sit under the twinkling outdoor lights and feel liberated.

Minimum stay: 2 nights. Logs provided.

Rooms	1 shepherd's hut for 2 (bathroom a short walk away): £70.
Meals	Pubs/restaurants 5 miles.
Closed	Never.

	Richard & Julie Robinson
	Edyn at Rose Cottage,
	Rose Cottage,
	Trenwheal, TR27 6BP
Tel	+44 (0)1736 850774
Email	edynrosecottage@gmail.com
Web	www.edynatrosecottage.co.uk

Entry 43   Map 1

Cornwall

Parc Mean

The 1903 house in its sylvan setting is half a mile from the sea; on stormy nights, you can hear the rollers pounding. You are surrounded by 1,200 acres of National Trust parkland, minutes from breathtaking coastal paths, magical Loe Pool, and Porthleven with its amazing choice of good places to eat – Michelin star Kota, twin restaurant Kota Kai, Rick Stein… Christine spoils you at breakfast at the pine table; country bedrooms have bags of old-fashioned comfort – sofas, dressing-tables, big beds, colourful Cornish art. All feels settled with no one to rush you, the house is filled with good cheer and you'll leave with a spring in your step.

Rooms	1 double, 1 twin/double, each with separate bath: £100.
Meals	Pubs/restaurants 1 mile.
Closed	Christmas & New Year.

	Chrissie Harvey
	Parc Mean,
	Penrose Estate (NT), Porthleven,
	Helston, TR13 0RB
Tel	+44 (0)1326 574290
Email	chrissie.parcmean1@gmail.com
Web	www.parcmean.com

Entry 44   Map 1

Cornwall

Nanspean Farmhouse

Head down long country lanes to arrive in this glorious setting overlooking the sea and Loe Pool – the largest natural freshwater lake in Cornwall. Simon and Sally have that happy knack of making you feel at home; Sally is a ceramicist and their whole house is full of art and interesting pieces. They give you a tucked away suite: a light, pretty bedroom, a comfy sitting room with flowers, views and lots of books; sunsets from the bedroom window are breathtaking. Simon bakes bread and the dining room is a lovely spot for breakfast: dark wood, oil family portraits, sun streaming in. Join the coastal path from the farmland... perfect!

Minimum stay: 2 nights in high season.

Rooms	1 suite for 2 with separate bath: £110-£125. Singles £80-£90.
Meals	Pubs/restaurant 1.5 miles.
Closed	Christmas & occasionally.

Simon & Sally Giles
Nanspean Farmhouse,
Gunwalloe,
Helston, TR12 7PX
Tel   +44 (0)1326 569525
Email   sallycgiles@yahoo.co.uk
Web   www.staywestcornwall.com

Entry 45   Map 1

Cornwall

Halzephron House

The coastal path runs through the grounds and the view is to die for – you can see St Michael's Mount on a clear day. Be greeted by homemade biscotti and organic coffee roasted in Cornwall: lovely Lucy and Roger are foodies as well as designers. The suite is contemporary, quirky and full of charm: space, art and bowls of wild flowers, velvet sofa and a big antique French bed; drift off under goose down to the sound of the waves. The drawing room leads onto a deck overlooking the garden and the sea; soak up the stunning sunsets. You can walk to three amazing beaches, a 13th-century church, a golf course and a gastropub. Heaven.

Rooms	1 suite for 2 with sitting room: £110-£130. Extra bed/sofabed available £30-£45 per person per night.
Meals	Pub 0.25 miles.
Closed	Rarely.

Lucy Thorp
Halzephron House,
Gunwalloe,
Helston, TR12 7QD
Mobile +44 (0)7899 925816
Email   info@halzephronhouse.co.uk
Web   www.halzephronhouse.co.uk

Entry 46   Map 1

Cornwall

The Hen House

A generous, peaceful oasis. Sandy and Gary are warmly welcoming, and have oodles of local information on places to visit, eat and walk – with OS maps on loan. Ground floor rooms, in individual barns, are spacious and colourful with bright fabrics, king-size beds and stable doors to the courtyard. Relax in the hot tub in the wildflower meadow, bask on the sun loungers, wander by the ponds and watch the ducks' antics; the central courtyard is fairy-lit at night. Scrumptious locally sourced breakfasts are served in the dining chalet surrounded by birdsong. Tai-chi in the meadow, reiki and reflexology in the Serpentine Sanctuary... bliss.

Minimum stay: 2 nights. Over 12s welcome.

Rooms	2 doubles: £80-£90.
Meals	Pub/restaurant 1 mile.
Closed	Rarely.

Sandy & Gary Pulfrey
The Hen House,
Tregarne, Manaccan,
Helston, TR12 6EW
Tel +44 (0)1326 280236
Mobile +44 (0)7809 229958
Email henhouseuk@btinternet.com
Web www.thehenhouse-cornwall.co.uk

Entry 47 Map 1

Cornwall

Bay House

Perched on the edge of the map, high on rugged, seapink-tufted cliffs, Bay House is almost as close to the sea as you can get. Rooms are spacious (one with a bay window), the dining room defers to stunning sunsets and the attention to detail is immaculate. Expect fine original artwork and antiques, Ralph Lauren dressing gowns, designer linen, Molton Brown lotions, iPod docks and DVD players. Scramble down to secluded beaches, stroll to the famous Lizard Lighthouse or relax to the sound of the surf in the beautiful garden under rustling palms and hovering kestrels. Breakfast is outstanding – with John's homemade bread and jams.

Children over 8 welcome.

Rooms	2 twin/doubles: £150-£175.
Meals	Pubs/restaurants 5-minute walk.
Closed	Christmas.

Carla Caslin
Bay House,
Housel Bay,
The Lizard, TR12 7PG
Tel +44 (0)1326 290235
Mobile +44 (0)7740 168805
Email carla.caslin@btinternet.com
Web www.mostsoutherlypoint.co.uk

Entry 48 Map 1

Cornwall

Trerose Manor

Follow winding lanes through glorious countryside to find the prettiest, listed manor house, a warm family atmosphere and welcoming tea in the beamed kitchen. Large, light bedrooms, one with floor-to-ceiling windows, sit peacefully in your own wing and have views over the stunning garden. All are dressed in pretty colours, have comfy seats for garden gazing and smartly tiled bathrooms. A sumptuous breakfast can be taken outside in summer, there are wonderful walks over fields to river or beach and stacks of interesting places to visit. Tessa and Piers are engaging hosts, and you're looked after very well – guests love it here.

French, German & Italian spoken.

Rooms	2 doubles, 1 twin/double: £120-£130. Singles £80.
Meals	Pubs/restaurants within walking distance.
Closed	Rarely.

Tessa Phipps
Trerose Manor,
Mawnan Smith,
Falmouth, TR11 5HX
Tel   +44 (0)1326 250784
Email   info@trerosemanor.co.uk
Web   www.trerosemanor.co.uk

Cornwall

Bosvathick

A huge old Cornish house that's been in Kate's family since 1760 – along with Indian rugs, heavy furniture, ornate plasterwork, pianos, portraits… even a harp. Historians will be in their element: pass three Celtic crosses dating from the 8th century before the long drive finds the imposing house (all granite gate posts and lions) and a rambling garden with grotto, lake, pasture and woodland. Bedrooms are traditional, full of books, antiques and pots of flowers; bathrooms are spick and span, one small and functional, one large. Come to experience a 'time warp' and charming Kate's good breakfasts. Close to Falmouth University, too.

French spoken. Post code has been changed from TR11 5RD; Sat Nav will find new post code if updated.

Rooms	2 twin/doubles: £100. 2 singles: £60-£70
Meals	Supper, from £25. Packed lunch £5-£10. Pubs 2 miles.
Closed	Rarely.

Kate & Stephen Tyrrell
Bosvathick,
Constantine,
Falmouth, TR11 5RZ
Tel   +44 (0)1326 340103
Email   kate@bosvathickhouse.co.uk
Web   www.bosvathickhouse.co.uk

Cornwall

Trevilla House

Come for the position: the sea and Fal estuary wrap around you, and the King Harry ferry gives you an easy reach into the glorious Roseland peninsula. Inside find comfortable airy bedrooms with homemade quilts on the beds – the twin with a sofa and old-fashioned charm, the double with stunning sea views. Jinty rustles up delicious locally sourced breakfasts and homemade jams, and you eat in the sunny conservatory that looks south over the sea. Trelissick Gardens, with its intriguing newly opened house, is nearby – worth visiting for the view down the Fal alone. From there you are able to take a ferry to Truro, St Mawes or Falmouth.

Rooms	1 double, 1 twin: £85-£95.
	1 single, sharing bath with double
	(let to same party only): £50-£55.
Meals	Pubs/restaurants 1-2 miles.
Closed	Christmas & New Year.

	Jinty & Peter Copeland
	Trevilla House,
	Feock, Truro, TR3 6QG
Tel	+44 (0)1872 862369
Mobile	+44 (0)7791 977621
Email	jinty.copeland@gmail.com
Web	www.trevilla.com

Entry 51   Map 1

Cornwall

Pollaughan Farm

B&B with a twist. Your own converted barn next to Valerie's farmhouse where you choose your breakfast style: a generous continental left in the fridge, or a full Monty platter ordered the night before and brought over in the morning. The beamed open-plan space is charming and light with seating at one end, a luxuriously dressed bed at the other (local chocs on the pillow), books, TV and doors on to a private sunny deck. Porthcurnick beach is a 20-minute walk – return to a great value supper: Valerie's delicious crumbly pies, pork chops with Cornish cider perhaps – and an excellent fish and chip van comes round twice a week!

Minimum stay: 2 nights.

Rooms	1 double: £110-£130.
Meals	Dinner £9-£12.
	Pubs/restaurants 3.5 miles.
Closed	Rarely.

	Valerie Penny
	Pollaughan Farm,
	Portscatho, Truro, TR2 5EH
Tel	+44 (0)1872 580150
Email	holidays@pollaughan.co.uk
Web	www.pollaughan-bandb.co.uk/
	bb-with-a-difference

Entry 52   Map 1

Cornwall

Hay Barton

Giant windows overlook many acres of farmland, and Jill and Blair look after you so well! Breakfasts are special with the best local produce, homemade granola, yogurt and more. Arrive for tea and lovely home-baked cake, laid out in a comfortable guest sitting room with a log fire and plenty of books and maps. Bedrooms are fresh and pretty with garden flowers, soft white linen on big beds and floral green walls. Gloriously large panelled bathrooms have long roll top baths and are painted in earthy colours. You can knock a few balls around the tennis court, and you're near to good gardens and heaps of places to eat.

Minimum stay: 2 nights in summer.

Rooms	3 twin/doubles: £85–£90.
	Singles £65.
Meals	Pubs 1-2 miles.
Closed	Rarely.

Jill & Blair Jobson
Hay Barton,
Tregony, Truro, TR2 5TF
Tel   +44 (0)1872 530288
Mobile   +44 (0)7813 643028
Email   jill.jobson@btinternet.com
Web   www.haybarton.com

Entry 53   Map 1

Cornwall

Tredudwell Manor

Winding lanes lead to this handsomely refurbished Queen Anne style house. Surrounded by lawns and mature trees the views are south to the sea and the total peace is just the tonic. Inside is a marble bar for more reviving and the mix of sofas, mini-ottomans, parquet floors with Persian rugs and family portraits make for a genteel atmosphere. First floor bedrooms are large enough to waltz in with toile de Jouy wallpaper, antiques and views. In the roof space are more compact but delightful rooms – uncluttered and calm with low beams, shuttered windows and modern bathrooms. Breakfast is a treat with the best produce from nearby Fowey.

Rooms	6 doubles: £85–£125.
	1 family room for 4: £125–£165.
	Singles £65–£100.
Meals	Pubs/restaurants 2 miles.
Closed	Rarely.

Justin & Valérie Shakerley
Tredudwell Manor,
Lanteglos,
Fowey, PL23 1NJ
Tel   +44 (0)1726 870226
Email   justin@tredudwell.co.uk
Web   www.tredudwell.co.uk

Entry 54   Map 1

Cornwall

Botelet B&B

The farmhouse at the end of the wild-flowered lane is an inspired synthesis of stone, wood, Shaker simplicity and comfy old chairs: the chicest of shabby chic. Rustic bedrooms reached by a steep stair have planked floors, antique beds and beautiful linen; the bathroom is just along the hallway. Breakfasts – organic, home-baked, home-picked, vegetarian – are enjoyed at a scrubbed table by the Rayburn. Drink in the pure air, explore the farm, walk the wooded valley; return to a therapeutic massage in the treatment room. Botelet has been in the family since 1860 and is quirky, friendly, artistic, huge fun. The yurts are amazing.

Children over 10 welcome.

Rooms	1 double, 1 twin/double sharing bath (let to same party only): £80-£100. 2 yurts for 2: £55-£90.
Meals	Continental breakfast (£15 for yurt). Pub 2 miles.
Closed	December – Easter.

The Tamblyn Family
Botelet B&B,
Herodsfoot,
Liskeard, PL14 4RD
Tel   +44 (0)1503 220225
Email   stay@botelet.com
Web   www.botelet.com

Cumbria

Chapelburn House

Yomp in the most dramatic scenery close to the best bits of Hadrian's Wall, then head for Chapelburn House. Matt and Katie are young, charming, unflappable, food is reared happily then cooked with more flavour than fuss. Honey is from their bees, bread is home-baked. You have a sitting room with an open fire, lots of books and squishy sofas, *and* a south-facing garden room for summer dreaming. Bedrooms are deeply comfortable and bathrooms (one definitely not for fatties!) brand spanking new. Children are more than welcome to join in. This would delight exhausted refugees from London, too.

Rooms	2 doubles: £75-£95.
Meals	Dinner, 3 courses, £25. Packed lunch £5-£7.50. Restaurant 5 miles.
Closed	Christmas & New Year.

Matthew & Katie McClure
Chapelburn House,
Low Row,
Brampton, CA8 2LY
Tel   +44 (0)1697 746595
Email   stay@chapelburn.com
Web   www.chapelburn.com

Cumbria

Hawksdale Lodge

Spring heaven! Bowl along blissfully quiet roads while sheep bleat and daffs bob in the breeze. This is supremely comfortable B&B at any time of the year though and your hosts look after you with great charm from their stunning 1810 gentleman farmer's house with pretty garden. Home baking and local produce at breakfast, sumptuously dressed bedrooms with plenty of space and seating, warm and inviting bathrooms with proper windows. The National Park is only six miles away for strenuous walking and cycling, the northern Lakes and fells beckon, Hadrian's wall is near. Return to something homemade and delicious. Lovely.

Minimum stay: 2 nights at Easter & New Year.

Rooms	1 double; 1 double with separate bath: £95-£150. Singles £70-£100.
Meals	Supper on request, 2 courses, £20. BYO. Packed lunch on request, from £5. Pubs/restaurants less than 1 mile.
Closed	Christmas.

Lorraine Russell
Hawksdale Lodge,
Dalston,
Carlisle, CA5 7BX
Mobile   +44 (0)7810 641892
Email   enquiries@hawksdalelodge.co.uk
Web   www.hawksdalelodge.co.uk

Entry 57   Map 11

Cumbria

Lazonby Hall

The pinky sandstone façade rises, château-like, from bright flowers, box hedges, crunchy gravel: enchanting. Views, from sash windows and garden folly, yawn over the Eden valley to the Pennines. Step past pillars to panelled, antique-filled rooms of heavy curtains, marble fires, mahogany and oils. Formal, yet not daunting – the Quines and their dachshunds bring life, flexibility, and delicious Cumbrian breakfasts. Wake to birdsong and garden views. This sweet area of winding lanes and dry stone walls is near the north Lakes, Penrith, Carlisle, Scotland – ripe for exploration by foot, bike, canoe or train.

Rooms	2 doubles; 1 double, 1 twin sharing bath: £90-£135. Singles £80-£100.
Meals	Dinner, 3 courses, £35-£50. Pub/restaurant 2 miles.
Closed	Rarely.

Mr & Mrs Quine
Lazonby Hall,
Lazonby,
Penrith, CA10 1AZ
Tel   +44 (0)1768 870300
Email   info@lazonbyhall.co.uk
Web   www.lazonbyhall.co.uk

Entry 58   Map 11

Cumbria

Johnby Hall

You are ensconced in the quieter part of the Lakes and have independence in this Elizabethan manor. Once a fortified Pele tower, it's a fascinating historic house yet very much a lived-in family home with a wonderful atmosphere. The airy suites have a sitting room each with books, children's videos, squashy sofas, pretty fabrics and whitewashed walls. Beds have patchwork quilts, windows have stone mullions and all is peaceful. Henry gives you sturdy breakfasts, and you can join him and Anna for convivial home-grown suppers by a roaring fire in the great hall. Children will have fun: hens and pigs to feed, garden toys galore and woods to roam.

Rooms	1 twin/double, with sitting room: £125. 1 family room for 4, with sitting room: £125. Singles £87. Extra bed/sofabed available £20 per person per night.
Meals	Supper, 2 courses, £20. Pub 1 mile.
Closed	Rarely.

Henry & Anna Howard
Johnby Hall,
Johnby,
Penrith, CA11 0UU
Tel   +44 (0)17684 83257
Email   bookings@johnbyhall.co.uk
Web   www.johnbyhall.co.uk

Entry 59   Map 11

Cumbria

Robyns Barn

Wow, fabulous views — fells and mountains in every direction including Blencathra, the most climbed fell in the Lakes. Robyns Barn is attached to the main house, and it's all yours. Step into a large, welcoming open-plan space: limewashed walls, big oak table, beams, antique pine, toasty wood-burner and plenty of DVDs, books and games. Inviting bedrooms, upstairs, have sheepskins on wooden floors. Wake when you want — Kathryn leaves a continental breakfast with homemade bread, muesli, fruit, yogurts; there's a farm shop close by serving excellent cooked breakfasts too. The garden has a picnic area, barbecue — and those views!

Minimum stay: 2 nights. Children over 8 welcome.

Rooms	Barn – 1 double, 1 twin with sitting/dining room & kitchenette (let to same party only): £90.
Meals	Continental breakfast. Supper £20. Pubs/restaurants 1 mile.
Closed	Rarely.

Adrian & Kathryn Vaughan
Robyns Barn,
Lane Head Farm, Troutbeck,
Keswick, Penrith, CA11 0SY
Tel   +44 (0)1768 779841
Email   robynsbarn@hotmail.co.uk
Web   www.robynsbarn.co.uk

Entry 60   Map 11

Cumbria

Lowthwaite

Leave your worries behind as you head up the lanes to the farmhouse tucked into the fell. Jim, ex-hiking guide, and Danish Tine are charming, helpful and well-travelled. Their barn is dotted with Tanzanian furniture and your peaceful bedrooms are in the view-filled wing. Beds are made of recycled dhow wood, sparkling bathrooms sport organic soaps; the garden room has its own patio. Breakfasts with homemade granola, bread and muffins are delicious – perhaps halloumi with mushrooms, tomatoes and egg or smoked salmon with creamed spinach. Birds galore in the garden, a trickling stream… endless fells to explore too – advice is happily given.

Rooms	2 twin/doubles: £85-£90. 2 family rooms for 4: £90-£120. Singles £55-£65.
Meals	Packed lunch £6. Dinner £18-£27. Pubs 2.5 miles.
Closed	Christmas.

Tine & Jim Boving Foster
Lowthwaite,
Matterdale,
Penrith, CA11 0LE
Tel   +44 (0)1768 482343
Email   info@lowthwaiteullswater.com
Web   www.lowthwaiteullswater.com

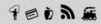

Entry 61   Map 11

Cumbria

Greenah

Tucked into the hillside off a narrow lane, this 1750s smallholding is surrounded by fells, so is perfect for walkers. Absolute privacy for friends or family with your own entrance to a beamed, stone-flagged sitting room with a wood-burning stove, and cheery floral curtains. Warm bedrooms have original paintings, good beds, hot water bottles, bathrobes and a sparkling bathroom with a loo with a remarkable view. Malcolm and Marjorie are totally committed to organic food – you get a welcoming pot of tea and cake on arrival and a fabulous breakfast. They'll give you good advice about the local area too. Fell walking is not compulsory!

Children over 8 welcome.

Rooms	1 double, 1 twin sharing shower (let to same party only): £94-£100. Singles £60-£65.
Meals	Pubs/restaurants 3 miles.
Closed	November – January.

Marjorie & Malcolm Emery
Greenah,
Matterdale, Penrith, CA11 0SA
Tel   +44 (0)1768 483387
Mobile   +44 (0)7767 213667
Email   info@greenah.co.uk
Web   www.greenah.co.uk

Entry 62   Map 11

Whitrigg House

On the edge of the National Park, a handsome 1700s house with original features galore. Period colours blend with contemporary pieces, eclectic finds and local art, the red sitting room is warmly inviting. Mike and Robbie live nearby and look after you well; the Whitrigg breakfast includes homemade bread, jams and muesli, fruit with crème fraîche and a full English. Beds are wonderfully comfy; towels thick and large. Stroll to the pub for supper, or if you arrive late tuck into a complimentary bowl of soup, or winter mulled wine. Just minutes from the M6 for a comfy stopover, and a good base for exploring the Lakes. Perfect!

Please check owners' website for availability before enquiring. Over 12s welcome.

Kelleth Old Hall

Glorious unimpeded views of fields, cows and the Howgill Fells from this fun and characterful B&B. Charlotte – chutney enthusiast, writer of three novels – has moved into an ancient manor (the fourth owner in 400 years); now it glows with paintings, antiques and books. Short steep stairs lead from 17th-century flagstones to a big canopied brass bed and yellow silk curtains at mullion windows. All is warm, charming, inviting, and that includes the roll top bath beneath a vaulted ceiling. Fuel up on a Cumbrian breakfast, return to a delicious supper of exotic flavours. Near the A685 but peaceful at night.

Rooms	2 doubles: £90–£110.
	1 single: £60.
Meals	Pubs/restaurants 5-minute walk.
Closed	Rarely.

Rooms	1 double (extra single bed
	available): £80–£90.
	Singles £60–£65.
Meals	Dinner, 2-3 courses, £18–£22.
	Pub/restaurant 5 miles.
Closed	Occasionally.

	Mike Taylor
	Whitrigg House,
	Clifton,
	Penrith, CA10 2EE
Tel	+44 (0)1768 895077
Email	info@whitrigghouse.co.uk
Web	www.whitrigghouse.co.uk

	Charlotte Fairbairn
	Kelleth Old Hall,
	Kelleth, Penrith, CA10 3UG
Tel	+44 (0)1539 623344
Mobile	+44 (0)7754 163941
Email	charlottefairbairn@hotmail.co.uk
Web	www.kelletholdhall.co.uk

Cumbria

Drybeck Hall

In the Yorkshire Dales National Park, looking south to fields, woodland and beck, this Grade II* listed, 1679 farmhouse has blue painted mullion windows and exposed beams. Expect a deeply traditional home with good furniture, open fire and pictures of Anthony's predecessors looking down on you benignly; the family has been in the area for 800 years. Comfortable bedrooms have pretty floral fabrics and oak doors; bathrooms are simple but sparkling. Lulie is relaxed and charming and a good cook: enjoy a full English with free-range eggs in the sunny dining room, and home-grown vegetables and often game for dinner. A genuine slice of history.

Rooms	1 double, 1 twin: £100. Singles £50.
Meals	Dinner, 3 courses, £25. Pub/restaurant 4 miles.
Closed	Rarely.

	Lulie & Anthony Hothfield
	Drybeck Hall,
	Appleby-in-Westmorland, CA16 6TF
Tel	+44 (0)1768 351487
Email	lulieant@aol.com
Web	www.drybeckhall.co.uk

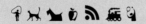

Entry 65 Map 12

Cumbria

Lapwings Barn

In the back of most-beautiful-beyond, down narrow lanes, this converted barn is a gorgeous retreat for two – or four. Delightful generous Gillian and Rick give you privacy and an upstairs sitting room with log stove, sofa and a balcony with views. Bedrooms downstairs (separate entrances) are pleasingly rustic with beams and modern stone-tiled bathrooms. Breakfast is delivered: sausages and bacon from their Saddlebacks, eggs from their hens, superb homemade bread and marmalade. Stroll along lowland tracks, watch curlews and lapwings, puff to the top of Whinfell. Ambleside and Beatrix Potter's house are near. One of the best.

Rooms	Barn – 2 twin/doubles & sitting room: £66-£90. Singles £55. Extra bed/sofabed available £20 per person per night.
Meals	Packed lunch £5. Dinner £20. Pub/restaurant 3.5 miles.
Closed	Rarely.

	Rick & Gillian Rodriguez
	Lapwings Barn,
	Whinfell, Kendal, LA8 9EQ
Tel	+44 (0)1539 824373
Mobile	+44 (0)7901 732379
Email	stay@lapwingsbarn.co.uk
Web	www.lapwingsbarn.co.uk

Entry 66 Map 12

Cumbria

Summerhow House

In four acres of fine landscaping and fun topiary is a large and inviting home of flamboyant wallpapers and shades of aqua, lemon and rose. Stylish but laid-back, grand but unintimidating, both house and hosts are a treat. Bedrooms have gilt frames and marble fireplaces, Molton Brown goodies and garden views, there are two sitting rooms to retreat to and breakfasts to delight you – fruits from the orchard, eggs from Sizergh Castle (John's family home). Two miles from Kendal: hop on the train to the Lakes. Walkers, sailors, skiers, food-lovers, dog-lovers will be charmed... aspiring actors too (talk to Janey!).

Rooms	1 double, 1 twin: £80-£120. Singles £50-£69.
Meals	Pub/restaurant 1.5 miles.
Closed	Occasionally.

Janey & John Hornyold–Strickland
Summerhow House,
Shap Road, Kendal, LA9 6NY

Tel	+44 (0)1539 720763
Mobile	+44 (0)7976 345558
Email	janeyfothergill@googlemail.com
Web	www.summerhowbedandbreakfast.co.uk

Entry 67   Map 11

Cumbria

Fellside Studios

Off the beaten tourist track, a piece of paradise in the Troutbeck valley: seclusion, stylishness and breathtaking views. Prepare your own candlelit dinners, rise when the mood takes you, come and go as you please. The flower beds spill with heathers, hens cluck, and there's a decked terrace for continental breakfast in the sun – freshly prepared by your gently hospitable hosts who live in the attached house. In your studio apartment you get oak floors, slate shower rooms, immaculate kitchenettes with designer touches, DVD players, comfy chairs, luxurious towels. Wonderful.

Minimum stay: 2 nights.

Rooms	1 double, 1 twin/double, each with kitchenette: £80-£100. Singles £50-£60.
Meals	Continental breakfast. Pub/restaurant 0.5 miles.
Closed	Rarely.

Monica & Brian Liddell
Fellside Studios,
Troutbeck,
Windermere, LA23 1NN

Tel	+44 (0)1539 434000
Email	brian@fellsidestudios.co.uk
Web	www.fellsidestudios.co.uk

Entry 68   Map 11

Cumbria

Gilpin Mill

Come to be seriously spoiled. Down leafy lanes is a pretty white house by a mill pond, framed by pastures and trees. Steve took a year off to build new Gilpin Mill, and Jo looks after their labs and guests – beautifully. In the country farmhouse sitting room oak beams span the ceiling and a slate lintel sits above the log fire. Bedrooms are equally inviting: beds are topped with duck down, luscious bathrooms are warm underfoot. Alongside is a lovely old barn where timber was made into bobbins; in the mill pond is a salmon and trout ladder and a dam, soon to provide power for the grid. And just six cars pass a day!

Children over 10 welcome.

Rooms	3 twin/doubles: £95-£115.
	Singles £63-£73.
Meals	Pub 2.5 miles.
Closed	Christmas.

Jo & Steve Ainsworth
Gilpin Mill,
Crook,
Windermere, LA8 8LN
Tel   +44 (0)1539 568405
Email info@gilpinmill.co.uk
Web   www.gilpinmill.co.uk

Entry 69   Map 11

Cumbria

Broadgate

Through stone pillars is a lovely Georgian house with stunning views to the sea. Vivid blue hydrangeas make a startling contrast to its white façade and smooth green lawns. Find elegant flowery bedrooms with high, comfortable beds and pretty furniture, a little sitting room with a wood-burner, and a beautifully laid table in the dining room. Diana, an accomplished cook, treats you to home-produced vegetables and fruits, local sausages, cakes and scones. Her walled garden, surrounded by woodland, is full of old roses, wide borders and places to sit. Head out for castles, gardens, Beatrix Potter's house, Coniston Water sailing and great walks.

Children over 10 welcome.

Rooms	2 doubles, both with separate bath: £55-£95.
	1 single with separate shower room: £55-£95.
Meals	Dinner, 3 courses, £25.
	Pub 5 miles.
Closed	Rarely.

Diana Lewthwaite
Broadgate,
Millom,
Broughton-in-Furness, LA18 5JZ
Tel   +44 (0)1229 716295
Email dilewthwaite@bghouse.co.uk
Web   www.broadgate-house.co.uk

Entry 70   Map 11

Cumbria

Broughton House

Down lanes edged with dry stone walls and hedges, with distant views of the Lakeland mountains… what peace! You feel instantly at home too, in a house full of books and colour. Bedrooms come with a jar of Cate's homemade brownies, a bowl of fruit and a deep mattress: owls hooting you to sleep in one, privacy in the wing, snug simplicity in Ben's Cabin. Wake to fresh juice, pancakes, homemade bread, local bacon and sausages, smoked salmon and scrambled eggs. Puffin the dog, Minty the cat, a host of hens and a large garden all add to the charm. Perfect for cycling, a hop from Windermere and eating out in pretty Cartmel is a treat.

Rooms	2 doubles: £85-£90.
	1 cabin for 2 (1 double, 1 single, kitchen & yurt sitting room): £60-£80.
	Singles £60.
Meals	Pub 1 mile.
Closed	Rarely.

Cate Davies
Broughton House,
Field Broughton,
Grange-over-Sands, LA11 6HN
Tel   +44 (0)1539 536439
Email   info@broughtonhousecartmel.co.uk
Web   www.broughtonhousecartmel.co.uk

Entry 71   Map 11

Cumbria

Viver Water Mill

Dianne and Ian have spent years renovating their attractive Lakeland stone water mill. Mentioned in the Domesday Book, it dates from the 13th century and one of the grinding stones is set in the traditional sitting room. Arrive to afternoon tea next to the fire, or by the summerhouse overlooking the mill stream and pretty valley. Fresh bedrooms have comfy beds and coordinating fabrics. Wake to home-grown fruits, homemade jams and eggs from the hens; Dianne is happy to do supper too. Wander the beautiful garden, visit historic homes and market town Kirkby Lonsdale; great walking and cycling, and close to the A590 so a good Scotland stop-over.

Rooms	1 double; 1 double with separate bathroom: £70-£80.
Meals	Supper £10. Dinner, 2 courses, £17.
	Pubs/restaurants 3 miles.
Closed	Rarely.

Dianne Woof
Viver Water Mill,
Viver Lane,
Hincaster, LA7 7NF
Tel   +44 (0)15395 61017
Email   info@viverwatermill.co.uk
Web   www.viverwatermill.co.uk

Entry 72   Map 11

Cumbria

The Malabar

Surrounded by stone walls, sheep and Howgill Fells… in the glorious Yorkshire Dales National Park. Well-travelled Fiona and Graham have restored the barn next to their farmhouse into deeply comfortable, smart spaces. Graham was born in India and tea plays a big part here! Arrive to a mound of scones, meringues, triple choc brownies. Sitting and dining rooms are upstairs: high rafters, Indian art, rugs, colourful elephant side tables. Tuck into breakfast at the big communal table: wild boar bacon, venison sausages, vegetarian choices, homemade bread. Sedburgh is a hop; return to a sunny terrace, toasty wood-burners and a wonderfully luxurious bed.

Minimum stay: 2 nights at weekends.

Rooms	3 doubles: £160–£180.
	3 suites for 2: £220–£240.
	Extra bed/sofabed available £15 per person per night.
Meals	Afternoon tea included.
	Pubs/restaurants 2 miles.
Closed	Rarely.

	Fiona Lappin
	The Malabar,
	Garths, Marthwaite, Sedbergh, LA10 5ED
Tel	+44 (0)15396 20200
Mobile	+44 (0)7594 550046
Email	info@themalabar.co.uk
Web	www.themalabar.co.uk

Entry 73   Map 12

Cumbria

Horse Market

Tucked away in the old part of town, 1 Horse Market started life as the police station. Much more stylish now… and Amorelle is delightful. You're greeted with tea and cake – settle on the sofa by the open fire. Bedrooms have luxurious linen; the airy Loft has low beams, antique French furniture and a roll-top bath with views over the fells; the cosy first floor Panelled Room looks on to Horse Market. Breakfast is a minute away at Plato's restaurant: full Cumbrian, toasted waffles with bacon, granola and berries. Markets, independent shops, the famous Ruskin's View… and walks are wonderful; Amorelle can organise a Lake Windermere boat trip too.

Minimum stay: 2 nights at weekends.

Rooms	2 doubles: £75–£100.
	Singles £60–£80.
Meals	Breakfast served at local restaurant Plato's. Restaurants 1-minute walk.
Closed	Rarely.

	Amorelle Hughes
	Horse Market,
	1 Horse Market, Kirkby Lonsdale,
	Carnforth, LA6 2AS
Tel	+44 (0)1524 272697
Email	stay@horsemarketbandb.co.uk
Web	www.horsemarketbandb.co.uk

Entry 74   Map 12

Derbyshire

Underleigh House

A Derbyshire longhouse in Brontë country built by a man called George Eyre. The position is unbeatable – field, river, hill, sky – but the stars of the show are Philip and Vivienne, dab hands at spoiling guests rotten. There's a big sitting room with maps for walkers, a dining room hall for hearty breakfasts, and tables and chairs scattered about the garden. Back inside, bedrooms vary in size, but all have super beds, goose down duvets and stunning views; a couple have doors onto the garden, the suites have proper sitting rooms. Fantastic walks start from the front door, Castleton Caves are on the doorstep and Chatsworth is close.

Minimum stay: 2 nights at weekends. Over 12s welcome.

Rooms	1 double: £90–£100.
	3 suites for 2: £105–£115.
	Singles £75–£90.
Meals	Packed lunches £6.
	Pubs/restaurants 0.5 miles.
Closed	Christmas & January.

Philip & Vivienne Taylor
Underleigh House,
Lose Hill Lane, Hope,
Hope Valley, S33 6AF
Tel   +44 (0)1433 621372
Email   underleigh.house@btconnect.com
Web   www.underleighhouse.co.uk

Entry 75   Map 12

Derbyshire

The Lodge at Dale End House

One of those places where you get your own annexe – in this case, the former milking parlour of the listed farmhouse. It certainly has scrubbed up nicely. The ground-floor bedroom has a finely dressed antique bed and magnificent chandelier while the well-equipped kitchen is a boon if you don't fancy venturing out for supper. Friendly, helpful Sarah takes orders for breakfasts – eggs from her hens, local sausages and bacon – and delivers to your door. No open fire but cosy underfloor heating warms you after a blustery yomp in any direction. Bring your four-legged friends – canine or equine – to this happy house.

Rooms	Lodge: 1 double with
	kitchen/dining/sitting room: £85–£95.
Meals	Pubs/restaurants 2.5 miles.
Closed	Rarely.

Sarah & Paul Summers
The Lodge at Dale End House,
Gratton,
Bakewell, DE45 1LN
Tel   +44 (0)1629 650380
Email   thebarn@daleendhouse.co.uk
Web   www.daleendhouse.co.uk

Entry 76   Map 8

Derbyshire

Manor Farm

Between two small dales, close to great houses (Chatsworth, Hardwick Hall, Haddon Hall), lies this cluster of ancient farms and a church; welcome to the 16th century! Simon and Gilly, warm, delightful and fascinated by the history, have restored the east wing to create big, beamy rooms in the old hayloft and a pretty garden room on the ground floor; a cosy and quaint bedroom overlooks the church. Wake to a scrumptious breakfast in the cavernous Elizabethan kitchen. There's a 'book exchange' in the old milking parlour and a lovely garden with sweeping views across the valley and distant hills.

Children over 6 welcome.

Rooms	1 double, 2 twin/doubles: £80-£90.
	1 family room for 2-4: £80-£140.
	Singles £55-£70.
Meals	Pubs within 10-minute drive.
Closed	Rarely.

Simon & Gilly Groom
Manor Farm,
Dethick, Matlock, DE4 5GG
Tel +44 (0)1629 534302
Mobile +44 (0)7944 660814
Email gilly.groom@w3z.co.uk
Web www.manorfarmdethick.co.uk

Entry 77 Map 8

Derbyshire

Mount Tabor House

On a steep hillside between the Peaks and the Dales, a chapel in a pretty village with a peaceful aura and great views. Enter a hall where light streams through stained-glass windows – this is a relaxed, easy place to stay with a distinctive and original interior, a log-burner to keep you toasty and a sweet dog called Molly. Fay is charming and generous and breakfast, in a dining room with open stone walls, is delicious: mainly from the village shops and as organic as possible; you can eat on the balcony in summer. Walk to the pub for dinner, come home to a fabulous wet room and a big inviting bed.

Usually minimum two nights at weekends.

Rooms	1 twin/double: £90-£95.
	Extra bed/sofabed available
	£10-£30 per person per night.
Meals	Occasional dinner £25.
	Pub 100 yds.
Closed	Rarely.

Fay Whitehead
Mount Tabor House,
Bowns Hill, Crich,
Matlock, DE4 5DG
Tel +44 (0)1773 857008
Mobile +44 (0)7813 007478
Email mountabor@msn.com

Entry 78 Map 8

Derbyshire

Alstonefield Manor

Country manor house definitely, but delightfully understated and cleverly designed to look natural. This family home, sitting in walled gardens, is high in the hills above Dovedale. Local girl Jo spoils you with homemade scones and tea when you arrive, served on the lawns or by the fire in the elegant drawing room. Beautiful bedrooms have antiques, flowers, lovely fabrics, painted floors and garden views; wood panelled bathrooms have showers or a roll top tub. Wake to birdsong – and a candlelit breakfast with local bacon and Staffordshire oatcakes. After a great walk, stroll across the village green for supper at The George. A joy.

Minimum stay: 2 nights. Over 12s welcome.

Rooms	1 double; 2 doubles, each with separate bathroom: £120–£150. Singles £100.
Meals	Pub 100 yds.
Closed	Christmas & occasionally.

	Robert & Jo Wood
	Alstonefield Manor,
	Alstonefield,
	Ashbourne, DE6 2FX
Tel	+44 (0)1335 310393
Email	stay@alstonefieldmanor.com
Web	www.alstonefieldmanor.com

Entry 79   Map 8

Derbyshire

Hinchley Wood

Glorious Georgian house with the most engaging, friendly hosts: you're in for a treat. The pineapple-topped gateposts are a symbol of hospitality, and you arrive for tea and cake by the fire in the splendid drawing room. Sleep well in elegant bedrooms; beds are topped with good linen, there are interesting books to browse and the views are stunning. Rosemaré's breakfasts are "legendary" – a local, usually organic, spread with her wonderful Staffordshire oat cakes. Pretty villages, historic houses, Nordic walking, riding, fly fishing on the river Dove... the area is dreamy and Cedric is happy to arrange activities.

Minimum stay: 2 nights at weekends. Children over 10 welcome. Pets by arrangement.

Rooms	1 double, 1 four-poster: £120–£140.
Meals	Pubs/restaurants 3-minute walk.
Closed	December/January.

	Cedric & Rosemaré Stevenson
	Hinchley Wood,
	Mappleton,
	Ashbourne, DE6 2AB
Tel	+44 (0)1335 350219
Email	rose-stevenson@hotmail.co.uk

Entry 80   Map 8

Devon

North Walk House

Sea views, brass bedsteads and big rooms at this calm retreat, perfectly positioned on a cliff-top path – super for walkers and foodies. Ian and Sarah welcome you with homemade cake in a cosy guest lounge, and give you light bedrooms with sparkling bathrooms and seductive beds. Enjoy the coastal and Exmoor walks, or genteel Lynton and Lynmouth; return to log fire and armchairs. Take your tea on a sea-view terrace, or be tempted by Sarah's four-course dinner, seasonal and mostly organic. Everything here has been carefully thought out, from the welcome to the décor and the refreshments: arrive, unpack, unwind…

Devon

Victoria House

Beachcombers, surfers and walkers will be in their element here. You stay in the beach-hut annexe with a big romantic deck facing the sea; complete with funky daybed and a magnificent view. The owners live next door in the Edwardian seaside villa: Heather is lively and fun; she and David are ex-RAF. They go out of their way to give you the best tour de force breakfasts – fruits, yogurts, waffles, eggs Benedict or the full Monty. Sip a sundowner on the deck or stir yourself to go further; you are on the coastal road to Woolacombe (of surfing and kite-surfing fame) and the beach is a ten-minute walk. A top spot for couples.

Check-in 4pm-9pm, unless arranged. Special diets catered for.

Rooms	2 doubles, 1 twin/double: £106–£164. Singles £50–£100.
Meals	Dinner, 4 courses, from £27. Pub/restaurant 0.25 miles.
Closed	Rarely.

Rooms	1 double: £100–£120. Singles £80–£90.
Meals	Pubs/restaurants 200 yds.
Closed	Rarely.

	Ian & Sarah Downing
	North Walk House,
	North Walk,
	Lynton, EX35 6HJ
Tel	+44 (0)1598 753372
Email	walk@northwalkhouse.co.uk
Web	www.northwalkhouse.co.uk

	Heather & David Burke
	Victoria House,
	Chapel Hill, Mortehoe,
	Woolacombe, EX34 7DZ
Tel	+44 (0)1271 871302
Email	heatherburke1959@gmail.com
Web	www.victoriahousebandb.co.uk

Entry 81   Map 2

Entry 82   Map 2

Devon

Beachborough Country House

Welcome to this gracious 18th-century rectory with stone-flagged floors, lofty windows, wooden shutters and glorious rugs. Viviane is vivacious and spoils you with dinners and breakfasts from the Aga; dine in the elegant dining room before a twinkling fire. Hens cluck, horses whinny but otherwise the peace is deep. Ease any walker's pains away in a steaming roll top tub; lap up country views from big airy bedrooms. There's a games room for kids in the outbuildings and a stream winds through the garden – a delicious three acres of vegetables and roses. Huge fun.

Rooms	2 doubles, 1 twin/double (extra single available): £85-£90.
Meals	Dinner, 2-3 courses, £20-£25. Catering for house parties. Pub 3 miles.
Closed	Rarely.

Viviane Clout
Beachborough Country House,
Kentisbury,
Barnstaple, EX31 4NH
Tel   +44 (0)1271 882487
Mobile   +44 (0)7732 947755
Email   viviane@beachboroughcountryhouse.co.uk
Web   www.beachboroughcountryhouse.co.uk

Entry 83   Map 2

Devon

Coombe Farm

Easy-going, foodie, country-lovers fit right in here. Lisa and Matt, passionate about real food, cook home-grown dinners; charcuterie a speciality. They're reinvigorating this fine old Devon long house in its green fold of farmland and you're free to wander the garden, chat to the pigs, plunge in the invigorating pool. The dramatic Blue Room has a fab bathroom; the smaller, equally comfortable Cloud Room, eponymous wallpaper; décor is a quirky mix of family and brocante finds. Breakfast – homemade continental – in your room or the sitting/dining room. 20 minutes to the coast and Exmoor walks; the No 3 cycle route is close by.

Min. stay: 2 nights at weekends & in high season. Children over 2 welcome. Pets by arrangement.

Rooms	1 double, 1 twin/double: £65-£85.
Meals	Dinner from £25. Restaurants 15-minute walk.
Closed	Rarely.

Lisa Eckford
Coombe Farm,
Coombe Farm, Goodleigh,
Barnstaple, EX32 7NB
Tel   +44 (0)1271 324919
Mobile   +44 (0)7771 346501
Email   info@coombefarmgoodleigh.co.uk
Web   www.coombefarmgoodleigh.co.uk

Entry 84   Map 2

Devon

Devon

Hollamoor Farm

If it's a civilised retreat you're after then head to where the Taw and Torridge meet... to Tarka country, and this rambling 300-year-old farm. Roses ramble, swallows swoop and there are 500 acres to explore. One bedroom is in a barn next to the house and combines stone rusticity and country house grandeur with aplomb; the soft furnishings are exquisite. The bedroom in the house is equally plush and both have fun bathrooms. There's a huge fireplace in the dining room and a well-loved sitting room where you can meet the Wreys (past and present). A real family home where the door is always open – elegant informality at its very best.

Tabor Hill Farm

From nearly 1,000-feet up the moorland views roll away to the south and down to the church spire in the village. Bring walking boots, perhaps even your horse, and enjoy being well away from it all in this beautiful Exmoor National Park spot. Smart rooms come with super-comfortable Hypnos beds, new oak floors and a stylish country feel; bathrooms are modern and spotless. A wood-burner warms the dining room and you may tinkle the Bechstein if you wish as sociable Astley fries eggs from her own hens. There are trails to walk, romantic Exmoor to explore, a wildlife hide and the clearest night skies. Wonderful.

Over 14s welcome.

Rooms	1 twin/double with separate bath; Barn – 1 twin/double: £90. Singles £45.
Meals	Dinner, 3 courses, £35. Pubs/restaurants 3 miles.
Closed	Rarely.

Rooms	1 double, 1 twin: £90. Singles £55.
Meals	Dinner £20. Pubs/restaurants 2-6 miles.
Closed	Rarely.

	Sir George & Lady Caroline Wrey Hollamoor Farm, Tawstock, Barnstaple, EX31 3NY
Tel	+44 (0)1271 373466
Mobile	+44 (0)7766 700904
Email	carolinewrey@gmail.com

	Astley Shilton Barlow Tabor Hill Farm, Heasley Mill, South Molton, EX36 3LQ
Tel	+44 (0)1598 740036
Mobile	+44 (0)7985 577175
Email	enquiries@taborhillfarm.co.uk
Web	www.taborhillfarm.co.uk

Entry 85   Map 2

Entry 86   Map 2

Devon

Sannacott

On the southern fringes of Exmoor you're in peaceful rolling hills, hidden valleys and a Designated Dark Sky area. The Trickeys breed horses from their Georgian style farmhouse; find roaring log fires, antiques, pretty fabrics, fresh flowers and a relaxed feel. Bedrooms are traditional and comfortable (one in an annexe), some with views over the garden and countryside. Generous breakfasts include homemade bread and jams and organic or local goodies. There's a pretty bird-filled garden to wander, walkers can enjoy the North Devon coastal path, birdwatchers and riders will be happy and there are well-known gardens to visit.

Stabling available and advice on rides.

Rooms	1 double, 1 twin/double sharing bath/shower (let to same party only); Annexe – 1 twin with kitchenette: £80. Singles £45.
Meals	Occasional dinner, 3 courses, £25. Pub 2.5 miles.
Closed	Rarely.

Clare Trickey
Sannacott,
North Molton, EX36 3JS
Tel   +44 (0)1598 740203
Email   mct@sannacott.co.uk
Web   www.sannacott.co.uk

Entry 87   Map 2

Devon

South Yeo

Down windy lanes with tall grassy banks and the smell of the sea is a lovely Georgian country house with two walled gardens and barns at the back. You'll fall for this place the moment you arrive, and its owners: Jo runs an interiors business; Mike keeps the cattle and sheep that graze all around. Bedrooms are inviting; the double, overlooking the valley, has a cream French bed, a pretty quilted cover, a claw-foot bath and a little sitting room (adjoining) with TV. There's an elegant drawing room with a real fire too. Delicious breakfasts with home-laid eggs and homemade jams are brought to a snug room that catches the morning sun.

Rooms	1 double with sitting room; 1 twin/double with separate bath: £80–£105. Singles £75.
Meals	Pub 1.5 miles.
Closed	Rarely.

Joanne Wade
South Yeo,
Yeo Vale, Bideford, EX39 5ES
Tel   +44 (0)1237 451218
Mobile   +44 (0)7766 201191
Email   stay@southyeo.com
Web   www.southyeo.com

Entry 88   Map 2

Devon

Beara Farmhouse

The moment you arrive at the whitewashed farmhouse you feel the affection your hosts have for their home and gardens. Richard is a lover of wood and a fine craftsman – every room echoes his talent; he also created the pond that's home to mallards and geese. Ann has laid brick paths, stencilled, stitched and painted, all with an eye for colour; bedrooms and guest sitting room are delectable and snug. Open farmland all around, sheep, hens in the yard, the Tarka Trail on your doorstep and hosts happy to give you 6.30am breakfast should you plan a day on Lundy Island. Guests love this place.

Minimum stay: 2 nights at weekends, bank holidays & June-September.

Rooms	1 double, 1 twin: £80. Singles by arrangement.
Meals	Pub 1.5 miles.
Closed	20 December to 5 January.

Ann & Richard Dorsett
Beara Farmhouse,
Buckland Brewer,
Bideford, EX39 5EH

Tel	+44 (0)1237 451666
Email	bearafarmhouse@gmail.com
Web	www.bearafarmhouse.co.uk

Entry 89   Map 2

Devon

The Linhay

Your own peaceful hideaway. The open valley has a running stream, views are of orchard, friendly sheep and a bright yellow vintage tractor. Andrei and Holly live in the main house, and they've created a quirky, natural feel in the lovely old barn: jaunty red rocking chairs by a wood-burner, art, flowers; up spiral steps to a colourfully clad bed in the eaves, down to a little kitchen area. They bring over a cooked breakfast: home-laid eggs, sausages from the pigs; help yourself to organic muesli, artisan bread, homemade jams – out on the balcony if you want. Borrow wellies and maps, return from Dartmoor to a great value supper. Bliss.

Arrival after 3pm, departure by 12 noon if possible. With a bit of notice can collect guests from the local stations.

Rooms	The Linhay Annexe – 1 suite for 2 with kitchenette: £95.
Meals	Homecooked supper for 2 £25. Pubs/restaurants 3 miles.
Closed	Rarely.

Holly Carter & Andrei Szerard
The Linhay,
Brendon Cottage, Copplestone,
Crediton, EX17 5NZ

Tel	+44 (0)1363 84386
Email	enquiries@smilingsheep.co.uk
Web	www.smilingsheep.co.uk

Entry 90   Map 2

Devon

Burnville House

Granite gateposts, Georgian house, rhododendrons, beech woods and rolling fields of sheep: that's the setting. But there's more. Beautifully proportioned rooms reveal subtle colours, elegant antiques, squishy sofas and bucolic views, stylish bathrooms are sprinkled with candles, there are sumptuous dinners and pancakes at breakfast. Your hosts left busy jobs in London to settle here, and their place breathes life – space, smiles, energy. Swim, play tennis, walk to Dartmoor from the door, take a trip to Eden or the sea. Or... just gaze at the moors and the church on the Tor and listen to the silence, and the sheep.

Rooms	3 doubles: £85-£95. Singles £65.
Meals	Dinner from £23. Pub 2 miles.
Closed	Rarely.

Victoria Cunningham
Burnville House,
Brentor, Tavistock, PL19 0NE
Tel   +44 (0)1822 820443
Mobile   +44 (0)7881 583471
Email   burnvillef@aol.com
Web   www.burnville.co.uk

Entry 91   Map 2

Devon

Lavender House

Right on the edge of Dartmoor, this creatively renovated house was originally five miners' cottages. Susie and Nigel's home is a happy mix of Art Deco finds, Victorian pieces and soft colours; find books, a wood-burner in the snug sitting room, and scones and jam for your arrival. Downstairs bedrooms have heaps of pillows, gowns, flowers, a silver tea tray with vintage china and homemade biscuits. Wake for an Aga breakfast round a sunny table – homemade bread and granola, kedgeree perhaps or ham and egg muffin parcels. Tavistock has a lively Saturday market; good pubs are a walk. Return to sit by the fire pit in the pretty garden.

Rooms	2 doubles: £85-£95. Singles £75-£85.
Meals	Dinner £25. Pubs/restaurants 2 miles.
Closed	Rarely.

Susie Bateman
Lavender House,
Brentor Road,
Mary Tavy,
Tavistock, PL19 9PY
Tel   +44 (0)1822 811048
Email   whiteginger@hotmail.co.uk

Entry 92   Map 2

Devon

Rose Cottage

On a quiet country road on the edge of Peter Tavy is a pretty slate-hung cottage and a garden full of birds: Pippin's delight. Enter to find a dining room with a shining wooden floor, a fine Georgian table and a smart Aga to keep things cosy. Bedrooms are sunny; 'Blue Room' and 'Rose Room' have lovely fabrics, watercolours, luxuriously comfy king-size beds and TVs; the sweet twin shares a bathroom with 'Rose' so is perfect for families. After a generous breakfast, pull on your boots and stride onto Dartmoor — or visit Pippin's favourite gardens. Then it's home to a delicious dinner — and hot water bottles on chilly nights.

Minimum stay: 2 nights at weekends. Babes in arms and children over 8 welcome.

Rooms	2 doubles, both with separate bath (can form a family suite for 4 with extra interconnecting twin): £70–£105. Singles £40.
Meals	Dinner, 2 courses, £20. Pubs/restaurants 0.5 miles.
Closed	Christmas.

Pippin Clarke
Rose Cottage,
Peter Tavey,
Tavistock, PL19 9NP
Tel   +44 (0)1822 810500
Email   rose.pippin@gmail.com
Web   www.rosecottagedartmoor.co.uk

Entry 93   Map 2

Devon

Kilbury Manor

You can stroll down to the Dart from the garden and onto their little island, when the river's not in spate! Back at the Manor — a listed longhouse from the 1700s — are four super-comfortable bedrooms, the most private in the stone barn. Your genuinely welcoming hosts (with dogs Dillon and Buster) moved to Devon to renovate the big handsome house and open it to guests. Julia does everything beautifully so there's organic smoked salmon and delicious French toast for breakfast, baskets of toiletries by the bath, the best linen on the best beds and a drying room for wet gear — handy if you've come to walk the Moor. Spot-on B&B.

Rooms	1 double; 1 double with separate bath: £79–£95. Barn – 2 doubles: £79–£95. Singles from £65.
Meals	Pubs/restaurants 1.5-4 miles.
Closed	Rarely.

Julia & Martin Blundell
Kilbury Manor,
Colston Road,
Buckfastleigh, TQ11 0LN
Tel   +44 (0)1364 644079
Email   info@kilburymanor.co.uk
Web   www.kilburymanor.co.uk

Entry 94   Map 2

Devon

Garfield House

Tony grew up here, came back and renovated this wooded-valley home with a generous spirit. He lives at one end in the coach house and every original watercolour and eclectic piece has a story. Art Deco mixes with vintage maps and a French vibe, wood fires burn, sash windows look out to the moor, elegant bedrooms (one downstairs) have space, light and roses. The snug, romantic shepherd's hut has its own bathroom. Breakfast is an informal Aga affair round a long table; tuck into heaps of local things, Riverford tomatoes, organic bread. Orchard, pretty stream, Dartmoor and views from the door, an easy river walk and 10 miles to the coast...

Rooms	3 doubles: £95.
	1 shepherd's hut for 2: £95.
	Discounts available for multiple
	night bookings.
Meals	Pubs/restaurants 1 mile.
Closed	Rarely.

Tony Harley
Garfield House,
Aish, South Brent, TQ10 9JQ
Tel +44 (0)1364 649242
Mobile +44 (0)7768 327253
Email tonyharley@aol.com
Web www.garfieldhouse.co.uk

Entry 95 Map 2

Devon

Seaview House

Morning sun pours into the dining room... tuck in to breakfast to the sound of seagulls and classical music. Your host is fun and well-travelled, and this house has heaps of personality: driftwood carvings above an open fire, a charcoal nude, a Rajasthani mirror embroidery hanging, polished antiques and French style painted furniture. Your ground floor bedroom has a richly dressed bed, the bathroom a cheery seaside feel. Enjoy views from the living rooms to Bigbury Bay and Thurlestone Rock, walk to great beaches and across the river to Burgh Island; there's a cliff-top golf club and Kingsbridge and Salcombe are a short drive.

Rooms	1 twin/double: £75-£90.
	Singles £60.
Meals	Pub 0.25 miles.
Closed	Rarely.

J Meredith
Seaview House,
Thurlestone,
Kingsbridge, TQ7 3NE
Mobile +44 (0)7711 704193
Email jan.meredith1@gmail.com

Entry 96 Map 2

Devon

Keynedon Mill

Welcome to an ancient stone mill, and beautiful rooms in the old miller's house. There's a big friendly kitchen with stone floors and a cheerful red Aga, a beamed dining room with a long polished table, a guest sitting room with a wood-burner, and a pretty garden with a stream running through – picnic, read, enjoy a glass of wine in peaceful corners. Elegant bedrooms have superb beds, antique linen curtains, fresh flowers, morning tea trays and decanters of port. A delicious breakfast of home-baked bread and local produce will set you up for the day: walk the coastal path, discover secluded coves.

Over 12s welcome.

Rooms	2 doubles; 1 double, 1 twin both with separate bath/shower: £95-£120. Singles £60-£80. Extra bed £30.
Meals	Pub 0.5 miles.
Closed	Rarely.

Stuart & Jennifer Jebb
Keynedon Mill,
Sherford, Kingsbridge, TQ7 2AS
Tel +44 (0)1548 531485
Mobile +44 (0)7775 501409
Email bookings@keynedonmill.co.uk
Web www.keynedonmill.co.uk

Entry 97   Map 2

Devon

Stokenham House

Lovely Stokenham House gazes at the sea and the bird-rich Slapton Ley. Iona and Paul – an energetic and thoughtful, imaginative couple – have created a super South Hams base: huge chill-out cushions on the lawn, summerhouse in the pretty banked garden, BBQ by the pool. It's grand yet laid-back, with a fine drawing room, big conservatory and a family-friendly feel. Learn to cook or grow veg, invite friends for dinner, host your own party: Iona is a superb cook. The funky large annexe suite is very private; generous bedrooms in the house are decked in vintage fabrics and papers, and have single rooms off.

Dogs welcome in downstairs room.

Rooms	1 twin/double sharing bath with single: £120. 1 suite for 2: £140. 1 family room for 4 (extra bed/cots available): £140-£210. 1 single: £80. Child over 5 £35. Cots & highchairs available.
Meals	Dinner from £30. Pubs/restaurants 2-minute walk.
Closed	Rarely.

Iona & Paul Jepson
Stokenham House,
Stokenham, Kingsbridge, TQ7 2ST
Tel +44 (0)1548 581257
Mobile +44 (0)7720 443132
Email ionajepson@googlemail.com
Web www.stokenhamhouse.co.uk

Entry 98   Map 2

Devon

Lodge on the Lake

Retreat from the world surrounded by water, woodland and silence. John is entirely affable, asking only that you make yourself at home among the comfortable sofas, stunning views, family photos, books, musical instruments, hats and cases of stuffed fish (most of them caught by him). Borrow a rod to fish the lower lake, wander along paths through acres of woods (bluebells in spring), admire the stunning classic car collection, have yourself a BBQ supper out on the bunting-festooned pontoon, hurl yourself into the water on scorching days. Your sleep will be unruffled and you wake to a breakfast egg from the chickens (strictly no fry-ups). Restful.

Minimum stay: 2 nights. Children over 10 welcome.

Rooms	1 double; 1 double with separate bath: £85–£130.
Meals	Pubs/restaurants 2 miles.
Closed	December to March/April.

John Bishop
Lodge on the Lake,
Sherford,
Kingsbridge, TQ7 2BG
Tel   +44 (0)1548 531574
Mobile   +44 (0)777 3920780
Email   jbishop27@hotmail.co.uk

Entry 99   Map 2

Devon

Strete Barton House

Contemporary, friendly, exotic and exquisite: French sleigh beds and Asian art, white basins and black chandeliers, and a garden with sofas for the views. So much to love – and best of all, the coastal path outside the door. Your caring hosts live the dream, running immaculate B&B by the sea, in an old manor house at the top of the village. Breakfasts are exuberantly local (village eggs, sausages from Dartmouth, honey from the bay), there's a wood-burner in the sitting room, warm toasty floors and Kevin and Stuart know exactly which beach, walk or pub is the one for you. Heavenly.

Children over 8 welcome. Dogs welcome in the cottage suite only.

Rooms	3 doubles, 1 twin/double; 1 twin/double with separate shower: £105–£145. Cottage – 1 suite for 2 & sitting room: £150–£165.
Meals	Pub/restaurant 50 yds.
Closed	Rarely.

Stuart Litster & Kevin Hooper
Strete Barton House,
Totnes Road, Strete,
Dartmouth, TQ6 0RU
Tel   +44 (0)1803 770364
Email   info@stretebarton.co.uk
Web   www.stretebarton.co.uk

Entry 100   Map 2

Devon

Lighthouse

Perched high above town with astonishing views... Pippa is an interior designer and art collector and her home has colourful furnishings galore, a huge state of the art wood-burner and masses of drawings. Pale wood floors give a Scandinavian feel and contemporary pieces mix well with antiques; ground floor bedrooms have goose down bedding, smart bathrooms – and those inspiring views. Breakfast, in the open-plan kitchen or on the sun terrace, is a local treat. Hop on a boat to Agatha Christie's house, or the ferry to Kingswear and a steam train along the coast. The steps back up will get you puffing... the sunset and an aperitif are the reward.

Parking available on-site & parking permits available in town.

Rooms	2 doubles: £100–£150.
Meals	Pubs/restaurants 2-minute walk.
Closed	Rarely.

Pippa Clague
Lighthouse,
50 Above Town,
Dartmouth, TQ6 9RG

Tel	+44 (0)1803 835225
Mobile	+44 (0)7815 107032
Email	pippaclague@me.com

Entry 101   Map 2

Devon

Fingals

Welcome to an institution from our first B&B book. We call it an 'institution' not because it has been going so long that some of the original guests' grandchildren now take their girlfriends, but because it has always been beyond categorisation. Richard and Sheila are moving back into their Queen Anne manor farmhouse and winding down – but as ever doing it their own way. Stay in a best hotel room, or self-cater in rooms nattily converted into apartments. The old laissez-faire atmosphere remains: honesty bar, wood-panelled dining room (dinner on occasion), grass court, pool and gym. Not your run-of-the-mill B&B... but nor are Richard and Sheila.

Minimum stay: 2 nights at weekends.

Rooms	3 doubles: £110–£210.
	1 suite for 2: £300–£700 per week (self-catering).
	1 barn for 5, 1 barn for 6: £400–£1,200 per week (self-catering). Extra bed/sofabed available £15 per person per night.
Meals	Dinner £36.
	Pub 1 mile; restaurants 6 miles.
Closed	Mid-January to mid-March.

Richard & Sheila Johnston
Fingals,
Dittisham,
Dartmouth, TQ6 0JA

Tel	+44 (0)1803 722398
Email	info@fingals.co.uk
Web	www.fingals.co.uk

Entry 102   Map 2

Devon

Devon

Kerswell Farmhouse

Close to Totnes and Dartmouth yet out in the wilds, this ridge-top house and barn have glorious views to the moor. A Devon longhouse that was once in poor repair, all has been transformed by oak – seasoned and new – while the front sports a gorgeous conservatory. Graham sells British art (on fabulous display), Nichola is an interior designer, together they run truly welcoming B&B. Find lots of delicious choices at breakfast including bacon from their own pigs and homelaid eggs; super-comfy bedrooms with electronic blinds; state of the art bathrooms; a suite with its own slice of garden. Books and DVDs on tap, local tipples in the honesty bar too.

No minimum stay. Over 12s welcome.

Riverside House

The loveliest 18th-century house with the tidal river estuary bobbing past with boats and birds; dip your toes in the water while sitting in the garden. Felicity, an artist, and Roger, a passionate sailor, give you pretty bedrooms with paintings, poetry, little balconies, wide French windows and binoculars; spot swans at high tide, herons (perhaps a kingfisher) when the river goes down. Stroll to the pub for quayside barbecues and jazz in summer; catch the ferry from Dittisham to Agatha Christie's house; discover delightful Dartmouth. Kayaks and inflatables are welcome by arrangement.

Minimum stay: 2 nights at weekends.

Rooms	3 doubles: £110-£120. Barn – 1 twin/double: £110-£120. Barn – 1 suite for 2 with sitting room & private garden: £140. Singles £82.50-£105.
Meals	Restaurants 2 miles.
Closed	Part of the winter season.

Rooms	1 double; 1 double with separate shower: £80-£100. Singles from £75. Extra bed/sofabed available £30 per person per night.
Meals	Pubs 100 yds.
Closed	Rarely.

Graham & Nichola Hawkins
Kerswell Farmhouse,
Kerswell,
Cornworthy, Totnes, TQ9 7HH
Tel   +44 (0)1803 732013
Email   gjnhawkins@rocketmail.com
Web   www.kerswellfarmhouse.co.uk

Felicity & Roger Jobson
Riverside House,
Tuckenhay, Totnes, TQ9 7EQ
Tel   +44 (0)1803 732837
Mobile +44 (0)7710 510007
Email   felicity.riverside@hotmail.co.uk
Web   www.riverside-house.co.uk

Devon

Brooking

A whitewashed, wisteria-clad house in a gorgeous village... tea and cake will be waiting. Alison's is a relaxed and friendly home. You will sleep well in a peaceful, charming bedroom: luxurious linen on a brass bed, floral cushions, a jug of wild flowers on an antique wooden chest. Alison's breakfasts change with the seasons: homemade granola, jams and bread, fruit compotes and tasty cooked choices. The garden is walled, rambling and pretty with a tangle of climbers, a bright wooden summerhouse and places to sit in the sun. Head out for nearby Totnes (bustling and arty), great wood or moorland walks and fun on the river Dart.

Travel cot, high chair, toys and books in house! Babysitting happily arranged if needed.

Rooms	1 double: £80-£90. Extra room available (let to same party only).
Meals	Soup, bread & local cheeses (price on request). Children's meals available by arrangement. Pubs 2-minute walk.
Closed	Rarely.

	Alison Carlyon
	Brooking,
	Ashprington,
	Totnes, TQ9 7UL
Tel	+44 (0)1803 731037
Email	w.carlyon@btinternet.com

Entry 105   Map 2

Devon

Avenue Cottage

The tree-lined approach is steep and spectacular; the cottage sits in 11 wondrous acres which overlook the River Dart and Sharpham Estate (local vineyard.) Richard is a gifted gardener and happy to guide you round his fascinating gardens with its magical woodland trail and enviable range of hydrangeas. Find a quiet spot to read or absorb the tranquility with tea on the terrace. The house itself is comfortable and calm – rooms look over the sweeping valley and garden. The old-fashioned twin room has a balcony and large, recently refurbished bathroom with a walk in shower. The pretty village, vineyard café and pub are a short walk away.

Rooms	1 twin/double; 1 double sharing shower room with owner: £70-£90. Singles £55-£75.
Meals	Pub 0.25 miles.
Closed	Rarely.

	Richard Pitts & David Sykes
	Avenue Cottage,
	Ashprington, Totnes, TQ9 7UT
Tel	+44 (0)1803 732769
Mobile	+44 (0)7719 147475
Email	richard.pitts@btinternet.com
Web	www.avenuecottage.com

Entry 106   Map 2

Devon

Beacon House

Perched above Brixham's bustling harbour (a scamper downhill for the sprightly) is this pretty Victorian villa and immaculate B&B. Here live Amanda, Nigel and Henry the springer spaniel, happily sharing garden, house and views. In 'Bay View' the bed is positioned so that you wake to the sun as it rises above the headland and shimmers across the bay... but every room is special and each gets the view. Torbay vistas compete with delicious breakfasts brought to small tables (Devon haddock; apricots stewed in tea and orange; local honey; Amanda's take on the old favourite, the 'Full Beacon'). Dartmouth is five miles, the coastal path a few steps.

Minimum stay: 3 nights on events weekends & bank holidays.

Rooms	3 doubles, 1 twin/double: £79-£129.
Meals	Pubs/restaurants 5-minute walk.
Closed	Rarely.

Nigel Makin
Beacon House,
Prospect Steps, South Furzeham Road,
Brixham, TQ5 8JB

Mobile	+44 (0)7768 565656
Email	enquiries@beaconbrixham.co.uk
Web	www.beaconbrixham.co.uk

Entry 107   Map 2

Devon

Orchard Barn House B&B

A weaver with a strong sense of the past, Susie has an incredible eye for detail. She and David have restored and created a calm, rustic-chic space filled with natural colour, wood, stone, art and reclaimed everything; each beautiful piece has a history and Susie's striking woven works (cushions, a wall hanging) are dotted about. They live next door. Come with friends, or meet new ones here; breakfast is delivered: a communal, DIY, continental affair with free-range eggs – the sleek kitchen is yours to rustle up snacks whenever. Have coffee on the sunny patio overlooking their flax beds, hire a kayak on the river Dart.

Minimum stay: 2 nights.

Rooms	2 doubles; 1 double with separate shower room: £80. Singles £50.
Meals	DIY continental breakfast provided. Pubs/restaurants 2 miles away.
Closed	Rarely.

Susie Gillespie & David Hughes
Orchard Barn House B&B,
Yalberton Farm House, Yalberton
Road, Paignton, TQ4 7PE

Mobile	+44 (0)7738162038
Email	emaildh@btinternet.com
Web	www.susiegillespie.com/accommodation/

Entry 108   Map 2

Devon

Penpark

Clough Williams-Ellis of Portmeirion fame did more than design an elegant house; he made sure it communed with nature. High on a hill overlooking the valley, light pours in to this lovely house from every window, and the views stretch across rolling farmland to Dartmoor and Hay Tor. One bedroom has a comfy sofa and its own balcony; the spacious private suite has arched French windows to gardens, pretty woodland beyond, and an extra room for young children. All is traditional and comforting: antiques, heirlooms, African carvings, silk and fresh flowers, richly coloured rugs. Your charming, generous hosts look after you well.

Rooms	2 twin/doubles, each with separate bath/shower: £76-£90.
	1 family room for 4 with separate shower (ground floor garden suite, dogs welcome): £76-£114.
	Singles by arrangement.
Meals	Pubs/restaurants 3 miles.
Closed	Rarely.

Madeleine & Michael Gregson
Penpark,
Bickington,
Ashburton, TQ12 6LH

Tel	+44 (0)1626 821314
Email	maddy@penpark.co.uk
Web	www.penpark.co.uk

Entry 109   Map 2

Devon

Bulleigh Barton Manor

Tea and scones will be waiting. Find long, leafy views to wake up to, a pool for lazy summer days, ponds and a big colourful garden with a summerhouse. Liz and Mark have restored their house with care, uncovering beams and lovely bits of old wood and filling it with original art and books. Bedrooms are inviting: sink-into beds, china pieces on white window sills, a pot of garden flowers, local fudge and homemade cake. They are keen on sourcing the best local produce and their host of hens lay your breakfast eggs. Dartmoor and the south coast are at your feet; return to a friendly hello from Zennor the dog by the fire.

Doggie welcome pack with homemade dog biscuits, guide & blanket.

Rooms	2 doubles: £80-£125.
	1 suite for 2 (with kitchenette): £81-£110.
	Dogs £5 per dog per night.
Meals	Pubs/restaurants 0.5 miles.
Closed	Rarely.

Liz & Mark Lamport
Bulleigh Barton Manor,
Ipplepen,
Newton Abbot, TQ12 5UA

Tel	+44 (0)1803 873411
Email	liz.lamport@btopenworld.com
Web	www.escapetosouthdevon.co.uk

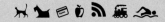

Entry 110   Map 2

Devon

Corndonford Farm

An ancient Devon longhouse and an engagingly chaotic haven run by warm and friendly Ann and Will, along with their Dartmoor ponies. Steep, stone circular stairs lead to bedrooms: bright colours, a four-poster with lacy curtains, gorgeous views over the cottage garden and a bathroom with a beam to duck. A place for those who want to get into the spirit of it all – maybe help catch an escaped foal, chatter to the farm workers around the table; not for fussy types or Mr and Mrs Tickety Boo! Delicious Aga breakfasts and good for walkers too – the Two Moors Way is on the doorstep. Return home for a convivial whisky or sloe gin in front of the fire.

Under 10s by arrangement.

Rooms	1 twin with separate bathroom; 1 four-poster: £80. Singles £40.
Meals	Pub 2 miles.
Closed	Rarely.

Ann & Will Williams
Corndonford Farm,
Poundsgate,
Newton Abbot, TQ13 7PP
Tel   +44 (0)1364 631595
Email   corndonford@btinternet.com

Entry 111   Map 2

Devon

Cyprian's Cot

A charming 16th-century terraced cottage filled with beams and burnished wood. The old stone fireplace is huge, the grandfather clock ticks, the views are stunning and Shelagh is warm and welcoming. Guests have their own sitting room with a crackling fire; up the narrow stairs and into cosy bedrooms – a small double and a tiny twin. Tasty breakfasts, served in the dining room, include free-range eggs, sausages and bacon from the local farm and garden fruits. Discover the lovely town with its pubs, fine restaurants and interesting shops. With the Dartmoor Way and the Two Moors Way on the doorstep, the walking is wonderful too.

Rooms	1 twin; 1 double with separate bath: £65-£75. Singles £32-£35.
Meals	Pubs/restaurants 4-minute walk.
Closed	Rarely.

Shelagh Weeden
Cyprian's Cot,
47 New Street, Chagford,
Newton Abbot, TQ13 8BB
Tel   +44 (0)1647 432256
Email   shelaghweeden@btinternet.com
Web   www.cyprianscot.co.uk

Entry 112   Map 2

Devon

Archerton

Arrive to tea and cake — you're looked after well here! Find attractive things throughout: a rather splendid chandelier over the breakfast table, floral wallpapers, shabby-chic leather sofas, open fires. Elegant bedrooms have snazzy bathrooms, spectacular views and homemade cookies for peckish moments. Wake for breakfast in the sunny dining room with views across to Haytor: Lizzie does a hearty feast with eggs from her rare breed hens and homemade jams. Simple suppers can be rustled up too — or Richard will ferry you to and from the pub. There are 20 acres to roam (take a picnic), walks galore and Exeter and the coast are less than an hour away.

Minimum stay: 2 nights. Children over 11 welcome.

Rooms	2 doubles: £95–£120. Extra beds for children available £20 per night (inc breakfast).
Meals	Supper £20. Picnic £7.50. Pubs/restaurants 2.5 miles.
Closed	Rarely.

Lizzie Jones
Archerton,
Dartmoor, Postbridge,
Yelverton, PL20 6TH
Tel   +44 (0)1822 880286
Email   lizjones100@btconnect.com
Web   www.archerton.com

Entry 113   Map 2

Devon

Hannaford House

An inviting home with fabulous views across the valley to Haldon Forest. If staying in the main house, Kay and Simon give you your own sitting room with wood-burner, bookcases stuffed with books and hare-inspired art and sculpture. Upstairs to a cosy bedroom: soft linen on a pretty iron bed, heaps of towels, lovely big shower. Or choose privacy in the comfy Boot Room with its own sunny courtyard. Breakfast is home-produced and tasty: sausage and bacon from the pigs, eggs from the hens, tomatoes in season, homemade bread and jams. Find hammocks in the colourful garden, woods to explore, Exmouth estuary for boating fun and Dartmoor for hearty walks.

Rooms	1 double: £85–£100. 1 annexe for 2: £75–£100. Singles £65–£90.
Meals	Pub 1.5 miles.
Closed	Rarely.

Kay & Simon Wisker
Hannaford House,
Kennford,
Exeter, EX6 7XZ
Tel   +44 (0)1392 833577
Email   kay@hannafordhouse.co.uk
Web   www.hannafordhouse.co.uk

Entry 114   Map 2

Devon

Devon

Brook Farmhouse

Tuck yourself up in the peace and quiet of Paul and Penny's whitewashed, thatched cottage, surrounded by glorious countryside. Inside find your own charming sitting room with a huge inglenook, good antiques, fresh flowers, and comfy sofa and chairs; breakfast here on homemade apple juice, eggs from the owners' hens and delicious local bacon and sausages. Up the ancient spiral stone stairs is your warm, beamed bedroom with smooth linen, chintzy curtains, lots of cushions. You are near Dartmoor and can reach Devon beaches and the north Cornish coast; perfect for hearty walkers, birdwatchers, surfers and picnic-lovers.

Langdale Farm

Victoria loves having people to stay. Cross the stream, then bump up the steep track to arrive at her friendly, whitewashed, slate-roofed farmhouse. It's a home full of art and quirky touches; the guest sitting room has a toasty wood-burner and gorgeous views; the big pretty bedrooms, up your own stairs, have sink-into linen, a posy of primroses, small bathrooms (mind your head here and there!) and chocs in a little basket. Wake to breakfast in the sun – inside or out on a terrace – fruits and yogurt, a tasty full English from the Aga, a pain au chocolat or two. Explore acres of fields and woodland, head off into Dartmoor National Park.

Rooms	1 double with separate bathroom: £80-£90. Singles £55-£65.	Rooms	1 double; 1 double with separate bath (let to same party only): £80. Singles £65.
Meals	Pub 2 miles.	Meals	Pubs 5 miles.
Closed	Rarely.	Closed	Rarely.

	Paul & Penny Steadman		**Victoria Machin**
	Brook Farmhouse,		Langdale Farm,
	Tedburn St Mary,		Dunsford,
	Exeter, EX6 6DS		Exeter, EX6 7BQ
Tel	+44 (0)1647 270042	Tel	+44 (0)1392 811323
Email	penny.steadman@btconnect.com	Email	victoriamachin@btinternet.com
Web	www.brook-farmhouse.co.uk	Web	www.langdalefarm.co.uk

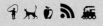

Entry 115   Map 2

Entry 116   Map 2

Devon

Larkbeare Grange

Expectations rise as you follow the tree-lined drive to the immaculate Georgian house... to be warmly greeted with homemade cakes. The upkeep is perfect, the feel is chic and the whole place exudes well-being. Sparkling sash windows fill big rooms with light, floors shine and the grandfather clock ticks away the hours. Expect the best: good lighting, goose down duvets, luxurious fabrics and fittings, a fabulous suite for a small family, flexible (and delicious) breakfasts and lovely views from the bedrooms at the front. Charlie, Savoy-trained, and Julia are charming and fun and there are bikes to borrow. Exceptional B&B!

Rooms	2 doubles, 1 twin/double: £112–£145. 1 suite for 4: £175–£195. Singles £85–£120.
Meals	Pub 1.5 miles.
Closed	Rarely.

Charlie & Julia Hutchings
Larkbeare Grange,
Larkbeare, Talaton, Exeter, EX5 2RY

Tel	+44 (0)1404 822069
Mobile	+44 (0)7762 574915
Email	stay@larkbeare.net
Web	www.larkbeare.net

Entry 117   Map 2

Devon

Lower Allercombe Farm

Horses in the paddock and no-frills bedrooms at this down-to-earth, friendly B&B. Susie, a retired eventer, lives at one end of the listed longhouse; a scented red rose rambles up one wall, and you step in to a sunny kitchen with a cat snoozing behind the Aga. There's a sitting room with horsey pictures and wood-burner, and bedrooms that reflect the fair price. You'll feast on home-grown fruit compote with Greek yogurt, homemade bread, garden tomatoes, home-laid eggs, honey from Susie's neighbour, rashers from local award-winning pigs. Handy for Exeter, the south coast and Dartmoor; the airport is ten minutes away, the A30 one mile.

Rooms	1 double, 1 twin; 1 double with separate bath: £60–£85. Singles £50–£65.
Meals	Pub/restaurant 2 miles.
Closed	Rarely.

Susie Holroyd
Lower Allercombe Farm,
Rockbeare, Exeter, EX5 2HD

Tel	+44 (0)1404 822519
Mobile	+44 (0)7980 255107
Email	holroyd.s@gmail.com
Web	www.lowerallercombefarm.co.uk

Entry 118   Map 2

Devon

The Dairy Loft

The beautiful East Devon Way brings you almost to the door of this smart, new B&B for the independent-minded. Up the exterior stair is your bright, refreshingly opinionated studio with cleverly arranged workstation and wet room with double-headed shower. The funky red leather sofa and big bed (or twins) opposite French windows invite lazing, star-gazing, Merlin-spotting. You're free to concoct your own lavish breakfast beneath the Italian lamp whenever you fancy. Oak-floored inside, larch clad out and with kind, interesting owners across the flowered yard who'll advise on all things local, from sea and river fishing to Exe Trail cycling.

Minimum stay: 2 nights. Pets by arrangement.

Rooms	1 twin/double: £90–£120.
Meals	Pubs/restaurants 2 miles.
Closed	Rarely.

Rob & Annie Jones
The Dairy Loft,
Valley Barn, Hawkerland, Colaton
Raleigh, Sidmouth, EX10 0JA
Tel +44 (0)1395 568411
Email robertjones@eclipse.co.uk
Web www.thedairyloft.co.uk

Entry 119   Map 2

Devon

Glebe House

Set on a hillside with fabulous views over the Coly valley, this late-Georgian vicarage is now a heart-warming B&B. The views will entice you, the hosts will delight you and the house is filled with interesting things. Chuck and Emma spent many years at sea – he a Master Mariner, she a chef – and have filled these big light rooms with cushions, kilims and treasured family pieces. There's a sitting room for guests, a lovely conservatory with vintage vine, peaceful bedrooms with blissful views and bathrooms that sparkle. All this, two sweet pygmy goats, wildlife beyond the ha-ha and the fabulous coast a hike away.

Minimum stay: 2 nights July & August weekends & bank holidays.

Rooms	1 double, 1 twin/double: £80.
	1 family room for 4: £80–£110
	Singles £50.
Meals	Dinner, 3 courses £25.
	Pubs/restaurants 2.5 miles.
Closed	Christmas & New Year.

Emma & Chuck Guest
Glebe House,
Southleigh, Colyton, EX24 6SD
Tel +44 (0)1404 871276
Mobile +44 (0)7867 568569
Email guestsatglebe@gmail.com
Web www.guestsatglebe.com

Entry 120   Map 2

Devon

West Colwell Farm

Devon lanes, pheasants, bluebell walks *and* sparkling B&B. The Hayes clearly love what they do; ex-TV producers, they have converted this 18th-century farmhouse and barns into a snug and stylish place to stay. Be charmed by original beams and pine doors, heritage colours and clean lines. Bedrooms are very private and luxurious, two have terraces overlooking the wooded valley and the most cosy is tucked under the roof. Linen is tip-top, showers are huge and breakfasts (Frank's pancakes, lovely bacon, eggs from next door) are totally flexible. A welcoming glass of wine, starry night skies, beaches nearby, peace all around. Bliss.

Minimum stay: 2 nights at weekends.

Rooms	3 doubles: £105. Singles £85. 10% off double room rate for 3+ nights.
Meals	Restaurants 3 miles.
Closed	December – February.

Frank & Carol Hayes
West Colwell Farm,
Offwell,
Honiton, EX14 9SL
Tel   +44 (0)1404 831130
Email   stay@westcolwell.co.uk
Web   www.westcolwell.co.uk

Entry 121   Map 2

Devon

Barton View

The feel is contemporary with a hint of brocante and breakfast is… whenever! There's a happy self-catering twist to this bright B&B. As well as a pretty bedroom and shower room, you've a sitting room – sofa and leather chair by the log-burner – and a kitchen area stocked with good homemade and local breakfast choices and all the kit for you to rustle it up. The Magranes, in the adjoining house, are relaxed and on hand to pop in. Views are of 15th-century Shute Barton and richly rolling AONB countryside. Train and bike here, walk along the Jurassic Coast from Beer to Branscombe, be a birder – and try the many good eateries in the area.

Minimum stay: 2 nights.

Rooms	Apartment – 1 double with sitting room & kitchen area (child's bed available): £95. Reduced rates for longer stays. Book 4 nights and get 5th free.
Meals	Pub 30-minute walk.
Closed	Rarely.

Paddy & Di Magrane
Barton View,
Shute,
Axminster, EX13 7QR
Tel   +44 (0)1297 35197
Email   paddymagrane@onetel.com
Web   www.bartonview.co.uk

Entry 122   Map 2

Devon

Applebarn Cottage

A tree-lined drive leads to a long white wall, and a gate opening to an explosion of colour – the garden. Come for a deliciously restful place and the nicest, most easy-going hosts; the wisteria-covered 17th-century cottage is full of books, paintings and fresh flowers. Bedrooms – one in an extension that blends in beautifully – are large, traditional, wonderfully comfortable, and the views down the valley are sublime. Patricia trained as a chef and dinners at Applebarn are delicious and great fun. Breakfast, served in a lovely oak-floored dining room, includes honey from the neighbour's bees.

Minimum stay: 2 nights.

Rooms	2 suites for 2: £78–£83. Dinner, B&B (including aperitif) £41.50–£67 p.p.
Meals	Dinner, 3 courses with aperitif, £28.
Closed	November to mid-March.

Patricia & Robert Spencer
Applebarn Cottage,
Bewley Down,
Axminster, EX13 7JX
Tel   +44 (0)1460 220873
Email   paspenceruk@yahoo.co.uk
Web   www.applebarn.wordpress.com

Entry 123   Map 2

Devon

Pounds Farm

A flock of white geese trot across the field, the cottage garden is a summer-blooming feast of colour and the Blackdown Hills are the green backdrop. Inside is just as good: polished wood, original lithographs, oil paintings, comfy seats by the fire, airy bedrooms in apple-pie order and freshly picked flowers in every room. Enjoy the pool, wander the gorgeous gardens, chat to Georgia the spaniel and Molly the horse, have breakfast (free-range and delicious) outside in the sun – Diana wants you to feel at home. Exmoor is close and you can wander down the hill for a pint in the local. A friendly house with a timeless charm.

Rooms	1 double; 1 double with separate bath: £70–£80. Singles £40–£50.
Meals	Pubs/restaurants 10-minute walk.
Closed	Rarely.

Diana Elliott
Pounds Farm,
Hemyock,
Cullompton, EX15 3QS
Tel   +44 (0)1823 680802
Email   diana@poundsfarm.co.uk
Web   www.poundsfarm.co.uk

Entry 124   Map 2

Dorset

Arty BnB By the Sea

Hugh & Candida – busy, travelled artists and environmentalists – make this place very special. You'll be at ease in a blink if you go for easy-going, arty, ramshackling in places, inspiring in others. Revel in the creativity of it all, from Hugh's bold paintings and wallpaper to great homemade bread and jam. You share the dining room, the lawn and veranda (with a nod to Cape Cod), looking sideways to the sea and Golden Cap, and could help in the veg garden. Rooms don't have sea views but plenty of comfort and charm; one has a handsome four-poster; both have brand new shower rooms. Plenty to do in Lyme on foot; forget the car.

Please check owners' website for availability before enquiring.

Rooms	2 doubles: £100.
Meals	Restaurant 5-minute walk.
Closed	Rarely.

	Candida & Hugh Dunford Wood
	Arty BnB By the Sea,
	The Little Place, Silver Street,
	Lyme Regis, DT7 3HR
Mobile	+44 (0)7932 677540
Email	hugh@dunfordwood.com
Web	www.artybnbbythesea.com

Entry 125 Map 2

Dorset

Denhay Corner House

Charlie runs a cut flower business, so her mellow stone cottage has beautiful blooms in every corner. The garden is dreamy, awash with colour. Step inside to find fantastic fabrics and artwork, wall hangings from all over the world, kilims and antiques. Bedrooms have down duvets, a morning tea tray if you wish, and the scent from jugs of old fashioned roses; dated bathrooms are spotless. Expect scrumptious Aga breakfasts – sausages and bacon from friends' pigs, homemade bread, orchard compotes. You can read in the garden, good walks start from the door, Bridport is arty and foodie and it's a short drive to the sea. Wonderfully relaxed.

Rooms	1 double; 1 double with separate bath: £90-£100. Singles £65.
Meals	Dinner, 2 courses, £15. Pubs/restaurants 2.5 miles.
Closed	January/February.

	Charlie Ryrie
	Denhay Corner House,
	Denhay Corner, Broadoak,
	Bridport, DT6 5NN
Tel	+44 (0)1308 427355
Email	charlie@cutflowergarden.co.uk
Web	www.denhaycorner.co.uk

Entry 126 Map 3

Dorset

Old Harbour View

Perch in the bow-fronted window and gaze down on the harbour where the fishing boats dock. What a position – in the heart of Old Weymouth. As for the house, built in 1805, it is uniquely 12 feet wide, yet all is spacious inside, and brimming with light. Imagine stained-glass windows, huge gilt mirrors, fragrant lilies, amusing etchings and posters, sumptuous sofas, and the most delightful hosts. Boat trips, seafood restaurants galore… then it's back home to ivory-white beds in soft-carpeted rooms. Wake to Anna's breads and jams, and locally-smoked haddock: outstanding breakfasts served on lovely china.

Ask about permits for parking, on booking. Minimum stay: 2 nights.

Rooms	1 double, 1 twin/double: £98. Singles £80.
Meals	Pubs/restaurants within walking distance.
Closed	Rarely.

Peter Vincent
Old Harbour View,
12 Trinity Road,
Weymouth, DT4 8TJ
Tel   +44 (0)1305 774633
Email   info@oldharbourview.co.uk
Web   www.oldharbourviewweymouth.co.uk

Entry 127   Map 3

Dorset

Lulworth House

Down through hills, wild heaths and pine forests to beautiful Lulworth. Carole and John's home is set back from this popular cove in a peaceful lane; artist and garden designer, their 1980s house is a creative treasure, inside and out. The garden has a tropical feel with banana trees, ferns, deep borders and abundant grapes over a pergola. Inside is a sparkling white canvas dotted with colour: paintings, glass vases, antique desk, old grandfather clock, cubist furniture. Garden bedrooms are delightful – one has a king-size bed and opens to its own terrace; breakfast is upstairs in the stunning open-plan living space. Walks galore from the door.

Minimum stay: 2 nights at weekends. Over 12s welcome.

Rooms	1 double; 1 double with separate shower room: £85-£125.
Meals	Pubs/restaurants within walking distance.
Closed	Occasionally.

John & Carole Bickerton
Lulworth House,
Bindon Road, West Lulworth,
Wareham, BH20 5RU
Tel   +44 (0)1929 406192
Email   info@lulworthhousebandb.co.uk
Web   www.lulworthhousebandb.co.uk

Entry 128   Map 3

Dorset

Gold Court House

Anthea and Michael have created a mood of restrained luxury and uncluttered, often beautiful, good taste in their Georgian townhouse. Restful bedrooms have antiques, beams, linen armchairs, radios and TVs. There's an eye-catching collection of aquamarine glass, interesting art, and a large drawing room and pretty walled garden in which to relax after a day out. Views are soft and lush yet you are in the small square of this attractive town with cafes and galleries a short walk. Your hosts are delightful – "they do everything to perfection" says a guest; both house and garden are a refuge.

Children over 10 welcome.

Rooms	1 double; 1 twin/double with separate bath: £85. Singles £70.
Meals	Restaurants 50 yds.
Closed	Rarely.

	Anthea & Michael Hipwell
	Gold Court House,
	St John's Hill,
	Wareham, BH20 4LZ
Tel	+44 (0)1929 553320
Email	info@goldcourthouse.co.uk
Web	www.goldcourthouse.co.uk

Entry 129   Map 3

Dorset

Bering House

Fabulous in every way. Renate's attention to detail reveals a love of running B&B: the fluffy dressing gowns and bathroom treats, the biscuits, fruit and sherry... she and John are welcoming and delightful. Expect pretty sofas, golden bath taps, a gleaming breakfast table, and a big sumptuous suite with views across sparkling Poole harbour to Brownsea Island and the Purbeck Hills. Breakfasts are served on blue and white Spode china: exotic fruits with Parma ham, smoked salmon with poached eggs and muffins, kedgeree, smoked haddock gratin, warm figs with Greek yogurt and honey: the choice is superb. An immaculate harbourside retreat.

Rooms	1 twin/double: £85. 1 suite for 2 with kitchenette: £100. Suite available as self-catering option from £85, singles from £80.
Meals	Pub 400 yds. Restaurant 500 yds.
Closed	Rarely.

	Renate & John Wadham
	Bering House,
	53 Branksea Avenue,
	Hamworthy, Poole, BH15 4DP
Tel	+44 (0)1202 673419
Email	johnandrenate1@tiscali.co.uk
Web	www.beringhouse.co.uk

Entry 130   Map 3

Dorset

52 Anthony's Avenue

A generous home with gregarious, travelling/sailing hosts. Homemaking and catering are second nature to Susie so expect a good breakfast with homemade granola, a fruit bowl groaning with melons, and a continental or full English spread; you sit at one large table in the sunny garden room. Your bedroom is up in the eaves – young children can hop through to the next door twin. Nearby beaches are award-winning, the harbour brims with colourful yachts, and you can catch the boat at Poole for the 5-minute journey to car-free Brownsea Island. Return to an elegant sitting room – or to sit out in the secluded garden by pots of geraniums.

Minimum stay: 2 nights. Parking on driveway.

Rooms	1 family room for 2-4: £100-£140.
	Discounts for longer stays.
Meals	Pubs/restaurants 5-minute walk.
Closed	February/March.

Susie Creighton
52 Anthony's Avenue,
Lilliput,
Poole, BH14 8JH
Tel   +44 (0)1202 707048
Email   susie.creighton@googlemail.com

🦜 🐕 🔊 🚂

Dorset

7 Smithfield Place

Valerie is creative and her home an elegant blend of old and new: tapestries and art, large restored mirrors, antiques and modern pieces in your own sitting room. She's also unstinting with treats, from wine to shortbread, kettle chips and chocolates. And breakfast is equally lavish: fruits and yogurts, excellent coffee, pastries, kedgeree or the full works served outdoors on sunny days. Built in 1880, the house sits on a quiet cul-de-sac off the high street, two miles from Bournemouth town centre with easy public transport. The garden is lit up in spring by blooming camellias and cherry blossom, and the whole house sparkles.

Rooms	1 double: £85-£90.
	Singles £60.
Meals	Packed lunch £15.
	Pub/restaurant 100 yds.
Closed	Christmas.

Valerie Johns
7 Smithfield Place,
Winton, Bournemouth, BH9 2QJ
Tel   +44 (0)1202 520722
Mobile   +44 (0)7398 665195
Email   valeriejohns@btinternet.com
Web   www.smithfieldplace.co.uk

🐈 🐕 🔊 🚂

Dorset

Crawford House

Below, the river Stour winds through the valley and under the medieval, nine-arched bridge. Above, an Iron Age hill fort; between is Crawford House. Elegant and Georgian, it sits in an acre of attractive walled gardens full of roses; inside is pretty too, with an easy, relaxed atmosphere. Bedrooms with period furnishings are homely and warm; one room has flowery four-poster twin beds. The sun streams through the tall windows of the downstairs rooms, and charming oil paintings hang in the dining room. Andrea is fun, and a great host, with lots of local knowledge; the North Dorset Trailway starts from her garden.

One night stays available.

Rooms	1 twin/double; 1 twin with separate bath; 1 twin with separate shower: £75-£80. Singles £40.
Meals	Pub in village.
Closed	Rarely.

Andrea Lea
Crawford House,
Spetisbury,
Blandford Forum, DT11 9DP
Tel   +44 (0)1258 857338
Email   andrea@lea8.wanadoo.co.uk

Entry 133   Map 3

Dorset

The Old Mill

Ancient willow trees cast shade over stretches of lawn as kingfishers flit from branch to branch. A secret paradise unfurls before you, as through the Mill's gardens the Stour and its tributaries flow, their banks a-shimmer with hostas, irises, day lilies, gunneras and ferns. Find privacy and independence in your own comfortably contemporary bolthole above the detached garage; a chandelier sparkles in the sun, a mini kitchen hides behind louvre doors, and relaxed Caroline brings you a fine continental breakfast. Walk across the water meadows to little Spetisbury for a pint; discover the delights of Brownsea Island and Blandford Forum.

Min stay: 2 nights at weekends during high season & bank holidays. Self-catering by arrangement.

Rooms	1 family room for 2 (self-contained with sofabed & kitchenette): £95. Singles £80 (mid-week only). £12 per child per night.
Meals	Continental breakfast. Pub 10-minute walk.
Closed	Rarely.

Caroline Ivay
The Old Mill,
Spetisbury,
Blandford Forum, DT11 9DF
Tel   +44 (0)1258 456014
Mobile   +44 (0)7786 096803
Email   c.ivay@btinternet.com
Web   www.theoldmillspetisbury.com

Entry 134   Map 3

Dorset

Stickland Farmhouse

Charming Dorset... welcome to a soft, delightful thatched cottage in an enviably rural setting. Sandy and Paul have poured love into this listed farmhouse and garden, the latter bursting with lupins, poppies, foxgloves, clematis, delphiniums. Sandy gives you delicious breakfasts with homemade muesli, eggs from the hens and soda bread from the Aga. Pretty, cottagey bedrooms have crisp white dressing gowns and lots of books and pictures – one room opens onto your own seating area in the garden. The village has a good pub, and Cranborne Chase, rich in barrows and hill forts, is close by.

Minimum stay: 2 nights at weekends in summer. Children over 10 welcome.

Rooms	2 doubles, 1 twin: £70–£80. Singles £60–£65.
Meals	Pub 3-minute walk.
Closed	Rarely.

Sandy & Paul Crofton-Atkins
Stickland Farmhouse,
Winterborne Stickland,
Blandford Forum, DT11 0NT
Tel +44 (0)1258 880119
Mobile +44 (0)7932 897774
Email sandysticklandfarm@gmail.com
Web www.sticklandfarmhouse.co.uk

Entry 135   Map 3

Dorset

Marren

On the Dorset coastal path overlooking Weymouth Bay – a blissful spot for Jurassic Coast adventures. The owners have transformed this 1920s house, set in six acres of terraced and wooded garden, and their style reflects their penchant for natural materials and country life. Bedrooms are elegant and comfortable; one has a door onto the garden; from the other you can marvel at the sun setting over the sea. Enjoy superb spreads of farm produce and homemade bread, then head off to the secluded beach below and a turquoise sea swim. There's a sense of slow living here. Leave the low-slung Morgan at home: the track is steep!

Minimum stay: 2 nights at weekends. Over 12s welcome.

Rooms	2 doubles: £95–£135.
Meals	Pub 1 mile.
Closed	Rarely.

Peter Cartwright
Marren,
Holworth,
Dorchester, DT2 8NJ
Tel +44 (0)1305 851503
Mobile +44 (0)7957 886399
Email marren@lineone.net
Web www.marren.info

Entry 136   Map 3

Dorset

Yoah Cottage

Rose and Furse are ceramic sculptors; she makes delicate, sometimes humorous, pieces, he creates bold animals and birds; their thatched, rambling house is a jaw-dropping gallery of modern art, ceramics and fabrics. The prettiest of cottage gardens brims with colour and scent – lots of seats and a summerhouse for sitting and admiring. Originally two cottages, you sleep on one side in lovely bedrooms under the eaves, sharing (with friends or family) a bathroom and a sitting room with log fire. Breakfast (full English, homemade jams) is next to the couple's studio. Such warm-hearted, artistic owners – and you're deep in Hardy country.

Minimum stay: 2 nights.

Rooms	1 double, 1 twin sharing bath (let to same party only): £70-£90. Singles £40-£50.
Meals	Pub/restaurant next door.
Closed	Christmas & Easter.

Furse & Rosemary Swann
Yoah Cottage,
West Knighton,
Dorchester, DT2 8PE

Tel   +44 (0)1305 852087
Email roseswann@tiscali.co.uk
Web   www.yoahcottage.co.uk

Entry 137 Map 3

Dorset

Manor Farm

You are high up on the chalk hills that fall to the Jurassic Coast. Tessa's family have lived in the flint and stone house since 1860 and it is crammed with history: solid antiques, books galore, pictures, maps and photographs. From all the windows views soar to sheep-dotted hills. Settle by the wood-burner in the dining room for your Aga-cooked breakfast or supper; in the summer you can eat outside in the garden; cooking is one of Tessa's passions so food is good! Bedrooms are without frills but clean and comfortable; the bathroom is large and sparkling. Outdoor heaven is yours; find a pet pig called Pork!

Rooms	1 double, 1 twin sharing bath (let to same party only): £80-£95.
Meals	Dinner, 2-3 courses, from £15. Pub/restaurant 4 miles.
Closed	Rarely.

Tessa Russell
Manor Farm,
Compton Valence,
Dorchester, DT2 9ES

Tel   +44 (0)1308 482227
Mobile +44 (0)7818 037184 (signal unreliable)
Email tessa.nrussell@btinternet.com
Web   www.manor-farm.uk.com

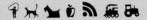

Entry 138 Map 3

Dorset

Tudor Cottage

There are gentle walks from this thatched cottage along the river Frome valley, and rugged coastal paths nearby for heartier souls. Return to homemade scones, a sitting room with lots of art and a roaring fire on chilly days – architecture buffs will swoop upon the medieval over mantle and ancient stone archway. Sleep soundly in crisp white linen with thick fabrics at the windows (you are on the road but it's quiet at night); bathrooms are gleaming. Charming Louise can make anybody feel at home and cooks delicious breakfasts and suppers from local ingredients. Fossils abound and you can track down public gardens too.

Over 12s welcome.

Rooms	1 double, 1 twin: £85-£110.
Meals	Dinner, 2-3 courses, £22-£27. Afternoon tea £7.50 (complimentary on arrival). Pub 2 miles.
Closed	Rarely.

Louise Clarke
Tudor Cottage,
9 Dorchester Road,
Frampton, Dorchester, DT2 9NB
Tel   +44 (0)1300 320382
Mobile   +44 (0)7970 282151
Email   stay@tudorcottagedorset.co.uk
Web   www.tudorcottagedorset.co.uk

Entry 139   Map 3

Dorset

Manor Farm

Pheasants stroll along grassy lanes, kestrels fly overhead and this stunning stone manor house is a delight. Ashley is easy-going and you have your own wing as well as a private courtyard next to the orangery; take a book and sit by the koi ponds. Bedrooms come in comfy country style; the Rose suite with antique linen and pretty wallpaper is charming. The dining room gleams with antiques, silver and flowers; feast on a breakfast of home-laid eggs, homemade jams and local sausages. Climb Eggardon Hill, visit Bridport and Sherborne; Lyme Regis and the Jurassic Coast are a short drive. Friendly lurchers add to the relaxed feel.

Minimum stay: 2 nights. Coarse fishing available on estate lake.

Rooms	1 double, 1 twin, each with separate bath/shower: £100-£140. 1 suite for 2: £120-£150. Singles £80-£100. Extra bed/sofabed available £50 per person per night.
Meals	Pubs within 3 miles.
Closed	Rarely.

Ashley Stewart
Manor Farm,
West Compton,
Dorchester, DT2 0EY
Tel   +44 (0)1300 320400
Email   ashley@manorfarmwestcompton.com
Web   www.westcomptonmanor.co.uk

Entry 140   Map 3

Dorset

The Old Rectory

Hills and meadows surround this lovely old rectory on the river Frome. Guests have an inviting suite of rooms on the first floor, independent from the happy hub of family life. Nessie is delightful! A foodie too – you arrive to a home-baked something with tea, and breakfast comes with garden raspberries or gingery rhubarb perhaps, homemade jam and a cooked spread. The elegant dining room is charming with antiques, candles, family photos. Bridport is a short drive: independent shops and a great Saturday market; Dorchester, for Hardy fans, is nearby too. Summer fields brim with wild flowers; walk to a pub in Cattistock for supper.

Minimum stay: 2 nights in high season. Pets by arrangement (sleeping in kennel).

Rooms	1 suite for 3 with extra child's bed, hall & living room: £100-£115. Singles £70. Extra bed/sofabed available £20 per person per night.
Meals	Dinner, 2 courses, £25. Pubs/restaurants 0.5 miles.
Closed	Christmas.

Nessie Owen
The Old Rectory,
Chilfrome,
Dorchester, DT2 0HA
Mobile   +44 (0)7973 927208
Email   nessieowen@emailitis.com

Entry 141   Map 3

Dorset

Fullers Earth

Such an English feel: the village with pub, post office and stores, the rose-filled walled garden with fruit trees beyond, the tranquil church view. This listed house – its late-Georgian frontage added in 1820 – is a treat: flowers and white linen, a lovely sitting room where you settle with tea and cake by the fire, roomy bedrooms with comfortable beds, books and views. At breakfast enjoy perfect compotes and jams from the garden, homemade muesli and local produce. Friendly Ian and Wendy will plan great walks with you in this AONB, the Jurassic coast is 20 minutes away and you can walk to the pub through the garden.

Rooms	1 double; 1 double sharing bath/shower room with single (let to same party only): £105-£115. 1 single: £45-£50.
Meals	Pub 5-minute walk.
Closed	Christmas.

Wendy Gregory
Fullers Earth,
Cattistock, Dorchester, DT2 0JL
Tel   +44 (0)1300 320190
Mobile   +44 (0)7792 654543
Email   stay@fullersearth.co.uk
Web   www.fullersearth.co.uk

Entry 142   Map 3

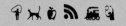

Dorset

Old Forge

Snug in a stream-tickled hamlet, deep in Hardy country, this B&B is as pretty as a painting and wonderfully peaceful. Judy is charming and friendly – this is a happy place, a real country home, a no-rules B&B. The one guest double, sharing the former forge with a self-catering pad for two, is inviting and cosy with yellow hues, thick carpets and trinkets from travels. Sit outside in a sunny patch by a beautiful copper beech. The 17th-century farmhouse opposite is where you breakfast: Judy, ex Prue Leith, serves a neighbour's eggs, a friend's sausages and good coffee in an eclectically furnished room with bucolic views to garden, meadows and hills.

Dorset

Urless Farm

In its own beautiful valley, this extended, refurbished 19th-century family house does seriously smart B&B. You'll want to linger over breakfast – local bacon, their hens' eggs, homemade jams, their own tomato sauce – in the light-filled orangery with breathtaking views across rich farmland to the distant Mendips. Luxuriate in traditional bedrooms with antiques and colourful rugs on polished floors; sensors control the lighting in peerless bathrooms with heated floors. Watch for wildlife by the ponds in the large, well-kept grounds. It's a short walk to a good pub and Dorset's delights surround you.

Over 16s welcome.

Rooms	Old Forge: 1 double: £100; 2 or more nights: £80-£90. Singles £60-£70.	Rooms	2 doubles, 1 twin; 1 double with separate shower: £100-£120.
Meals	Pub 1.5 miles.	Meals	Pubs/restaurants 15-minute walk.
Closed	Rarely.	Closed	Rarely.

Judy Thompson
Old Forge,
Lower Wraxall Farmhouse,
Lower Wraxall, Dorchester, DT2 0HL
Tel   +44 (0)1935 83218
Email   judyjthompson@hotmail.co.uk
Web   www.lowerwraxall.co.uk

Charlotte Hemsley
Urless Farm,
Corscombe,
Dorchester, DT2 0NP
Tel   +44 (0)1935 891528
Email   charlie.urless@gmail.com
Web   www.urlessdorset.com

Entry 143   Map 3

Entry 144   Map 3

Dorset

Wooden Cabbage House

Leafy lanes and a private drive lead you to Martyn and Susie's beautifully restored hamstone house, hidden in rolling West Dorset. Leave the hubbub behind, savour the stunning valley views, relax in this spacious stylish home amongst flowers, fine antiques and paintings. Cosy bedrooms have country-house charm. A delicious breakfast is served in the garden room – homemade muesli, a fresh fruit platter, local eggs and sausages – and French windows open to a productive potager and terraced gardens. Walks are good and the Jurassic coast is half an hour away; return to comfy sofas by the log fire. Fabulous hosts – nothing is too much trouble.

Minimum stay: 2 nights at weekends.

Rooms	2 doubles, 1 twin: £110.
	Singles £100.
Meals	Pubs/restaurants 3 miles.
Closed	Rarely.

Martyn & Susie Lee
Wooden Cabbage House,
East Chelborough,
Dorchester, DT2 0QA

Tel	+44 (0)1935 83362
Email	relax@woodencabbage.co.uk
Web	www.woodencabbage.co.uk

Entry 145   Map 3

Dorset

Holyleas House

In a lovely village, a fabulous house, comfortable, peaceful and easy – and Tia and her two friendly dogs give the warmest welcome. You breakfast in an elegant dining room, by a log fire in winter, on free-range eggs, bacon and sausages from the farmers' market, homemade jams and marmalade. Sleep in light, softly coloured bedrooms with lovely views across well-tended gardens; bathrooms are spotless. Walkers and explorers will be happy to roam the Dorset Downs, then return to a roaring fire and a cosy book in the drawing room.

Minimum stay: 2 nights in high season & at weekends.

Rooms	1 double: £80–£90.
	1 family room for 3: £100–£120.
	1 single with separate bath: £40.
Meals	Pub a short walk.
Closed	Christmas & New Year.

Tia Bunkall
Holyleas House,
Buckland Newton,
Dorchester, DT2 7DP

Tel	+44 (0)1300 345214
Mobile	+44 (0)7968 341887
Email	tiabunkall@holyleas.fsnet.co.uk
Web	www.holyleashouse.co.uk

Entry 146   Map 3

Dorset

Lower Fifehead Farm

A passion for cooking here! The dramatic dining room has church pews at an oak refectory table; the log fire will be lit in winter, and you can eat on the terrace in summer. Hearty breakfasts include bacon and sausages from home-reared pigs, devilled mushrooms or eggs Benedict; Jessica makes the bread and preserves, and there's always freshly squeezed orange juice. It's a gorgeous house too – it's been in Jasper's family for over years and shines with pretty fabrics, antiques, hand-painted furniture, vintage pieces, rich colour – and seriously comfortable brass beds. Don't miss the candlelit dinners.

Minimum stay: 2 nights at weekends.

Rooms	2 doubles, 1 twin/double: £75-£95. Singles from £55.
Meals	Dinner, 2-3 courses, £20-£30. Pubs/restaurants 2 miles.
Closed	Christmas & New Year.

	Jessica Miller
	Lower Fifehead Farm,
	Fifehead St Quinton,
	Sturminster Newton, DT10 2AP
Tel	+44 (0)1258 817335
Email	lowerfifeheadfm@gmail.com
Web	www.lowerfifeheadfm.co.uk

Entry 147 Map 3

Dorset

Munden House

This is a super B&B – farm cottages and assorted outbuildings beautifully stitched together. It's run with great warmth by Colin and Annie, who buy and sell colourful rugs and have travelled the world to do it. Outside, long views shoot off over open country; inside, airy interiors, pretty bedrooms and lots of colour. The garden cottages are more private; one has a galleried bedroom above a lovely sitting room. Annie cooks a great breakfast – organic porridge with toffee sauce is a winter treat, and the bread comes from the 100-year-old bakery next door. You eat at smartly dressed tables in the sunny dining room overlooking the garden.

Dogs and children welcome in Garden Cottage and Dairy Cottage.

Rooms	3 doubles, 1 twin/double, 1 four-poster: £85-£140. Garden Cottage & Dairy Cottage – both with 1 double & extra sofabed: £85-£140. Summer House – 1 double: £85-£140. Singles from £70.
Meals	Pub 2 miles.
Closed	Christmas.

	Annie & Colin Fletcher
	Munden House,
	Mundens Lane, Alweston,
	Sherborne, DT9 5HU
Tel	+44 (0)1963 23150
Email	stay@mundenhouse.co.uk
Web	www.mundenhouse.co.uk

Entry 148 Map 3

Dorset

Caundle Barn

Take the pretty route... ramble through rich pasture, tiny hamlets and woodland to reach this attractive 17th-century stone barn. All is spotless, from the oak stairs and galleried landing to the antiques and exquisite curtains; Sarah has blended old and new beautifully. Your bedroom is sunny and sumptuous; the little shower room has scented oils and luxurious towels. Sarah cooks with the seasons and you'll enjoy homemade marmalade, fruits, local eggs, bacon and sausages. Views and walks are sublime, Sherborne is fun, there are gourmet pubs galore and Poppy the Jack Russell adds her charm to this friendly home.

Rooms	1 double: £80–£110. Singles £50.
Meals	Pubs/restaurants 4 miles.
Closed	Rarely.

Sarah Howes
Caundle Barn,
Purse Caundle,
Sherborne, DT9 5DY
Tel   +44 (0)1963 251264
Email   howes20@btinternet.com

Entry 149   Map 3

Dorset

Lawn Cottage

In a quiet village in Blackmore Vale, the path to this spacious cottage is lined with tulips and vegetables. Easy-going June is a collector of pretty things; art, antiques and china blend charmingly with soft colours and zingy kilims. Bedrooms are sunny – one is downstairs (en suite) with a private entrance; there's a sweet very comfy shepherd's hut too if you fancy a night under the stars and sunset views. Breakfasts are generous; hut dwellers can come in to the dining room or have a hamper delivered. Visit Sherborne (abbey, castle, smart shops), walk from the gate to Duncliffe Wood. Return to a tiny snug sitting room. Perfect Dorset B&B!

Rooms	1 twin/double; 1 double with separate bathroom: £80. 1 shepherd's hut for 2 with separate bathroom in main house: £90. Singles £40. Extra bed/sofabed available at no charge.
Meals	Pub/restaurant 1 mile.
Closed	Rarely.

June Watkins
Lawn Cottage,
Stour Row, Shaftesbury, SP7 0QF
Tel   +44 (0)1747 838719
Mobile   +44 (0)7809 696218
Email   enquiries@lawncottagedorset.co.uk
Web   www.lawncottagedorset.co.uk

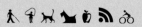

Entry 150   Map 3

Dorset

St Andrews Farm East

Deeply rural bliss! The part-thatched house is lovely: roses and clematis around the door, its tranquil garden keenly tended. The approach is pure Hardy: up a no through lane, verges rampant with wild flowers, old walls penning tiny cottage gardens, the pond where cartwheels were washed. Then there's Diana's creation – as designer and seamstress – of the elegant interiors. Bleached oak timbers frame the superb, chandeliered master bedroom. More gentle cream, antiques and flowers in the second charming double. Traditional, cosseting bathrooms too. Breakfasts are terrific – orchard fruit salad a speciality. Luxurious and friendly.

Rooms	1 double; 1 double with separate bathroom: £75-£85. Singles £50-£60.
Meals	Pubs/restaurants 1 mile.
Closed	Rarely.

Diana Man
St Andrews Farm East,
Bedchester,
Shaftesbury, SP7 0JU
Tel +44 (0)1747 812242
Email mrsdianaman@hotmail.com
Web www.bedchester.net

Entry 151 Map 3

Dorset

The Old Forge, Fanners Yard

Step back in time in this beautifully restored forge: retro signs, museum pieces, ponies in the paddock and a slower way of life... Tim and Lucy's smallholding gives you a taste of harmonious living with the seasons, and they recycle everything. This includes Tim's classic cars, cosy gypsy caravan and vintage shepherd's hut. Attic bedrooms in the main house are snug with Lucy's quilts, antiques, sparkling bathrooms. Breakfasts are renowned: eggs from the hens, organic bacon and sausages, home-grown jams, orchard apple juice; if you stay in the Smithy, a tasty hamper is left for you so rise when you want. A happy place, a tonic to stay.

Children over 8 welcome. Minimum stay: 2 nights in Gypsy caravan, huts and Smithy.

Rooms	1 double with separate bath: £90. 1 family room for 3: £95-£150. Smithy – 1 double with kitchen: £125. 2 shepherd's huts for 2 (shower/wc close by): £95. 1 Gypsy caravan for 2: £95. Singles £60-£75.
Meals	Pub/restaurant within 1 mile.
Closed	Rarely.

Tim & Lucy Kerridge
The Old Forge, Fanners Yard,
Compton Abbas,
Shaftesbury, SP7 0NQ
Tel +44 (0)1747 811881
Email theoldforge@ymail.com
Web www.theoldforgedorset.co.uk

Entry 152 Map 3

Dorset

Glebe Farm

You're in Dorset's highest village – the views sprawl for miles. Tessa and Ian's home has eclectic art, green oak beams, uncluttered rooms and a great sense of space. Light floods in through the floor to ceiling windows that frame those views out beyond the decking, past the chickens to Win Green. ("Emmerdale meets Grand Designs" to quote a happy guest). Aga-cooked breakfasts include local bacon and home-laid eggs; dinner might be roast pheasant – served on the terrace in summer (Tessa does shoot catering). Bedrooms, one up, one down, are hotel-swish with big beds, bold colours and flowers. Join the Wessex Ridgeway from the village.

Over 14s welcome.

Rooms	2 twin/doubles: £100-£120. Singles from £60.
Meals	Dinner, 2 courses, £30. Pubs 2 miles.
Closed	Christmas & New Year.

Tessa & Ian Millard
Glebe Farm,
High Street, Ashmore,
Salisbury, SP5 5AE
Tel   +44 (0)1747 811974
Mobile   +44 (0)7799 858961
Email   stay@glebefarmashmore.co.uk
Web   www.glebefarmashmore.co.uk

Entry 153   Map 3

Durham

Burnhopeside Hall

It's peaceful, traditional, pristine, and nothing is too much trouble for Christine. Welcome to a listed Georgian house on a 475-acre estate near Durham, its elegant sitting rooms furnished with pictures and photos, log fires and big sofas, billiards and a baby grand, and great sash windows with garden and woodland views. Resident springer spaniel Max loves all dogs, so bring yours; stroll the magnificent lawns, cycle alongside the river. Breakfast? Eggs from the hens, bacon from the pigs, honey and fruits from the walled garden: a perfect start to the day. Enormous beds, luxurious linen and fresh flowers await your return.

Rooms	4 doubles: £85-£120. 1 apartment for 4: £100-£150. Singles £70-£85.
Meals	Pubs/restaurants 4 miles.
Closed	Rarely.

Christine Hewitt
Burnhopeside Hall,
Durham Road,
Lanchester, DH7 0TL
Tel   +44 (0)1207 520222
Email   harmerchristine@hotmail.com
Web   www.burnhopeside-hall.co.uk

Entry 154   Map 12

Durham

The Coach House

There's so much to gladden your heart – the cobbled courtyard that evokes memories of its days as a coaching inn, the river running through the estate, the far-reaching views, the drawing room's log fire, the delicious breakfasts... and Peter and Mary, your kind, unstuffy, dog-adoring hosts (they have two well-behaved ones). All your creature comforts are attended to in this small, perfect, English country house: lined chintz, pure cotton linen, cushioned window seats looking onto a lovely garden, heated towel rails, cut flowers. Friendly, delightful, and the perfect stepping stone to Scotland or the south.

Pets by arrangement.

Rooms	1 twin/double; 1 twin/double with separate bath/shower: £95. Singles £70.
Meals	Restaurant within walking distance. Many more pub/restaurants within 3 miles.
Closed	Rarely.

Peter & Mary Gilbertson
The Coach House,
Greta Bridge,
Barnard Castle, DL12 9SD
Tel   +44 (0)1833 627201
Email   info@coachhousegreta.co.uk
Web   www.coachhousegreta.co.uk

Entry 155 Map 12

Essex

The Old Pottery

Tubs of flowers at the door, Twiglet the dog to pat and a friendly feel throughout. Jacky moved from London to this charming village house and has restored and decorated with natural style: new oak floors, stripped beams, polished antique pieces. Bedrooms have well-dressed beds and thick curtains; the extra little room is just right for a child. Jacky is a good cook, so hop downstairs for a delicious breakfast – the best sausages and bacon or continental with home-baked ham; she's happy to do light suppers, and makes Christmas puds to sell. There are fun events at the Norman motte-and-bailey castle; thriving Long Melford and Clare are close.

Children over 8 welcome.

Rooms	1 twin/double; 1 double with separate bathroom: £90-£95. 1 single sharing bathroom with double (let to same party only): £55-£65.
Meals	Light supper from £20. Pubs/restaurants 2-minute walk.
Closed	Rarely.

Jacky Short
The Old Pottery,
37 St James Street, Castle
Hedingham, Halstead, CO9 3EW
Tel   +44 (0)1787 582168
Email   jackyshort@outlook.com
Web   www.hedinghamoldpottery.com

Entry 156 Map 10

Essex

Hill House

The Romer-Lees converted this listed brick Coach House and it's rather special: light and airy with pale beams, oatmeal carpets and merry gingham blinds. Downstairs is a private entrance hall; upstairs is a generous open-plan bedroom/living area with a queen-sized bed and en suite bathroom. On the other side of the room, separated by the stairs, are two cream sofas that open into double beds, a TV, DVDs and board games. No garden but you get a balcony with stunning views across the Colne Valley, breakfast (all the usuals plus bacon and sausages from the owners' rare-breed pigs) is served here on warm days. Cambridge is close.

Minimum stay: 2 nights at weekends.

Rooms	Coach House – 1 suite for 2 with sitting room & sofabeds (can sleep up to 6 people): £95-£120. Extra bed/sofabed available £15 per person per night.
Meals	Pub/restaurant 5-minute walk.
Closed	Rarely.

	Hattie Romer-Lee
	Hill House,
	Chappel Hill, Chappel,
	Colchester, CO6 2DX
Mobile	+44 (0)7802 601144
Email	hattieromerlee@yahoo.co.uk
Web	www.hillhousechappel.co.uk

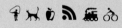

Entry 157   Map 10

Gloucestershire

The Old School

So comfortable and filled with understated style is this 1854 Cotswold stone house. Wendy and John are generous, beds are huge, linen is laundered, towels and robes are fluffy. Your own mini fridge is carefully hidden and pretty lamps cast a warm glow. Best of all is the upstairs sitting room: a chic, open-plan space with church style windows letting light flood in and super sofas, good art, lovely fabrics. A wood-burner keeps you toasty, Wendy is a grand cook and all is flexible. A gorgeous, relaxing place to stay – on the A44 but peaceful at night – that positively hums with hospitality. Guests say "even better than home!"

Over 12s welcome.

Rooms	3 doubles, 1 twin/double: £130-£150. Singles £100-£130.
Meals	Dinner, 4 courses, £32. Supper, 2 courses, £18. Supper tray £12. Pub 0.5 miles.
Closed	Rarely.

	Wendy Veale & John Scott-Lee
	The Old School,
	Little Compton,
	Moreton-in-Marsh, GL56 0SL
Tel	+44 (0)1608 674588
Mobile	+44 (0)7831 098271
Email	wendy@theoldschoolbedandbreakfast.com
Web	www.theoldschoolbedandbreakfast.com

Entry 158   Map 8

Gloucestershire

Trinity House

Meet Zelic: generous, charming, and passionate about the Cotswolds. Off a lane in dreamy Upper Oddington is a smart modern house with a crisp gravel drive and newly planted borders. Inside, a country elegance prevails. Antique furniture shines with care and polish, walls are covered with 20th-century art and splendid sofas front the fire. Bedrooms and bathrooms ooze comfort and joy: one with a private balcony, another with its own terrace, all with village views. But don't snuggle under the goose down for too long: breakfast verges on the sinful and is locally sourced and delicious. Prepare to be thoroughly spoiled!

Rooms	1 double, 2 twin/doubles: £110–£120. Singles £70–£85.
Meals	Pubs within walking distance.
Closed	Rarely.

Zelie Mason
Trinity House,
Upper Oddington,
Moreton-in-Marsh, GL56 0XH

Tel	+44 (0)1451 831284
Mobile	+44 (0)7809 429365
Email	info@trinityhousebandb.co.uk
Web	www.trinityhousebandb.co.uk

Entry 159   Map 8

Gloucestershire

Wren House

Barely two miles from Stow-on-the-Wold, this peaceful house sits charmingly on the edge of a tiny hamlet. It was built before the English Civil War and Kiloran spent two years stylishly renovating it; the results are a joy. Downstairs, light-filled, elegant rooms with glowing rugs on pale Cotswold stone; upstairs, delicious bedrooms, spotless bathrooms and a doorway to duck. Breakfast in the vaulted kitchen is locally sourced and organic, where possible, and the well-planted garden, in which you are encouraged to sit, has far-reaching views. Explore rolling valleys and glorious gardens; Kiloran can advise.

Minimum stay: 2 nights. Premium for 1 night stays and public holidays/weekends.

Rooms	1 twin/double; 1 twin/double with separate bath; 1 twin/double with separate bath/shower: £110–£120. Singles from £95.
Meals	Pubs/restaurants 1 mile.
Closed	Rarely.

Mrs Kiloran McGrigor
Wren House,
Donnington,
Stow-on-the-Wold, GL56 0XZ

Tel	+44 (0)1451 831787
Mobile	+44 (0)7802 676673
Email	enquiries@wrenhouse.net
Web	www.wrenhouse.net

Entry 160   Map 8

Gloucestershire

Gloucestershire

Clapton Manor

Karin and James's 16th-century manor is as all homes should be: loved and lived-in. And, with three-foot-thick walls, rich Persian rugs on flagstoned floors, sit-in fireplaces and stone-mullioned windows, it's gorgeous. The garden, enclosed by old stone walls, is full of birdsong and roses. One bedroom has a secret door leading to a fuchsia-pink bathroom; the other room, smaller, has a Tudor stone fireplace and wonderful garden views. Wellies, dogs, a comfy guest sitting room with lots of books... and breakfast by a vast fireplace: homemade bread, award-winning marmalade and eggs from the hens. A happy, charming family home.

Aylworth Manor

Set in a peaceful Cotswolds valley and surrounded by attractive gardens, John and Joanna's gorgeous manor is immaculate. Sit beside the wood-burner in the comfy snug or play the piano in a grand drawing room, rich with art and family photos: your hosts have that happy knack of making you feel instantly at home. Large sunny bedrooms come with garden and valley views, perfect linen on seriously cushy beds, antiques and lavish bathrooms. Wake refreshed for breakfast in the dining room: homemade bread, eggs from the ducks and hens, coffee in a silver pot. The Windrush Way passes the gate at the end of the drive. What a treat!

Over 12s welcome.

Rooms	1 double, 1 twin/double: £110–£130. Singles from £100.
Meals	Pub/restaurants within 15-minute drive.
Closed	Rarely.

Rooms	1 double; 1 double, 1 twin/double, both with separate bath: £100–£120. Singles £60.
Meals	Pub 1 mile.
Closed	Rarely.

Karin & James Bolton
Clapton Manor,
Clapton-on-the-Hill, GL54 2LG

Tel	+44 (0)1451 810202
Mobile	+44 (0)7967 144416
Email	bandb@claptonmanor.co.uk
Web	www.claptonmanor.co.uk

John & Joanna Ireland
Aylworth Manor,
Naunton, Cheltenham, GL54 3AH

Tel	+44 (0)1451 850850
Mobile	+44 (0)7768 810357
Email	enquiries@aylworthmanor.co.uk
Web	www.aylworthmanor.co.uk

Gloucestershire

North Farmcote

Step back 50 years, to a solid 19th-century farmhouse high on the escarpment, and views falling away to the west; on a clear day you can see Hay Bluff. A brilliant spot for North Cotswolds' exploration, it is run by charming and gently self-deprecating David – farmer of cereals and sheep, keen walker, good shot. The exploits of his family decorate the walls (racing at Brooklands, hunting in Africa), there's a floral three-piece to sink into, a terrace with outstanding views, and a great pub you can stride to across fields. Bedrooms and bathrooms are old-fashioned, spacious, comfortable and spotless.

Rooms	1 double, 1 twin; 1 twin with separate bath: £85–£100. Singles £60.
Meals	Pub 2 miles.
Closed	January/February.

David Eayrs
North Farmcote,
Winchcombe,
Cheltenham, GL54 5AU
Tel   +44 (0)1242 602304
Email   davideayrs@yahoo.co.uk
Web   www.northfarmcote.co.uk

Entry 163   Map 8

Gloucestershire

The Courtyard Studio

This smart first-floor studio, attractive in reclaimed red brick, is reached via its own wrought-iron staircase; you are beautifully private. Find a clever, compact, contemporary space with a light and uncluttered living area, a mini window seat opposite two very comfortable boutiquey beds, fine linen, wicker armchair, and a patio area for balmy days. John and Annette live next door, and you stroll over to their friendly home for a tasty, locally sourced breakfast: artisan bread, homemade jams, marmalade and muesli, a traditional full English. It's a 20-minute easy walk to the centre of Cheltenham and you're a quick canter from the races.

Minimum stay: 2 nights.

Rooms	Studio: 1 twin: £85.
Meals	Restaurants/pubs within 1 mile.
Closed	Rarely.

John & Annette Gill
The Courtyard Studio,
1 The Cleevelands Courtyard,
Cleevelands Drive,
Cheltenham, GL50 4QF
Tel   +44 (0)1242 573125
Mobile   +44 (0)7901 978917
Email   courtyardstudio@aol.com

Entry 164   Map 8

Gloucestershire

Detmore House

Down a private drive, sitting in seven acres, this elegant house has been the home of poets, artists and writers. Gill carries on the creativity with her cooking, interior design, jewellery, gardening and chickens; she and Hugh are easy natural hosts. Comfortable bedrooms have a smart hotel feel, bathrooms are immaculate, and you and your dinner party guests will be spoiled with organic garden produce. Find wide lawns, mature trees – and wonderful views across Charlton Hills from lovely sitting spots. Walk the Cotswold Way from the door, head off to one of Cheltenham's many festivals (literary, science, jazz, folk…) or the races.

Gloucestershire

Calcot Peak House

A treat to stay in such a handsome old house with such relaxed owners – lovely Alex is full of enthusiasm for her B&B enterprise. There's an excellent butcher in Northleach so breakfasts are tip-top, and the bedrooms are a sophisticated mix of traditional and contemporary: Farrow & Ball colours, rich florals, fresh flowers, and fluffy white robes for trots to the bathroom. You also have your own charming drawing room: tartan carpet, pink sofas, family oils. Outside: 19 acres for Dexie the dog and a bench on the hill for the view. Tramp the Salt Way, dine in Cirencester, let the owls hoot you to sleep.

Dogs very welcome to sleep in utility room (comfortable and warm!) but not in bedrooms.

Rooms	2 twin/doubles, 1 twin: £85-£95. 1 family room for 3: £120-£150. Singles from £65.
Meals	Dinner from £28.50 (for groups of 6+). Packed lunch £6. Pub 1 mile.
Closed	Christmas & New Year.

Rooms	1 double, 1 twin sharing bathroom & drawing room (let to same party only; children's room available): £95. Singles £75.
Meals	Pub 2 miles.
Closed	Rarely.

	Gill Kilminster
	Detmore House,
	London Road, Charlton Kings,
	Cheltenham, GL52 6UT
Tel	+44 (0)1242 582868
Email	gillkilminster@btconnect.com
Web	www.detmorehouse.com

	Tom & Alexandra Pearson
	Calcot Peak House,
	Northleach,
	Cheltenham, GL54 3QB
Tel	+44 (0)1285 721047
Mobile	+44 (0)7738 468798
Email	pearsonalex5@gmail.com

Entry 165   Map 8

Entry 166   Map 8

Gloucestershire

The Priest House

This romantic, ancient cottage is all yours. Tucked behind the owners' farm, and next to the Saxon church of St Andrew, part remains an atmospheric ruin. You sleep under soaring oak beams in the airy attic bedroom: sumptuous feather mattress, white linen, flowers; downstairs, you'll find a bathroom, and a big swish open-plan kitchen/sitting area. Delightful Jo leaves all you need to rustle up a full breakfast. The medieval-style vegetable garden is a perfect spot for a sundowner – the views are glorious – and it's a short drive to a good pub for supper.

Gloucestershire

The Guest House

Your own timber-framed house with masses of light and space, a sunny terrace, and spectacular valley and woodland views... A peaceful secluded place, it's full of books and mementoes of Sue's treks across the world; the large living room has wooden floors, lovely old oak furniture and French windows onto the rose-filled garden. Sue brims with enthusiasm and is a flexible host: breakfast can be over in her kitchen with delicious farm shop sausages and bacon, or continental in yours at a time to suit you. There's a wet room downstairs, and you hop up the stairs to your charming up-in-the-eaves bedroom with oriental rugs and a big comfy bed. Wonderful!

Min stay: 2 nights at weekends Easter – October.

Rooms	Cottage – 1 double with kitchen/sitting room: £110.
Meals	Pub 1 mile.
Closed	Rarely.

Rooms	1 double with sitting room & kitchenette: £140-£160. 3-6 night breaks £133-£152 per night, 7 nights £935.
Meals	Dinner, 2 courses, from £17.50; 3 courses, from £22.50; 4 courses, from £28 per person. Pub 1 mile.
Closed	Christmas.

	Joanna Davies The Priest House, Coln Rogers, Cirencester, Cheltenham, GL54 3LB
Tel	+44 (0)1285 720246
Email	priesthouse29@gmail.com

	Sue Bathurst The Guest House, Manor Cottage, Bagendon, Cirencester, GL7 7DU
Tel	+44 (0)1285 831417
Email	thecotswoldguesthouse@gmail.com
Web	www.cotswoldguesthouse.co.uk

Gloucestershire

The Old Rectory

English to the core – and to the bottom of its lovely garden, with a woodland walk and plenty of quiet places to sit. Sweep into the circular driveway to this beautiful, 17th-century high gabled house. Inside, all is comfortably lived-in with an understated décor, antiques, creaky floorboards and a real sense of atmosphere and history. The bedrooms, one with a garden view, have good beds, TVs and a chaise longue or easy chair; bathrooms are vintage and functional but large. Caroline is charming and serves breakfasts with eggs from friends' hens and local bacon at the long table in the rich red dining room. A welcoming place.

Rooms	1 double, 1 twin/double (extra bed available): £85–£110. Extra bed and cot for children available. Singles £60–£100.
Meals	Pub 200 yds.
Closed	December/January.

Roger & Caroline Carne
The Old Rectory,
Meysey Hampton,
Cirencester, GL7 5JX
Tel   +44 (0)1285 851200
Email   carocarne13@gmail.com
Web   www.meyseyoldrectory.co.uk

Entry 169   Map 8

Gloucestershire

Ashley Barn

On the edge of a hamlet... a beautifully restored, traditional converted barn. Huge doorways and floor to ceiling timber-framed windows let the light flood in. You have your own entrance and can come and go as you please. Your suite has good linen, plump pillows, flowers and views onto the garden; the roomy bathroom is gleaming. Walk through for breakfast by a log fire in the huge dining hall in the main barn: local sausages and bacon, eggs from the hens on pretty Poole pottery; Amanda is happy to cook dinner too. Badminton Horse Trials are a hop, Cirencester too; return for a wander round the rose garden, and a snooze by the fire.

Rooms	1 suite for 2: £100–£110. Singles £75.
Meals	Dinner, 3 courses, £25. Pub/restaurant 5-minute drive.
Closed	Rarely.

Amanda Montgomerie
Ashley Barn,
Ashley, Tetbury, GL8 8SU
Tel   +44 (0)1666 575156
Mobile +44 (0)7785 505548
Email   amanda@montgomerie.org
Web   www.ashleybarn.co.uk

Entry 170   Map 3

Gloucestershire

The Moda House

A fine house and a big B&B, but one that retains a deeply homely feel; Duncan and Jo are hugely well-travelled and have filled it with pictures and artefacts from all over the world. Bedrooms differ (three are in a neat annexe) but all are cosy and well decorated with lovely colours, good fabrics, pocket sprung mattresses and bright bathrooms with thick towels. Breakfast – locally sourced, cooked on the Aga and brought to round tables – sets you up for fabulous walks: you are a mile from the Cotswold Way. Return to a basement sitting room with comfy armchairs and lots of books, and a bustling town full of restaurants and shops.

Minimum stay: 2 nights over busy weekends & 3 nights during Badminton.

Rooms	8 doubles: £82-£95.
	3 singles: £62-£67.
Meals	Pubs/restaurants within 100 yards.
Closed	Rarely.

Duncan & Jo MacArthur
The Moda House,
1 High Street,
Chipping Sodbury, BS37 6BA
Tel +44 (0)1454 312135
Email enquiries@modahouse.co.uk
Web www.modahouse.co.uk

Entry 171   Map 3

Gloucestershire

The Close

Up a hill of pretty Cotswold-stone houses, this large Queen Anne house with handsome sash windows delivers what it promises. Step into a stone-flagged hall with grandfather clock and Georgian oak staircase; take welcoming tea with Karen in the drawing room – all gracious sofas and charming chandelier; then upstairs to three light and airy bedrooms softly furnished with antiques. Window seats, shutters and views over garden or pretty street add to the restful atmosphere. Karen, as gracious and relaxed as her house, serves excellent breakfasts in the polished dining room. An elegantly hospitable base for exploring the Cotswolds.

Minimum stay: 2 nights at weekends.

Rooms	2 doubles, 1 twin: £85-£95.
	Singles £65-£75.
Meals	Pubs/restaurants 1-minute walk.
Closed	January.

Karen Champney
The Close,
Well Hill, Minchinhampton,
Stroud, GL6 9JE
Tel +44 (0)1453 883338
Email theclosebnb@gmail.com
Web www.theclosebnb.co.uk

Entry 172   Map 8

Gloucestershire

Well Farm

Perhaps it's the gentle, unstuffy attitude of Kate and Edward. Or the great position of the house with its glorious views across the Slad valley. Whichever, you'll feel comforted and invigorated by your stay. It's a real family home and you get both a fresh, pretty bedroom that feels very private and the use of a comfy, book-filled sitting room opening to a flowery courtyard; Kate is an inspired garden designer. Sleep soundly on the softest of pillows, wake to deep countryside peace and the delicious prospect of eggs from their own hens and good bacon. Friendly dogs Jaffa and Dot add to the charm, the area teems with great walks – lovely pubs too.

Rooms	1 twin/double, with sitting room: £95.
Meals	Dinner from £25.
	Pubs nearby.
Closed	Rarely.

Kate & Edward Gordon Lennox
Well Farm,
Frampton Mansell,
Stroud, GL6 8JB
Tel   +44 (0)1285 760651
Email   kategl@btinternet.com
Web   www.well-farm.co.uk

Entry 173   Map 8

Gloucestershire

St Annes

Step straight off the narrow pavement into a sunny hall and a warm and welcoming family home. Iris and Greg have made their pretty 17th-century house, in the heart of this bustling village, as eco-friendly as possible. Comfy bedrooms are charming; the four-poster room has a tiny en suite shower room. Farmers' market breakfasts are a feast, the Aga kitchen is a friendly space, and Rollo the dog (who has his own sofa) loves children. Painswick is known as 'the Queen of the Cotswolds': enjoy superb rambles through orchid meadows and beech woods carpeted with bluebells; visit good pubs on the way. Great value and perfect for walkers without a car.

Parking available within 100 yds.

Rooms	1 double, 1 twin, 1 four-poster: £75.
Meals	Packed lunch £6.
	Pubs/restaurants in village.
Closed	Rarely.

Iris McCormick
St Annes,
Gloucester Street, Painswick,
Stroud, GL6 6QN
Tel   +44 (0)1452 812879
Email   iris@st-annes-painswick.co.uk
Web   www.st-annes-painswick.co.uk

Entry 174   Map 8

Gloucestershire

Mayfield Studio

A small lane runs past the studio, and oak doors open to a stylish interior. Slate floors are warmed from beneath and the double height ceiling lends an airy feel. A lime-washed staircase leads to a mezzanine bedroom of uncluttered simplicity with views across the valley. Quirky industrial lighting, stone walls, 1930s woodcut prints, and Ercol furniture all marry superbly. There's no garden – although with permission you may use Sara's next door; choose to stay on a B&B or self-catering basis, with breakfasts delivered or left for you as you wish. Walk to Laurie Lee's favourite pub or dine locally, it's all on your doorstep.

Minimum stay: 2 nights at weekends.

Rooms	Studio – 1 double: £110–£140. One well-behaved dog welcome, £10 per night.
Meals	Breakfast arranged on booking. Pubs/restaurants 2-4-minute walk.
Closed	Rarely.

Sara Kirby
Mayfield Studio,
Vicarage Street,
Painswick,
Stroud, GL6 6XP
Tel +44 (0)1452 814858
Email sara.kirby@mac.com

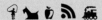

Entry 175   Map 8

Gloucestershire

Frampton Court

Deep authenticity in this magnificent Grade I-listed house. The manor of Frampton on Severn has been in the Clifford family since the 11th century and although Rollo and Janie look after the estate, it is cooking enthusiasts Polly and Craig who greet you on their behalf and look after you. There are exquisite examples of decorative woodwork and, in the hall, a cheerful log fire; perch on the Mouseman fire seat. Bedrooms are traditional with antiques, panelling and long views. Beds have fine linen, one with embroidered Stuart hangings. Stroll around the ornamental canal, soak up the old-master views. An architectural masterpiece.

Children over 10 welcome.

Rooms	1 double, 1 twin/double, 1 four-poster: £150–£250.
Meals	Dinner from £45. Pub across the green. Restaurant 3 miles.
Closed	Christmas.

Polly Dugdale
Frampton Court,
Frampton on Severn, GL2 7EX
Tel +44 (0)1452 740267
Email framptoncourt@framptoncourtestate.co.uk
Web www.framptoncourtestate.co.uk/
framptoncourthomepage.htm

Entry 176   Map 8

Gloucestershire

Grove Farm

Boards creak and you duck, in a farmhouse of the best kind: simple, small-roomed, stone-flagged, beamed, delightful. The walls are white, the polished furniture is good and there are pictures everywhere. In spite of great age (16th century), it's light, with lots of pretty windows. The 400 acres are farmed organically and Penny makes a grand breakfast – continental at busy times. Stupendous views across the Severn estuary to the Cotswolds, the Forest of Dean on the doorstep, and woodland walks carpeted with spring flowers. And there is simply no noise – unless the guinea fowl are in voice.

Rooms	1 double; 1 twin/double with separate bath: £70–£80. Singles £40–£45. Extra bed/sofabed available £10–£20 per person per night.
Meals	Packed lunch £5. Pub 2 miles.
Closed	Rarely.

Penny & David Hill
Grove Farm,
Bullo Pill, Newnham, GL14 1EA

Tel	+44 (0)1594 516304
Mobile	+44 (0)7990 877984
Email	davidaghill48@gmail.com
Web	www.grovefarmbnb.co.uk

Entry 177   Map 8

Gloucestershire

Pauntley Court

If a rural hideaway is what you seek then beat a path here and prepare to be enchanted. The house is a historical corker and was home to the Whittington family for 300 years – Dick is reputed to have been born here. Plush traditional rooms with beautiful beds look over unspoilt countryside; smart bathrooms have Neal's Yard toiletries. Breakfast in the ballroom on fresh local produce, some from the garden, and enjoy the special juice of the day. Surrounded by romantic gardens you can wander at will amidst the yew 'ruins' or gaze at Pan over a glass of Chablis. Delightful Melissa adds the finishing touch to a blissful place.

Fishing & stable available.

Rooms	2 twin/doubles: £125–£140. Singles £80.
Meals	Pub 6 miles.
Closed	Rarely.

Mark & Melissa Hargreaves
Pauntley Court,
Pauntley Court Drive, Redmarley,
Gloucester, GL19 3JA

Tel	+44 (0)1531 828627
Mobile	+44 (0)7798 865979
Email	melissa@pauntleycourt.com
Web	www.pauntleycourt.com

Entry 178   Map 8

Hampshire

Little Cottage

Just 45 minutes from Heathrow but the peace is deep, the views are long and the wildlife thrives – watch fox and deer, listen out for the rare nightjar. Chris and Therese grow summer salads and soft fruits and give you superb breakfasts; eat in a big conservatory filled with greenery. Guests have a lovely sitting room with an eclectic mix of modern and antique furniture, and a pretty terrace overlooks the garden; bedrooms, likewise, are on the ground-floor, fresh and light, the double with distant views. Perfect for walkers and those who seek solace from urban life but don't want to stray too far.

Minimum stay: 2 nights at weekends (April-October). Over 12s welcome.

Rooms	1 double, 1 twin/double: £80-£95. 1 single: £55.
Meals	Pubs/restaurants nearby.
Closed	Christmas, New Year & occasionally.

Chris & Therese Abbott
Little Cottage,
Hazeley Heath, Hartley Wintney,
Hook, RG27 8LY

Tel	+44 (0)1252 845050
Mobile	+44 (0)7721 462214
Email	info@little-cottage.co.uk
Web	www.little-cottage.co.uk

Entry 179 Map 4

Hampshire

Meadow Lodge

A summerhouse treat, tucked away beside the handsome Lodge, overlooking a pool and pretty landscaped gardens. French windows open to a terrace of tumbling wisteria, shrubs and pots. The huge bedroom is elegant and light, the bathroom luxurious; beds are well-dressed, there are books to read, rattan sofa and chairs, wide-screen TV, CDs and a lovely mix of family pieces, antiques and Liza's art. An English breakfast with home-laid eggs is brought over; help yourself to cereals, patisserie, toast, coffee... and your fridge is stocked with nibbles and drinks. Amble over the trout-filled river Anton and meadows for a pub supper.

Rooms	Summerhouse: 1 double, 2 singles (single room and extra beds available too): £75-£200. £140 for 3; £180 for 4; £200 for 5. Singles £85.
Meals	Dinner, 2 courses, £20. Pubs 5-minute walk.
Closed	Rarely.

Elizabeth Butterworth
Meadow Lodge,
Green Meadow Lane, Goodworth
Clatford, Andover, SP11 7HH

Tel	+44 (0)1264 352965
Mobile	+44 (0)7930 532822
Email	liza.butterworth@googlemail.com
Web	www.greenmeadowlodge.co.uk

Entry 180 Map 3

Yew Tree House

Philip and Janet's house is artistic and tranquil. The views, the house and the villagers are said to have inspired Dickens, who escaped London for the peace of the valley. The exquisite red brick house was there 200 years before him; the rare dovecote in the next door churchyard, to which you may have the key, 300 years before that. Thoughtful hosts, interesting to talk to, have created a home of understated elegance: a yellow-ochre bedroom with top quality bed linen, cashmere/silk curtains designed by their son, enchanting garden views, flowers in every room, a welcoming log fire. Breakfast with good coffee is delicious too.

Brymer House

Complete privacy in a B&B is rare. Here you have it, just a 12-minute walk from town, cathedral and water meadows. Relax in your own half of a Victorian townhouse immaculately furnished and decorated, and with a garden to match – all roses and lilac in the spring. Breakfasts are sumptuous, there's a log fire in the guests' sitting room and fresh flowers abound. An 'honesty box' means you may help yourselves to drinks. Bedrooms are small and elegant, with antique mirrors, furniture and bedspreads; bathrooms are warm and spotless. Guy and Fizzy have charmed Special Places guests for many years.

Children over 7 welcome.

Rooms	1 double: £85. Twin by arrangement.
Meals	Pub within 50 yds.
Closed	Rarely.

Rooms	1 double, 1 twin: £85–£95. Singles £65–£70. Extra bed/sofabed available £20 per person per night.
Meals	Pubs/restaurants nearby.
Closed	Rarely.

Philip & Janet Mutton
Yew Tree House,
Broughton,
Stockbridge, SO20 8AA
Tel   +44 (0)1794 301227
Email   mutton@mypostoffice.co.uk

Guy & Fizzy Warren
Brymer House,
29-30 St Faith's Road, St Cross,
Winchester, SO23 9QD
Tel   +44 (0)1962 867428
Email   brymerhouse@aol.com
Web   www.brymerhouse.co.uk

Beechwood

In a popular residential area of town you find the best of both worlds: a bedroom that overlooks a huge garden, and the joys of Winchester a walk away – the cathedral is 15 minutes. Tony and Cecile love their big Victorian house, offer you a cosy room with an elegant bed, a private sitting room (Dickens on the shelves, glowing coals in the grate), and a claw-foot bath for a luxurious soak. It's a family home, a place to relax, and flexible too; if you'd like breakfast outside you can have it. Catch the bus to Jane Austen's house at Chawton, dine finely in Winchester, pop into the local pub.

Bridge House

A beautifully tended garden, with a paved breakfast area, surrounds this 1920s family home and the Grettons couldn't be more hospitable: tea, cake and good talk on arrival; stacks of local knowledge. Family photos and evidence of Michael's naval career personalise the elegant sitting room, with its open fire and doors onto the garden. Bedrooms – Yellow and Blue – are comfortable, pretty, immaculate, and the double overlooks the garden. Steph's breakfasts are a happy mix of good things homemade and local. The old Watercress Line is nearby, Winchester is a draw and have you been to Jane Austen's Chawton?

Rooms	1 double: £75.
	Singles £60.
Meals	Pub 5-minute walk.
Closed	Rarely.

Rooms	1 double; 1 twin with separate bath: £90–£105.
Meals	Pubs/restaurants 5-minute drive.
Closed	Rarely.

Cecile Pryor
Beechwood,
Worthy Road,
Winchester, SO23 7AG
Tel   +44 (0)1962 869561
Email tony_cecile@yahoo.co.uk
Web   www.beechwood-winchester.com

Stephanie & Michael Gretton
Bridge House,
Chillandham Lane, Martyr Worthy,
Winchester, SO21 1AS
Tel   +44 (0)1962 779379
Email bh@itchenvalleybandb.com
Web   www.itchenvalleybandb.com

Hampshire

Hampshire

9 Langtons Court

Approached through a private courtyard Araminta's house sits in a small group of red brick homes. She's an interior designer with projects here and in France, where she has a house too. Her home is simple yet elegant: antiques, paintings, bronze figures, books and piano. Bedrooms are comfy with pretty patchwork and armchairs. The drawing room has French windows on to a leafy garden; wake for a full English breakfast, fruit and croissants. It's a stroll to the centre of Alresford with its market, coloured Georgian houses and lively Music and Watercress Festivals; the Watercress Line, well-known by train enthusiasts, is a five-minute walk.

Dunhill Barn

Arrive for Jan's homemade cake and feel quite at home. Her relaxed, rustic house is full of natural tones, quirky pieces, candles and twinkling wood fires. Bedrooms brim with beamy character; the main barn has the odd steep stair and low bit; Cartshed is ideal for a sharing party; snug Granary is on two floors – hop across stepping stones for a bathroom in the barn. Breakfast is in the stunning living area of the barn – light streams in through big windows while you tuck into home-baked banana muffins, granola, berries, a full cooked spread. You're in the heart of South Downs National Park; thriving Petersfield and heaps of good pubs are nearby.

Minimum stay: 2 nights at weekends.

Rooms	2 doubles sharing bath: £65. Singles £50.
Meals	Dinner £12.50. Pubs/restaurants 10-minute walk.
Closed	Rarely.

Rooms	2 doubles: £120. Granary – 1 double with separate bath: £110. 1 family room for 4: £150. Cartshed – 1 family room for 4: £100–£180.
Meals	Pubs/restaurants 2-minute walk.
Closed	Christmas & New Year.

	Araminta Stewart 9 Langtons Court, Sun Lane, Alresford, SO24 9UE
Tel	+44 (0)1962 809861
Mobile	+44 (0)7979 694779
Email	amintys@aol.com
Web	www.langtonscourtbandb.co.uk

	Jan Martin Dunhill Barn, Steep, Petersfield, GU32 2DP
Tel	+44 (0)1730 268179
Mobile	+44 (0)7789 002342
Email	dunhillbarn@gmail.com
Web	www.dunhillbarn.co.uk

Entry 185   Map 10

Entry 186   Map 4

Hampshire

Shafts Farm

The 1960s farmhouse has many weapons in its armoury: a tremendous South Downs thatched-village setting, owners who know every path and trail, comfortable generous bedrooms and a stunning rose garden designed by David Austin Roses (parterres, obelisks, meandering paths). The two bedrooms are fresh in cream, florals and plaids, each with a shower room with heated floors to keep toes toasty. Homemade granola, garden fruit and the full English make a fine start to the day; the airy, cane-furnished conservatory is the place for afternoon tea and a read. Your hosts are both geographers and have created an intriguing display of maps.

Quiet village – motorbikes not encouraged!

Rooms	2 twins: £90.
	Singles £55.
Meals	Pubs/restaurants 500 yds.
Closed	Rarely.

Rosemary Morrish
Shafts Farm,
West Meon,
Petersfield, GU32 1LU
Tel   +44 (0)1730 829266
Email info@shaftsfarm.co.uk
Web   www.shaftsfarm.co.uk

Entry 187   Map 4

Hampshire

Broadcroft

Tucked down a leafy lane, the Howards' happy home is full of art, porcelain, antiques and traditional furnishings. Comfy bedrooms with new digital shower rooms are in a separate wing and face south over the pretty garden. Relax in the large, light and lovely drawing room which leads outside – perfect for children and dogs on sunny days. Breakfast on the terrace in summer, or in the conservatory – a colourful spot with grandchildren's drawings and Heather's collection of wire/pottery chickens topping the windowsills. Tuck into a hearty continental or full English. Lymington is fun: restaurants, shops and a great Saturday market.

Very pet friendly with secure garden. Minimum stay: 2 nights preferred at weekends.

Rooms	1 double, 1 twin: £75–£85. Both
	rooms can be let as a family suite.
	Singles £60–£65.
Meals	Pubs/restaurants 0.5 miles.
Closed	Rarely.

Heather Howard
Broadcroft,
28 Broad Lane,
Lymington, SO41 3QP
Tel   +44 (0)1590 672741
Email whoward@uwclub.net
Web   www.broadcroft-lymington.co.uk

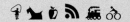

Entry 188   Map 3

Hampshire

Bay Trees

The Isle of Wight and the Needles loom large as you approach Milford on Sea: the beach is shingle, the views are amazing. Mark and Sarah have become dab hands at B&B and welcome you in to a sun-filled conservatory with Ercol elm and beech tables and chairs; the home-bakes and award-winning breakfasts are delicious. Comfortable bedrooms, with good linen, are spotless and warm; bathrooms ooze white towels. One room opens to the lush garden: magnolias, weeping willow and pond; and chickens that lay your breakfast eggs! With Mark's background in hospitality and Sarah's passion for cooking the service here is second to none.

Minimum stay usually: 2 nights at weekends.

Rooms	1 double, 1 four-poster, 1 family room for 3: £100–£120. Singles £80–£100.
Meals	Restaurants 100 yds.
Closed	Rarely.

Mark & Sarah Clayson
Bay Trees,
8 High Street, Milford on Sea,
Lymington, SO41 0QD

Tel	+44 (0)1590 642186
Email	mark.clayson@btinternet.com
Web	www.baytreebedandbreakfast.co.uk

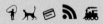

Entry 189   Map 3

Hampshire

Vinegar Hill Pottery

A sylvan setting, stylish pottery, a young and talented family. The cobalt blues and rich browns of David's ceramics fill the old stables of a Victorian manor house. Take pottery courses (one hour to a long weekend) or just enjoy the creative Mexican-inspired décor. A narrow staircase spirals up to a modern loft: crisp whites, cathedral ceiling with sunny windows, brilliant shower. The ground-floor garden suite has a patio (with a gorgeous Showman's wagon!), sitting room, painted bed and optional children's beds. Lucy brings breakfast to your room. Stroll to the beach: stretch out and you almost touch the Isle of Wight.

Minimum stay: 2 nights at weekends (April–October), 3 on bank holidays.

Rooms	1 double: £85. 1 suite for 2-4: £95. 1 wagon for 2 (available in summer, with separate wet room): £80. Singles from £60.
Meals	Pub/restaurant 0.25 miles.
Closed	Rarely.

Lucy Rogers
Vinegar Hill Pottery,
Vinegar Hill,
Milford on Sea, SO41 0RZ

Tel	+44 (0)1590 642979
Email	info@vinegarhillpottery.co.uk
Web	www.vinegarhillpottery.co.uk

Entry 190   Map 3

Herefordshire

Bunns Croft

The timbers of this medieval yeoman's house are quite possibly a thousand years old. Little of the structure has ever been altered and it is sheer delight. Stone floors, rich colours, a piano, dogs, books, cosy chairs – all give a homely, warm feel. Cruck-beamed bedrooms are snugly small, the stairs are steep, and the twin's bathroom has its own sweet fireplace. The countryside is 'pure', too, with 1,500 acres of National Trust land a short hop away. Anita is charming, loves to look after her guests, grows her own fruit and vegetables and makes fabulous dinners. Just mind your head.

Herefordshire

Staunton House

This handsome Georgian rectory has a traditional, peaceful feel. Step into light, colourful and well-proportioned rooms that brim with family photographs, antiques, china and masses of books. The original oak staircase leads to inviting bedrooms with comfortable beds, pretty fabrics and garden posies; the blue room looks onto garden and pond. Wander through the beautiful garden, drive to Hay or Ludlow, stride across ravishing countryside, play golf near Offa's Dyke; return to Rosie and Richard's lovely home to relax in their drawing room before enjoying a delicious dinner in the elegant dining room. You will be well looked after here.

Pets by arrangement.

Rooms	1 double, sharing bath with 2 singles. Let to same party only, 1 twin: £80-£90. 2 singles: £40.	Rooms	1 double, 1 twin/double: £85-£95. Singles £55-65.
Meals	Dinner, 3 courses, £25. Pub 7 miles.	Meals	Dinner, 3 courses, £30. Pub/restaurant 2.5 miles.
Closed	Rarely.	Closed	Rarely.

	Anita Syers-Gibson
	Bunns Croft,
	Moreton Eye,
	Leominster, HR6 0DP
Tel	+44 (0)1568 615836

	Rosie & Richard Bowen
	Staunton House,
	Staunton-on-Arrow, Pembridge,
	Leominster, HR6 9HR
Tel	+44 (0)1544 388313
Mobile	+44 (0)7780 961994
Email	rosbown@aol.com
Web	www.stauntonhouse.co.uk

Entry 191   Map 7

Entry 192   Map 7

Wickton Court

At the end of a no-through road, two miles from little Stoke Prior, is a rambling old place steeped in history, a courthouse that dates from the 15th century; ask Sally to show you the wig room! Be welcomed by ducks on the pond, sheep in the field, dogs by the fire, and lovely hosts who make you feel at home. The hallway is flagged, the sitting room panelled, the fireplace huge and often lit; all feels authentic and atmospheric. Visit Hampton Court Castle, antique-browse in Leominster, play golf, walk to the pub. Return to cosseting bedrooms with generous curtains, big bathrooms, wonky floors and ancient beams; one room even has a wood-burner.

Rooms	1 twin with separate bathroom: £95.
	1 four-poster suite for 2: £95–£120.
	Singles £85–£95.
Meals	Dinner, 3 courses, £25–£30.
	Cold platter for late arrivals, £12.50.
	Pubs/restaurants 5 miles.
Closed	Rarely.

	Sally Kellard
	Wickton Court,
	Stoke Prior,
	Leominster, HR6 0LN
Email	sally@wickton.co.uk
Web	www.wickton.co.uk

Entry 193   Map 7

Grendon Manor

The best of traditional meets modern country living: this 16th-century manor house is a super mix of the very old and very new. A working sheep and cattle farm is wrapped around it and you can walk over fields and down to a pretty Norman church. Jane is easy company and looks after you well. Guests in their own wing will rejoice in bedrooms with old beams, crisply comfortable linen and new bathrooms, while the guest sitting room downstairs has marvellous dark oak panelling, rich colours and glowing lamps. A farmhouse-tasty breakfast sets you up for beautiful Herefordshire walks, and Ludlow is close.

Rooms	2 doubles, 1 twin: £100.
	Singles £50.
Meals	Dinner £25 (groups only).
	Pub/restaurant 2 miles.
Closed	Rarely.

	Jane Piggott
	Grendon Manor,
	Bredenbury, Bromyard, HR7 4TH
Tel	+44 (0)1885 482226
Mobile	+44 (0)7977 493083
Email	jane.piggott@btconnect.com
Web	www.grendonmanor.com

Entry 194   Map 7

Orchard Ridge

Pass pretty well-kept hedges, fruit trees and sheep and arrive at Belinda's Georgian farmhouse for tea and homemade cake – in the sitting room or under an apple tree in the garden. The views towards the Malvern Hills are a treat. Inside is lived-in and friendly: wood fires, family photos, comfy sofas and inviting bedrooms with goose down duvets. Breakfast includes compotes from local fruit, honey from a neighbour, homemade granola; Belinda is happy to cook supper too. Malvern Three Counties Showground is close, foodie Ludlow an hour; you can bring your own horse and go trekking, and the Herefordshire Trail runs past the end of the garden.

Rooms	2 doubles: £65-£100.
Meals	Dinner £30.
	Restaurants 1.5 miles away.
Closed	Rarely.

Belinda McMullen
Orchard Ridge,
Hill End, Rushall, Ledbury, HR8 2PB
Tel +44 (0)1531 660213
Mobile +44 (0)7759 975951
Email bel42@btinternet.com
Web www.orchard-ridge.co.uk

Entry 195 Map 7

49 St Martin's Street

Rick and Andrea have filled their Georgian townhouse with rich colour and music. Find maps, etchings, books, flowers and teapots on mantelpieces; Rick's chic-upcycling includes a headboard from old doors. Your cosy bedroom at the top has its own sitting room next door; your friendly Dutch hosts leave you a carafe of port and brimming trolley of nice things; a Japanese-style foldaway can be set up for an extra guest. Breakfast on delicious choices: organic bacon and sausages, juices, veggie and vegan options; Andrea can do high tea of savoury and sweet treats, and dinner too. Hereford Cathedral, swimming pool, park and shops are all a stroll away.

Minimum stay: 2 nights at weekends. 2 parking spaces available (1 on-street space with a visitors' permit & 1 in private car park across the road).

Rooms	1 twin/double with separate
	shower: £90.
Meals	Dinner, 3 courses, £20.
	High tea £20, served in the guests' sitting room.
	Pubs/restaurants 2-minute walk.
Closed	Rarely.

Rick & Andrea Noordegraaf-Teeuw
49 St Martin's Street,
Hereford, HR2 7RD
Tel +44 (0)1432 340183
Email andrea@teacosy.nl

Entry 196 Map 7

Herefordshire

East Friars

Laid back, lively and on the banks of the river Wye... Polly and Roger's family house will scoop you up and make you feel at home. Find a jumble of books, music and art in every corner, comfy armchairs in the lived-in sitting room and generous sunny bedrooms. Watch swans and ducks from the conservatory or terrace, while you tuck into Polly's local, seasonal, yummy breakfast with homemade bread and marmalade; she's a chef and holds pop-up restaurant nights in the conservatory too. Fish from the pontoon, borrow a canoe, bounce on trampolines, stroll to the city centre. Ted Hughes the Jack Russell and Bea the Cockerton love guests too!

Herefordshire

Yew Tree House

Sue and John's gorgeous 19th-century home is surrounded by gardens bejewelled with roses and fruit trees – plus stunning views across the Golden Valley to Hay Bluff. Meet these delightful people over tea and homemade cake in a tastefully decorated guest sitting room with comfy sofas, an open fire and shelves groaning with books. Generous bedrooms in pretty pastels are supremely comfortable, bathrooms have plenty of fluffy towels. Wake to the smell of baking bread, hasten to the dining room for a delicious breakfast of local produce. Dore Abbey's down the road, and Hay-on-Wye a half-hour jaunt. The countryside is glorious.

Rooms	1 twin/double: £75–£115.
	1 family room for 4: £85–£120
Meals	Pubs/restaurants 10-minute walk.
Closed	Rarely.

Rooms	1 double, 1 twin: £80–£100.
	1 suite for 3: £80–£100.
Meals	Dinner, 3 courses, £25.
	Pub/restaurant 3.5 miles.
Closed	Rarely.

	Polly Ernest
	East Friars,
	Greyfriars Avenue,
	Hereford, HR4 0BE
Tel	+44 (0)1432 276462
Email	polly@eastfriars.co.uk
Web	www.eastfriars.co.uk

	John & Susan Richardson
	Yew Tree House,
	Batcho Hill, Vowchurch,
	Hereford, HR2 9PF
Tel	+44 (0)1981 251195
Email	enquiries@yewtreehouse-hereford.co.uk
Web	www.yewtreehouse-hereford.co.uk

Entry 197   Map 7

Entry 198   Map 7

Rock Cottage

Birds, books and beautiful Black Mountain views highlighted by morning sun, turning to an inky black line at dusk; the cottage glows. There's an instant feeling of warmth and friendliness as you step into the snug hall; find rich autumnal colours, old rugs, a big wood-burner and comfy sitting rooms. Local art and photos line the walls, bedrooms have sumptuous beds, perfect linen and garden posies. You eat (very well) en famille at the communal oak table, or out on the pretty terrace. Thoughtful Chris and Sue will take you to hear the dawn chorus and there are food and literary festivals, bookshops and walks galore.

Minimum stay: 2 nights. Pets by arrangement.

The Bridge Inn

Getting here is huge fun. The 16th-century inn (with a pretty garden) and farmhouse sit by the river beneath the Black Hill of Bruce Chatwin fame and willows line the footbridge. Walkers descend, as do local farmers and shooting parties, and Glyn is a great host. Comfy country bedrooms lie in the farmhouse; find antiques, flagstone floors and a dark panelled sitting room below. Breakfast on the best bacon and local eggs in the huge farmhouse kitchen, visit Hay for bookshops, yomp in the Beacons. Return to a piping hot bath then wander down to the pub for a tasty supper and a pint of Butty Bach (small friend) by the wood-burner.

Rooms	2 doubles: £70–£90.
Meals	Packed lunch £6.
	Dinner, 1 course, £15 or 3 courses, £23.
	Pub/restaurant 4 miles.
Closed	Christmas & New Year.

Rooms	1 double, 2 twin/doubles: £95.
	Hay Festival price for 2 per night: £165.
Meals	Lunch £8–£22.
	Dinner £12–£22.
Closed	Rarely.

Chris & Sue Robinson
Rock Cottage,
Newton St Margerets,
Hereford, HR2 0QW
Tel   +44 (0)1981 510360
Email robinsrockcottage@googlemail.com
Web   www.rockcottagebandb.co.uk

Glyn Bufton & Gisela Vargas
The Bridge Inn,
Michaelchurch Escley,
Hereford, HR2 0JW
Tel   +44 (0)1981 510646
Email thebridgeinn@hotmail.com
Web   www.thebridgeinnmichaelchurch.co.uk

Entry 199   Map 7

Entry 200   Map 7

Home Farm Dulas

Two miles off a main road you are pitched into rural England and the lively old-fashioned village of Ewyas Harold. And there, up a narrow lane, are the attractive red-brick barns and house of Home Farm, a working hub in amongst unspoilt countryside. The friendly Bradleys – she a keen horsewoman, he a farmer of sheep and beef – give you fine breakfasts from local ingredients (and their own apple juice) and three bedrooms off the landing, airy, big, comfortable, light, and rugs on polished floors, baths and showers, TVs and views. You're in the Golden Valley next to Dore Abbey, on the edge of the beautiful Brecon Beacons.

Minimum stay: 2 nights. Children over 8 welcome. Pets by arrangement.

The Old Post Office

Simple, laissez faire B&B in the most glorious surroundings. Linda lives at one end of her house and you have the other. Bedrooms are colourful; art dots the walls in the dining and sitting rooms. The larder is full of vegetarian breakfast things: fruits, different milks, yogurts, granola, free-range eggs, mushrooms, vine tomatoes; the communal table is laid for you – rustle up breakfast when you want. There's space to store supper stuff too, or you can walk two miles across fields to bustling Hay-on-Wye. Have fun in the Black Mountain then return to the summerhouse for drinks as the sun goes down – fridge and glasses waiting.

Minimum stay: 2 nights. Children over 5 welcome.

Rooms	2 doubles, 1 twin: £75-£85. Stays of 2 or more nights: £75. Singles £65-£75.
Meals	Restaurants 1 mile away.
Closed	Rarely.

Rooms	1 double, 2 twin/doubles: £80. Singles £60. Child £15.
Meals	Pubs/restaurants 2 miles.
Closed	Winter months & occasionally.

Maddy Bradley
Home Farm Dulas,
Dulas,
Ewyas Harold, HR2 0HJ

Tel +44 (0)1981 241108
Email willandmaddy@homefarmdulas.co.uk
Web www.homefarmdulas.co.uk

Linda Webb
The Old Post Office,
The Old Post Office, Llanigon,
Hay-on-Wye, HR3 5QA

Tel +44 (0)1497 820008
Email lindalewebb@gmail.com
Web www.oldpost-office.co.uk

Entry 201   Map 7

Entry 202   Map 7

Herefordshire

Westbrook Court

A smoothly contemporary stables renovation with views over the Wye Valley. Each suite opens on to the sun deck, most have a mezzanine bedroom above your sitting space and Australian interior designer Kari has thought of everything... Vintage pieces, unusual books and Welsh throws add colour to white-washed floors; smart bathrooms have aromatics and bath sheets. You can book boutique extras too – bubbles, cheeseboard, flowers and spa treatments. Breakfasts are local and generous: on weekdays a hamper is delivered; on weekends tuck into a full cooked spread over in the farmhouse. Wild swim at The Warren on the Wye, hike up Hay Bluff, browse in Hay.

Minimum stay: 2 nights on weekends in peak season. Cot available on request. Parking on-site.

Rooms	1 four-poster: £90–£100. 3 doubles, 1 twin/double, all with mezzanine: £90–£100. Extra camp beds £15.
Meals	Pubs/restaurants 2.5 miles.
Closed	Rarely.

Chris & Kari Morgan
Westbrook Court,
Westbrook,
Hay-on-Wye, HR3 5SY
Tel   +44 (0)1497 831752
Email   stay@westbrookcourtbandb.co.uk
Web   www.westbrookcourtbandb.co.uk

Entry 203   Map 7

Hertfordshire

Number One

It's worth hopping out of bed for Annie's breakfast: luxury continental with raspberry brioche or the full delicious Monty. Her house is a sparkling Aladdin's cave of mirrors, bunches of white twigs with birds atop, candles, cherubs, painted wooden floors, big open fires and generous bunches of roses. Bedrooms are lavishly done; nifty bathrooms have Italian tiles – and more roses! Close to the centre, this good-looking Georgian terrace house featured in Pevsner's guide to Hertfordshire, and the market town is busy with theatre, shops and galleries. Return for a gourmet dinner in the magical courtyard garden – when the sun is shining!

Over 12s welcome.

Rooms	1 double with separate bath/shower; 2 twin/doubles: £105–£130.
Meals	Dinner £40. BYO. Pubs/restaurants 5-minute walk.
Closed	Rarely.

Annie Rowley
Number One,
1 Port Hill, Hertford, SG14 1PJ
Tel   +44 (0)1992 587350
Mobile   +44 (0)7770 914070
Email   annie@numberoneporthill.co.uk
Web   www.numberoneporthill.co.uk

Entry 204   Map 9

Isle of Wight

Westbourne House

Watch the yachts go by from this elegant townhouse on the waterfront. A welcoming drink and chat with Richard in the drawing room sets you up well: antiques, oil paintings, a bevy of guitars, family photos – and stunning views. Bedrooms (one downstairs) have WiFi, home-baked biscuits, cosy well-dressed beds. Kate gives you breakfast: with the view: lots of choice, homemade marmalade – and Bucks Fizz too; if you're an early bird you can help yourself to a continental spread. You're between the two main marinas and close to the high street, so attractive shops, bars and restaurants (as well as the Southampton ferry) are all a saunter.

Over 13s welcome.

Rooms	2 doubles: £110.
Meals	Pubs/restaurants 1-minute walk.
Closed	Rarely.

	Kate Gough
	Westbourne House,
	43 Birmingham Road,
	Cowes, PO31 7BH
Tel	+44 (0)1983 290009
Email	katec56@gmail.com
Web	www.westbournehousecowes.co.uk

Entry 205   Map 4

Isle of Wight

Arreton Manor

A dream of a manor... Jacobean, grand and gorgeous. Owned by a parade of English monarchs, including Edward the Confessor and Henry VIII, it rests peacefully in five acres of landscaped gardens. Snooze by a fire in the atmospheric Old Hall, breakfast in the wonderful dining room: ancient oak panelling, polished table and gilt-framed pictures of nobility. Gleaming bedrooms have rich fabrics and excellent linen. Wake for Julia's award-winning breakfast: local sausages and bacon, famous Arreton tomatoes, homemade jams. Village pubs are a stroll, festival sites a short drive; it's a treat to stay in this friendly, very special home.

Rooms	2 doubles: £115-£130.
Meals	Pubs 5-minute walk.
Closed	Rarely.

	Julia Gray-Ling
	Arreton Manor,
	Main Road,
	Newport, PO30 3AA
Tel	+44 (0)1983 522604
Email	julia@arretonmanor.co.uk
Web	www.arretonmanor.co.uk

Entry 206   Map 4

Isle of Wight

Redway Farm

Immerse yourself in the rolling landscape of the sunny Arreton Valley... up a winding lane find a handsome, south-facing Georgian farmhouse and friendly Linda. Bedrooms are quiet, large, light and sumptuous with thick mattresses, gorgeous linen and lovely views over the gardens; warm bathrooms sparkle. Downstairs is delightful with antiques, roaring fires and fresh flowers. You breakfast on fresh croissants from the Aga – or the full works with eggs from the hens, in the sun-filled morning room or the dining room with wood-burner. Explore acres of bird-sung garden, cycle to sandy beaches. Bliss.

Rooms	2 doubles, each with separate bath: £89-£99. Extra bed/sofabed available £20 per person per night.
Meals	Pub 3 miles.
Closed	Rarely.

Linda James
Redway Farm,
Budbridge Lane, Merstone,
Newport, PO30 3DJ
Tel   +44 (0)1983 865228
Mobile   +44 (0)7775 480830
Email   lindajames.redway@gmail.com
Web   www.bedbreakfast.redwayfarm.co.uk

Entry 207   Map 4

Isle of Wight

Northcourt

A Jacobean manor in matchless grounds: 15 acres of terraced gardens, exotica and subtropical flowers. The house is magnificent too; huge but a lived-in home with big comfortable guest bedrooms in one of the wings. The formal dining room has separate tables, where delicious homemade bread and jams, garden fruit, honey and local produce are served. There's a snooker table in the library, a chamber organ in the hall and a grand piano in the vast music room. Groups are welcome and John offers garden tours. The peaceful village is in lovely downland – and you can walk from the garden to the Needles.

Rooms	3 twin/doubles: £78-£105. Singles £50-£68.
Meals	Pub 3-minute walk through gardens.
Closed	Rarely.

John & Christine Harrison
Northcourt,
Shorwell, PO30 3JG
Tel   +44 (0)1983 740415
Mobile   +44 (0)7955 174699
Email   christine@northcourt.info
Web   www.northcourt.info

Entry 208   Map 4

Isle of Wight

Gotten Manor

Miles from the beaten track and bordered by old stone barns, the guest wing of this Saxon house is charmingly simple. Up steep stone steps (you must be nimble!) and through a low doorway find big bedrooms in laid-back rustic, funky French style: beams, limewashed stone, wooden floors, Persian rugs and a sweet window. Sleep on a rosewood bed and bathe by candlelight – in a roll top tub in your room. Friendly, informal Caroline serves breakfast in the old creamery: homemade yogurts, compotes and organic produce. There's a walled garden and a guest living room with cosy wood-burner.

Minimum stay: 2 nights at weekends. Over 12s welcome.

Rooms	2 doubles: £95–£105.
Meals	Pub 1.5 miles.
Closed	Rarely.

Caroline Gurney-Champion
Gotten Manor,
Gotten Lane,
Chale, PO38 2HQ

Tel	+44 (0)1983 551368
Mobile	+44 (0)7746 453398
Email	as@gottenmanor.co.uk
Web	www.gottenmanor.co.uk/bed-breakfast

Entry 209   Map 4

Kent

Ightham

Lord it through electric oak gates to find B&B in your own modern barn. Gardening enthusiast Caroline's house is close but not hugely visible: you're wonderfully independent. Bedrooms on the ground floor are eclectic and appealing, with pine floors, dazzling white walls and slatted wooden blinds for a moody light; the bathroom is big and contemporary with a walk-in shower. Upstairs: an enormous family space for sitting, eating, playing, and glass doors on to a terrace for outdoor fun. Breakfast is delivered: eggs from the hens, pancakes, French toast. Great walks start from the door; return for supper – Caroline loves to cook.

Rooms	Barn – 1 double, 1 twin (let to same party only): £115–£125. Extra bed/sofabed available £25 per person per night.
Meals	Pub/restaurant 5-minute walk.
Closed	Rarely.

Caroline Standish
Ightham,
Hope Farm,
Sandy Lane, Ightham,
Sevenoaks, TN15 9BA

Tel	+44 (0)1732 884359
Email	clstandish@gmail.com
Web	www.ighthambedandbreakfast.co.uk

Entry 210   Map 5

Kent

Charcott Farmhouse

The 1750s farmhouse is rustic and family orientated, and if you don't come expecting an immaculate environment you will enjoy it here. In the old bake house there's a small sitting room with original beams and bread oven, TV and WiFi; relax in here on cooler days, with cats and a dog to keep you company. On sunny days tea is served in the garden. Bedrooms are pretty and comfy with blankets and eiderdowns, oriental rugs and antique furniture. Nicholas – a tad eccentric for some – is half French and cooks amazing breakfasts on the Aga, while Ginny's great grandfather (Arnold Hills) founded West Ham football team. Come and go as you please.

Rooms	2 twins; 1 twin with separate bath: £80-£90.
	Singles from £65.
Meals	Pub 5-minute walk.
Closed	Rarely.

Nicholas & Ginny Morris
Charcott Farmhouse,
Charcott,
Tonbridge, TN11 8LG

Tel	+44 (0)1892 870024
Mobile	+44 (0)7734 009292
Email	charcottfarmhouse@btinternet.com
Web	www.charcottfarmhouse.com

Entry 211   Map 5

Kent

Merzie Meadows

This lovely ranch-style house has huge windows, pergolas groaning with climbers and a Mediterranean-style swimming pool. Sitting in landscaped gardens, paddocks and woodland there are horses, hens, wild flowers and lots of twittering birds. Pamela gives you a locally sourced breakfast with fruits, organic bread and just-laid eggs. Bedrooms are beautifully dressed with pretty fabrics, handmade mattresses are topped with good linen and goose down pillows; the suite has a sitting area looking onto the garden, a study and a bathroom sleek with Italian marble and plump towels. All is peaceful; garden and nature lovers will adore it here.

Minimum stay: 2 nights at weekends April-September.

Rooms	1 double: £115-£120.
	1 suite for 2-3: £115-£150.
	Singles £98.
	Extra bed/sofabed available £50 per person per night.
Meals	Pub 2.5 miles.
Closed	Mid-December to February.

Pamela Mumford
Merzie Meadows,
Hunton Road, Marden,
Maidstone, TN12 9SL

Tel	+44 (0)1622 820500
Mobile	+44 (0)7762 713077
Email	merziemeadows@me.com
Web	www.merziemeadows.co.uk

Entry 212   Map 5

Kent

Reason Hill

Brian and Antonia's 200-acre fruit farm is perched on the edge of the Weald of Kent, with stunning views over orchards and oast houses. The farmhouse has 17th-century origins (low ceilings, wonky floors, stone flags) and a conservatory for sunny breakfasts; colours are soft, antiques gleam, the mood is relaxed. Pretty bedrooms have garden views, TVs and magazines; there's a comfy sitting room too. Come in spring for the blossom, in summer for the fruit and veg from the garden; chickens roam free. The Greensand Way runs along the bottom of the farm, you're close to Sissinghurst Castle and 45 minutes from the Channel Tunnel.

Rooms	1 double, 2 twins: £85-£90.
	1 single, sharing shower with double
	(let to same party only): £50.
Meals	Pubs within 1 mile.
Closed	Christmas & New Year.

Brian & Antonia Allfrey
Reason Hill,
Linton, Maidstone, ME17 4BT

Tel	+44 (0)1622 743679
Mobile	+44 (0)7775 745580
Email	antonia@allfrey.net
Web	www.reasonhill.co.uk

Entry 213   Map 5

Kent

Pullington Barn

Up a private drive and straight in to a vast, beamed expanse of bright light, warm colours, beautiful art and a cheery welcome from Gavin and Anne in their converted barn. There are endless books to choose: settle in the comfy drawing room with its grand piano, or sit in the pretty south-facing garden on a fine day. On the other side, views from the orchard spread over oast houses and church spires. Big bedrooms (one on the ground floor) have good mattresses, coordinated bed linen and feather pillows. You breakfast well on local and homemade produce, served at the travertine table in the dining hall. Lovely walks from the door.

Children over 9 welcome, younger ones by arrangement.

Rooms	1 double, 1 twin: £85-£100.
	Singles £60-£75.
	Dogs £5 per night.
Meals	Pub/restaurant 0.5 miles.
Closed	Christmas.

Gavin & Anne Wetton
Pullington Barn,
Benenden, TN17 4EH

Tel	+44 (0)1580 240246
Mobile	+44 (0)7849 759929
Email	anne@wetton.info
Web	www.wetton.info/bandb

Entry 214   Map 5

Kent

Beacon Hall House

A family home and Julie truly enjoys having guests. Aga breakfasts are full of delicious homemade, home-grown things; supper too, perhaps cottage pie or Hastings sea bass with veg from the garden. Find sweet herbs on your pillow, home-baked biscuits, flowers and beautiful eclectic furnishings in comfortable bedrooms. Explore seven acres of paddocks, cutting garden and mature elevated terraces, with gorgeous views across rolling Kent and Sussex. Sissinghurst and Great Dixter, castles and pretty villages are close. Return to a sitting room with huge relaxing sofas and fat cushions; Buster and Hetty the spaniels are an added boon.

Rooms	1 double, 1 twin/double: £95-£110. 1 family room for 4: £110-£140. Singles £75-£95.
Meals	Supper from £20. Pubs within 10 miles.
Closed	Christmas.

Julie Jex
Beacon Hall House,
Rolvenden Road,
Benenden, TN17 4BU
Tel   +44 (0)1580 240434
Email   julie.jex@btconnect.com
Web   www.beaconhallhouse.co.uk

Entry 215   Map 5

Kent

Ramsden Farm

The views across the Wealds are stunning! These former farm buildings have been renovated with flair, and Sally has created a gorgeous, comfortable home. Unhurried, very good breakfasts are eaten in the huge kitchen by the jaunty lemon Aga, and floor to ceiling glass doors open on to a wooden deck; spill outside on warm days. After a hearty walk you can doze in front of a tree-devouring inglenook. Find lovely sunny bedrooms with more of that view from each, natural colours, tip-top mattresses and the crispest white linen – chocolates too; bathrooms have travertine marble and underfloor heating. Friendly, spoiling and completely peaceful.

Rooms	1 double, 1 twin; 1 double with separate bath: £95-£120.
Meals	Pub 1 mile.
Closed	Rarely.

Sally Harrington
Ramsden Farm,
Dingleden Lane,
Benenden, TN17 4JT
Tel   +44 (0)1580 240203
Email   sally@ramsdenfarmhouse.co.uk
Web   www.ramsdenfarmhouse.co.uk

Entry 216   Map 5

Kent

Lamberden Cottage

Down a farm track find two 1780 cottages knocked into one, with flagstone floors, a cheery wood-burner in the guest sitting room and welcoming Beverley and Branton. There's a traditional country-cottage feel with pale walls, thick oak beams, soft carpeting and very comfortable bedrooms (the twin has an adjoining bedroom); views from all are across the Weald of Kent. Wander the lovely gardens to find your own private spot, sip a sundowner on the terrace, eat a hearty breakfast in the family dining room: home-grown fresh fruits, homemade marmalades and yogurts. Near to Sissinghurst, Great Dixter and many historic places.

Rooms	1 double, 1 twin with adjoining twin room: £75–£100. Singles from £65.
Meals	Pub 1 mile.
Closed	Christmas & New Year.

Beverley & Branton Screeton
Lamberden Cottage,
Rye Road, Sandhurst,
Cranbrook, TN18 5PH

Tel	+44 (0)1580 850743
Mobile	+44 (0)7768 462070
Email	thewalledgarden@lamberdencottage.co.uk
Web	www.lamberdencottage.co.uk

Entry 217   Map 5

Kent

Barclay Farmhouse

Lynn's breakfasts are fabulous: fresh fruit, warm croissants, home-baked breads and a daily changing twist on the traditional English. The weatherboarded guest barn may be in perfect trim but it has a been-here-for-ever feel; you have country-cosy dining tables for breakfast, a patio for summer, a big peaceful garden. Gleaming bedrooms have handmade oak bedheads, chocolates, slippers, discreet fridges, radios, TVs; shower rooms are in perfect order. Couples, honeymooners, garden lovers – many would love it here (but no children: the garden pond is deep). Warm-hearted B&B, and glorious Sissinghurst nearby.

Minimum stay: 2 nights at weekends in high season.

Rooms	Barn: 3 doubles: £95. Singles from £70.
Meals	Pubs/restaurants 1 mile.
Closed	Rarely.

Lynn Ruse
Barclay Farmhouse,
Woolpack Corner,
Biddenden, TN27 8BQ

Tel	+44 (0)1580 292626
Email	info@barclayfarmhouse.co.uk
Web	www.barclayfarmhouse.co.uk

Entry 218   Map 5

Kent

Hereford Oast

Jack the Jack Russell will meet you, swiftly followed by Suzy who'll bring you tea and cake in the garden: sheer heaven in summer. The 1876 oast house, set back from a country road and gazing on lush fields, has become the loveliest B&B. Downstairs is the dining room, as unique as it is round. Upstairs is the guest room, sunny, fresh and bright, with a blue and white theme and a rural view. As for the village – white-clapboard cottages, pubs, fine church – it's the prettiest in Kent. Sausages from Pluckley and homemade soda bread set you up for cultured jaunts: Leeds Castle, Sissinghurst, Great Dixter... all marvellously close.

Rooms	1 twin/double: £85-£90. Singles £50-£55.
Meals	Pubs 1 mile.
Closed	Rarely.

Suzy Hill
Hereford Oast,
Smarden Bell Road, Smarden,
Ashford, TN27 8PA
Tel   +44 (0)1233 770541
Email   suzy@herefordoast.fsnet.co.uk
Web   www.herefordoast.co.uk

Entry 219   Map 5

Kent

Romden

Guarded by trees and birds, lording it over meadows and lanes, this rambling 'castle' with its 16th-century tower has a charmingly lived-in feel. Lovely laid-back Miranda and Dominic make you feel at home; help yourself to cereals while they drum up your bacon and eggs, enjoy the flower-filled terrace, play croquet or use their pool and tennis court (by arrangement). Bedrooms, sitting room and hall are decked out with pretty wallpapers, antiques, art, rugs and throws; one of the twins has a tiny shower room; log fires keep things toasty. And if you're hankering after a real castle, Sissinghurst and Leeds are down the road.

Rooms	1 double, 1 twin; 1 twin with separate bath: £70-£95. Singles £55-£75.
Meals	Pubs/restaurants 1.5 miles.
Closed	Rarely.

Miranda Kelly
Romden,
Smarden,
Ashford, TN27 8RA
Tel   +44 (0)1233 770687
Email   miranda_kelly@hotmail.com
Web   www.romdencastle.co.uk

Entry 220   Map 5

Snoadhill Cottage

You'll feel at home the moment you arrive at Yvette and Philip's friendly cottage. Once a medieval 'hall house', it's awash with huge oak beams. Up steep stairs and past shelves of books find fresh, sunny bedrooms with lovely views. Enjoy a flagstone terrace for summery breakfasts or a fireside spot in the dining room; expect eggs from the hens, homemade jams, kippers perhaps or a full English. You're surrounded by glorious open countryside, walks and cycle rides start from the door and it's just 25 minutes from the Channel Tunnel. Dip in the swimming pond, chat to Rocky the labrador… and wander the blooming gardens.

The Old Rectory

On a really good day (about once every year) you can see France. But you'll be more than happy to settle for the superb views over Romney Marsh, the Channel in the distance. The big, friendly house, built in 1845, has impeccable, elegant bedrooms and good bathrooms; the large, many-windowed sitting room is full of books, pictures and flowers from the south-facing garden. Marion and David are both charming and can organise transport to the Channel Tunnel for you. It's remarkably peaceful – perfect for walking (right on the Saxon Shore path), cycling and bird watching.

Children over 10 welcome.

Rooms	1 double with separate shower, 1 twin with separate bath: £80-£85. Singles £65.
Meals	Pub 1 mile.
Closed	Rarely.

Rooms	1 twin; 1 twin with separate bath/shower: £90. Singles £60.
Meals	Pubs within 4 miles.
Closed	Christmas & New Year.

Yvette James
Snoadhill Cottage,
Snoadhill, Bethersden,
Ashford, TN26 3DY
Tel +44 (0)1233 820245
Email enquiries@snoadhillcottage.co.uk
Web www.snoadhillcottage.co.uk

Marion & David Hanbury
The Old Rectory,
Ruckinge,
Ashford, TN26 2PE
Tel +44 (0)1233 732328
Email oldrectory@hotmail.com
Web www.oldrectoryruckinge.co.uk

Entry 221   Map 5

Entry 222   Map 5

Kent

Stowting Hill House

A classic manor house in an idyllic setting, close to Canterbury and the North Downs Way. This warm, civilised home mixes Tudor beams with Georgian proportions; find a huge conservatory full of greenery, a guest sitting room with sofas and log fire, and breakfasts fresh from the Aga. Traditional bedrooms are carpeted and cosily furnished. Your charming, country-loving hosts welcome you with tea and flowers from the garden – a perfect spot with its lawns, tree-lined avenue, bluebell woods and stone obelisk. Not much more than a half hour train ride from London – and ten minutes from the Chunnel, but this is worth more than one night.

Rooms	1 twin/double, 1 twin: £100.
	Singles from £65.
Meals	Dinner from £30.
	Pub 1 mile.
Closed	Christmas & New Year.

Richard & Virginia Latham
Stowting Hill House,
Stowting,
Ashford, TN25 6BE

Tel	+44 (0)1303 862881
Email	lathamvj@gmail.com
Web	www.stowtinghillhouse.co.uk

Kent

Park Gate

Peter and Mary are a generous team and their conversation is informed and easy. Behind the wisteria-clad façade are two sitting rooms with inglenook fireplaces, ancient beams and polished wood. Fresh comfortable bedrooms have TVs, gorgeous views over the garden to the fields beyond and gleaming bathrooms. Meals are delicious! More magic outside: croquet, tennis and thatched pavilions, wildlife and roses and a sprinkling of sheep to mow the paddock. The house dates back to 1460 and has a noble history: Sir Anthony Eden lived here and Churchill visited during the war. Great value, and convenient for Channel Tunnel and ferries.

Rooms	2 twin/doubles: £85.
	1 single with separate shower: £45.
Meals	Occasional dinner, 3 courses, £30.
	Simple supper £17.50.
	Pubs/restaurants 1 mile.
Closed	Christmas, New Year & January.

Peter & Mary Morgan
Park Gate,
Elham,
Canterbury, CT4 6NE

| Tel | +44 (0)1303 840304 |
| Email | marylmorgan@hotmail.co.uk |

Kent

Waterlock House

A stylish Georgian town house with your own airy loft apartment on two floors. Judith gives you a key to a separate entrance, so come and go as you please. The vast bedroom/sitting room has French antique quirky pieces, a painted black and white diamond floor, a sink-into sofa and a very comfortable big bed with a colourful cover. Hop downstairs for a continental breakfast with croissants, local ham, boiled eggs – and the papers too. There's a fantastic, authentic Provençal-style walled garden behind, Sophie and Judith's decorative antique shop next door – have a browse – and you're surrounded by pretty villages and marvellous walks.

Well-behaved pets welcome (no access to garden).

Rooms	1 apartment for 2 with sitting room & kitchenette: £120.
Meals	Continental breakfast. Pubs/restaurants 2-minute walk.
Closed	Rarely.

Sophie Norton
Waterlock House,
Canterbury Road
Wingham,
Canterbury, CT3 1BH
Tel +44 (0)1227 721792
Email branchingoutwingham@gmail.com
Web www.branchingoutwingham.co.uk

Kent

7 Longport

A delightful, unexpected hideaway bang opposite the site of St Augustine's Abbey and a five-minute walk to the Cathedral. You pass through Ursula and Christopher's elegant Georgian house to emerge in a pretty courtyard, with fig tree and rambling rose, to find your self-contained cottage. Downstairs is a cosy sitting room with pale walls, tiled floors and plenty of books, and a clever, compact wet room with mosaic tiles. Then up steep stairs to a swish bedroom with crisp cotton sheets on a handmade bed and views of magnolia and ancient wisteria. You breakfast in the main house or in the courtyard on sunny days. Perfect.

Rooms	Cottage – 1 double with sitting room: £90-£100. Singles £70.
Meals	Restaurants 5-minute walk.
Closed	Rarely.

Ursula & Christopher Wacher
7 Longport,
Canterbury, CT1 1PE
Tel +44 (0)1227 455367
Email info@7longport.co.uk
Web www.7longport.co.uk

Kent

Huntingfield House

A sleepy setting... a long drive through parkland brings you to this Georgian-fronted manor house and delightful host Emma. It's a friendly family home with chickens, ponies and two stable cats who like to go for walks with the basset hounds. Classic country-house bedrooms have garden views, flowers and tea trays. Hop down for breakfast in the sunny elegant dining room: home-reared bacon and sausages, homemade bread and marmalade. Lots of treats nearby will keep you happy: Leeds Castle, Sissinghurst, shopping in Canterbury... Emma is a keen cook – so you might return to a tasty informal supper (or three-course spread) too.

Minimum stay: 2 nights in high season.

Kent

The Linen Shed

A weatherboard house with a winding footpath to the front door and a pot-covered veranda out the back: sit here and nibble something delicious and homemade while you contemplate the pretty garden with its gypsy caravan. Vickie, wreathed in smiles, has created a 'vintage' interior: find wooden flooring, reclaimed architectural pieces, big old roll tops, a mahogany loo seat. Bedrooms (two up, one down) are painted in the softest colours, firm mattresses are covered in fine cotton or linen, dressing gowns hang in the smart bathrooms. Food is seriously good here, and adventurous – try a seaside picnic hamper!

Rooms	1 double, 1 twin: £90-£100. Singles £60-£70. Extra bed/sofabed available £30 per person per night.
Meals	Supper, 2 courses, £20. Dinner, 3 courses, £30. Pubs/restaurants 2 miles.
Closed	Rarely.

Rooms	2 doubles with separate bath/shower, 1 double with separate bath (occasionally shared with family): £85-£110. Singles from £75.
Meals	Picnic hamper from £20. Pub/restaurant 300 yds.
Closed	Rarely.

	Emma Norwood
	Huntingfield House,
	Stalisfield Road,
	Eastling,
	Faversham, ME13 0HT
Tel	+44 (0)1795 892138
Email	emma@huntingfieldhouse.co.uk
Web	www.huntingfieldhouse.co.uk

	Vickie Hassan
	The Linen Shed, 104 The Street,
	Boughton-under-Blean,
	Faversham, Kent ME13 9AP
Tel	+44 (0)1227 752271
Mobile	+44 (0)7714 646469
Email	bookings@thelinenshed.com
Web	www.thelinenshed.com

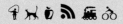

Entry 227   Map 5

Entry 228   Map 5

Kent

Northwood Lodge

Emma is happy to share her friendly home. Bedrooms have pretty beds and rugs on painted floors; the huge guest bathroom is gorgeous: freestanding bath, fluffy towels, scented lotions, a jug of flowers. A delicious breakfast with a dish of the day and homemade jam is served in the big, bright kitchen, or outside in the sun. You can settle in the drawing room for a film/dinner night (book beforehand), and there's another sitting room with heaps of books, open fire and large antique mirrors. Head out for seaside walks, Whitstable Oyster Festival and Faversham with its medieval market place; Canterbury and Margate are a short drive too.

Minimum stay: 2 nights at weekends & in high season. Children over 8 welcome.

Rooms	2 doubles sharing bath: £110. Singles £85.
Meals	Dinner from £25. Dinner and movie from £35. Pubs/restaurants 5 miles.
Closed	Rarely.

Emma Clarke
Northwood Lodge,
Bullockstone Road,
Herne Bay, CT6 7NR
Tel   +44 (0)1227 634549
Email emma@stellarproductions.co.uk

🐈 🥗 📶 🚂

Entry 229   Map 5

Kent

Great Selson Manor

A gem of a restoration in a blooming garden. Graham (film maker) and Yolanda's home is one of the earliest Dutch-influenced buildings in east Kent, and you step inside to wonderful features at every turn: a striking brick hall floor, a Jacobean oak staircase, Graham's artwork, oriental musical instruments, an elegant library. Inviting bedrooms, claw foot baths, and cushiony sofas in the sitting room add to the comfortable vibe. Breakfast includes a neighbour's award-winning apple juice, best-sourced sausages, homemade jams, eggs from the hens. Graham and Yolanda exude cheerfulness and interest – it's a treat to stay with them.

Over 13s welcome.

Rooms	2 doubles: £100-£130.
Meals	Continental breakfast available. Pubs/restaurants 2.5 miles away.
Closed	Rarely.

Graham Johnston
Great Selson Manor,
Selson Lane, Eastry,
Sandwich, CT13 0EF
Mobile +44 (0)7957 160385
Email   g.j3@btinternet.com

📖 🥗 📶 🚂 🚜 🚲

Entry 230   Map 5

Kent

Kingsdown Place

A huge white Italianate villa set in terraced gardens running down to the sea – on clear days you can see France! Tan has renovated house and garden with panache: modern art festoons the walls, statues lurk and all is light and contemporary. Upstairs are superb bedrooms: one four-poster with garden views, and, up a spiral staircase in the loft, a private suite with a sitting room, terrace and view of the sea. All have Conran mattresses and white linen. Breakfast on scrambled eggs, smoked salmon or the full works, out on the terrace in good weather. Relaxed seaside chic and a mere hop from Deal, Dover, Walmer and Sandwich.

Lancashire

Challan Hall

The wind in the trees, the boom of a bittern and birdsong. That's as noisy as it gets. On the edge of the village, delightful Charlotte's former farmhouse overlooks woods and Haweswater Reservoir; deer, squirrels and Leighton Moss Nature Reserve are your neighbours. The Cassons are well-travelled and the house, filled with a colourful collection of mementos, is happily and comfortably traditional. Expect a sofa-strewn sitting room, a smart red and polished-wood dining room and two freshly floral bedrooms (one with a tiny shower room). Morecambe Bay and the Lakes are on the doorstep – come home to lovely views and stunning sunsets.

Rooms	1 double, 1 four-poster, each with separate bath & sitting room: £95-£100. 1 suite for 2 with sitting room & terrace: £120-£130. Singles from £75.
Meals	Packed lunch £10. Dinner £25. Restaurant 500 yds. Pub 0.5 miles.
Closed	Christmas & New Year.

Rooms	1 twin/double; 1 twin/double with separate bath: £75. 2 nights or more: £70 (Mon-Fri). Singles from £50.
Meals	Dinner, 2 courses, £25. Packed lunch available. Pubs 1 mile.
Closed	Rarely.

	Tan Harrington Kingsdown Place, Upper Street, Kingsdown, CT14 8EU
Tel	+44 (0)1304 380510
Email	tan@tanharrington.com

	Charlotte Casson Challan Hall, Silverdale, LA5 0UH
Tel	+44 (0)1524 701054
Mobile	+44 (0)7790 360776
Email	cassons@btopenworld.com
Web	www.challanhall.co.uk

Lancashire

Sagar Fold House

In a spectacular setting, a 17th-century dairy and two perfect studios, one up, one down. Private entrances lead to big beamed spaces that marry immaculate efficiency with unusual beauty. A gorgeous Indian door frame serves as the en suite door upstairs, soft colours and contemporary touches lift the spirit, plentiful books and DVDs entertain you and a continental breakfast is supplied – homemade and organic whenever possible. The gardens are amazing with lovely places to sit, a sweet old summer house and an Italian knot garden – very Wolf Hall! Take walks in deeply peaceful countryside; top-notch places to eat are an easy drive.

Rooms	2 studios for 2, each with kitchenette: £90.
Meals	Continental breakfast in fridge. Pubs/restaurants 1-2 miles.
Closed	Rarely.

Helen & John Cook
Sagar Fold House,
Higher Hodder, Clitheroe, BB7 3LW
Tel   +44 (0)1254 826844
Mobile   +44 (0)7850 750709
Email   helencook14@gmail.com
Web   www.sagarfoldhouse.co.uk

Entry 233   Map 12

Leicestershire

Breedon Hall

Through high walls find a listed Georgian manor house in an acre of garden, and friendly Charlotte and Charles. Make yourselves at home in the fire-warmed drawing room full of fine furniture, art and furnishings in the richest reds and golds. Charlotte is a smashing cook: homemade granola and marmalade, local eggs, bacon and sausages for breakfast; you can book a three-course dinner too. Bedrooms are painted in soft colours, beds are covered in goose down; bathrooms are immaculate. The old stabling now houses three neat self-catering cottages too. Borrow a bike and discover the glorious countryside right on the cusp of two counties.

Check availability calendar on owners' website.

Rooms	5 doubles: £75-£150. Extra bed/sofabed available at no charge.
Meals	Supper £25. Dinner, 3 courses, £35. Pub/restaurant 1-minute walk.
Closed	Occasionally.

Charlotte Meynell
Breedon Hall,
Main Street, Breedon-on-the-Hill,
Derby, DE73 8AN
Tel   +44 (0)1332 864935
Mobile   +44 (0)7973 105467
Email   charlottemeynell1963@gmail.com
Web   www.breedonhall.co.uk

Entry 234   Map 8

Leicestershire

Curtain Cottage

A pretty village setting for this cottage on the main street, next door to Sarah's interior design shop. You have your own entrance by the side and through a large garden, which backs onto fields with horses and the National Forest beyond. A conservatory is your sitting room: wicker armchairs, wooden floors, a contemporary take on the country look. Bedrooms are light and fresh: linen from The White Company on sumptuous beds, slate-tiled bathrooms, stunning fabrics. Breakfast is full English with eggs from the hens or fresh fruit and croissants from the local shop – all is delivered to you. Perfect privacy.

Leicestershire

The Gorse House

Passing cars are less frequent than passing horses – this is a peaceful spot in a pretty village. Lyn and Richard's 17th-century cottage has a feeling of lightness and space; there's a fine collection of paintings and furniture, and oak doors lead from dining room to guest sitting room. Country style bedrooms have green views and are simply done. The garden layout was designed by Bunny Guinness, you can bring your horse (there's plenty of stabling) and it's a stroll to a good pub dinner. The house is filled with laughter, breakfasts with home-grown fruits are tasty and the Cowdells are terrific hosts who love having guests to stay.

Rooms	1 double, 1 twin: £90–£95.
	Singles £65–£70.
Meals	Pubs/restaurants 150 yds.
Closed	Rarely.

Rooms	1 double: £75.
	1 family room for 4: £90–£125.
	Stable – 1 triple with kitchenette: £75–£112.
	Singles £45.
Meals	Packed lunch £5.
	Pub 75 yds (closed on Sun eves).
Closed	Rarely.

	Sarah Barker
	Curtain Cottage,
	92-94 Main Street,
	Woodhouse Eaves, LE12 8RZ
Tel	+44 (0)1509 891361
Mobile	+44 (0)7906 830088
Email	sarah@curtaincottage.co.uk
Web	www.curtaincottage.co.uk

	Lyn & Richard Cowdell
	The Gorse House,
	33 Main Street, Grimston,
	Melton Mowbray, LE14 3BZ
Tel	+44 (0)1664 813537
Mobile	+44 (0)7780 600792
Email	cowdell@gorsehouse.co.uk
Web	www.gorsehouse.co.uk

Entry 235   Map 8

Entry 236   Map 9

Lincolnshire

The Old Farm House

You will feel at home in this rambling, quirky house – Nicola loves having guests to stay. Three cottages combined, the house is 300 years old and it's said that Dick Turpin, on the run, once hid in the roof. Read the papers by a winter fire, flop into worn leather chairs, sip an evening glass of wine in the garden, sleep soundly on a fine brass bed. Rooms are named after the men of the extended family – King Henry, George and James – and all are colourful, comfortable and cushioned. There are cycle routes, walks and golf courses galore (Nicola has all the info), racing at Market Rasen, quaint churches to visit and an annual classic car rally.

Rooms	2 doubles: £85.
	1 family room for 4: £120
	(£90 for 3, £80 for 2).
	Singles £55.
Meals	Pub 2.5 miles.
Closed	Christmas, New Year & occasionally.

Nicola Clarke
The Old Farm House,
Low Road, Hatcliffe,
Grimsby, DN37 0SH

Tel	+44 (0)1472 824455
Mobile	+44 (0)7818 272523
Email	clarky.hatcliffe@btinternet.com
Web	www.oldfarmhousebandbgrimsby.com

Entry 237   Map 13

Lincolnshire

The Manor House

At the end of a neatly raked gravel drive, a new manor house with wide views and stunning sunsets over the peaceful Trent valley. The Days have farmed in the village since 1898 and look after you with rich warm comfort and friendly ease. You have your own entrance hall leading to a bedroom with opulent curtains, period furniture, comfy sofa and rural art. There's a sunny patio outside your annexe, and the beautiful gardens are awash with roses, ducks on the pond, horses in the paddock. Shooting can be arranged and you can fish for carp in the lake, or play golf nearby; there are music and art festivals, antique fairs and walks in abundance too.

Rooms	Annexe – 1 twin/double with kitchenette: £75.
	Singles £50.
Meals	Pub/restaurant 3.5 miles.
Closed	Christmas & New Year.

Judy Day
The Manor House,
Manton, Kirton Lindsey,
Gainsborough, DN21 4JT

Tel	+44 (0)1652 649508
Mobile	+44 (0)7712 766347
Email	enquiries@manorhousebedandbreakfast.co.uk
Web	www.manorhousebedandbreakfast.co.uk

Entry 238   Map 13

Lincolnshire

Grayingham Lodge

An attractive stone farmhouse surrounded by fields. Jane and Peter's house is a working sheep farm, and you arrive to a welcoming cup from a silver teapot and delicious cake by the fire. If you're peckish later too, there are homemade flapjacks in pretty, very comfortable bedrooms. In the morning, the sideboard holds an impressive spread: homemade marmalade, fruit salad, compote, cereals – and a tasty cooked breakfast to follow. Have a day sightseeing in Lincoln – the Cathedral is magnificent and the castle has a copy of the Magna Carta; explore the Lincolnshire Wolds and coast; head off early for some exciting racing at Blyton Park.

Rooms	3 doubles: £85.
	Singles £55.
Meals	Pubs/restaurants 3 miles.
Closed	Rarely.

Jane Summers
Grayingham Lodge,
Gainsborough Road,
Northorpe,
Gainsborough, DN21 4AN

Tel	+44 (0)1652 648544
Email	janesummers@btinternet.com
Web	www.grayinghamlodge.co.uk

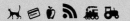

Lincolnshire

The Grange

Wide open farmland and an award-winning farm on the edge of the Lincolnshire Wolds. This immaculately kept farm has been in the family for generations; Sarah and Jonathan are delightful and make you feel instantly at home. Find acres of farmland and a two-mile farm trail to explore, a trout lake to picnic by and an open fire to warm you in an elegant drawing room with Georgian windows. Sarah gives you delicious homemade cake on arrival and huge Aga breakfasts with home-laid eggs and local produce. Comfortable bedrooms have TVs, tea trays and gleaming bathrooms. Fabulous views stretch to Lincoln Cathedral and the walks are superb.

Rooms	2 doubles: £74–£80.
	Singles £52–£54.
Meals	Supper from £18.
	Dinner, 2 courses, from £25. BYO.
	(No meals during harvest.)
	Pub/restaurant 1 mile.
Closed	Christmas & New Year.

Sarah & Jonathan Stamp
The Grange,
Torrington Lane,
East Barkwith, LN8 5RY

Tel	+44 (0)1673 858670
Mobile	+44 (0)7951 079474
Email	sarahstamp@myfwi.co.uk
Web	www.thegrange-lincolnshire.co.uk

Lincolnshire

Baumber Park

Lincoln red cows and Longwool sheep surround this attractive rosy-brick farmhouse – once a stud that bred a Derby winner. The old watering pond is now a haven for frogs, newts and toads; birds sing lustily. Maran hens conjure delicious eggs, and charming Clare, a botanist, is hugely knowledgeable about the area. Bedrooms are light and traditional with mahogany furniture; two have heart-stopping views. Guests have their own wisteria-covered entrance, sitting room with an open fire, dining room with local books and the lovely garden to roam. This is good walking, riding and cycling country; seals and rare birds on the coast.

Minimum stay usually: 2 nights at weekends in high season.

Rooms	2 doubles; 1 twin with separate shower: £68-£80. Singles £40-£65.
Meals	Pubs 1.5 miles.
Closed	Christmas & New Year.

Clare Harrison
Baumber Park,
Baumber, Horncastle, LN9 5NE

Tel	+44 (0)1507 578235
Mobile	+44 (0)7977 722776
Email	mail@baumberpark.com
Web	www.baumberpark.com

Entry 241   Map 9

Lincolnshire

The Barn

Surrounded by meadows this 17th-century barn is in a quiet spot in a conservation village. Step in to a light-filled home with old beams and good antiques; a fireplace glows and heated floors keep toes warm. Above the high-raftered main living/dining room is a comfy, good-sized double; two adjoining rooms share a shower and are perfect for family or friends sharing; the single has an antique brass bed. Jane is helpful and friendly, there are endless extras and nothing is too much trouble; her delicious breakfasts and suppers are entirely local or home-grown. Views are to sheep-dotted fields and the village is on a 25-mile cycle trail.

Rooms	1 twin/double; 2 twin/doubles sharing a shower: £80. 1 single with separate bath/shower: £55.
Meals	Supper, 2 courses, £17.50. Dinner, 3 courses, £25. BYO. Pubs in village & 2 miles.
Closed	Rarely.

Jane Wright
The Barn,
Spring Lane, Folkingham,
Sleaford, NG34 0SJ

Tel	+44 (0)1529 497199
Mobile	+44 (0)7876 363292
Email	sjwright@farming.co.uk
Web	www.thebarnspringlane.co.uk

Entry 242   Map 9

London

Arlington Avenue

This 1848 townhouse is a real find – from here you can follow the canal up to Islington. Inside you find a world of books and art; immaculate bedrooms (the double very spacious) are colourful and filled with pictures, etchings and pretty furniture, with views over several gardens to the back. The grey marble shared guest bathroom is two flights down, but if you don't mind that, you've struck gold. Shop locally, eat picnic suppers in the red and gold dining room, chill drinks in the fridge. You help yourself to breakfast in a lemon coloured country-style kitchen; this is laissez-faire B&B and fantastic value.

Tube: Angel & Old Street (15-minute walk). Buses: 5 mins to stops for City, St Paul's, Tate Modern. Limited parking (by arrangement).

Rooms	1 double, sharing bath with single: £55–£70.
	1 single: £45–£65.
Meals	Pubs/restaurants 100 yds.
Closed	Rarely.

Thomas Blaikie
Arlington Avenue,
Islington, N1 7AX
Mobile +44 (0)7711 265183
Email thomas@arlingtonavenue.co.uk
Web www.arlingtonavenue.co.uk

Entry 243   Map 22

London

66 Camden Square

A modern, architect designed house made of African teak, brick and glass. Climb wooden stairs under a glazed pyramid to light-filled, Japanese-style bedrooms with low platform beds, modern chairs and private sitting room/study. Sue and Rodger have travelled widely so there are pictures, photographs and ethnic pieces everywhere – and a burst of colour from Peckam the parrot. Share their lovely open-plan dining space overlooking a verdant bird-filled courtyard at breakfast – a delicious start to the day. Cool Camden's bustling market is close, along with theatres, restaurants, bars and zoo.

Minimum stay: 2 nights. Children over 8 welcome.

Rooms	1 double: £110–£120.
	1 single, sharing bath with double, let to same party only: £65–£75.
Meals	Pubs/restaurants nearby.
Closed	Occasionally.

Sue & Rodger Davis
66 Camden Square,
Camden Town, NW1 9XD
Tel +44 (0)20 7485 4622
Email suejdavis@btinternet.com

Entry 244   Map 22

London

30 King Henry's Road

Shops, restaurants and sublime views of Primrose Hill are a five-minute stroll from this interesting 1860s house; walls are covered in a lifetime collection of watercolours, drawings and maps. Your room on the top floor has a comfortable brass bed, a sisal floor, fine pieces of furniture, a wall of books, digital TV and a smart new bathroom. Breakfast on homemade bread and jams, bagels, croissants, yogurts and fresh fruit salad in the large kitchen/dining room with a big open fire and garden views. There's open-air theatre in Regent's Park in summer; Carole and Ted know London well and will happily advise.

Min stay: 2 nights at weekends. Tube: Chalk Farm, 5-minute walk. Parking free on street 6pm-8.30am & all weekend.

Rooms	1 double: £130.
	Singles £120.
Meals	Continental breakfast.
	Pubs/restaurants 2-minute walk.
Closed	Occasionally.

Carole & Ted Cox
30 King Henry's Road,
Primrose Hill, NW3 3RP
Tel   +44 (0)20 7483 2871
Mobile   +44 (0)7976 389350
Email   carole.l.cox@gmail.com

Entry 245   Map 22

London

The Roost

The immaculate pale blue-painted front door sets the tone for this large and lofty Victorian home. This is boutique B&B and you get smart hotel-standard rooms at a fraction of the price. The furniture is excellent: fine family pieces and clever Liz's handsome finds. There is a conservatory for continental breakfast, a delightful Parson Russell dog and art everywhere. Liz, a former fashion pattern cutter and dancer, is a natural and lovely hostess. The Roost is brilliantly positioned for whizzing into town, yet here you have a lovely park, an irresistible bakery, great restaurants and a farmers' market on Sundays. Marvellous.

Minimum stay: 2 nights. Free parking weekends. Tube & overground within walking distance.

Rooms	3 doubles (2 with bath/shower;
	1 with shower): £120-£135.
	Singles £95-£115.
Meals	Continental breakfast.
	Pubs/restaurants 5-minute walk.
Closed	Rarely.

Liz Crosland
The Roost,
37 Lynton Road,
Queen's Park, NW6 6BE
Tel   +44 (0)20 7625 6770
Mobile   +44 (0)7967 354477
Email   liz@boutiquebandblondon.com
Web   www.boutiquebandblondon.com

Entry 246   Map 22

London

101 Abbotsbury Road

The area is one of London's most desirable and Sunny's family home is opposite the borough's loveliest park, with open-air opera in summer. The top floor is for visitors. Warm, homely bedrooms are in gentle beiges and greens, with pale carpets, white duvets, pelmeted windows and a pretty dressing table for the double. The bathroom, marble-tiled and sky-lit, shines. You are well placed for Kensington High Street, Olympia, Notting Hill, Portobello Market, Kensington Gardens, the Albert Hall, Knightsbridge and Piccadilly! Relax, unwind, feel free to come and go.

Children over 6 welcome. Tube: Holland Park, 7-min walk. Off-street parking sometimes available.

Rooms	1 double, sharing bath with single: £110-£120.
	1 single: £65-£75.
Meals	Continental breakfast.
	Pubs/restaurants 5-minute walk.
Closed	Occasionally.

Sunny Murray
101 Abbotsbury Road,
Holland Park, W14 8EP

Tel	+44 (0)20 7602 0179
Mobile	+44 (0)7768 362562
Email	sunny.murray@gmail.com

Entry 247   Map 22

London

31 Rowan Road

Terrific value for money in leafy Brook Green. The two studios are fantastic spaces: one under the eaves (comfy twin beds and armchairs, a deep cast-iron bath from which you can gaze at the birds), the other larger and more contemporary in style, on the lower ground floor, with its own wisteria-clad entrance. All independent with a continental breakfast popped in your fridge. Or join in with family life and stay in the little pink bedroom with books and hats, and take breakfast in the pretty conservatory with Vicky and Edmund. A friendly home with flowers, art, photos and a relaxed vibe – Tiger the terrier and a blossoming garden too.

Tube: Hammersmith. Off-street parking £20 a day.

Rooms	1 double with separate bath/shower: £75-£90.
	2 studios for 2 with kitchenette: £75-£130.
	Singles £75. Extra bed/sofabed available £20 per person per night.
Meals	Continental breakfast.
	Pubs/restaurants 2 minutes.
Closed	Occasionally.

Vicky & Edmund Sixsmith
31 Rowan Road,
Brook Green,
Hammersmith, W6 7DT

Tel	+44 (0)20 8748 0930
Mobile	+44 (0)7966 829359
Email	vickysixsmith@me.com
Web	www.abetterwaytostay.co.uk

Entry 248   Map 22

London

1 Peel Street

Pretty, gabled and surprisingly quiet with central London on your doorstep. Fascinating old maps, photos from Susie's world travels and objets d'art all create an unusual and elegant feel. The top floor is all yours: the bedroom is full of character, framed by the slanting angles of the roof and soothingly decorated in neutral shades; the shelf above the snug-looking bed is crammed with interesting reads. Breakfast is at a table overlooking the patio: organic bread, pastries, fruit and excellent coffee. Just a stroll to good tapas, wine bars, Hyde Park and Notting Hill. Hop on a bus or tube to explore further. Guests love it here.

Rooms	1 double with separate bath/shower: £130. Singles £95.
Meals	Continental breakfast. Pubs/restaurants 2-minute walk.
Closed	Occasionally.

	Susan Laws 1 Peel Street, Kensington, W8 7PA
Tel	+44 (0)20 7792 8361
Mobile	+44 (0)7776 140060
Email	susan@susielaws.co.uk

Entry 249   Map 22

London

Colet Gardens

This smart Victorian terraced house is an easy base for Kensington and a ten-minute walk from the hustle of Hammersmith. A home of art, sculptures, books and music, and Jane and Rod offer you a large modern loft studio with floor to ceiling windows, colourful rug and a day bed, or a smaller comfy double on the first floor; both have little shower rooms. A continental breakfast is served at the kitchen table; French windows lead out to a palm-dotted courtyard where you can have your coffee in the sun. Convenient for tube or bus, and close to the Lyric Theatre, Riverside Studios, and a Thames riverside amble with good pubs along the way.

Minimum stay: 2 nights.

Rooms	1 studio room with kitchenette: £60-£105. Garden Room – 1 double: £60-£105.
Meals	Continental breakfast. Pub/restaurant 5-minute walk.
Closed	Rarely.

	Jane Kennard Colet Gardens, West Kensington, W14 9DH
Mobile	+44 (0)7958 932749
Email	janekennard@btinternet.com
Web	www.guestinlondon.com

Entry 250   Map 22

London

15 Delaford Street

A pretty Victorian, terraced Fulham home, inside all charming and spacious. In a tiny, sun-trapping courtyard you can have continental breakfast in good weather – tropical fruits are a favourite and the coffee is very good; a second miniature garden bursts with life at the back. The bedroom, up a spiral staircase, looks down on it all. Expect perfectly ironed sheets on a comfy bed, a quilted throw, books in the alcove, a sunny bathroom and fluffy white towels. The tennis at Queen's is in June and on your doorstep. Tim and Margot – she's from Melbourne – are fun, charming and happy to pick you up from the nearest tube.

Tube: West Brompton. Parking free eves & weekends; otherwise pay & display. Bus: 74 to West End nearby.

Rooms	1 double: £100–£105.
	Singles £80.
Meals	Restaurants nearby.
Closed	Occasionally.

Margot & Tim Woods
15 Delaford Street,
Fulham, SW6 7LT
Tel   +44 (0)20 7385 9671
Email   woodsmargot@hotmail.co.uk

Entry 251   Map 22

London

22 Marville Road

Smart railings help a pink rose climb, orange lilies add a touch of colour, and breakfast is in the pretty back garden on sunny days. Ben, the springer and Tizzie the cocker spaniel, and Christine – music lover, traveller, rower – make you feel at home. Your big light-filled bedroom is high up in the eaves and comes in elegant French grey with comfortable beds, crisp linen, pretty lamps, a smart bathroom and a chaise longue for lounging and reading. The house is friendly with treasures from Christine's travels and gentle music at breakfast; there's a baby grand to play too. Restaurants and shops are a stroll away and the Boat Race down the river.

Children over 10 welcome.

Rooms	1 twin/double: £105.
	Singles £95.
Meals	Continental breakfast.
	Pubs/restaurants nearby.
Closed	Rarely.

Christine Drake
22 Marville Road,
Fulham, SW6 7BD
Tel   +44 (0)20 7381 3205
Email   chris@christine-drake.com
Web   www.londonguestsathome.com

Entry 252   Map 22

35 Burnthwaite Road

Near Queen's Club and Wimbledon for tennis and Fulham Broadway's tube, a sweet terraced house on the sunny side of the street. A fresh aqua carpet ushers you up to a bright bedroom on the second floor, and a spotless white bathroom squeezed under the eaves. It's as peaceful as can be. No sitting room but a rather smart dining table for breakfast – croissants, cereals, fresh fruit salad. A traditional and civilised feel prevails, thanks to lovely family pieces, fine china, touches of chintz – and friendly Diana who helps you plan your day. Buses to Piccadilly and Westminster, a stroll to the Thames, all of London at your feet.

Min. stay: 2 nights. Children over 10 welcome.

Rooms	1 twin/double: £100–£120.
Meals	Continental breakfast.
	Pubs/restaurants within walking distance.
Closed	Rarely.

Diana FitzGeorge-Balfour
35 Burnthwaite Road,
Fulham, SW6 5BQ

Tel	+44 (0)20 7385 8081
Mobile	+44 (0)7831 571449
Email	diana@dianabalfour.co.uk
Web	www.dianabalfour.co.uk

Entry 253   Map 22

Chelsea Park Garden

A super-central B&B tucked behind the Kings Road, just a saunter away from bustling shops and restaurants. Return to a deeply comfortable bedroom up in the eaves with rosebud papered walls, blue and white china bedside lights, plenty of hanging space and views over swaying treetops; a single room is next door and shares the bathroom. There's a guest sitting room (with honesty bar) overlooking the garden and an antique dark wood trestle table for proper breakfasts of bacon, Lincolnshire sausages and eggs how you like them. Suzie, a cook, can rustle up a light supper or a full blown dinner party. Invite friends!

Children over 5 welcome.

Rooms	1 double with separate bathroom: £140–£170.
	1 single sharing bath with double (let to same party only): £60.
	Extra bed/sofabed available £40 per child per night.
Meals	Dinner from £20.
	Restaurants 2-minute walk.
Closed	Christmas & New Year, July/August.

Suzie Hyman
Chelsea Park Garden,
Chelsea, SW3 6AE

Mobile	+44 (0)7885 586181
Email	suziehyman@gmail.com

Entry 254   Map 22

London

90 Old Church Street

In a quiet street facing the Chelsea Arts Club is an enticing, contemporary haven. Softly spoken Nina is passionate about the arts, knows Chelsea inside out and takes real pleasure in looking after her guests. Antique shop spoils stand alongside more modern delights, the attention to detail is amazing and there are plentiful bunches of flowers. A lush carpet takes you up to the second floor and your super-private, surprisingly peaceful and deliciously designed bedroom and bathroom. Breakfast – fruit platters, yogurt and croissants – is shared with Nina in the kitchen. We love No. 90 – and the little black poodles!

Minimum stay: 2 nights on weekdays, 3 nights at weekends, 4 nights in high season.

Rooms	1 double: £120–£150.
	Singles £100–£130.
Meals	Continental breakfast £10.
	Restaurants nearby.
Closed	Occasionally.

	Nina Holland
	90 Old Church Street,
	Chelsea, SW3 6EP
Tel	+44 (0)20 7352 4758
Mobile	+44 (0)7831 689167
Email	ninastcharles@gmail.com
Web	www.chelseabedbreakfast.com

Entry 255   Map 22

London

Kew Gardens B&B

All is tip-top in Ragini's cool annexe to her house. Deeply comfortable bedrooms, on the second floor, display a rich blend of influences: French, contemporary English, Moorish patterns, designer furniture. Hop downstairs to the first-floor communal kitchen for a vegetarian breakfast: juices, sourdough, pastries, granola, berries…. coconut chutney and sambar sometimes (or have a continental tray in your room). Ragini and her daughter are passionate cooks and a treasure trove of talent – sign up for chapatti making, intros to herbal remedies or Ayurveda, herbal tours of Kew… picnic baskets too! Two-minute walk to the tube, central London half an hour.

Minimum stay: 2 nights.

Rooms	3 doubles: £100–£140.
	Singles £80–£120.
	Dinner £30.
Meals	Vegetarian breakfast.
	Pubs/restaurants 2-minute walk.
Closed	Rarely.

	Ragini Annan
	Kew Gardens B&B,
	8A Broomfield Road,
	Richmond, TW9 3HR
Mobile	+44 (0)7973 327662
Email	reservations@kewgardensbandb.com
Web	www.kewgardensbandb.com

Entry 256   Map 22

London

20 St Philip Street

Come to retreat from the frenzy of city life. In the 1890 Victorian cottage all is peaceful and calm and Barbara looks after you beautifully. The dining room, with the odd oriental piece from past travels, is where you have your full English breakfast – unusual for London – and across the hall is the elegant sitting room, with gilt-framed mirrors, sumptuous curtains, and a piano which you are welcome to play. Upstairs is a bright, restful bedroom with pretty linen and a cloud of goose down. The large bathroom next door is all yours – fabulous. Nothing has been overlooked and the tiny courtyard garden is a summer oasis.

Train: 6-min Waterloo, 3-min Victoria. Bus: 137, 452 (Sloane Sq) & 156 (Vauxhall). Tube: 10 mins. Parking: £2.50/hr or £10 day permit. Weekends free.

Rooms	1 double with separate bath & shower: £115. Singles £85. Stays of 2 or more nights: £110 double, £80 single.
Meals	Pubs/restaurants 200 yds.
Closed	Occasionally.

	Barbara Graham 20 St Philip Street, Battersea, SW8 3SL
Tel	+44 (0)20 7622 5547
Email	batterseabedandbreakfast@gmail.com
Web	www.batterseabandb.co.uk

Entry 257   Map 22

London

The Glebe House

Surely one of London's most village-y spots? Find a pretty Georgian house snuggling up to the church, a community pottery and beehives and allotments in a walled garden. Alix writes for interiors magazines and has weaved her magic into every corner. The sitting room, with velvet and linen sofas on toasty stone floors, was once an archway for horses and carriages – now a lofty space with huge doors onto a courtyard. Your bed is antique, your room peaceful, the bathroom bright with white Metro brick tiles. Help yourself to a continental breakfast of cereal, fruit, and artisan breads in the funky kitchen. Alix, son and dog are a delight.

Rooms	2 doubles sharing family bathroom (let to same party only, extra futon available): £110. Singles £80.
Meals	Continental breakfast. Pubs/restaurants 0.2 miles.
Closed	Rarely.

	Alix Bateman The Glebe House, Clapham Old Town, SW4 0DZ
Tel	+44 (0)20 7720 3844
Email	talixjones@hotmail.com
Web	www.theglebehouselondon.com

Entry 258   Map 22

London

28 Old Devonshire Road

In a quiet part of Balham — close to leafy common, tube and train — are Georgina's lovely home and award-winning garden. Enjoy breakfast under the pear tree, or at the long wooden table in the dining room, with a marble fireplace and a friend's watercolours. You have the top floor to yourself: a sunny, cosy bedroom, with city views, a TV, lots of books; a big bathroom too, with a fab shower and comforting waffle robes to pad about in. Georgina lays on a special breakfast and all sorts of thoughtful extras. She loves to chat (speaks French and Italian too) really knows her London and will help plan your stay.

Minimum stay: 2 nights. 7-minute walk from Balham mainline & tube stations. Visitors' Parking Permits available £7 per day excluding Sunday.

Rooms	1 double: £100–£105. Singles £80–£85.
Meals	Pubs/restaurants 500 yds.
Closed	Rarely.

Georgina Ivor
28 Old Devonshire Road,
Balham, SW12 9RB

Tel	+44 (0)20 8673 7179
Mobile	+44 (0)7941 960199
Email	georgina@balhambandb.co.uk
Web	www.balhambandb.co.uk

London

The Coach House

A rare privacy: you have your own coach house, separated from the Notts' home by a stylish terracotta-potted courtyard with Indian sandstone paving and various fruit trees (peach, pear, nectarine). Breakfast in your own sunny kitchen, or let Meena treat you to a full English in hers (she makes great porridge, too). The lovely big attic bedroom has beams, cream curtains, rugs on polished wood floors; the brick-walled ground-floor twin is pleasant and airy; both look over the peaceful garden. Urban but bucolic — just perfect as a romantic retreat, or a family getaway.

Minimum stay: 3 nights; 2 nights January & February. Tube: Balham Station to Leicester Square & Oxford Street or train to Victoria.

Rooms	1 twin with separate shower (same-party bookings only): £120–£200. 1 family room for 2-3: £190–£200. £200 for the whole Coach House.
Meals	Pub/restaurant 200 yds.
Closed	Occasionally.

Meena & Harley Nott
The Coach House,
2 Tunley Road,
Balham, SW17 7QJ

Tel	+44 (0)20 8772 1939
Email	coachhouse@chslondon.com
Web	www.coachhouse.chslondon.com

London

108 Streathbourne Road

It's a handsome house in a conservation area that manages to be both elegant and cosy. The cream-coloured double bedroom has an armchair, a writing desk, pretty curtains and a big comfy walnut bed; the twin is light and airy. The dining room overlooks a secluded terrace and garden and there are newspapers at breakfast. You can eat in – David, who works in the wine trade, always puts a bottle on the table – or out, at one of the trendy new restaurants in Balham. A friendly city base on a quiet, tree-lined street – maximum comfort, delicious food and good value for London. Delightful.

Children over 12 welcome.

Rooms	1 double, 1 twin: £98-£100. Singles £80-£85.
Meals	Dinner £35. Restaurants 5-minute walk.
Closed	Occasionally.

Mary & David Hodges
108 Streathbourne Road,
Balham, SW17 8QY
Tel   +44 (0)20 8767 6931
Email   davidandmaryhodges@gmail.com
Web   www.southwestlondonbandb.co.uk

Entry 261   Map 22

London

38 Killieser Avenue

On a quiet leafy street, the Haworths have brought country-house chic to South London. Philip and Winkle have filled their elegant Victorian townhouse with attractive fabrics, sunny colours and treasures from far-flung travels. The house glows, the garden is ravishing with parterre, arbour, brimming borders and secluded seats. Breakfasts are delicious and bedrooms are spacious: fine linen, lambswool throws, waffle robes, the scent of roses. Few people do things with as much natural good humour as Winkle, whose passions are cooking, gardening and garden history. Transport is close and you can be in Victoria in 15 minutes.

Minimum stay: 2 nights at weekends. Free and unrestricted parking on street outside the house.

Rooms	1 twin: £115-£120. 1 single with separate bath: £95-£100. Stays of 2 or more nights: £110-£115 double; £90-£95 single.
Meals	Dinner £30-£35.
Closed	Occasionally.

Winkle Haworth
38 Killieser Avenue,
Streatham Hill, SW2 4NT
Tel   +44 (0)20 8671 4196
Email   winklehaworth@hotmail.com
Web   www.thegardenbedandbreakfast.com

Entry 262   Map 22

London

24 Fox Hill

This part of London is full of sky, trees and wildlife; Pissarro captured on canvas the view up the hill in 1870 (the painting is in the National Gallery). There's good stuff everywhere – things hang off walls and peep over the tops of dressers; bedrooms are stunning, with antiques, textiles, paintings and big, firm beds. Sue, a graduate from Chelsea Art College, employs humour and intelligence to put guests at ease and has created a special garden too. Tim often helps with breakfasts: eggs to order, good coffee. Owls hoot at night, woodpeckers wake you in the morning, in this lofty, peaceful retreat.

Train: Crystal Palace. Tube: East London line. Collection possible. Good buses to West End & Westminster. Victoria 20 minutes by train.

Rooms	1 twin/double; 1 double, 1 twin sharing shower: £90–£120. Singles £60. Extra bed available £30 per person per night; sofabed £50 per night.
Meals	Dinner £35. Pubs/restaurants 5-minute walk.
Closed	Rarely.

	Sue & Tim Haigh
	24 Fox Hill,
	Crystal Palace, SE19 2XE
Tel	+44 (0)20 8768 0059
Email	suehaigh@hotmail.co.uk
Web	www.foxhill-bandb.co.uk

Entry 263   Map 22

London

113 Pepys Road

This Victorian terraced house overlooks the first landscaped park of its kind in south-east London; the pretty garden, designed by David's father, is graced with majestic magnolias. Find a quirky mix of classic British furniture and oriental antiques. Picking up from his Chinese mother Anne, David has now taken on the B&B (helped by his housekeeper) and breakfast can be English or oriental. It's a convivial, lived-in home full of family portraits, batiks and books; the Chinese 'Peony' room downstairs has a huge bed, bamboo blinds, kimonos for the bathroom. A short walk to buses and tubes… and blissfully quiet for London.

Rooms	1 double, 1 twin/double; 1 twin with separate bath: £110. Singles £85.
Meals	Restaurant 0.5 miles.
Closed	Rarely.

	David Marten
	113 Pepys Road,
	New Cross, SE14 5SE
Tel	+44 (0)20 7639 1060
Email	pepysroad@gmail.com
Web	www.pepysroad.com

Entry 264   Map 22

London

16 St Alfege Passage

The peaceful approach is along the passage between Hawksmoor church and its graveyard, away from Greenwich hubbub. At the end of the lane is a 'cottage' set about with greenery, lamp posts and benches; inside, bold art and antiques – and tea with flapjack awaiting you in an eccentrically furnished (stuffed cat on dentist chair, huge parasol) sitting room. Bedrooms are cosy and colourful, with double beds (not huge) that positively encourage intimacy. Breakfast – delicious – is in the basement, another engagingly furnished room awash with character. Robert, an actor, is easy, funny, chatty – and has created an unusual, attractive place.

3-min walk from Greenwich train & Docklands Light Railway station or Cutty Sark DLR station. Parking free from 5pm (6pm Sundays) to 9am.

Rooms	1 double, 1 four-poster: £110-£150. 1 single: £90.
Meals	Pubs/restaurants 2-minute walk.
Closed	Rarely.

Nicholas Mesure & Robert Gray
16 St Alfege Passage,
Greenwich, SE10 9JS

Tel	+44 (0)20 8853 4337
Email	info@st-alfeges.co.uk
Web	www.st-alfeges.co.uk

Entry 265   Map 22

Norfolk

Narborough Hall

Fairy lights wind up stone stairs to vast romantic bedrooms… flowers, art, wood fires galore. Gorgeous rooms, gardens with lake and pool, barns for parties – Joanne and family love having people to stay. There's a creeper-covered little cottage in the grounds too. Delicious food comes out of the restaurant kitchen – carefully sourced and seasonal with home-grown veg, herbs, nuts and fruits from the Victorian walled garden. Breakfast is in "the pretty kitchen" next to the Aga, lunch and dinner in an atmospheric dining room; Sunday lunch helpfully runs until 4 o'clock – so walk the Nar Valley Way first. An amazing place…

Rooms	5 doubles (1 available in winter only): £90-£120. 1 cottage for 4: £90-£120.
Meals	Dinner, 2-3 courses, £20-£25. Pubs/restaurants 5 miles.
Closed	21 December to 21 January.

Joanne Merrison
Narborough Hall,
Narborough, PE32 1TE

Tel	+44 (0)1760 339923
Email	narboroughfood@gmail.com
Web	www.narboroughhallgardens.com

Entry 266   Map 10

Norfolk

Tudor Lodgings

A treasured family home on the site of Castle Acre's medieval defences, with dogs, ducks and views of the lovely Nar valley. A cosy guest sitting room leads to the ancient, dark-beamed dining room hung with portraits, where you breakfast on good things homemade and local; do try a Swaffham Sizzler. Cottagey bedrooms are cream-carpeted and have coordinated fabrics, attractive wildlife prints and small shower rooms. Julia is passionate about garden history, Gus is a keen fisherman; both know their history and horses. Peddars Way runs close by and you're not far from the coast – or the village pub!

Rooms	2 twins: £80. Singles £60.
Meals	Pub within walking distance.
Closed	Rarely.

Julia Stafford-Allen
Tudor Lodgings,
Castle Acre,
King's Lynn, PE32 2AN
Tel   +44 (0)1760 755334
Email   jstaffordallen@btinternet.com
Web   www.tudorlodgings.co.uk

Entry 267   Map 10

Norfolk

Litcham Hall

For the whole of the 19th century this was Litcham's doctor's house; the Hall is still at the centre of the community. The big-windowed guest bedrooms look onto stunning gardens with yew hedges, a lily pond and herbaceous borders. This is a thoroughly English home with elegant proportions – the hall, drawing room and dining room are gracious and beautifully furnished, and there's a large sitting room for guests. The garden fills the breakfast table with soft fruit in season and John and Hermione are friendly and most helpful. Close to Fakenham, and only 30 minutes from Burnham Market and the coast.

Children & pets by arrangement. Outside pool heated in high summer; use by arrangement.

Rooms	2 doubles; 1 twin with separate bath: £80-£100. Singles by arrangement.
Meals	Pub in village & more within 5 miles.
Closed	Christmas.

John & Hermione Birkbeck
Litcham Hall,
Litcham,
King's Lynn, PE32 2QQ
Tel   +44 (0)1328 701389
Email   hermionebirkbeck@hotmail.com
Web   www.litchamhall.co.uk

Entry 268   Map 10

Norfolk

Meadow House

A beautifully traditional new-build with handmade oak banisters and period furniture. Step into a large drawing room, where you find a warm, sociable atmosphere with squashy sofas and comfy chairs. Breakfast is served in here or in the conservatory. One bedroom is cosy and chintzy, the other is larger and more neutral; brand-new bathrooms gleam. Amanda looks after you well; she's lived in Norfolk most of her life and is delighted to advise. There are footpaths from the door and plenty to see, starting with Walpole's Houghton Hall, a short walk. A bucolic setting for a profoundly comfortable stay, perfect for country enthusiasts.

Rooms	2 twin/doubles: £70-£80. Singles £40-£45.
Meals	Packed lunch £5-£7. Pub 9-minute walk.
Closed	Rarely.

Amanda Case
Meadow House,
Harpley,
King's Lynn, PE31 6TU

Tel	+44 (0)1485 520240
Mobile	+44 (0)7890 037134
Email	amandacase@amandacase.plus.com
Web	www.meadowhousebandb.co.uk

Entry 269   Map 10

Norfolk

Bagthorpe Hall

Ten minutes from Burnham Market, yet here you are immersed in peaceful countryside. Tid is a pioneer of organic farming and the stunning 700 acres include a woodland snowdrop walk. Gina's passions are music, dance and gardens and she organises open days and concerts for charity. Theirs is a large, elegant house with a fascinating hall mural chronicling their family life; bedrooms – one with a tiny en suite shower room – have big comfy beds and lovely views. Breakfasts are delicious with local sausages and bacon, homemade jams and raspberries from the garden. Birdwatching, cycling and walking are all around.

Rooms	1 double; 1 twin/double with separate shower: £90. Singles £50.
Meals	Pubs/restaurants 2 miles.
Closed	Rarely.

Gina & Tid Morton
Bagthorpe Hall,
Bagthorpe, Bircham,
King's Lynn, PE31 6QY

Tel	+44 (0)1485 578528
Mobile	+44 (0)7979 746591
Email	dgmorton@hotmail.com
Web	www.bagthorpehall.co.uk

Entry 270   Map 10

Norfolk

Heacham House

Rebecca is a dab hand at soft furnishings and creating delicious things. Step in to a home full of pretty fabrics and flowers. All is homemade from the welcoming cake to the granola, potato farls and home-grown roasted tomatoes on brioche; honey, bacon and eggs are sourced from local suppliers, hand-knitted tea cosies and hand-embroidered tablecloths add a thoughtful touch. Immaculate, comfortable bedrooms have all sorts of extra goodies. It's paradise for bird-watchers, you can take a boat trip to spot seals, and it's a short walk to the beach. Norfolk Lavender is minutes away too – buy some pots to take home. Lovely!

Minimum stay: 2 nights.

Rooms	2 doubles; 1 twin/double with separate bath: £85-£95.
Meals	Pubs/restaurants 5-minute walk.
Closed	Christmas & New Year.

Rebecca Bradley
Heacham House,
18 Staithe Road,
Heacham,
King's Lynn, PE31 7ED
Tel   +44 (0)1485 579529
Email   info@heachamhouse.com
Web   www.heachamhouse.com

Norfolk

Troon Cottage

No cottage this! Rather, a large Edwardian terraced house at the far end of town, lovingly renovated, sumptuously furnished and a ten-minute walk from glorious sands. Marian and Barry have been in the antiques business for years, serve brilliant breakfasts, offer you cream teas, and know exactly how to pamper. After a day acquainting yourselves with grand or royal houses (Holkham Hall, Royal Sandringham) and the shops and restaurants of lovely old Hunstanton, what nicer than to come home to a sofa by the wood-burner, a delicious bath scented with lavender and an irresistible king-size bed?

Rooms	2 doubles: £95.
Meals	Pubs/restaurants 5-minute walk.
Closed	Rarely.

Marian Sanders
Troon Cottage,
4 Victoria Avenue,
Hunstanton, PE36 6BX
Tel   +44 (0)1485 532918
Mobile   +44 (0)7503 276485
Email   marianatmoreau@hotmail.com
Web   www.trooncottage.co.uk

Norfolk

The Merchants House

The oak four-poster – a beauty – came with the house. Part of the building (1400) is the oldest in Wells; in those days, the merchant could bring his boats up to the door. Liz and Dennis know the history, and happily share it. Inside is friendly and inviting: the mahogany shines, bathrooms sparkle, there are books to borrow and pretty sash windows overlook salt marshes. Breakfasts are a treat: homemade bread and jams, local produce and flowers on the table. As for Wells, it's on the famous Coastal Path, has a quay bustling with boats and 16 miles of sands. Birdwatch by day, dine out at night – easy when you're in the centre.

Minimum stay: 2 nights in July & August.

Rooms	1 double; 1 four-poster with separate bath/shower: £90–£100. Singles £70–£75.
Meals	Pubs/restaurants 300 yds.
Closed	Rarely.

Elizabeth & Dennis Woods
The Merchants House,
47 Freeman Street,
Wells-next-the-Sea, NR23 1BQ

Tel	+44 (0)1328 711877
Mobile	+44 (0)7816 632742
Email	denniswoods@talktalk.net
Web	www.the-merchants-house.co.uk

Norfolk

The Control Tower

A unique slice of history. This iconic landmark on the former RAF North Creake airfield was built in the 1940s to command 199 and 171 Squadrons. The restoration has been a labour of love and Ni and Claire's attention to detail is remarkable: modernism and Art Deco design in full flow. Be greeted with tea or locally roasted coffee in the art-filled sitting room; sink into goose down in bright bedrooms; enjoy shiny bathrooms with period fittings and lavender soaps. Vegetarian breakfasts are good! House tours include the open roof deck; you can lunch al fresco in the wild flower garden; Wells-next-the-Sea and Blakeney seal trips are close.

Rooms	3 doubles: £110–£120. 1 suite for 2: £110–£120. Extra bed/sofabed available £25 per person per night.
Meals	Restaurants 3 miles.
Closed	Rarely.

Claire Nugent & Nigel Morter
The Control Tower,
Bunkers Hill, Egmere,
Walsingham, NR22 6AZ

Tel	+44 (0)1328 821574
Email	mail@controltowerstays.com
Web	www.controltowerstays.com

Stonegate

A welcoming entrance hall full of books and art sets the tone here. Carved banisters, family portraits, wonky floors, Persian rugs, flowers and open fires… and Liz greeting you with tea, homemade cake and chat. Lovely! Bedrooms are crammed with character, antiques, a comfy armchair or fire here and there, and more books; one's in the eaves, one has a kitchen, all are charming (lots of stairs). Garden treats too: a vine to sit under, pots of summer colour, quirky old flint and brick walls. Head off for coastal walks and boat trips. The farm shop down the road (providing your delicious breakfast) is award-winning and a treat to visit too.

Min stay: 2 nights at weekends & in high season.

Green Farm House

This Norfolk farmhouse has been beautifully restored. Choose to stay in the 'Garden Room' wing, or upstairs in the main house – both well-dressed bedrooms have smart bathrooms. Sun streams in through the French windows of the garden room; find books, DVDs, rugs on slate floors, art, pots of flowers and a comfy sofa by the wood-burner. The 'Guest Room' has field views and morning sun. Breakfast in the conservatory on local sausages, bacon and eggs, homemade marmalade and muesli – in the pretty, sheltered garden on sunny days. Friendly Lucy can arrange sailing; good for walkers, cyclists and birdwatchers too.

Cyclists welcome; secure bike shed available.

Rooms	1 double with separate bath: £85. 2 family rooms for 3: £75-£95
Meals	Pubs/restaurants 5-minute walk.
Closed	Rarely.

Rooms	House – 1 double: £95-£125. Garden Room – 1 double: £95-£125. Singles £90-£105. Extra bed/sofabed available £15-£25 per person per night.
Meals	Pub within 2 miles.
Closed	Rarely.

Liz Downing
Stonegate,
Walsingham, NR22 6BS
Mobile +44 (0)7818 237561
Email lizrenwick@hotmail.co.uk
Web www.walsinghambedandbreakfast.co.uk

Lucy Jupe
Green Farm House,
Balls Lane, Thursford,
Fakenham, NR21 0BX
Tel +44 (0)1328 878507
Mobile +44 (0)7768 542645
Email ljupe@greenfarmbarns.co.uk
Web www.greenfarmbarns.co.uk

Entry 275 Map 10

Entry 276 Map 10

Norfolk

Holly Lodge

The whole place radiates a lavish attention to detail, from the spoilingly comfortable beds to the complimentary bottle of wine. It's perfect for those who love their privacy: these three snug guest 'cottages' have their own entrances as well as smart bedsteads and rugs on stone tiles, neat little shower rooms and tapestry-seat chairs, and books, music and TVs. Enjoy the Mediterranean garden, the handsome conservatory and the utter peace; Holt and historic Little Walsingham are nearby. Your hosts are delightful: ex-restaurateur Jeremy who cooks enthusiastically, ethically and with panache, and Canadian-raised Gill.

Rooms	3 cottages for 2: £100-£130. Singles £80-£110.
Meals	Dinner, 2-3 courses with wine, £18-£22. Pubs/restaurants 1 mile.
Closed	Rarely.

Jeremy Bolam
Holly Lodge,
Thursford Green,
Fakenham, NR21 OAS
Tel   +44 (0)1328 878465
Email   info@hollylodgeguesthouse.co.uk
Web   www.hollylodgeguesthouse.co.uk

Entry 277   Map 10

Norfolk

Beck Farmhouse

A self-contained country pad on the Stody Estate by the river Glaven. Settle by the wood-burner with a book, sink into spruce white linen, rustle up breakfast at a time to suit you – a continental basket is left for you with local jams and bread, yogurt, fruit compote, homemade granola, eggs and croissants. Ex-chef Bella can bring over a one-pot supper too – or you can walk to the estate's own Hunny Bell pub. Georgian Holt is dotted with lanes of shops and cafés; further fun can be had with crabbing, seal trips, gardens, historic houses, great walks. There's room for a cot – and a sunny patch of garden for relaxing with a glass of wine.

Babes in arms welcome. A basket of logs is provided.

Rooms	1 double with separate bathroom: £80-£100. Beach hut available by arrangement £40 per day.
Meals	Pubs/restaurants 1 mile.
Closed	Rarely.

Bella Philippi
Beck Farmhouse,
Hunworth,
Holt, NR25 7QL
Mobile +44 (0)7775 628208
Email   bellaphilippi@hotmail.co.uk
Web   www.beckfarmhouse.co.uk

Entry 278   Map 10

Church Farm House

Step into a hall where a bookcase opens to reveal steep secret stairs up to your cosy self-contained suite… (the less nimble can use the main staircase). It's a friendly home, and Mary settles you in with homemade cake or scones. Find attractive bedrooms with good linen, watercolours, flowers and local chocs; a jolly collection of jugs on the landing; a kitchen where you breakfast on tasty homemade treats. The pretty walled garden has a veg patch, grass tennis court, summerhouse and sunny seats. Children can help walk the dog and feed the chickens; trips out include seal watching, walks, cycle rides; nearby Holt has independent shops to browse.

Minimum stay: 2 nights (July / August).

Sloley Hall

A grand and gracious yellow-brick Georgian house with formal gardens, tree-studded parkland and glorious views from every window. It has also been beautifully renovated, with flagstoned floors, Persian rugs, gleaming circular tables and vases of garden-grown flowers. Your hosts are delightful – Barbara and Simon were married here and are easy-going and helpful. A huge light-flooded dining room is perfect for breakfast; the drawing room is comfy and uncluttered with a marble fireplace and long views. Bedrooms are large and elegant with sumptuous bed linen; generous bathrooms glow with warmth.

Minimum stay: 2 nights in high season.

Rooms	1 suite for 4 (2 doubles with kitchen, let to same party only): £90–£180. £10 per dog.
Meals	Pubs/restaurants 5 miles.
Closed	Rarely.

Rooms	1 double with separate bath, 1 double with separate shower: £80–£90. 1 suite for 2: £90–£100. Singles from £50. Child bed available.
Meals	Pubs/restaurants 2–4 miles.
Closed	Rarely.

Mary Lintott
Church Farm House,
Church Street,
Plumstead, Norwich, NR11 7LG
Tel   +44 (0)1263 577718
Email   mary.lintott57@btinternet.com
Web   www.cargocollective.com/
            churchfarmhouse

Barbara Gorton
Sloley Hall,
Sloley, Norwich, NR12 8HA
Tel   +44 (0)1692 538582
Mobile +44 (0)7748 152079
Email   babsgorton@hotmail.com
Web   www.sloleyhall.com

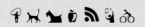

Entry 279   Map 10

Entry 280   Map 10

Norfolk

Hoveton Hall

A Regency house snoozing in beautiful parkland and gardens. Formal and grand, yet comfortably friendly, Harry and Rachel's home brims with wonderful woodwork, decorated ceilings, art old and new. Their children are keen to play with visiting young ones, there's a lovely collection of hare sculptures up the stairs and the views over the 620 acres are stunning. Airy bedrooms have well-dressed beds, tea trays, biscuits and flowers. Morning sun lights up the panelled library/sitting room where you have breakfast, shelves are crammed with books and there's a large fire to sit by. Explore the estate, head off for beaches and The Broads.

Minimum stay: 2 nights at weekends.

Rooms	1 double: £130.
	1 family room for 4: £160.
Meals	Pubs/restaurants 1 mile.
Closed	Rarely.

Rachel Buxton
Hoveton Hall,
Hoveton Hall Estate,
Hoveton,
Norwich, NR12 8RJ

Tel	+44 (0)1603 784 297
Email	rachel@hovetonhallestate.co.uk
Web	www.hovetonhallestate.co.uk

Entry 281   Map 10

Norfolk

Washingford House

Tall octagonal chimney stacks and a Georgian façade give the house a stately air. In fact, it's the friendliest of places to stay and Paris gives you a delicious, locally sourced breakfast including plenty of fresh fruit. The house, originally Tudor, is a delightful mix of old and new. Large light-filled bedrooms have loads of good books and views over the four-acre garden, a favourite haunt for local birds. Bergh Apton is a conservation village seven miles from Norwich and you are in the heart of it; perfect for cycling, boat trips on the Norfolk Broads and the twelve Wherryman's Way circular walks.

Rooms	1 twin/double; 1 twin/double (with
	separate bath & shower): £75–£90.
	1 single with separate bath: £40–£60.
	Singles £35–£65.
Meals	Pubs/restaurants 4-6 miles.
Closed	Christmas.

Paris & Nigel Back
Washingford House,
Cookes Road, Bergh Apton,
Norwich, NR15 1AA

Tel	+44 (0)1508 550924
Mobile	+44 (0)7900 683617
Email	parisb@waitrose.com
Web	www.washingford.com

Entry 282   Map 10

Gothic House

Silver tea and coffee pots and Portmeirion china, pictures and prints from far-flung places, and an unexpected peace in the centre of the city – welcome to Gothic House. The building is listed and Regency and your host, enthusiastic, charming, knows the history. As for breakfast, it is fresh, lavish and locally sourced; in short, a treat. Bedrooms are stylish and spacious with a strong period feel, the double and the two bathrooms on the first floor, and the twin above. Norwich is blessed with culture, character and pubs, and a cathedral with the second tallest spire in England. Fabulous!

Parking space available.

The Buttery

Down a farm track, a treasure: your own thatch-and-flint octagonal dairy house perfectly restored by local craftsmen and as snug as can be. You get a jacuzzi bath, a little kitchen and a fridge stocked with delicious bacon and ground coffee so you can breakfast when you want; take it to the sun terrace in good weather. The sitting room is terracotta-tiled and has a music system, a warming fire and a sofabed for those who don't want to tackle the steep wooden stair to the cosy bedroom on the mezzanine. You can play a game of tennis, and walk from the door into peaceful parkland and woods. Lovely!

Minimum stay: 2 nights at weekends.

Rooms	1 double with separate bathroom, 1 twin with separate bathroom & wc: £95. Singles £65.
Meals	Pubs/restaurants 5-minute walk.
Closed	Rarely.

Rooms	1 double, with sitting room & small kitchen: £90-£110.
Meals	Pub 10-minute walk.
Closed	Rarely.

Clive Harvey
Gothic House,
King's Head Yard,
42 Magdalen Street,
Norwich, NR3 1JE
Tel   +44 (0)1603 631879
Email   charvey649@aol.com
Web   www.gothic-house-norwich.com

Deborah Meynell
The Buttery,
Berry Hall,
Honingham,
Norwich, NR9 5AX
Tel   +44 (0)1603 880541
Email   thebuttery@paston.co.uk
Web   www.thebuttery.biz

Norfolk

Stable Cottage

Sarah's home is set in the grounds of Heydon, one of Norfolk's finest Elizabethan houses. In the Dutch-gabled stable block, fronted by Cromwell's Oak, is her cottage – fresh, sunny and enchanting. Each room is touched by her warm personality and love of beautiful things: seagrass floors, crisp linen and pretty china; the cosy sitting room is set with tea and biscuits for your arrival. Bedrooms are cottagey and immaculate; bathrooms have baskets of treats. Sarah serves a delicious breakfast with golden eggs from her hens, homemade marmalade and garden fruit. Thursford is close and you're 20 minutes from the coast.

Minimum stay: 2 nights at weekends.

Rooms	2 twin/doubles: £100.
	Stays of 2 or more nights: £90 per
	night.
	Singles from £50.
Meals	Pub 1 mile.
Closed	Christmas.

Sarah Bulwer-Long
Stable Cottage,
Heydon Hall, Heydon,
Norwich, NR11 6RE
Tel   +44 (0)1263 587343
Mobile +44 (0)7780 998742
Web   www.heydon-bb.co.uk

Entry 285   Map 10

Norfolk

The Old Rectory

Conservation farmland all around; acres of wild heathland busy with woodpeckers and owls; the coast two miles away. Relax in the spacious drawing room of this handsome 17th-century rectory and friendly family home, set in lovely mature gardens (NGS) full of trees and unusual planting. Fiona loves to cook and bakes her bread daily, food is delicious, seasonal and locally sourced, jams are homemade. Comfortable bedrooms have *objets* from diplomatic postings and the spacious suite comes with mahogany furniture and armchairs so you can settle in with a book. Super views, friendly dogs, tennis in the garden and masses of space.

Self-catering available in the Garden Room.

Rooms	1 double with kitchenette &
	separate bath/shower: £75-£85.
	1 suite for 2: £75-£90.
	1 studio for 2 (self-catering):
	£235-£420 per week.
	Singles £50.
Meals	Dinner from £25.
	Pubs 2 miles.
Closed	Rarely.

Peter & Fiona Black
The Old Rectory,
Ridlington, NR28 9NZ
Tel   +44 (0)1692 650247
Mobile +44 (0)7774 599911
Email   ridlingtonoldrectory@gmail.com
Web   www.oldrectorynorthnorfolk.co.uk

Entry 286   Map 10

Norfolk

Norfolk Courtyard

Walk straight in through French windows to your own, underfloor-heated room in the courtyard; independence from the main house where friendly Simon and Catherine live. The rooms are decorated in soft colours, mattresses are perfect, cotton sheets are smooth and your handsome bathroom has limestone tiles – all rather luxurious; there's a welcome tea tray and a fridge to cool a bottle too. Continental breakfast is next door in the old, beamed barn – help yourself to croissants, crumpets, homemade jams, compotes and muesli – and home-laid eggs that you cook in an easy egg steamer: very popular! Stunning walks await on the coast.

Minimum stay: 2 nights at peak season weekends.

Rooms	3 doubles, 1 twin/double: £105–£110. Extra bed/sofabed available £20–£30 per person per night.
Meals	Pub/restaurant 0.5 miles.
Closed	Rarely.

Simon & Catherine Davis
Norfolk Courtyard,
Westfield Farm, Foxley Road,
Foulsham, Dereham, NR20 5RH

Tel	+44 (0)1362 683333
Mobile	+44 (0)7969 611510
Email	info@norfolkcourtyard.co.uk
Web	www.norfolkcourtyard.co.uk

Entry 287   Map 10

Norfolk

Carrick's at Castle Farm

This warm-bricked farmhouse is up a long drive and surrounded by 720 acres; John's family have lived here since the 1920s. He and Jean are passionate about conservation and the protection of wildlife, and here you have absolute quiet – for birdwatching, fishing or walking. Return to the drawing room with its open fire, books, and decanter of sherry. Your friendly hosts give you coffee and cake, or wine, when you arrive, and bedrooms are light and luxurious with pretty fabrics and homemade biscuits. Breakfasts and candlelit dinners are delicious, and the garden leads to a footpath alongside the river.

Rooms	1 double, 2 twin/doubles; 1 double with separate bath: £95. Singles £70.
Meals	Dinner, 3 courses, £30. BYO. Pub 0.5 miles.
Closed	Rarely.

Jean Wright
Carrick's at Castle Farm,
Castle Farm,
Swanton Morley,
Dereham, NR20 4JT

Tel	+44 (0)1362 638302
Email	jean@castlefarm-swanton.co.uk
Web	www.carricksatcastlefarm.co.uk

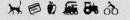

Entry 288   Map 10

Norfolk

College Farm

Katharine is a natural at making guests feel like friends. Her beautiful farmhouse tucks itself away on the edge of the village and the big friendly kitchen is filled with delicious smells of home baking. Meals are served by the large wood-burner in the grand Jacobean dining room, filled with good antiques, period furnishings and cosy places to sit; food is home-grown, seasonal and local. Sleep well in charming bedrooms with smooth linen, pretty furniture and garden views; bathrooms are small and simple. A fascinating area teeming with pingos, wildlife, old churches... and glorious antique shops.

Over 12s welcome.

Northamptonshire

Bridge Cottage

A truly peaceful place, yet only a few miles from Peterborough. Sip a glass of wine on the decking down by the Willowbrook; beautiful countryside envelops you, cattle doze, kingfishers flash by and you may see a red kite (borrow some binoculars). Inside find pretty bedrooms with sloping ceilings, the purest cotton sheets and proper blankets; bathrooms are thickly towelled and full of lotions and bubbles. Breakfast is local, scrumptious and served in the friendliest kitchen facing that heavenly view. Walks and cycle rides start from the door; return and settle with a book in the conservatory. A hidden gem, and Judy and Rod are brilliant hosts.

Pets by arrangement.

Rooms	3 twin/doubles: £100-£125. Singles £50-£75.	Rooms	1 double, 1 twin; 1 double with separate bath: £87-£90.
Meals	Dinner from £20. Pub 1 mile.	Meals	Pub/restaurant 500 yds.
Closed	Christmas.	Closed	Christmas.

Katharine Wolstenholme
College Farm,
Thompson,
Thetford, IP24 1QG
Tel   +44 (0)1953 483318
Email info@collegefarmnorfolk.co.uk
Web   www.collegefarmnorfolk.co.uk

Judy Young
Bridge Cottage,
Oundle Road, Woodnewton,
Peterborough, PE8 5EG
Tel   +44 (0)1780 470860
Mobile +44 (0)7979 644864
Email   enquiries@bridgecottage.net
Web   www.bridgecottage.net

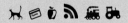

Northamptonshire

The Old House

Northamptonshire is the county of spires and squires. And here, on the through-road of this fascinating medieval town, is a listed squire's house – once home to a merchant who traded in the marketplace opposite. Enter the heavy oak door and step back 400 years. William, courteous, hospitable and renovating with aplomb, is full of plans. Facing the courtyard at the back (furnished for summery breakfasts and aperitifs) are the quietest rooms; all have sumptuous fabrics and wallpapers, dramatic touches and divine beds. Delightfully quirky, spanking new bathrooms with walk-in showers are as special as all the rest.

Northamptonshire

Staverton Hall

Through impressive iron gates to a grand house in a spectacular setting. Find masses of room, and friendly owners who have young children of their own; they love having families to stay. Relaxed breakfasts at flexible times are served at one table; all is local and delicious. Large, light bedrooms and super-modern bathrooms are upstairs, have good views and feel private. Relax in the huge, creamy-yellow guest sitting room with sash windows, log fire, board games and comfy sofas; there's also a heated pool, a play area, acres of garden, and the pub a walk away. Family heaven.

Minimum stay: 2 nights in high season.

Rooms	3 doubles, 1 twin/double: £80. Singles £60.
Meals	Pubs/restaurants 150 yds.
Closed	Rarely.

Rooms	2 doubles, each with separate private bathroom: £90. 2 singles, each with separate private bathroom: £70. Extra bed/sofabed available £10 per person per night.
Meals	Pub 3-minute walk.
Closed	Rarely.

William Evans
The Old House,
5 Market Square,
Higham Ferrers,
Rushden, NN10 8BP

Tel   +44 (0)1933 314006
Email   theoldhousehighamferrers@gmail.com
Web   www.theoldhousehighamferrers.co.uk

Entry 291   Map 9

Serena Frost
Staverton Hall,
Manor Road,
Staverton,
Daventry, NN11 6JD

Tel   +44 (0)1327 878296
Email   serenasutherland@hotmail.com
Web   www.stavertonhall.co.uk

Entry 292   Map 8

Northamptonshire

Northamptonshire

Colledges House

Huge attention to comfort here, and a house full of laughter. Liz clearly derives pleasure from sharing her 300-year-old stone thatched cottage, immaculate garden, conservatory and converted barn with guests. Sumptuous bedrooms have deep mattresses with fine linen, sparkling bathrooms are a good size. The house is full of interesting things: a Jacobean trunk, a Bechstein piano, mirrors and pictures, pretty china, bright fabrics, a beautiful bureau. Cordon Bleu dinners are elegant affairs – and great fun. Stroll around the conservation village of Staverton – delightful.

Babes in arms & children over 8 welcome.

The Vyne

Weighed down by wisteria, this 16th-century cottage rests in a honey-hued conservation village on the cusp of Oxfordshire. Beams and wonky lines abound; rooms are filled with good antiques and eclectic art. The twin overlooking the garden is enchanting, tucked under the rafters, its beds decorated in willow-pattern chintz, its walls glinting with gilded frames; the double has a Georgian four-poster and a sampler-decorated bathroom that's a quick flit next door. Warm and charming, Imogen not only works in publishing but is a contented gardener and Cordon Bleu cook – enjoy supper in her sunny secluded garden.

Babies welcome.

Rooms	Cottage – 1 double, 1 twin; 1 double with separate bath: £99. 1 single: £70. Stays of 3 or more nights: £95 for 2 per night.
Meals	Dinner, 3 courses, £35. Pub 4-minute walk.
Closed	Rarely.

Rooms	1 twin; 1 four-poster with separate bath: £85. Singles £55-£60.
Meals	Supper £20. Dinner £30. BYO. Pub 2-minute walk.
Closed	Rarely.

	Liz Jarrett
	Colledges House,
	Oakham Lane, Staverton,
	Daventry, NN11 6JQ
Tel	+44 (0)1327 702737
Mobile	+44 (0)7710 794112
Email	liz@colledgeshouse.co.uk
Web	www.colledgeshouse.co.uk

	Imogen Butler
	The Vyne,
	High Street,
	Eydon,
	Daventry, NN11 3PP
Tel	+44 (0)1327 264886
Mobile	+44 (0)7974 801475
Email	imogenbutler@outlook.com

Entry 293   Map 8

Entry 294   Map 8

Northamptonshire

The Old Vicarage

A golden ironstone vicarage overlooking the 12th-century church. The pretty porch leads you into Tim and Alison's traditional home of family portraits, antiques, books and cosy armchairs. There's a trio of comfortable bedrooms; all are fresh and light with well-dressed beds and a private bath or powerful shower. The main double has a neat basin in a cupboard; another flight of stairs takes you to the lovely room at the top. Breakfast with a leafy view is in the dining room at a long polished table. Sunny seats in the garden, Silverstone a short drive, plenty of handsome houses to visit and you can join the Macmillan Way from the door.

Pets by arrangement.

Rooms	1 double: 1 twin/double with separate shower; 1 twin with separate bath: £95. Singles £65.
Meals	Pubs 2 miles.
Closed	Christmas & New Year.

Tim Eastwood
The Old Vicarage,
Banbury Road,
Moreton Pinkney,
Daventry, NN11 3SQ

Tel	+44 (0)1295 760057
Email	tjs.eastwood@btinternet.com
Web	www.theoldvicaragemp.com

Entry 295   Map 8

Northumberland

West Coates

Slip through the gates of this Victorian townhouse and you're in the country. Two acres of leafy gardens, with pretty spots to relax, belie the closeness of Berwick's centre. From the lofty ceilings and sash windows to the soft colours, paintings and gleaming furniture, the house has a calm, ordered elegance. Bedrooms have antiques and garden views; one has a roll top bath; fruit, homemade cakes, flowers welcome you. Warm, friendly Karen is a stunning cook, inventively using local produce and spoiling you – she runs a cookery school here too. The coastline is stunning and there are castles and country houses galore to visit.

Min. stay: 2 nights at weekends & in high season.

Rooms	2 twin/doubles: £90–£110. Singles £70.
Meals	Supper £20. Pub/restaurant 15-minute walk.
Closed	December/January.

Karen Brown
West Coates,
30 Castle Terrace,
Berwick-upon-Tweed, TD15 1NZ

Tel	+44 (0)1289 309666
Mobile	+44 (0)7814 281973
Email	westcoatesbandb@gmail.com
Web	www.westcoates.co.uk

Entry 296   Map 16

Northumberland

Chain Bridge House

Overlooking an idyllic stretch of the river Tweed is the last house in England – Scotland is 100 yards away across the magnificent Union Chain Bridge. In the sitting room: a log fire and books galore. In the bedrooms: goose down duvets and a fresh, airy feel. Livvy, a professional cook, is an active supporter of the Slow Food movement and local producers. Visit the neighbouring honey farm, glorious Bamburgh, Holy Island, the Farnes, or the unspoilt borders beyond: return to a revolving summerhouse in the garden for tea. Children and dogs get a generous welcome in this delightful family home.

Children over 2 welcome.

Rooms	1 double, 1 twin: £90-£95. Singles £60-£65.
Meals	Dinner £30. Supper £15. Packed lunch from £7.50. Pubs/restaurants 5-7 miles.
Closed	Rarely.

Livvy Cawthorn
Chain Bridge House,
Horncliffe,
Berwick-upon-Tweed, TD15 2XT
Tel   +44 (0)1289 382541
Email   info@chainbridgehouse.co.uk
Web   www.chainbridgehouse.co.uk

Entry 297   Map 16

Northumberland

Laundry Cottage

History lovers, peace seekers and observers of nature will mellow further in this glorious spot overlooking the Cheviot hills. On arrival enjoy cake and tea with the evening sun – in the sun room, or in the garden on warm days. Indulge yourself with one of Ginia's wonderful big breakfasts, stride through iron age forts and the remains of Saxon palaces or visit long white beaches; return to Welsh slate floors, wood-burners, a delicious dinner, feather and down on deep comfy mattresses and fluffy towels; the twin beds have cheerful patchwork quilts made by Ginia. She and Peter are amiable hosts and the super garden is filled with roses in summer.

Over 14s welcome. Pets by arrangement.

Rooms	1 double, 1 twin: £70-£75. Singles £60-£70.
Meals	Dinner £18-£23, coffee included. Pub/restaurant 5 miles.
Closed	December – March.

Peter & Ginia Gadsdon
Laundry Cottage,
East Horton,
Wooler, NE71 6EZ
Tel   +44 (0)1668 215383
Email   peter@gadsdon.me.uk
Web   www.laundry-cottage-bnb.co.uk

Entry 298   Map 16

Northumberland

Old Rectory Howick

Christine and David's house on the edge of the village is surrounded by fields and woods, and is only minutes from the beautiful Northumberland coast, a designated AONB. Breakfasts are hearty: Craster kippers from down the road, eggs from Erica, Sylvia and Ella. Scamper about with wide beaches, stunning castles, rugged walks, golf courses and Holy Island, return to a cosy sitting room with a wood-burner. Sleep well in large, airy bedrooms with good bouncy mattresses, chintzy fabrics, top-of-the-range cotton sheets, warm showers and white towels. Wander the peaceful garden – there's a tree house and a croquet lawn.

Minimum stay: 2 nights.

Rooms	2 doubles; 1 twin with separate bathroom: £75-£100. 1 suite for 4 with separate bathroom: £140-£170. Singles £65-£90. Extra bed/sofabed available £25 per person per night.
Meals	Pubs/restaurants 1 mile.
Closed	November – February.

Christine & David Jackson
Old Rectory Howick,
Howick, Alnwick, NE66 3LE

Tel	+44 (0)1665 577590
Mobile	+44 (0)7879 681753
Email	stay@oldrectoryhowick.co.uk
Web	www.oldrectoryhowick.co.uk

Entry 299   Map 16

Northumberland

Courtyard Garden

In the county town of Northumberland, with its grand castle and innovative gardens, step directly off the pavement and enter a courtyard surrounded by shrubs and pretty pots; sit out here on sunny days and sip a glass of something cool. Bedrooms (one overlooking the church, the other the garden) are traditional and immaculate; bathrooms, one with a roll top bath, have original wooden floors, thick towels. Friendly Maureen gives you breakfast in the comfortable sitting room at a round Georgian table underneath the window. Explore the town on foot, stride along white beaches, discover more castles; history is all around you.

Rooms	1 double, 1 twin/double: £80-£100. Singles £60-£80.
Meals	Pub/restaurant within 300 yds.
Closed	Rarely.

Maureen Mason
Courtyard Garden,
10 Prudhoe Street,
Alnwick, NE66 1UW

Tel	+44 (0)1665 603393
Email	maureenpeter10@btinternet.com
Web	www.courtyardgarden-alnwick.com

Entry 300   Map 16

Northumberland

Redfoot Lea

Prepare to be thoroughly spoiled. This fine renovation of an old farmsteading lies just off the A1 up a quiet lane – perfect for touring the county or a great stopover. Amiable Philippa gives you a super south-facing sitting room and ground-floor bedrooms with comfortable beds, crisp linen, fluffy bathrobes and heated floors; bathrooms are smart and spotless. You breakfast at a large table in the magnificent open-plan hall, scented with glorious flower arrangements; enjoy freshly squeezed orange juice, homemade compotes, local produce, excellent coffee. A short hop from Alnwick Castle and gardens, and stunning beaches.

Rooms	1 double: £90-£100.
	1 suite for 2: £90-£100.
	Singles £65.
Meals	Pubs/restaurants 0.25 miles.
Closed	Rarely.

Philippa Bell
Redfoot Lea,
Greensfield Moor Farm,
Alnwick, NE66 2HH

Tel	+44 (0)1665 510700
Mobile	+44 (0)7870 586214
Email	info@redfootlea.co.uk
Web	www.redfootlea.co.uk

Entry 301   Map 16

Northumberland

Bilton Barns

A solidly good farmhouse B&B whose lifeblood is still farming. The Jacksons know every inch of the surrounding countryside and coast; it's a pretty spot. They farm the 400 acres of mixed arable land that sweeps down to the sea yet always have time for guests. Dorothy creates an easy and sociable atmosphere with welcoming pots of tea and convivial breakfasts – all delicious and locally sourced. Comfortable, smartly done bedrooms have a traditional feel, bathrooms have underfloor heating, the huge conservatory is filled with sofas and chairs and there's an elegant guest sitting room with an open fire and views to the sea.

Rooms	1 double, 1 twin, 1 four-poster:
	£80-£88.
	Singles £40-£65.
Meals	Packed lunch £4-£6.
	Pub/restaurant 2 miles.
Closed	Christmas.

Brian & Dorothy Jackson
Bilton Barns,
Alnmouth, Alnwick, NE66 2TB

Tel	+44 (0)1665 830427
Mobile	+44 (0)7939 262028
Email	dorothy@biltonbarns.com
Web	www.biltonbarns.com

Entry 302   Map 16

Northumberland

Thistleyhaugh

The family thrives on hard work and humour, and if Enid's not the perfect B&B hostess, she's a close contender. Her passions are pictures, cooking and people, and certainly you eat well – local farm eggs at breakfast and their beef at dinner. Choose any of the five large, lovely bedrooms and stay the week; they are awash with old paintings, silk fabrics and crisp linen. Wake refreshed and nip downstairs, past the log fire, to a laden and sociable table, head off afterwards to find 720 acres of organic farmland and a few million more of the Cheviots beyond. Wonderful hosts, a glorious region, a happy house.

Rooms	3 doubles, 1 twin: £100.
	1 single: £70-£90.
	Extra bed/sofabed available £15 per person per night.
Meals	Dinner, 3 courses, £25.
	Pub/restaurant 2 miles.
Closed	Christmas, New Year & January.

Henry & Enid Nelless
Thistleyhaugh,
Longhorsley,
Morpeth, NE65 8RG
Tel   +44 (0)1665 570629
Email   thistleyhaugh@hotmail.com
Web   www.thistleyhaugh.co.uk

Entry 303   Map 16

Northumberland

Shieldhall

The converted 18th-century farm buildings are charming. Step in through your own entrance off the central courtyard to cosy bedrooms, flowers and homemade biscuits. Family run and friendly, it's a treat to stay. Stephen and his sons make bespoke, and restore antique, furniture, and the rooms are named after the different woods they use. Daughter Sarah and her husband John are great hosts; you pop over to the main house for meals. Delicious Aga-cooked breakfasts include homemade bread and eggs from the hens; Celia helps with the dinners – have a glass of wine in the beautiful library beforehand: the views over garden and parkland are stunning.

Rooms	1 double, 1 twin, 1 four-poster: £80.
	Singles £60.
Meals	Dinner, 4 courses, £28.
	Pub 7 miles.
Closed	Rarely.

Celia & Stephen Robinson-Gay
Shieldhall,
Wallington,
Morpeth, NE61 4AQ
Tel   +44 (0)1830 540387
Email   shieldhall@btconnect.com
Web   www.shieldhallguesthouse.co.uk

Entry 304   Map 16

Northumberland

Matfen High House

Bring the wellies – and jumpers! You are 25 miles from the border and the walking is a joy. Struan and Jenny are good company, love sporting pursuits and will advise on where to eat locally (and drive you there if needed). The sturdy stone house of 1735 is a lived-in, happily shabby-chic kind of place: the en suite bedrooms have fine fabrics and pictures, bathrooms are well-kept and the drawing room has books and choice pieces. Enjoy local bacon and sausages at breakfast, with Struan's marmalade and bread warm from the oven. The countryside is stunning, Hadrian's Wall and the great castles (Alnwick, Bamburgh) beckon.

Rooms	1 double, 2 twins; 1 double, 1 twin sharing bath: £60–£80. Singles £45.
Meals	Packed lunch £4.50. Restaurant 2 miles.
Closed	Rarely.

Struan & Jenny Wilson
Matfen High House,
Matfen,
Corbridge, NE20 0RG
Tel   +44 (0)1661 886592
Email   struan@struan.enterprise-plc.com
Web   www.matfenhighhouse.co.uk

Northumberland

The Grange

You're only seven miles away from Newcastle city centre but this couldn't be more peaceful. Kind owners let you wind down in their elegant Georgian house on the private Blagdon Estate, surrounded by mature trees and lovely gardens. Nod off in cosy, airy bedrooms with pale carpets (quiet at night), wake to eat like a lord at separate tables with Blagdon bacon, award-winning sausages and all the trimmings. There's a gentle woodland walk on the doorstep, rugged countryside and the nearby coast to explore. Newcastle airport is only four miles away (owners can arrange drop off and collection) and you can return to a roaring log fire.

Rooms	3 doubles: £100–£170. Extra bed/sofabed available £30–£70 per person per night.
Meals	Pubs/restaurants 1 mile.
Closed	Rarely.

Paul Wappat & Penny Dane
The Grange,
Great North Road, Seaton Burn,
Newcastle upon Tyne, NE13 6DF
Tel   +44 (0)1670 789666
Email   info@thegrangebandb.co.uk
Web   www.thegrangebandb.co.uk

Northumberland

The Hermitage

A magical setting, three miles from Hadrian's Wall, in a house of friendship and comfort. Through ancient woodland, up the drive, over the burn and there it is: big, beautiful and Georgian. Interiors are comfortable country-house, full of warmth and charm; bedrooms, carpeted, spacious and delightful, are furnished with antiques, paintings and superb beds; bathrooms have roll top baths. Outside are lovely lawns, a walled garden, wildlife, and breakfasts on the terrace in summer. Katie – who was born in this house – looks after you brilliantly.

Babes in arms & children over 7 welcome.

Rooms	1 double, 1 twin; 1 double with separate bath: £85–£90. Singles from £55.
Meals	Pub 2 miles.
Closed	October – February.

Simon & Katie Stewart
The Hermitage,
Swinburne,
Hexham, NE48 4DG
Tel   +44 (0)1434 681248
Mobile +44 (0)7708 016297
Email katie.stewart@themeet.co.uk

Entry 307   Map 16

Northumberland

3 Ada Crescent

Rosemary's end-terrace, Victorian house is in a quiet cul-de-sac, and the serenity of Hexham Abbey is just across the park. Calm and welcoming, it's filled with antiques, books, colourful rugs and paintings. The bedroom is fresh with country colours, handsome family pieces, flowers and books; the airy bathroom has big blue towels and good soaps. Breakfast, including homemade bread and muesli, is super-flexible; relax with newspapers and coffee in the snug, pretty sitting room or in the little south-facing courtyard. Rosemary, warm and cultured, and Garlic the terrier, greet you with homemade cake and encourage you to feel at home.

Children over 10 welcome. Extra room available.

Rooms	1 twin/double with separate bathroom: £90. Singles £55.
Meals	Pubs/restaurants 10-minute walk.
Closed	Rarely.

Rosemary Stobart
3 Ada Crescent,
Hexham, NE46 3DR
Tel   +44 (0)1434 694242
Mobile +44 (0)7850 375535
Email rosemary.stobart@btinternet.com

Entry 308   Map 12

Northumberland

Emley Farm

You will be happy here, deep in the rural bliss of Northumberland with its bleating sheep and spectacular views. The Smarts look after you beautifully in their elegant Georgian farmhouse surrounded by a charming garden and on the edge of the village. You have your own comfortable sitting room with open fire, and delicious meals are taken in the handsome dining room; do stay in for dinner – local lobster, fish or game perhaps? Margaret is an accomplished cook. Sleep soundly in your view-filled bedroom under a proper eiderdown and savour the total peace. Hadrian's Wall is near, and the Lakes close enough for a bracing day out.

Rooms	1 suite for 2 with separate bath: £95–£100.
Meals	Dinner on request. Pubs less than a mile away.
Closed	Rarely.

Margaret Smart
Emley Farm,
Whitfield,
Hexham, NE47 8HB
Tel   +44 (0)1434 345776
Email margiecook2001@yahoo.co.uk

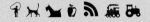

Entry 309   Map 12

Nottinghamshire

Willoughby House

A tall village house with an air of smart comfort. Step in to a warming log fire, antiques, quirky collections, art and lively colours. Bedrooms have tea, coffee and homemade flapjacks, fine linen and comfy sofas; Harry's and Bobby's are in the main house, Arthur's Stable and Top Barn are over the cobbles in Granary Annexe. Suzannah runs the family fruit farm and turns the produce into jams and juices; she and Marcus make scrumptious breakfasts. Norwell is on the edge of the Dukeries; head out for Sherwood Forest and the famous Major Oak, Lincoln and its cathedral, historic Newark and Southwell. Walk to the village pub for supper.

Rooms	1 twin/double; 1 double with separate bathroom: £100–£120. 1 family room for 4: £85–£200. Granary Annexe – 1 twin/double, 1 suite for 3: £120.
Meals	Pub 3-minute walk.
Closed	Rarely.

Suzannah Beatson-Hird
& Marcus Edward-Jones
Willoughby House,
Main Street, Norwell,
Newark, NG23 6JN
Tel   +44 (0)1636 636266
Mobile +44 (0)7780 996981
Email   willoughbyhousebandb@gmail.com
Web   www.willoughbyhousebandb.co.uk

Entry 310   Map 9

Nottinghamshire

Compton House

Two minutes from Newark's antique shops and old market, seek out this terraced Georgian townhouse where the mayor once lived. Naturally elegant, and overlooking Fountain Gardens, the drawing room has an open fire and books. Lisa – who won 'Friendliest Landlady of the Year' – has filled the place with lovely personal touches and rooms are named after friends, from red-gold Judy's room to Harry's bijou single; the best is Cooper's, with a four-poster, a roll top bath through a draped archway and a wall hand-painted by a local artist. Pad down to the sunny basement for Lisa's feast of a breakfast. Hotel comforts but a truly homely feel.

Dogs by arrangement.

Rooms	2 doubles, 1 twin/double, 2 twins, 1 four-poster: £95-£130. 1 single with separate shower: £50.
Meals	Packed lunch £5. Dinner, 3 courses, from £25. Pub/restaurant 0.5 miles.
Closed	Christmas.

Lisa Holloway
Compton House,
117 Baldertongate,
Newark, NG24 1RY
Tel   +44 (0)1636 708670
Mobile   +44 (0)7817 446485
Email   info@comptonhousenewark.com
Web   www.comptonhousenewark.com

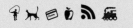

Entry 311   Map 9

Oxfordshire

Primrose Hill Farm

Surrounded by 80 acres dotted with munching sheep and horses... you've landed in a peaceful spot. All is polished and immaculate inside. Bedrooms are inviting: some have vaulted elm beams, all have deep beds, fat feather pillows, pretty lamps, vases of flowers. Elegant sitting and dining rooms look uphill to the woods; find silver pheasants atop a gleaming table, a trio of colourful sofas. Expect a hearty breakfast with compotes and a myriad of teas. The area teems with places to visit: Stratford, Warwick Castle, National Trust gems, Compton Verney art. John is warm and engaging – Trouble the terrier will help you feel at home too.

Children over 8 welcome.

Rooms	2 doubles, 1 twin/double, 1 twin: £95. Singles £85.
Meals	Pubs/restaurants 3 miles.
Closed	Rarely.

John Jeffries
Primrose Hill Farm,
Arlescote,
Banbury, OX17 1DQ
Mobile   +44 (0)7956 328359
Email   stay@primrose-hill-farm.com
Web   www.primrose-hill-farm.com

Entry 312   Map 8

Oxfordshire

Uplands House

Come to be spoiled at this handsome house, built in 1875 for the Earl of Jersey's farm manager. All is elegant and lavishly furnished; expect large light bedrooms, crisp linen, thick towels and vases of flowers. There are long views from the orangery, where you can have tea and cake; relax here with a book as the scents of the pretty garden waft by. Chat to Poppy while she creates delicious dinner – a convivial occasion enjoyed with your hosts. Breakfast is Graham's domain – try smoked salmon with scrambled eggs and red caviar. You're well placed for exploring – Moreton-in-Marsh and Stratford are close, Oxford just under an hour.

Oxfordshire

Minehill House

Wind your way up the farm track to the top of a beautiful hill and you arrive at a gorgeous family farmhouse with views for miles and warm, energetic Hester to care for you. Children will have fun with the ping-pong table and trampoline; their parents will enjoy the gleaming old flagstones, vibrant contemporary oils, wood-burning stove and seriously sophisticated food. Rest well in the big double room with its gloriously comfortable bed, verdant leafy wallpaper and stunning views; there's a cubby-hole door to extra twin beds (children love it!) and the bathroom is sparkling and spacious. Bracing walks start straight from the door.

Rooms	1 double, 1 twin/double, 1 four-poster: £100–£180. Singles £70–£110 (Mon–Thurs).	
Meals	Dinner, 2-4 courses, £20–£35. Pub 1.25 miles.	
Closed	Rarely.	

Rooms	1 double with adjoining twin room: £110–£170. Singles £75.
Meals	Dinner, 3 courses, £35. Pubs 1-5 miles.
Closed	Christmas & New Year.

	Poppy Cooksey & Graham Paul
	Uplands House,
	Upton, Banbury, OX15 6HJ
Tel	+44 (0)1295 678663
Mobile	+44 (0)7836 535538
Email	poppy@cotswolds-uplands.co.uk
Web	www.cotswolds-uplands.co.uk

	Hester & Ed Sale
	Minehill House,
	Lower Brailes, Banbury, OX15 5BJ
Tel	+44 (0)1608 685594
Mobile	+44 (0)7890 266441
Email	hester@minehillhouse.co.uk
Web	www.minehillhouse.co.uk

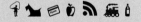

Entry 313   Map 8

Entry 314   Map 8

Oxfordshire

Court House

Climber-clad walls and terraced gardens wrap around Richard and Sara's 17th-century court house. Step in to find deep walls, ancient flags, polished elm and heaps of history. The old Court Room is now a gorgeous, high vaulted, beamed sitting room with piano, books, huge log-burner and mementoes of Richard's RAF years. Hop up to top-of-the-house bedrooms: attractive linen and fat pillows on seriously comfy beds, and a well-designed, small shared shower room. Tasty breakfasts include eggs from the hens, homemade bread and marmalade. Hammocks in the orchard, woodland and croquet, garden open days aplenty in the village… a peaceful, charming place.

Rooms	2 doubles sharing shower room: £85. Singles £60. Extra bed/sofabed available £20 per person per night.
Meals	Pub 3-minute walk.
Closed	Rarely.

Richard & Sara Thomas
Court House,
Main Street, Sibford Gower,
Banbury, OX15 5RW

Tel	+44 (0)1295 788797
Mobile	+44 (0)7976 221658
Email	enquiries@hillcrestsibford.co.uk
Web	www.hillcrestsibford.co.uk/ #!court-house/c7j1

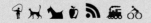

Entry 315   Map 8

Oxfordshire

Home Farmhouse

This 400-year-old house is charming… beams, inglenooks and winding stairs. Rosemary has been welcoming guests for over 20 years; her gently faded home brims with character, antiques and chintz. Pretty bedrooms have eiderdowns and traditional blankets; bathrooms are small and a little dated. Hop up old stone steps and enjoy independence in the barn room – a simple space with a mixture of family pieces. Breakfast is generous with garden compotes, homemade bread and conserves. The family's travels are evident all over, Samson the wire-haired dachshund is friendly and it's all so laid-back you'll find it hard to leave.

Rooms	1 double, 1 twin/double: £94. Barn – 1 twin/double: £94. Singles £65.
Meals	Pub 100 yds.
Closed	Christmas.

Rosemary Grove-White
Home Farmhouse,
Charlton, Banbury, OX17 3DR

Tel	+44 (0)1295 811683
Mobile	+44 (0)7795 207000
Email	grovewhite.rosemary@gmail.com
Web	www.homefarmhouse.co.uk

Entry 316   Map 8

Oxfordshire

The Old Post House

Great natural charm in the 17th-century Old Post House, where shiny flagstones, rich dark wood and mullion windows combine with handsome fabrics and furniture. Bedrooms are big, with antique wardrobes, oak headboards and a comfortably elegant feel. The walled gardens are lovely – with espaliered fruit trees, and a pool for sunny evenings. Christine, a well-travelled ex-pat, has an innate sense of hospitality; breakfasts are delicious (homemade granola, eggs Benedict, blueberry pancakes perhaps). There's village traffic but your sleep should be sound. Deddington is delightful – you will love Harry the friendly terrier too!

Over 12s welcome.

Rooms	1 twin/double; 1 double with separate bath, 1 four-poster with separate shower: £95. Singles £65.
Meals	Occasional dinner from £20. Pubs/restaurants 5-minute walk.
Closed	Rarely.

Christine Blenntoft
The Old Post House,
New Street, Deddington, OX15 0SP

Tel	+44 (0)1869 338978
Mobile	+44 (0)7713 631092
Email	kblenntoft@aol.com
Web	www.oldposthouse.co.uk

Entry 317   Map 8

Oxfordshire

Rectory Farm

This big country house has a wonderfully settled, tranquil feel – the family have farmed here for three generations. Find large, light bedrooms, floral and pretty, with bold chintz bed covers, draped dressing tables, thick mattresses and tea trays with delicious chocolate shortbread; all have garden views. Sink into comfortable sofas flanking a huge fireplace in the drawing room, breakfast on local bacon and sausage with free-range eggs, stroll the lovely garden, or grab a rod and try your luck on one of the trout lakes. Elizabeth knows her patch well, walkers can borrow maps and lively market town Chipping Norton is close.

Rooms	1 double, 1 twin/double; 1 twin/double with separate bath: £95-£120. Singles £65-£75.
Meals	Pub/restaurant 1.5 miles.
Closed	December/January.

Elizabeth Colston
Rectory Farm,
Salford, Chipping Norton, OX7 5YY

Tel	+44 (0)1608 643209
Mobile	+44 (0)7866 834208
Email	enquiries@rectoryfarm.info
Web	www.rectoryfarm.info

Entry 318   Map 8

Oxfordshire

Corner House at Churchill

Peter and Caroline, London escapees keen on the fine detail, have turned this handsome listed house into an immaculate home. All is beamed and inviting with warm colours, smart furniture, limestone floors, white linen on the refectory table; carbon-neutral too. Bedrooms are in a separate wing and named after local villages; find a headboard clad in tweed, Welsh rugs, plump pillows on comfy beds. Peter cooks you a generous classic breakfast along with compotes, yogurt, smoked salmon, pancakes with fruit. The Cotswolds is foodie heaven; there are literary and music festivals to attend, National Trust gems to visit. It's a treat to stay.

Minimum stay: 2 nights at weekends.

Rooms	2 doubles, 1 twin/double: £100-£130. Singles £90-£105.
Meals	Breakfast served until 10am. Pubs 2-minute walk.
Closed	Rarely.

Caroline & Peter Dunnicliffe
Corner House at Churchill,
Church Road, Churchill,
Chipping Norton, OX7 6NJ

Tel	+44 (0)1608 658432
Email	cornerhousepeter@icloud.com
Web	www.cornerhousechurchill.co.uk

Entry 319   Map 8

Oxfordshire

Heyford House

Old church and handsome house face each other down a village lane – and then the road runs out. In this timeless Oxfordshire valley, the white gate leads into gardens where pathways weave between borders to a kitchen garden and orchards. The house, warm-hearted and well-proportioned, has been in the family for years; your hosts (he a personal trainer, she a chef) live in one wing. Find contemporary art, bright old rugs and open fires – a happy mix of traditional and new. Bedrooms are handsome and comfortable, with excellent bath and shower rooms; Sonja's breakfasts, served by the Aga, are a treat.

Rooms	2 doubles, 2 twin/doubles: £100-£120. Singles £60-£80. Extra bed/sofabed available £25 per person per night.
Meals	Dinner for larger parties available, 2 courses from £20; 3 courses from £27 (enquire for further catering). Picnic from £10. Pubs/restaurants 4 miles.
Closed	Rarely.

Leo Brooke-Little
Heyford House,
Church Lane,
Lower Heyford,
Bicester, OX25 5NZ

Tel	+44 (0)1869 349061
Email	info@stayatheyfordhouse.co.uk

Entry 320   Map 8

Oxfordshire

The Glove House

Handmade chocolates from Turin (Francesco is Italian) and espresso machines in the bedrooms show proper respect for the important things in life. This handsome Georgian house in the heart of Woodstock combines calm contemporary comfort with warm smiles. The sitting room is panelled in golden oak; the suites, overlooking rooftops at the back, are discreet and delicious. Upholstered headboards, best feather duvets, Cotswolds wool throws, books, magazines and small buttoned armchairs... Enjoy a chilled prosecco by the garden's fountain before venturing out for supper; this lovely old town is awash with treats.

Ask about parking. Children over 10 welcome.

Rooms	1 double: £140-£175.
	2 suites for 3: £150-£220.
	Extra bed/sofabed available £55 per person per night.
Meals	Pubs/restaurants nearby.
Closed	Rarely.

Francesco & Caroline Totta
The Glove House,
24 Oxford Street,
Woodstock, OX20 1TS
Tel   +44 (0)1993 813475
Email   info@theglovehouse.co.uk
Web   www.theglovehouse.co.uk

Entry 321   Map 8

Oxfordshire

Green Close

This trim idyllic village abuts Blenheim Park and the parish church is famous for its medieval wall paintings. The Freelands' old stone house sits on the edge of one of the greens. The feel inside is harmonious and airy: high rafters, polished wood, a hall dining room with light streaming through mullioned windows, a winter fire in the lived-in sitting room, simple spotless bedrooms. Your hosts are easy-going, the retriever is smiley and children are welcome. An Aga breakfast will include compote, yogurt, eggs from the hens, homemade bread and good coffee. Woodstock and Oxford are a hop, and you can walk to supper at the pub.

Pets by arrangement.

Rooms	2 doubles;
	1 twin with separate bath: £90.
	Singles £55.
Meals	Pubs/restaurants 75 yds.
Closed	Rarely.

Caroline Freeland
Green Close,
West End, Combe,
Witney, OX29 8NS
Tel   +44 (0)1993 891223
Email   julian.freeland@btinternet.com
Web   www.greenclose.net

Entry 322   Map 8

Oxfordshire

Rectory Farm

Come for the happy relaxed vibe, and Mary Anne's welcome with tea and homemade shortbread. There's a wood-burner in the guest sitting room, and bedrooms have beautiful arched mullion windows. The huge twin with ornate plasterwork overlooks the garden and church, the pretty double is cosier and both have good showers and big fluffy towels. Wake for an excellent Aga breakfast with eggs from the hens, garden and hedgerow compotes, home or locally produced bacon and homemade jams. A herd of Red Ruby Devon cattle are Robert's pride and joy; the family have farmed for generations and you can buy the beef. It's a treat to stay.

Min stay: 2 nights at weekends & high season.

Rooms	1 double, 1 twin: £86–£90. Singles £65–£67.
Meals	Pub 2-minute walk.
Closed	Christmas & New Year.

Mary Anne Florey
Rectory Farm,
Northmoor, Witney, OX29 5SX

Tel	+44 (0)1865 300207
Mobile	+44 (0)7974 102198
Email	enquiries@visitrectoryfarm.co.uk
Web	www.visitrectoryfarm.co.uk

Entry 323   Map 8

Oxfordshire

Star Cottage

Classic Cotswolds – from the cottagey stone walls to the flower-bright garden – and swathes of open countryside for cyclists and walkers. Step inside to hand-sewn fabrics, cute lampshades, country furniture, fresh flowers and calm, pretty bedrooms: Sally delights in details. She and Peter, a plant biologist, love their winding stone-walled garden with its herbs, climbers and medlar tree; its jelly appears at breakfast, alongside smoked haddock and local sausages. The pub (yards away) offers dinner, Burford market town is a ten-minute walk, Cheltenham and Oxford a half-hour drive. Or kind Peter will fetch from the station.

Rooms	1 double, 1 family room for 3: £80–£110. Barn – 1 family room for 3 with kitchen: £80–£110. Singles £70–£80.
Meals	Pubs/restaurants within walking distance.
Closed	Rarely.

Peter & Sally Wyatt
Star Cottage,
Meadow Lane, Fulbrook,
Burford, OX18 4BW

Tel	+44 (0)1993 822032
Email	wyattpeter@btconnect.com
Web	www.burfordbedandbreakfast.co.uk

Entry 324   Map 8

Oxfordshire

Oxford University

Oxford at your fingertips – at a fair price. In the city's ancient heart are Wadham and Keble; in leafy North Oxford is friendly St Hugh's. Keble's sleeping quarters, functional though a good size, stand in stark contrast to the neo-gothic grandeur of its dining hall – pure Hogwarts! Wadham's hall, 17th century, soaring, is yet more glorious – with top breakfasts. Its student-simple bedrooms are reached via crenellated cloisters and lovely walled gardens; ask for a room facing the beautiful quad. At St Hugh's: three residences (one historic), a student café, 14 acres of romantic gardens and a 15-minute walk into town.

23 colleges in total.

Rooms	52 doubles, 121 twins: £69–£120. 12 family rooms for 3-4: £100–£165. 1,052 singles: £42–£93.
Meals	Breakfast included. Keble: occasional supper £22.50. Restaurants 2-15 minutes' walk.
Closed	Mid-January to mid-March, May/June, October/November; Christmas. A few rooms available throughout year.

University Rooms
Oxford University,
Oxford

Web	www.universityrooms.com/ en/city/oxford/home

Entry 325   Map 8

Oxfordshire

Willow Cottage

You are a short step from a village with an excellent pub (return across fields with a torch). Or treat yourself to dinner at Le Manoir aux Quat'Saisons. Katrina's delicious thatched cottage sits down a quiet lane. Through your own entrance find a guest dining room with armchairs by the old range, interesting prints and paintings, an eclectic mix of antiques and contemporary furniture. Bedrooms are warm, comfortable and stylish with views over the garden; shower rooms (not huge) are brand new and deeply smart. Breakfast, unhurried and bristling with local produce, sets walkers up for the Chiltern Way and the Ridgeway.

Rooms	3 doubles: £90–£110. Singles £65–£75. Extra bed/sofabed available £15 per person per night.
Meals	Pubs/restaurants 0.5 miles.
Closed	Rarely.

Katrina Sheldon
Willow Cottage,
Denton, Oxford, OX44 9JG

Tel	+44 (0)1865 874728
Email	katrinasheldon@aol.com
Web	www.willowcottage.info

Entry 326   Map 8

Oxfordshire

Fyfield Manor

A fabulous house in Oxfordshire (once owned by the de Montfort family) with water gardens providing a most romantic setting. The Browns have added solar panels too. Charming bedrooms in your own part of the house have views, slippers and comfy sofas. From the grand wood-panelled hall enter a beamed dining room with high-backed chairs, brass rubbings, wood-burner and pretty 12th-century arch; breakfast is largely locally sourced with organic bacon and eggs and garden fruit. Oxford Park & Ride is nearby, there's walking from the door and delightful Christine has wangled you a free glass of wine in the local pub if you walk to get there! Superb.

Children over 10 welcome.

Rooms	1 twin/double: £85-£95.
	1 family room for 2-4 with sofabed & separate bath (£20 extra per person): £85-£90.
	Singles £65-£75.
Meals	Pubs within 1 mile.
Closed	Rarely.

Christine Brown
Fyfield Manor,
Benson,
Wallingford, OX10 6HA

Tel	+44 (0)1491 835184
Email	chris_fyfield@hotmail.co.uk
Web	www.fyfieldmanor.co.uk

Entry 327   Map 4

Rutland

Old Hall Coach House

A rare and special setting; the grounds of the house meet the edge of Rutland Water, with far-reaching lake and church views. There's a terrace with table and chairs, a stunning garden and a croquet lawn. Inside: high ceilings, stone archways, antiques, a log fire to sit by. Comfortable and traditional bedrooms have smart, handsome bathrooms; the twin has glorious views from both windows. Wake for an Aga-cooked spread of home-laid eggs, sausages and homemade marmalade. Rutland is a mini-Cotswolds of stone villages and gentle hills; Georgian Stamford, Burghley House and Belvoir Castle are all near. Cecilie is a well-travelled, interesting host.

Minimum stay: 2 nights at weekends. Children over 6 welcome.

Rooms	1 double, 1 twin with separate bath: £95.
	Singles from £45.
Meals	Dinner £30.
	Pub/restaurant 5-minute walk.
Closed	Occasionally.

Cecilie Ingoldby
Old Hall Coach House,
31 Weston Road, Edith Weston,
Oakham, LE15 8HQ

Tel	+44 (0)1780 721504
Mobile	+44 (0)7767 678267
Email	cecilieingoldby@aol.com
Web	www.oldhallcoachhouse.co.uk

Entry 328   Map 9

Rutland

Old Rectory

Jane Austen fans will swoon. This elegant 1740s village house was used as Mr Collins's 'humble abode' by the BBC: you breakfast in the beautiful dining room that was 'Mr Collins's hall', and you can sleep in 'Miss Bennett's bedroom'. Victoria is wonderful – feisty, fun and gregarious – and looks after you beautifully with White Company linen in chintzy old-fashioned bedrooms, a log fire in the drawing room, fruit from the lovely garden, homemade jams and Aga-cooked local bacon and eggs. Guests love it here. You are near to some pleasant market towns and good walking and riding country. Don't forget the smelling salts!

Pets by arrangement.

Rooms	1 double, 1 twin: £85. Singles £45.
Meals	Pubs within 3 miles.
Closed	Rarely.

Victoria Owen
Old Rectory,
Teigh, Oakham, LE15 7RT
Tel   +44 (0)1572 787681
Mobile   +44 (0)7484 600721
Email   torowen@btinternet.com
Web   www.teighbedandbreakfast.co.uk

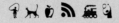

Entry 329   Map 9

Shropshire

Tybroughton Hall

Off a winding country lane, surrounded by 40 acres of grassland, find a pretty white listed farmhouse and a wonderful welcome from Daisy, her family and two dear dogs. Step into the hallway with its polished antique table and bright garden flowers and you know you've made the right choice: this is a house to unwind in. After a day's hiking or biking, bliss to return to bedrooms cosy and comfortable – the traditional double with its country view or the large lovely twin. Breakfasts are worth getting up for: Tim makes the preserves, bees make the honey, hens lay the eggs and the pigs (five beauties!) provide the bacon.

Rooms	1 double, 1 twin with separate bath: £80–£100. Singles £50–£65.
Meals	Dinner £20–£25. Pub 4 miles.
Closed	Rarely.

Daisy Woodhead
Tybroughton Hall,
Tybroughton, Whitchurch, SY13 3BB
Tel   +44 (0)1948 780726
Mobile   +44 (0)7850 395885
Email   daisy.woodhead@btinternet.com
Web   www.tybroughtonhall-bedandbreakfast.co.uk

Entry 330   Map 7

Shropshire

The Isle

History buffs and nature lovers rejoice. You drive through lion-topped stone pillars to a house built in 1682 (then extended) that stands in 800 acres enfolded by the river Severn. Charming Ros and Edward are down-to-earth and hands-on: eggs, bacon, ham, vegetables, and logs, come from the estate. Flop in front of a huge fire in the drawing room, homely with family antiques, big rug, magazines strewn on large tables. Peaceful bedrooms are large and light with pocket-sprung memory mattresses and snazzy upmarket bathrooms. Walk, fish, ride (there's a livery stable on site) and lap up the views – they're sublime.

Shropshire

Brimford House

Beautifully tucked under the Breidden Hills, farm and Georgian farmhouse have been in the Dawson family for four generations. Views stretch all the way to the Severn; the simple garden does not try to compete. Spotless bedrooms have flowers, and pretty china for morning tea; there's a half-tester with rope-twist columns, a twin with Victorian wrought-iron bedsteads, a double with a brass bed, a big bathroom with a roll top bath. Liz serves you farm eggs and homemade preserves at breakfast, and there's a food pub just down the road. Sheep and cattle outdoors, a lovely black lab in, and wildlife walks from the door. Good value.

Pets by arrangement.

Rooms	3 doubles, 1 twin: £80-£100. 1 family room for 4: £90-£145. Singles £50-£70.
Meals	Packed lunch £5. Dinner £15-£20. Pub/restaurant 4.3 miles.
Closed	Rarely.

Rooms	2 doubles, 1 twin: £75-£85. Singles £50-£60. Extra bed/sofabed available £15-£20 per person per night.
Meals	Packed lunch £4.50. Pub 3-minute walk.
Closed	Rarely.

	Ros & Edward Tate The Isle, Bicton, Shrewsbury, SY3 8EE
Mobile	+44 (0)7776 257286
Email	ros@isleestate.co.uk
Web	www.the-isle-estate.co.uk

	Liz Dawson Brimford House, Criggion, Shrewsbury, SY5 9AU
Tel	+44 (0)1938 570235
Mobile	+44 (0)7801 100848
Email	info@brimford.co.uk
Web	www.brimford.co.uk

Entry 331   Map 7

Entry 332   Map 7

Shropshire

Whitton Hall

Down a long private drive with fields on either side is a lovely 18th-century farmhouse, elegant but not intimidating, with a sense of timelessness. A large open hallway and a cosy sitting room where tea and a drinks tray are provided are peaceful spaces for relaxing with a book. You breakfast in the dining room, on local muesli, bread, marmalades and jams, milk from their Jersey cows, soft fruit from their garden, sausages and bacon from down the road. Peaceful, light and large bedrooms in an adjacent wing have modern bathrooms, country house furniture and long views to glorious gardens. Unwind in the peace.

Children over 10 welcome.

Rooms	1 double with separate bathroom, 1 twin/double with separate shower: £110. 1 family room for 4 with separate bathroom: £110-£140.
Meals	Supper in dining room £25 a head for 4+ guests. Cold supper tray in room or garden £20 for 2, £15 for 1. Restaurant 1.5 miles.
Closed	Christmas, New Year & Easter.

Christopher & Gill Halliday
& Kate Boscawen
Whitton Hall,
Westbury, Shrewsbury, SY5 9RD
Tel   +44 (0)1743 884270
Mobile   +44 (0)7974 689629
Email   accommodation@whittonhall.com
Web   www.whittonhall.co.uk

Entry 333   Map 7

Shropshire

Hardwick House

On a quiet street in the heart of Shrewsbury, this fine Georgian house has been in Lucy's family for generations. The dining room (oak panelling, a huge fireplace) is a lovely space to breakfast on locally sourced produce and homemade bread; vases of garden flowers are dotted all around this cheerful family home. Bedrooms are traditional and comfortable with pretty china tea cups; bathrooms are old-fashioned. The walled garden is fabulous; take tea in an 18th-century summerhouse. Birthplace of Darwin, this is a fascinating historic town; walk to the abbey, castle, theatre, festivals and great shops. Lucy is delightful.

Rooms	2 twin/doubles (one with adjoining twin can form a large suite): £85-£100. Singles £55-£75.
Meals	Pubs/restaurants 150 yds.
Closed	Christmas & New Year.

Lucy Whitaker
Hardwick House,
12 St John's Hill,
Shrewsbury, SY1 1JJ
Tel   +44 (0)1743 350165
Email   gilesandlucy@btinternet.com
Web   www.hardwickhouseshrewsbury.co.uk

Entry 334   Map 7

Shropshire

North Farm

Peaceful green Shropshire and a stunning garden surround this classic white farmhouse. Chickens, ducks and geese are happily dotted about and the veg patch blooms. Tess and family look after you well. Bedrooms have flowery fabrics, tip-top linen, Lloyd Loom chairs and pretty tea trays. Wake for a delicious breakfast served on Portmeirion china: homemade marmalade, compotes, eggs from the hens, bacon and sausages from home-reared pigs. Lots to do close by: historic Shrewsbury, Ironbridge, Ludlow, Powis Castle – and the walks are a treat. Settle by the log-burner on your return: books to browse, a glass of wine... lovely.

Rooms	1 double, 1 twin; 1 double with separate bath: £85. Singles £55.
Meals	Pubs/restaurants 4-minute drive.
Closed	Rarely.

Tess Bromley
North Farm,
Eaton Mascot, Cross Houses,
Shrewsbury, SY5 6HF
Tel   +44 (0)1743 761031
Mobile   +44 (0)7956 817705
Email   tessbromley@ymail.com
Web   www.northfarm.co.uk

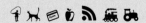

Entry 335   Map 7

Shropshire

5 Wilmore Street

Clare delights in making her home glow. Passionate about interior décor, she's designed an immaculate house crammed with creative touches and Georgian elegance; inviting sitting and breakfast rooms have comfy sofas, a wood-burner and refectory tables. An experienced cook too, so expect good breakfasts and dinners: homemade treats, eggs from a friend's hens, fish from the market. Soak in a slipper bath; sleep in a charming panelled bedroom with armchairs, hand-painted antiques and pictures; church bells keep time. The historic town is rich in timbered buildings, monastic ruins, arty festivals and award-winning independent shops.

Rooms	1 double: £110. Singles £85.
Meals	Dinner, 3 courses, £30. Pubs/restaurants 5-minute walk.
Closed	Rarely.

Richard & Clare Wozniak
5 Wilmore Street,
Much Wenlock, TF13 6HR
Tel   +44 (0)1952 727268
Mobile   +44 (0)7530 779568
Email   5wilmorestreet@gmail.com

Entry 336   Map 7

Shropshire

The Old Rectory

With its own spring water, horses, dogs and slow pace this Georgian rectory is comfortable country living at its best. Izzy and Andy are charming and interesting and give you scones and tea by the fire in a drawing room full of family photos, plump sofas and books. Elegant bedrooms have fluffy hot water bottles; smart bathrooms have scented lotions in pretty bottles, robes and slippers. Candlelit dinner will often be fish or game with garden vegetables; breakfast is local and leisurely with homemade granola and jams. There's a bootroom for muddy feet and paws, stabling and seven acres to roam.

Pets welcome, sleeping in bootroom.

Rooms	1 double, 1 twin/double; 1 double with separate bathroom: £85-£125. Singles £70-£110.
Meals	Dinner, 3 courses with coffee, drinks & canapes, £35. Supper tray (soup & sandwich) £10. Pubs 1.25-4 miles.
Closed	Rarely.

Isabel Barnard
The Old Rectory,
Wheathill, Ludlow, Bridgnorth,
WV16 6QT
Tel   +44 (0)1746 787209
Email   enquiries@theoldrectorywheathill.com
Web   www.theoldrectorywheathill.com

Entry 337   Map 7

Shropshire

Timberstone Bed & Breakfast

The house is young and engaging — as are Tracey and Alex, new generation B&Bers. Come for charming bedrooms — two snug under the eaves, two in the smart oak-floored extension — roll top baths, pretty fabrics, thick white cotton, beams galore... and reflexology or a sauna in the garden studios; Tracey, once in catering, is a reflexologist. In the warm guest sitting/dining room find art, books, comfortable sofas and glass doors onto the terrace. Breakfasts are special with croissants and local eggs and bacon; dinners are delicious too, or you can head off to Ludlow and its clutch of Michelin stars.

Whole house available for self-catering.

Rooms	2 doubles, 1 double, with sofabed: £85-£120. 1 family room for 4: £115-£120. Singles £60-£95. Dinner, B&B £67-£71 per person.
Meals	Dinner, 3 courses, £25. Pubs/restaurants 5 miles.
Closed	Rarely.

Tracey Baylis & Alex Read
Timberstone Bed & Breakfast,
Clee Stanton, Ludlow, SY8 3EL
Tel   +44 (0)1584 823519
Mobile +44 (0)7905 967263
Email   timberstone1@hotmail.com
Web   www.timberstoneludlow.co.uk

Entry 338   Map 7

Shropshire

35 Lower Broad Street

You're almost at the bottom of the town, near the river and the bridge. Elaine's terraced Georgian cottage is spotless and cosy; her office doubles as a sitting area for guests with leather armchairs, TV and a desk space for workaholics. Upstairs are two good-sized doubles with a country crisp feel, king-size beds and a pretty blue and white bathroom. Walkers, shoppers, antique- and book-hunters can fill up on a superb breakfast of homemade potato scones, black pudding, organic eggs and good coffee before striding out to explore. This is excellent value, comfortable B&B and can be enjoyed without a car.

Rooms	1 double with sitting room & separate bathroom; 1 double sharing bathroom (let to same party only): £75. Singles £50.
Meals	Pubs/restaurants 100 yds.
Closed	Rarely.

	Elaine Downs
	35 Lower Broad Street, Ludlow, SY8 1PH
Tel	+44 (0)1584 876912
Mobile	+44 (0)7970 151010
Email	a.downs@tesco.net

Entry 339   Map 7

Shropshire

Rosecroft

A pretty, quiet, traditional house with charming owners, well-proportioned rooms, an elegant sitting room and not a trace of pomposity. Breakfasts are huge enough to set you up for the day: Pimhill organic muesli, smoked or unsmoked local bacon, black pudding, delicious jams. The garden is a delight to stroll through – in summer you can picnic here – while serious walkers are close to the Welsh borders. Bedrooms and bathrooms are polished to perfection; there are fresh flowers, plenty of interesting books, home-baked cakes when you arrive. The village has a super pub and Ludlow is close by.

Over 12s welcome.

Rooms	1 double; 1 double with separate bath: £80-£90. Singles £65-£75.
Meals	Packed lunch £4. Pub 200 yds.
Closed	Rarely.

	Gail Benson
	Rosecroft, Orleton, Ludlow, SY8 4HN
Tel	+44 (0)1568 780565
Email	gailanddavid@rosecroftorleton.co.uk
Web	www.rosecroftbedandbreakfast.co.uk

Entry 340   Map 7

Shropshire

Walford Court

Come for a break from clock-watching and a spot of Shropshire air. Large bedrooms delight with the comfiest mattresses on king-size beds, scented candles, antiques, books, games and double-end roll top baths – one under a west facing window. Debbie and Craig's Aga-cooked breakfasts have won awards and include eggs from 'the ladies of the orchard'. Wander through the apple, plum and pear trees, find a motte and bailey, strike out for a long, leafy hike. Craig and Debbie are thoughtful and hugely keen on wildlife (you get binoculars) and this is the perfect place to bring a special person – and a bottle of champagne.

Minimum stay: 2 nights at weekends.

Rooms	1 double; 2 doubles, each with sitting room: £95–£105. Extra bed/sofabed available £30 per person per night.
Meals	Room platter of local pâté, cheeses, ham & homemade pickles & chutney. Packed lunch. Pubs/restaurants 1–3 miles.
Closed	Christmas & Boxing Day.

Debbie & Craig Fraser
Walford Court,
Walford, Leintwardine,
Ludlow, SY7 0JT

Tel	+44 (0)1547 540570
Email	info@romanticbreak.com
Web	www.romanticbreak.com

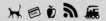

Entry 341   Map 7

Shropshire

Upper Buckton

This grand Georgian house, complete with heronry and point-to-point course, stands on a motte and bailey site. The Welsh Borders setting is beautiful and the gardens slope peacefully down to the millstream, meadows and river. Breakfasts are local and delicious, convivial dinners are preceded by drinks in the drawing room; Yvonne's cooking is upmarket and creative, Hayden's wine list is a treat. Retire to large bedrooms with huge beds made to perfection (proper blankets, lovely linen). Wander, admiring the roses and azaleas; join the Hereford Way from the farm; visit abundant castles and gardens. Ludlow is a ten-minute drive.

Children by arrangement.

Rooms	1 double, 1 twin/double; 1 twin/double with separate bath: £96–£120. Singles £70–£75.
Meals	Dinner, 4 courses, £30. Pub/restaurant 2 miles.
Closed	Rarely.

Hayden & Yvonne Lloyd
Upper Buckton,
Leintwardine, Craven Arms,
Ludlow, SY7 0JU

Tel	+44 (0)1547 540634
Email	ghlloydco@btconnect.com
Web	www.upperbuckton.co.uk

Entry 342   Map 7

Shropshire

Lower Buckton Country House

You are spoiled here in house-party style; Carolyn – passionate about Slow Food – and Henry, are born entertainers. Kick off with homemade cake in the drawing room with its oil paintings, antique furniture and old rugs; return for delicious nibbles when the lamps and wood-burner are flickering. Dine well at a huge oak table (home-reared pork, local cheeses, dreamy puddings), then nestle into the best linen and the softest pillows; bedrooms feel wonderfully restful. This is laid-back B&B: paddle in the stream, admire the stunning views, find a quiet spot with a good book. Great fun!

Pets by arrangement.

Rooms	2 doubles; 1 twin/double with separate bath: £100. Singles £75–£100. Extra bed/sofabed available £25–£45 per person per night.
Meals	Dinner, 4 courses, £35. BYO wine. Pub/restaurant 4 miles.
Closed	Rarely.

Henry & Carolyn Chesshire
Lower Buckton Country House,
Buckton, Leintwardine, SY7 0JU
Tel   +44 (0)1547 540532
Mobile +44 (0)7960 273865
Email   carolyn@lowerbuckton.co.uk
Web   www.lowerbuckton.co.uk

Entry 343   Map 7

Shropshire

Hopton House

Karen looks after her guests wonderfully and even runs courses on how to do B&B! Unwind in this fresh and uplifting converted granary with old beams, high ceilings and a sun-filled dining/sitting room overlooking the hills. The bedroom above has its own balcony; those in the barn, one up, one down, each with its own entrance, are as enticing: beautifully dressed beds, silent fridges, good lighting, homemade cakes. Bathrooms have deep baths (and showers) – from one you can lie back and gaze at the stars. Karen's breakfasts promise Ludlow sausages, home-laid eggs, fine jams and homemade marmalade.

Minimum stay: 2 nights. Over 16s welcome.

Rooms	1 double; Barn: 2 doubles: £110–£125. Check owner's website for availability calendar and booking engine.
Meals	Restaurant 3 miles.
Closed	19-27 December.

Karen Thorne
Hopton House,
Hopton Heath,
Craven Arms, SY7 0QD
Tel   +44 (0)1547 530885
Web   www.shropshirebreakfast.co.uk

Entry 344   Map 7

Shropshire

Clun Farm House

A relaxed country feel here, with heavenly hills all around. Friendly hosts Susan and Anthony are enthusiastic collectors of country artefacts and have filled their listed 15th-century farmhouse with eye-catching things; the cowboy's saddle by the old range echoes Susan's roots. Bedrooms have aged and oiled floorboards, fun florals and bold walls; there is space for children in the extra bunk room; bathrooms are small and simple. Walk Offa's Dyke and the Shropshire Way; return to rescue hens wandering the garden, a warm smile and a glass of wine by the cosy wood-burner – before supper at one of the local pubs. Good value.

Horses welcome.

Rooms	1 double with extra bunk bedroom; 1 twin/double with separate shower: £85. Singles by arrangement.
Meals	Packed lunch £4. Pubs/restaurants nearby.
Closed	Occasionally.

Anthony & Susan Whitfield
Clun Farm House,
High Street, Clun,
Craven Arms, SY7 8JB
Tel   +44 (0)1588 640432
Mobile +44 (0)7885 261391
Email anthonyswhitfield0158@btinternet.com
Web   www.clunfarmhouse.co.uk

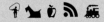

Entry 345   Map 7

Somerset

Taggart House

Past the church, up through the pretty village, to Andrew and Rachel's relaxed eco-friendly house. Through your own doorway, find a smart bedroom with tip-top linen, TV, a basket of books, French windows onto patios – perfect for an evening glass of wine – and a sleek bathroom with thick white towels. Wake for bacon and sausages from the Potting Shed Farm Shop, eggy bread, local jams. Walton Brook runs through the garden, a visiting pair of ducks can be spotted on the pond, and you can walk through ancient woodland to join the coastal path to Clevedon. Close to Portishead and only 25 minutes from Bristol. A leafy retreat.

Rooms	1 double, 1 twin/double: £95–£105.
Meals	Pubs/restaurants within 2 miles.
Closed	Rarely.

Andrew & Rachel Francis
Taggart House,
Walton Street, Walton-in-Gordano,
Clevedon, BS21 7AP
Tel   +44 (0)1275 316970
Email rachel@taggarthouse.co.uk
Web   www.taggarthouse.co.uk

Entry 346   Map 2

Somerset

Church House

All is tickety boo in this Georgian rectory with views over seaside homes and the Bristol Channel. Terry and Tracey look after you impeccably; help yourself to Tracey's homemade cakes on the landing. You'll sleep peacefully in light and airy bedrooms all named after islands in the channel; swish bathrooms have underfloor heating to keep you toasty warm. Take breakfast in the dining room at a mahogany table: home-baked bread, homemade jams and marmalade, eggs from down the hill and local bacon. Walk it off on the coastal path, cycle along quiet lanes, or head for Weston and old-fashioned seaside fun.

Pets by arrangement.

Rooms	4 doubles, 1 twin: £85-£110.
	Singles £85-£95.
	Extra bed/sofabed available £15-£25
	per person per night.
Meals	Pubs 400 yds.
Closed	Rarely.

Terry & Tracey Gill
Church House,
27 Kewstoke Road, Kewstoke,
Weston-super-Mare, BS22 9YD

Tel	+44 (0)1934 633185
Email	info@churchhousekewstoke.co.uk
Web	www.churchhousekewstoke.co.uk

Entry 347   Map 2

Somerset

Stonebridge

A country house with scrumptious food, a friendly black labrador and croquet on the lawn. Liz and Richard give you scones and tea, and your own independent wing of their listed house. You have two pretty bedrooms (one up, one down) with country furniture and super bathrooms. In winter, a wood-burner keeps your little sitting room cosy; in summer, laze in a sea of flowers. You feast on local eggs and homemade bread and jams for breakfast; Liz cooks memorable dinners too with home-grown veg. Just off the village road, it's close to Bristol airport, Wells – and the M5, so the perfect pit-stop if you're on your way to Devon or Cornwall.

Children over 2 welcome.

Rooms	1 double, 1 twin/double: £85-£95.
	Singles £65-£75.
Meals	Dinner, 2-3 courses, £25-£29.
	Pub 2 miles.
Closed	Christmas.

Richard & Liz Annesley
Stonebridge,
Wolvershill Road,
Banwell, BS29 6DR

Tel	+44 (0)1934 822549
Email	liz.annesley@talktalk.net
Web	www.stonebridgebandb.co.uk

Entry 348   Map 3

Somerset

Burrington Farm

High in the Mendips, Ros and Barry's 15th-century longhouse is blissfully rural, yet Bristol, Bath and Wells are close. Their wonderful house glows: rugs and flagstones, books, burnished beams, paintings and fine old furniture. Guests have a cosy sitting room and bedrooms are charming; you'll need to be nimble to negotiate ancient steps and stairs. For those who prefer a bit more privacy there's a lovely family room in a separate green oak barn – stunningly converted and with views over the enchanting garden. Wake for a locally sourced breakfast round a big table. A friendly, relaxed and special place.

Rooms	1 double; 1 double, 1 twin sharing bath (let to same party only): £85-£120. Barn – 1 family room for 4: £100-£120. Singles £65.
Meals	Pub 10-minute walk.
Closed	Christmas.

	Barry & Ros Smith Burrington Farm, Burrington, BS40 7AD
Tel	+44 (0)1761 462127
Mobile	+44 (0)7825 237144
Email	unwind@burringtonfarm.co.uk
Web	www.unwindatburringtonfarm.co.uk

Somerset

Harptree Court

A gorgeous Georgian house that has been in Charles' family for generations. Inside all is elegant and grand, but this is very much a family home; there's a welcoming log fire in the hall and Charles and Linda are charming and relaxed. The interior gleams with flowers, art and polished wood, and the dining room looks onto the beautiful garden; warm, sunny bedrooms have delicate fabrics, china pieces and antiques, and bathrooms sparkle. An excellent breakfast of garden fruits, local honey and sausages sets you up for a walk in the grounds: acres of parkland with ponds, an ancient bridge, carpets of spring flowers. A peaceful delight.

Rooms	3 doubles, 1 twin/double: £140. Singles £90.
Meals	Pub 300 yds.
Closed	December/January.

	Linda & Charles Hill Harptree Court, East Harptree, Bristol, BS40 6AA
Tel	+44 (0)1761 221729
Mobile	+44 (0)7970 165576
Email	bandb@harptreecourt.co.uk
Web	www.harptreecourt.co.uk

Somerset

The Old Vicarage

The vicarage sits at the foot of Jack and Jill's hill in a sleepy Mendip village. Both bedrooms have goose down comfort: one has an antique French bed and limestone wet room; the sunny blue room upstairs has a freestanding roll top. Your hosts are informal and friendly and their home exudes charm: a medieval stone floor in the hall, old flagstones, carpets designed by Lizzy, flowers, wood-burners and a pretty kitchen. Hens potter, carp laze in the canal pond; breakfast when you want on a full English, garden compotes and delicious coffee. National Trust gems and splendid walking on the Colliers Way will keep you busy.

Minimum stay: 2 nights.

Rooms	1 double with sitting room;
	1 four-poster with separate wc:
	£95–£110.
Meals	Pub 100 yds.
Closed	Rarely.

Elizabeth Ashard
The Old Vicarage,
Church Street, Kilmersdon,
Radstock, BA3 5TA

Tel	+44 (0)1761 436926
Email	lizzyashard@gmail.com
Web	www.theoldvicaragesomerset.co.uk

Entry 351   Map 3

Somerset

Jericho

'Jericho' means in the middle of nowhere and here above lovely Mells you have space around your ears and long views. Babington House and excellent pubs are close, yet sybarites may just want to wallow in the generous bedroom and sitting room with doors to a vine-hung loggia and parterre, French Grey panelling, original art, and a wet room with a drenching shower. Stephen, a product designer, has orchestrated the look, and furniture, rugs and fabrics chime contentedly with the architecture. Find top-notch coffee and tea on your tea tray, hand-pressed apple juice from the orchard, and exquisite vegetarian breakfasts delivered to you.

Rooms	1 suite for 2 with sitting room:
	£100–£110.
Meals	Pub 3 miles.
Closed	Rarely.

Stephen Morgan
Jericho,
Mells Down, Mells,
Frome, BA11 2RL

Tel	+44 (0)1373 813242
Email	mail@stayatjericho.co.uk
Web	www.stayatjericho.co.uk

Entry 352   Map 3

Somerset

Somerset

Old Reading Room

Mells is a treasure with its medieval centre and liberal sprinkling of charming cottages; you'll find Vicky and John's attractive house down a track in the quiet wooded valley. It's a home with a friendly feel: books, art, pots of flowers, intriguing finds from family travels, comfy sofas around the wood-burner. Beds are wrapped in fine cotton and colourful quilts; sweet bathrooms have scented candles. Come down for breakfast in the kitchen – homemade bread, eggs from happy hens – delivered by a friend on a pony! Sunny cottage garden, walks from the door, a five-minute drive to Babington House… and entertaining hosts.

Penny's Mill

The old part of Nunney village, with its small pretty streets, has a shop, a café and Rosie's gorgeous old stone millhouse down in the river valley. You are greeted warmly with tea and biscuits at a large wooden table in the kitchen, or in the drawing room upstairs with family photos, paintings and a big window looking over the millpond. Sunny bedrooms painted in gentle blues and greens have a mix of antique and modern furniture; bathrooms have Molton Brown soaps and white fluffy towels. You can book one of Rosie's cookery courses, and her fine breakfast sets you up for a short walk to Nunney Castle, or a yomp further afield.

Rooms	2 doubles: £95.
	Singles £85.
Meals	Pubs/restaurants 5-minute walk.
Closed	Rarely.

Rooms	1 double, 1 twin/double with own
	living room: £90.
	1 family room for 4: £150.
Meals	Dinner £25-£35.
	Pub 300 yds.
Closed	Rarely.

Vicky & John Macdonald
Old Reading Room,
Mells,
Frome, BA11 3QA

Tel	+44 (0)1373 813487
Email	johnmacdonaldm@gmail.com

Rosie Davies
Penny's Mill,
Horn Street, Nunney,
Frome, BA11 4NP

Tel	+44 (0)1373 836210
Email	stay@pennysmill.com
Web	www.stayatpennysmill.com

Entry 353   Map 3

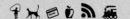

Entry 354   Map 3

Somerset

Broadgrove House

Head down the long, private lane and arrive at Sarah's peaceful 17th-century stone house with its pretty walled cottage garden and views to Alfred's Tower and Longleat. Inside is just as special. Beams, flagstones and inglenook fireplaces have been sensitively restored; rugs, pictures, comfy sofas and polished antiques add warmth and serenity. The twin, at the end of the house, has a little shower room and its own sitting room. Breakfast on homemade and farmers' market produce before exploring Stourhead, Wells, Glastonbury. Sarah, engaging, well-travelled and a great cook, looks after you warmly.

Children by arrangement. Minimum stay: 2 nights at weekends in the summer season. Dogs welcome in twin room (own door into garden).

Rooms	1 twin with sitting room, 1 double with separate bath: £85–£95. Singles £65.
Meals	Pub/restaurant 1 mile.
Closed	Christmas.

	Sarah Voller Broadgrove House, Leighton, Frome, BA11 4PP
Tel	+44 (0)1373 836296
Mobile	+44 (0)7775 918388
Email	broadgrove836@tiscali.co.uk
Web	www.broadgrovehouse.co.uk

Entry 355   Map 3

Zzzzomerzet

Bee & Bee at Honeycomb Farm

Who hasn't dreamt of sleeping in a beehive at one point or other? Oh, maybe it's just me. Well anyway, now you can at our latest discovery, Bee & Bee. Nectar farmers, Bee and Buzz, have lifted the lid of their amazing home – a modernist masterpiece where identical, hexagonal rooms, dripping in gold, have a sweet charm. Buzz stays in and drones on a bit while busy sister Bee, clad antennae to toe in black and gold velvet, goes out and about, stocking up on supplies. If you're not good with crowds, then possibly this place isn't for you but if you love a buzzy atmosphere and a chance to see the queen, you've struck gold. (Happy Birthday Ma'am.)

Direct Beesyjet flights every day.

Rooms	100,000 singles; no bathrooms: don't get stung.
Meals	Honey for breakfast, lunch and tea.
Closed	Heaven help us if it ever is.

	Bee & Buzz Honeybun Bee & Bee at Honeycomb Farm, Wildflower Lane, Pollen, BUZ Z1E
Tel	Just give them a buzz
Web	www.beenbeebnb.co.uk

The Manor House

Late medieval, this is a house teeming with colour and stories. Discover a Jacobean staircase, open fireplaces, oil portraits, and embroideries and finds from Harriet's time in Central Asia. Each bedroom has its own charm with a beautiful blend of intricately carved pieces and rustic touches: sea blue walls with paintings of sailing boats, and a small stairway leading up to an attic room; fuchsia print wallpaper and a rich ethnic feel in the master 'Cheese room'. Breakfast with homemade marmalade and blackcurrant jam is a delicious local spread, the garden has roses, a knot garden and woodland, and Bryan and Harriet are friendly and engaging.

Rooms	2 doubles sharing bathroom (let to same party only): £80-£95; singles £60. 1 single sharing bathroom (let to same party only): £50.
Meals	Pubs/restaurants 3 miles.
Closed	Christmas & occasionally.

Harriet & Bryan Ray
The Manor House,
West Compton,
Shepton Mallet, BA4 4PB
Tel   +44 (0)1749 890582
Email   rayswestcompton@btinternet.com
Web   www.themanorhousebandb.co.uk

Entry 356   Map 3

Hillview Cottage

Catherine is a wonderful host: warm-spirited, cultured and humorous. She knows the area well, and is happy to show you around Wells Cathedral – she's an official guide. This is a comfy tea-and-cakes family home with rugs on wooden floors and antique quilts. Bedrooms have a French feel, the bathroom an armchair for chatting and there's a friendly sitting room with an open fire. The stunning vaulted breakfast room has huge beams, an old Welsh dresser with hand painted mugs, a cheerful red Aga, a wood-burner to sit by and glorious views; breakfasts are superb. Guests love it here; excellent value too.

Rooms	1 twin/double, 1 twin sharing bath (let to same party only): £80-£90. Singles £50.
Meals	Pubs 5-minute walk.
Closed	Rarely.

Michael & Catherine Hay
Hillview Cottage,
Paradise Lane,
Croscombe, Wells, BA5 3RN
Tel   +44 (0)1749 343526
Mobile   +44 (0)7801 666146
Email   cathyhay@yahoo.co.uk
Web   www.hillviewcottage.me.uk

Entry 358   Map 3

Coach House

Take a glass of wine to your private courtyard and absorb the peace; or picnic in the gardens. In the hamlet of Dulcote, a mile from Wells, is your own two-storey, two-bedroom coach house flooded with light, full of character and the latest mod cons. Downstairs, a black and white zebra theme; upstairs, white walls, crisp linen, high beams, a glimpse of Wells Cathedral and views that reach to the Mendips. Friendly Chumba the dog greets you and your (well-behaved) waggy friend. Karen leaves eggs from her hens and other goodies in your fridge so you can breakfast in your jim-jams. A delightful B&B for nature lovers and dog-walkers.

Minimum stay: 2 nights. Over 12s welcome.

Rooms	Annex – 1 double, 1 twin sharing sitting room, sofabeds & kitchen (let to same party only): £95 per night for 1 bedroom plus £35 per extra person per night. Singles £90.
Meals	Pubs within 2 miles.
Closed	Rarely.

Karen Smallwood
Coach House,
Little Fountains, Dulcote,
Wells, BA5 3NU

Tel	+44 (0)1749 678777
Mobile	+44 (0)7789 778880
Email	stay@littlefountains.co.uk
Web	www.littlefountains.co.uk

Entry 359   Map 3

Caro

Come for a creative take on B&B. You step into Caro, Natalie's coffee bar and design shop, your stylish bedroom is upstairs and you stroll down to At the Chapel for breakfast. Natalie has thought of everything: Roberts radio and tea, roll top bath, big shower and Aesop Aromatiques. Expect good food at the bakery Chapel: bread from the wood fire, Somerset ham, granola, pancakes; lunch and dinner too. Explore popular Bruton, head off on one of the walks helpfully described in your room, visit Hauser and Wirth gallery; return for a browse in the shop and a delicious coffee – the locally made cakes and Florentines are works of art too.

Minimum stay: 2 nights in high season. Over 14s welcome.

Rooms	1 double: £120.
	1 single (sharing bath with double; let to same part only): £70.
Meals	Breakfast 2-minute walk to The Chapel restaurant.
	Pubs/restaurants 4-minute walk.
Closed	Christmas & New Year.

Natalie Jones
Caro,
9 Quaperlake Street,
Bruton, BA10 0HF

Tel	+44 (0)1749 813931
Email	hello@carosomerset.com
Web	www.carosomerset.com

Entry 360   Map 3

Somerset

Ansford Park Cottage

An old farmworker's house, modernised and freshly spruced, stands proud in verdant countryside. Long views from the clipped garden drift into the distance; warm Sue (plus cute Jack Russells) greets you. You sleep in the extension to the front of the house; one bedroom has valley views, the other has views over the Mendips. Both have comfy beds, books, homely touches and peacefulness. Breakfast is a leisurely affair of local bacon and eggs. Tramp off on an inspiring walk – Leland trail, Macmillan Way – you're spoilt for choice. Escape London by train (95 minutes) – collection from the station can be arranged.

Rooms	1 twin/double; 1 twin/double with separate bath: £75.
Meals	Dinner £25. Packed lunch £5. Pub/restaurant 1 mile.
Closed	Christmas & rarely.

	Susan Begg
	Ansford Park Cottage,
	Ansford Park,
	Maggs Lane,
	Castle Cary, BA7 7JJ
Tel	+44 (0)1963 351066
Email	nigelbegg@lineone.net
Web	www.ansfordparkcottage.co.uk

Entry 361   Map 3

Somerset

Cary Place

In the heart of town yet sitting in three acres... a honey-stoned gem. Debra's home has an open-house vibe – helped along perfectly by Humphrey the terrier. Step into a generous hall to find an elegant sitting room for guests, polished floors, original art and gorgeous colours in every room. Bedrooms are a delight: sofas at the end of sleigh beds, tip-top linen and pretty fabrics. Hop down for breakfast in the airy dining room, or out on a sunny terrace: fruits from the orchard, croissants, organic sausages and bacon. Come and go as you want – walk to cafés, delis and independent shops; Glastonbury and Stourhead are close.

Rooms	1 double, 1 twin; 1 double with separate bath: £105. Extra room available.
Meals	Pubs/restaurants within walking distance.
Closed	Rarely.

	Debra Henderson
	Cary Place,
	4 Upper High Street,
	Castle Cary, BA7 7AR
Tel	+44 (0)1963 359269
Mobile	+44 (0)7956 972552
Email	info@caryplace.co.uk
Web	www.caryplace.co.uk

Entry 362   Map 3

Somerset

Yarlington House

A mellow Georgian manor surrounded by impressive parkland, romantic rose gardens, apple tree pergola and laburnum walk. Your hosts are friendly and flexible artists with an eye for quirky detail; Carolyn's embroideries are everywhere, and there's something to astound at every turn: fine copies of 18th-century wallpapers, elegant antiques, statues with hats atop and tremendous art. Traditional bedrooms with glorious garden views and proper 50s bathrooms have a faded charm. Enjoy a full English breakfast, grape juice from the glasshouse vines, log fires and lovely local walks. Surprising, unique.

Heated swimming pool in the summer.

Rooms	1 double; 1 double with separate bath: £140. 1 family room for 4 with separate bath: £140-£210. Singles £70.
Meals	Pubs/restaurants within 0.5 miles.
Closed	25 July to 23 August.

Carolyn & Charles de Salis
Yarlington House,
Yarlington,
Wincanton, BA9 8DY

Tel	+44 (0)1963 440344
Email	carolyn.desalis@yarlingtonhouse.com
Web	www.yarlingtonhouse.com

Entry 363   Map 3

Somerset

The Lynch Country House

Peace and privacy at this immaculate Regency house in a Somerset valley. First-floor bedrooms are traditionally grand, attic rooms are smaller but pretty; those in the coach house have a more modern feel. Rich colours prevail, fabrics are flowery and linen best Irish. You'll feel as warm as toast and beautifully looked after. A stone staircase goes right to the top where the observatory lets in cascading light; the flagged hall, high ceilings, long windows and private tables at breakfast create a country-house hotel feel. The lovely garden has black swans on a lake, hundreds of trees and a terrace from which to drink it all in.

Rooms	1 double, 1 four-poster, 2 twin/doubles with extra single bed; 1 double with separate bath & extra single bed: £80-£115. Coach House – 2 doubles, 2 twin/doubles: £80-£115. Singles £70-£95.
Meals	Pubs 5-minute walk.
Closed	Rarely.

Lynne Vincent
The Lynch Country House,
4 Behind Berry,
Somerton, TA11 7PD

Tel	+44 (0)1458 272316
Email	thelynchcountryhouse@gmail.com
Web	www.thelynchcountryhouse.co.uk

Entry 364   Map 3

Somerset

Keepers Cottage

Restored stable, hayloft and cottage... take your pick from imaginatively restored spaces. Oak-beamed bedrooms have well-dressed beds, sofas, reclamation finds, books and biscuits; 'Hayloft' has a wood-burner; 'Paddock' and 'Orchard' can interconnect for a family. Amble over to the friendly kitchen in the main house for breakfast: homemade granola, organic porridge, all sorts of cooked choices – pop your menu-sheet in the 'bread bin' by the back door in the evening; Emma will bring over a continental breakfast to your room if preferred. Sunny sitting spots in the garden, a scramble up Glastonbury Tor, a stroll to a good supper at the pub...

Minimum stay: 2 nights at weekends. Children over 10 welcome.

Rooms	3 doubles: £100-£120. Singles £75-£85. Extra bed/sofabed available £30 per person per night.
Meals	Pubs/restaurants 5-minute walk.
Closed	Christmas.

Emma Taylor
Keepers Cottage,
Wood Lane, Butleigh,
Glastonbury, BA6 8TR
Tel +44 (0)1458 850353
Email info@keeperssomerset.com
Web www.keeperssomerset.com

🐾 🐕 🔊

Entry 365   Map 3

Somerset

Studio Farrows

An appealingly quirky studio hidden in the luxuriant garden of artists Paul and Tracey. They live in the main house and are relaxed, helpful hosts. They'll arrange a swim in a friend's walled pool, and all sorts of courses from baking to glass blowing; or you can simply relax in this comfy, peaceful retreat. You have a big living space with giant wood-burner, books, and eclectic art and furniture (including an Anglia!); bedrooms are colourful, bathrooms sleek. Breakfasts are gorgeous, a continental feast and scrambled eggs to die for! Sit out on the veranda, light the fire baskets, gaze at the stars... Bliss.

Email can be unreliable: please phone! Min. 4 person booking. Min. stay: 2 nights. Pets by arrangement. Smoking permitted on the veranda.

Rooms	2 doubles with sitting room and kitchen: £114. Singles £57. 15% discount for weekly stays. Sofabed in its own space available on request.
Meals	Vegetarian & vegan meals available on request. Pub 3 miles.
Closed	Rarely.

Tracey Baker
Studio Farrows,
Aller,
Langport, TA10 0QW
Tel +44 (0)1458 252599
Email tracey@studiofarrows.com
Web www.studiofarrows.com

♿ 🚶 🎣 🐕 🐾 🔊 🚂

Entry 366   Map 3

Somerset

Church Byres

Meander down lanes and a tree-lined drive to a courtyard flanked by farm buildings: four solid stone farm byres. One side is your hosts', the other is yours, so you have your own wing; it's great value for a family – and your dog is very welcome too. Peter and Jenny, attentive and fun, give you breakfast out on a terrace on sunny mornings, and can direct you to some good local country pubs for supper. It's a treat to come home to your own wood-burner and deep sofas, white bathrobes and muted tones: the mood is warmly contemporary. Take a chilled beer from your own fridge to the guest terrace by the front lawn – lovely!

Rooms	1 double, 1 twin sharing bathroom (let to same party only): £80-£100. Singles £60.
Meals	Pubs/restaurants 3 miles.
Closed	Christmas.

Jenny Cox
Church Byres,
South Barrow,
Yeovil, BA22 7LN
Mobile +44 (0)7765 175058
Email bookings@somerset-bb.co.uk
Web www.somerset-bb.co.uk

Somerset

Barwick Farm House

A 17th-century farmhouse sitting in organically managed land dotted with hens, horses and Dorset sheep. Angela is delightful and has worked wonders with gorgeous limewash colours in every room. Step into a beautiful hall to find a house full of ancient elm boards, colourful rugs, open fires, books, china and pots of flowers. Pretty bedrooms have good linen on comfy beds; the downstairs one has its own breakfast room and garden entrance, and a big copper tub; one bathroom is cleverly clad in reclaimed grain store panels. Wake to birdsong and sizzling local bacon; excellent walking and cycling start from the door.

Rooms	2 doubles, 1 twin/double: £80-£90. Singles £50-£60.
Meals	'Early Bird' packed breakfasts also available. Restaurant 100 yds.
Closed	Rarely.

Angela Nicoll
Barwick Farm House,
Barwick, Yeovil, BA22 9TD
Tel +44 (0)1935 410779
Mobile +44 (0)7967 385307
Email info@barwickfarmhouse.co.uk
Web www.barwickfarmhouse.co.uk

Somerset

Fairways

The food, the views – amazing! Tim is a passionate cook, and he and Sarah want you to enjoy their friendly open house. Settle in with tea and Tim's high-rise scones and look out over Seaborough Hill. Their 1960s bungalow is immaculate: white walls, gleaming oak floors, toasty wood-burner and French windows onto the garden. Perfect bedrooms have inviting beds and pots of sweet peas; bathrooms sparkle. Pad through to breakfast in the airy sitting/dining room – or out on the sunny deck: eggs from across the valley, smoked salmon, homemade bread, granola and jams; dinner is equally good with organic local veg and charcuterie. A treat!

Over 16s welcome.

Rooms	2 doubles: £100.
	Singles £80.
Meals	Dinner, 3 courses with tea/coffee,
	£27.50. BYO.
	Pub/restaurant 3 miles.
Closed	Rarely.

Sarah & Tim Dommett
Fairways,
Hewish Lane, Crewkerne, TA18 8RN

Tel	+44 (0)1460 271093
Mobile	+44 (0)7768 753045
Email	info@fairwaysbandb.co.uk
Web	www.fairwaysbandb.co.uk

Entry 369 Map 3

Somerset

Brook House

A relaxed home with no rules; arrive to tasty cake and tea or a tipple, settle in the sitting room by one of the wood-burners, chat in the kitchen, wander mown paths in the garden. The sunny open-plan kitchen/living room is the heart of the house; Becky is a keen cook so food is good, local, homemade; Crumpet, one of the terriers, snoozes by the Aga. Quiet, comfy bedrooms have tip-top linen, painted furniture, pots of flowers, garden views; the larger twin has a sofa by tall windows. Next door Cider Mill has a farm shop, museum and tea rooms, the walks are great, the Jurassic coast is a short drive. A friendly place, a treat to stay.

Over 12s welcome.

Rooms	1 double, 1 twin/double: £85–£95.
	Singles £65–£75.
Meals	Dinner, 3 courses, from £20.
	Pub 3 miles.
Closed	Occasionally.

Becky Jam
Brook House,
Dowlish Wake, Ilminster, TA19 0NY

Tel	+44 (0)1460 250860
Mobile	+44 (0)7841 594342
Email	becky@brookhousesomerset.com
Web	www.brookhousesomerset.com

Entry 370 Map 3

Somerset

The Beeches

This relaxed, beautiful old house sits in a peaceful Somerset village. Step in to find interesting furniture, good art and family photos, thick curtains, flickering fires and views from every window. Abby encourages unwinding: sleep on the fattest hand-stitched mattresses, choose pretty much what you want for breakfast (try panettone eggy bread), help yourself to homemade cake in the sitting room at teatime. There are heaps of good walks and the Jurassic coast to discover (borrow a map), museums and gardens galore and nearby pubs for supper. On sunny days you can just loll in Abby's leafy garden if you prefer and watch the pottering chickens.

Rooms	1 double, 1 twin/double: £90. Singles £60.
Meals	Pubs/restaurants 2-minute walk.
Closed	Rarely.

Abby Norton
The Beeches,
Water Street, Seavington St
Michael, Ilminster, TA19 0QH
Tel   +44 (0)1460 241123
Email   abigail@southsomersetbandb.co.uk
Web   www.southsomersetbandb.co.uk

Entry 371   Map 2

Somerset

Park Farmhouse

'Artisan Baker' says the sign on the lane… you're in for a treat here. Buy bread and pastries on Saturdays, learn how to bake them on Sundays, tuck into Friday pizza, enjoy the most delicious croissants (all French butter and flour) for breakfast. Frank is bonkers about bread! He and Carolyn like you to feel part of the family. Their Georgian farmhouse has classic elegance with a French rustic twist: furniture painted in soft tones (Carolyn's creations), original oak parquet floor in the pretty bread-shop room, big comfy sitting room with wood-burner, airy bedrooms with pots of roses. Supper with your hosts too, or walk across fields to the pub.

Rooms	1 double; 1 double with separate bath: £70-£90. Singles £50-£60.
Meals	Supper from £15. Pubs/restaurants 15-minute walk.
Closed	Rarely.

Carolyn & Frank Heuff
Park Farmhouse,
Bickenhall,
Taunton, TA3 6TZ
Tel   +44 (0)1823 480878
Email   breadbedandbreakfast@gmail.com
Web   www.breadbedandbreakfast.co.uk

Entry 372   Map 2

Somerset

Frog Street Farmhouse

Through a pastoral landscape, past green paddocks and fine thoroughbreds, to a beautiful longhouse set in pretty secluded gardens surrounded by 130 acres. Its heart dates back to 1436 and its renovation is remarkable, highlighting beamed ceilings, Jacobean panelling and open fireplaces. Louise and David, brimful of enthusiasm for both house and visitors, give you four exquisite bedrooms in French country style, one with its own sitting room – very romantic. Louise happily does evening meals and hosts small house parties with ease. After a day out, return to great leather sofas and a wood-burning stove. Guests love it here!

Rooms	3 doubles: £90-£120.
	1 family room for 4: £120-£160.
	Singles £80-£120.
	Extra bed/sofabed available £15 per person per night.
Meals	Dinner, 3 courses, £27.50 (for parties of 6 or more).
	Pubs within 2.5 miles.
Closed	Christmas.

Louise & David Farrance
Frog Street Farmhouse,
Hatch Beauchamp,
Taunton, TA3 6AF
Tel   +44 (0)1823 481883
Mobile +44 (0)7811 700789
Email   frogstreet@hotmail.com
Web   www.frogstreet.co.uk

Entry 373   Map 2

Somerset

Brook Farm

The front door is open for your arrival... Step into the rich red hallway of this traditional Georgian-fronted farmhouse, and find cosy corners for reading, period prints, polished wood, and open fires in the winter. Maria gives you breakfast in a sunny dining/sitting room, where doors open out to the patio and garden beyond; the guest sitting room is snug with comfy sofas and plenty of books. Sink into luxurious beds in immaculate bedrooms; TVs are smart, WiFi is on tap, bathrooms gleam and views are green and peaceful. The Somerset Levels surround you, Glastonbury and Wells are close and there's a good pub in the village too.

Over 12s welcome.

Rooms	1 double, 1 twin/double: £90-£105.
	Singles £75-£85.
Meals	Pubs/restaurants 1.2 miles.
Closed	Rarely.

Maria Laing
Brook Farm,
Newport Road, North Curry,
Taunton, TA3 6DJ
Tel   +44 (0)1823 491124
Email maria.follett@hotmail.co.uk
Web   www.brookfarmbb.com

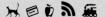

Entry 374   Map 2

Somerset

Causeway Cottage

Robert and Lesley are ex-restaurateurs, so guests heap praise on their food, most of which is sourced from a local butcher and fishmonger; charming Lesley is an author, runs cookery courses and once taught at Prue Leith's. This is the perfect, pretty Somerset cottage, with an apple orchard and views to the church across a cottage garden and a field. The bedrooms are light, restful and have a country-style simplicity with their green check bedspreads, white walls and antique pine furniture; guests have their own comfortable sitting room. Easy access to the M5 yet with a rural feel. Very special.

Children over 10 welcome.

Rooms	1 double, 2 twins: £80-£85. Singles £60.
Meals	Supper from £30. Pub/restaurant 0.75 miles.
Closed	Christmas.

	Lesley & Robert Orr
	Causeway Cottage,
	West Buckland, Taunton, TA21 9JZ
Tel	+44 (0)1823 663458
Mobile	+44 (0)7703 412827
Email	orrs@causewaycottage.co.uk
Web	www.causewaycottage.co.uk

Entry 375   Map 2

Somerset

Bashfords Farmhouse

A feeling of warmth and happiness pervades this exquisite 17th-century farmhouse in the Quantock Hills. The Ritchies love doing B&B – even after over 20 years! – and interiors have a homely feel with well-framed prints, natural fabrics, comfortable sofas, and a sitting room with inglenook, sofas and books. Bedrooms are pretty, fresh and large and look over the cobbled courtyard or open fields. Charles and Jane couldn't be nicer, know about local walks (the Macmillan Way runs by) and love to cook: local meat and game, tarte tatin, homemade bread and jams. A delightful garden rambles up the hill; the pub is just a minute away.

Rooms	1 twin/double; 1 twin/double with separate bath; 1 twin/double with separate shower: £80. Singles £50.
Meals	Dinner £27.50. Supper £22.50. Pub 75 yds.
Closed	Rarely.

	Charles & Jane Ritchie
	Bashfords Farmhouse,
	West Bagborough,
	Taunton, TA4 3EF
Tel	+44 (0)1823 432015
Email	info@bashfordsfarmhouse.co.uk
Web	www.bashfordsfarmhouse.co.uk

Entry 376   Map 2

Cider Barn

Set back from the lane is a newly converted and refurbished barn. Step in to find fine old proportions, heated oak floors and heaps of character. Louise's stunning living quarters spread under the beams and bedrooms lie privately below on the ground floor. One opens to the courtyard, and all are airy and peaceful with modern fabrics and cream walls. There's a sunny guest sitting room leading onto the garden, and delightful Louise, a great cook, serves breakfast at a long table by the wood-burner. You can walk through fields to the river or hills, stroll to the pub for supper – and alternative therapies can be arranged locally.

Huntstile Organic Farm

Catapult yourself into country life in the foothills of the Quantocks; make that connection between the rolling green hills, the idyllic munching animals and the delicious, organic food on your plate; here it is understood. Lizzie and John buzz with energy in this gorgeous old house with Jacobean panelling and huge walk-in fireplaces, two sitting rooms, sweet and cosy rustic bedrooms, a café, and a restaurant serving their own meat, eggs and vegetables. House parties, weddings, team building, a stone circle for hand-fasting ceremonies – all come under Lizzie's happy and efficient umbrella. And there are woodlands to roam.

Minimum stay: 2 nights in high season.

Rooms	1 double, 1 twin/double: £75–£90. Singles £60–£70.
Meals	Pub 1 mile.
Closed	Rarely.

Rooms	7 doubles: £85–£150. 3 family rooms for 4: £95–£150. Apartment – 1 double, 1 twin with sitting room: £85–£150. Singles £55–£75. Extra bed/sofabed £15–£25 p.p.n.
Meals	Dinner, 3 courses, £22.50–£27. Packed lunch from £6.50. Pub/restaurant 3 miles.
Closed	Rarely.

	Louise Bancroft
	Cider Barn,
	Runnington,
	Wellington, TA21 0QW
Tel	+44 (0)1823 665533
Email	louisegaddon@btinternet.com
Web	www.runningtonciderbarn.co.uk

	Lizzie Myers
	Huntstile Organic Farm,
	Goathurst,
	Bridgwater, TA5 2DQ
Tel	+44 (0)1278 662358
Email	huntstile@live.co.uk
Web	www.huntstileorganicfarm.co.uk

Entry 377   Map 2

Entry 378   Map 2

Somerset

Blackmore Farm

Come for atmosphere and architecture: the Grade I-listed manor-farmhouse is remarkable. Medieval stone, soaring beams, ecclesiastical windows, giant logs blazing in the Great Hall. Ann and Ian look after guests and busy dairy farm with equal enthusiasm. Furnishings are rich, bedrooms are large and the oak-panelled suite (with secret stairway) takes up an entire floor; there are worn corners here and there and the old bathroom in the family room has a makeover planned. The stable rooms are simpler. Aga breakfasts with local sausages and jams are eaten at the long polished table in the Hall. Don't miss the excellent farm shop – there's a café too.

Rooms	1 four-poster, 1 suite for 2, 1 family room for 3: £110–£120. Cider Press: 1 double, 1 twin. Singles £65.
Meals	Occasional dinner from £27 for parties (large parties only). Pubs/restaurants 5-minute walk.
Closed	Rarely.

	Ann Dyer Blackmore Farm, Cannington, Bridgwater, TA5 2NE
Tel	+44 (0)1278 653442
Email	dyerfarm@aol.com
Web	www.blackmorefarm.co.uk

Entry 379   Map 2

Somerset

Witheridge Farm

Head down the lane to this Exmoor farmhouse snoozing in the Exe valley. It's a home with a heart – Jackie and Michael have created a friendly, relaxed vibe and are past masters at restoring houses. Find window seats in every room, pots of flowers, beautiful fabrics and art. The sitting room is snug with comfy chairs by the wood-burner; bedrooms and bathrooms are inviting: good white linen, big towels, robes and views over the garden and hills. Tuck into an Aga breakfast round the polished table in the beamed dining room, simple suppers too. Characterful ponies add to the happy feel, there's a suntrap terrace and you can walk from the door onto Exmoor.

Stabling & turnout paddock available. Dogs are welcome but need to stay in the kennels provided.

Rooms	1 twin/double; 1 double with separate bathroom: £90. 1 bunk room for 2, sharing bathroom with double (let to same party only): £60. Singles £80.
Meals	Supper £20. Pubs/restaurants 1.5 miles.
Closed	Rarely.

	Michael & Jackie Archer Witheridge Farm, Winsford, Dulverton, TA22 9JY
Tel	+44 (0)1643 851895
Mobile	+44 (0)7779 749668
Email	jacksarcher@hotmail.co.uk
Web	www.witheridgefarmexmoorbandb.co.uk

Entry 380   Map 2

Staffordshire

Manor House Farm

A working rare-breed farm in an area of great beauty, a Jacobean farmhouse with oodles of history. Behind mullioned windows is a glorious interior crammed with curios and family pieces, panelled walls and wonky floors... hurl a log on the fire and watch it roar. Rooms with views have four-posters; one bathroom flaunts rich red antique fabrics. Chris and Margaret are passionate hosts who serve perfect breakfasts (eggs from their own hens, sausages and bacon from their pigs and home-grown tomatoes) and give you the run of a garden resplendent with plants, vistas, tennis, croquet, two springer spaniels and one purring cat. Heaven.

Min. stay: 2 nights at weekends during high season.

Rooms	1 double, 2 four-posters: £70-£80.
	1 family room for 4: £80-£100.
Meals	Pub/restaurant 1.5 miles.
Closed	Christmas.

Chris & Margaret Ball
Manor House Farm,
Prestwood, Denstone,
Uttoxeter, ST14 5DD
Tel   +44 (0)1889 590415
Mobile   +44 (0)7976 767629
Email   cmball@manorhousefarm.co.uk
Web   www.manorhousefarm.co.uk

Entry 381   Map 8

Staffordshire

Westmorland Cottage

The pretty village has hanging baskets decorating shops and riverside, and Tim and Caroline's house was built in the arboretum of Oswald Mosley's former family seat. Comfy sitting rooms have heaps of books, art, a log fire; bedrooms (one in the studio) have tip-top linen, garden views and shortbread. Wake for a generous Aga breakfast: homemade granola, Tim's bread, local bacon – or continental with croissants. You're on the edge of the Peak District National Park – head out for walks, cycling, National Trust houses galore. Return to the stunning garden for afternoon tea and cake: unusual trees, Italianate pond, sunny spots...

Rooms	1 double; 1 double with separate
	bathroom: £75-£85.
	1 studio for 2: £95.
	Singles £65.
Meals	Pubs/restaurants 5-minute walk.
Closed	Rarely.

Caroline Bucknall
Westmorland Cottage,
Hall Grounds, Rolleston-on-Dove,
Burton-on-Trent, DE13 9BS
Tel   +44 (0)1283 813336
Mobile   +44 (0)7814 849211
Email   bucknalltandc@gmail.com
Web   www.westmorlandcottage.co.uk

Entry 382   Map 8

Suffolk

Pavilion House

A conservation village surrounded by chalk grassland – famous for its flora, fauna and butterflies; marked walks are straight from this 16-year-old red-brick house. Friendly Gretta teaches cooking and you are in for a treat: homemade cake, enormous breakfasts with her own bread and jams, proper dinners or simple suppers. Sleep peacefully in traditional, comfortable bedrooms (all downstairs) with crisp linen and TVs. There's a guest sitting room too: English comfort with an oriental feel, parquet floors, antiques, original drawings, a cosy log-burner. Wander the superb garden. Newmarket and Cambridge are close.

Suffolk

The Old Vicarage

Up the avenue of fine white horse chestnut trees to find just what you'd expect from an old vicarage: a Pembroke table in the flagstoned hall, a refectory table sporting copies of *The Field*, a piano guests can play, silver pheasants, winter log fires in the breakfast and drawing rooms and homemade cake on arrival. The house is magnificent, with huge rooms and passageways. Comfy beds are dressed in old-fashioned counterpanes; the twin has stunning far-reaching views. Weave your way through the branches of the huge copper beech to Jane's colourful garden; she grows her own vegetables, keeps hens, makes jams and cooks delicious breakfasts.

Children over 7 welcome.

Rooms	1 double; 1 double, 1 twin/double, both with separate bath/shower: £85–£125. Singles £55–£60. Child bed available.	Rooms	1 twin/double with separate bath, 1 twin with separate bath: £80–£90. Extra single room available (let to same party only). Singles £50.
Meals	Lunch from £10. Dinner from £25. Supper from £15. BYO. Pub 1.5 miles.	Meals	Packed lunch £6. Pub 1 mile.
Closed	Christmas.	Closed	Christmas.

	Gretta & David Bredin Pavilion House, 133 Station Road, Dullingham, Newmarket, CB8 9UT		**Jane Sheppard** The Old Vicarage, Great Thurlow, Newmarket, CB9 7LE
Tel	+44 (0)1638 508005	Tel	+44 (0)1440 783209
Mobile	+44 (0)7776 197709	Mobile	+44 (0)7887 717429
Email	gretta@thereliablesauce.co.uk	Email	s.j.sheppard@hotmail.co.uk
Web	www.pavilionhousebandb.co.uk	Web	www.thurlowvicarage.co.uk

Entry 383   Map 9

Entry 384   Map 9

Suffolk

The Old Stable

A rural ramble brings you to a flint and brick bolthole – tucked into the courtyard of the main house. Joanna has restored her stables with a blend of old and new: beams, lime washed walls, rustic window sills, modern log-burner, swish new bathrooms. Bedrooms ('Hayloft' up, 'Coach House' down) are fresh and comfy – one has a double sofabed for extra guests. Wide French windows in the big dining/sitting room open to the pool – have a dip on summer mornings; dahlias and roses fill the garden. Joanna brings over breakfast: homemade jams, home-buzzed honey, a full English spread. Walk from the door; hop on a bike and discover nearby Bury.

Over 13s welcome.

Rooms	1 twin/double, 1 twin (let to same party only): £90-£115. Extra bed/sofabed available £25 per person per night.
Meals	Occasional supper from £15. Packed lunch £7.50. Pubs/restaurants within 3 miles.
Closed	Occasionally.

Joanna Mayer
The Old Stable,
Cattishall Farmhouse, Great Barton,
Bury St Edmunds, IP31 2QT
Tel   +44 (0)1284 787340
Mobile   +44 (0)7738 936496
Email   joannamayer42@googlemail.com
Web   www.theoldstablebandb.co.uk

Suffolk

The Old Manse Barn

A large, lush loft apartment in sleepy Suffolk; this uncluttered living space of blond wood, white walls and big windows has an urban feel yet overlooks glorious countryside. Secluded from the main house, in a timber-clad barn, all is fabulous and spacious: leather sofas, glass dining table, stainless steel kitchenette. Floor lights dance off the walls, surround-sound creates mood and you can watch the stars from your bed. Homemade granola, fruits, cold meats, cheeses and fresh pastries are popped in the fridge – bliss. There's peace for romance, solitude for work, a garden to sit in and lovely Sue to suggest the best pubs.

Rooms	Apartment: 1 double & kitchenette: £80-£90.
Meals	Pubs within walking distance.
Closed	Mid-January to end February.

Sue & Ian Jones
The Old Manse Barn,
Chapel Road, Cockfield,
Bury St Edmunds, IP30 0HE
Tel   +44 (0)1284 828120
Mobile   +44 (0)7931 753996
Email   bookings@theoldmansebarn.co.uk
Web   www.theoldmansebarn.co.uk

Suffolk

Copinger Hall

A stunning bay-windowed house which has been in the family since the 16th century, yet is anything but ancient in feel. At the end of a sweeping gravel drive, past the church which adjoins the garden, it is 'country smart', deeply comfortable and very much a home – complete with two noisily amiable dogs. Lisa is someone to whom throwing open the doors to guests brings immeasurable pleasure, a gifted and generous host. Breakfasts (superb breakfast menu!) are in the elegant dining room, and guests have the use of the drawing room, garden and tennis court. Head out for Aldeburgh, Lavenham and the music at Snape Maltings.

Rooms	1 double, 1 twin/double; 1 double with separate bath/shower: £100-£130. Singles £95.
Meals	Pub & restaurant within 1 mile.
Closed	Occasionally.

Lisa & Stephen Minoprio
Copinger Hall,
Brettenham Road, Buxhall,
Stowmarket, IP14 3DJ
Tel   +44 (0)1449 736000
Mobile +44 (0)7775 621715
Email   lisa@copingerhall.com

Entry 387   Map 10

Suffolk

The Old Rectory

A handsome house surrounded by large gardens and sheep-dotted fields. Maggie's home is filled with beautiful things: old family china, prints, portraits, blue and white decorated lamps, polished wood – a piano you can play too. Bedrooms are peaceful and pretty; 'Rose' is reached up a few steps. Breakfast is well worth waking up for: granola, compote, homemade jams, home-buzzed honey, sausages and bacon from their own pigs; sourcing local food is a passion and Maggie loves to cook, so dinner will be equally good. Set off for Constable country, charming old wool town Lavenham, antiques in Long Melford, the coast… it's a fascinating spot.

Rooms	1 twin/double; 1 double with separate bathroom: £90-£100.
Meals	Dinner, 2-3 courses with wine, £20-£25. Pubs/restaurants 2 miles.
Closed	Rarely.

Maggie Lawrence
The Old Rectory,
Kettlebaston,
Ipswich, IP7 7QD
Tel   +44 (0)1449 740400
Email   theoldrectorykettlebaston@gmail.com
Web   www.theoldrectorykettlebaston.co.uk

Entry 388   Map 10

Suffolk

The Pink Cottage

Beamed and brimming with rich colours, polished antiques, art and flowers. Tom and Fiona welcome you to their 17th-century cottage as friends, and everything is generously done. Bedrooms are in a separate wing; beds are topped with a pile of towels, a box of truffles tied with ribbon, a patchwork quilt; you'll find TVs and wine, books and an immaculate bathroom too. Breakfast is a passion and there's a huge choice – organic, garden-grown or local and all delicious: homemade jams, berries, eggs Benedict, wild mushroom omelette... out on the terrace when sunny. Three miles to medieval Lavenham; Constable country is a treat.

Minimum stay: 2 nights in high season.

Rooms	1 double: £100–£125.
	1 single sharing bath with double
	(let to same party only): £75–£100.
Meals	Pubs/restaurants 2-minute walk.
Closed	Rarely.

Fiona Carville
The Pink Cottage,
Brent Eleigh Road,
Monks Eleigh,
Lavenham, Ipswich, IP7 7JG
Tel   +44 (0)1449 744211
Email   lavenhampink@gmail.com
Web   www.lavenhampink.com

Entry 389   Map 10

Suffolk

Poplar Farm House

Only a few miles from Ipswich but down a green lane, this rambling farmhouse has a pretty, whitewashed porch and higgledy-piggledy roof. All light, elegant and spacious with wonderful flowers, art, sumptuous soft furnishings (made by Sally) and quirky sculptures; expect comfy beds, laundered linen and smart bathrooms. Sally is relaxed and friendly and will give you eggs from her handsome hens, homemade bread, veg from the garden on an artistically laid table. Play tennis, swim, steam in the sauna or book one of Sally's arts and crafts courses, then wander in the woods beyond with beautiful dogs Shale and Rune. Great value.

Rooms	2 doubles, 1 twin sharing
	2 bath/shower rooms: £70.
	Yurt – 1 double: £70.
	Singles £45.
Meals	Dinner, 3 courses, £15–£25.
	Packed lunch £7. Pub 1 mile.
Closed	Rarely.

Sally Sparrow
Poplar Farm House,
Poplar Lane,
Sproughton, Ipswich, IP8 3HL
Tel   +44 (0)1473 601211
Mobile   +44 (0)7950 767226
Email   sparrowsally@aol.com
Web   www.poplarfarmhousesuffolkbb.eu

Entry 390   Map 10

Suffolk

Holbecks House

Up the drive through parkland studded with ancient trees and step into the flagstoned hall of this 18th–century house. Find gracious rooms, soft colours, Persian rugs, antiques, hunting prints and books to browse. Perry is delightful and looks after you well; settle into big peaceful bedrooms with good beds, chocolates and long rural views. Just beyond the market town of Hadleigh, the house snoozes on a hill with acres of garden, orchard, croquet lawn, rose walk and pond. Explore Constable Country, visit the Munnings Art Museum in Dedham, Gainsborough House in Sudbury and the cathedral city of Bury St Edmunds.

Minimum stay: 2 nights at weekends.

Rooms	1 double, 1 twin/double; 1 double with separate bath: £100-£145. Singles £85-£115.
Meals	Supper £20. BYO. Pubs/restaurants 0.5 miles.
Closed	Rarely.

Perry Coysh
Holbecks House,
Holbecks Lane,
Hadleigh, Ipswich, IP7 5PE

Tel	+44 (0)1473 823211
Mobile	+44 (0)7875 167771
Email	info@holbecks.com
Web	www.holbecks.com

Entry 391   Map 10

Suffolk

The Old Rectory Country House

In a hamlet of thatched cottages by the church of St Lawrence sits a handsome rectory, quietly steeped in ancient history. Find elegant proportions, family antiques and owner Frank who asks only that you feel at home. The drawing room has an honesty bar and walking maps, the garden is a delight and you can use the pool. Feel spoiled in big smart bedrooms with pretty fabrics, smooth linen and lovely views; the Stables are charming with books, a garden suite and comfy sofas. Be lazy and have continental breakfast in your room, or rouse yourself for local sausages and bacon by a log fire in the magnificent dining room. A treat.

Please check availability and book online through owner's website.

Rooms	2 doubles, 1 twin/double: £75-£229. Child's bed/cot available. Stables – 3 doubles, extra single in 2, sharing sitting/dining room & kitchen (self-catering option available): £75-£189. Singles £65-£85 (Sunday-Thursday).
Meals	Meals £40 for guests booking the whole house only. Pub 1 mile.
Closed	Rarely.

Frank Lawrenson
The Old Rectory Country House,
Great Waldingfield,
Lavenham,
Sudbury, CO10 0TL

Tel	+44 (0)1787 372428
Email	info@theoldrectorycountryhouse.co.uk
Web	www.theoldrectorycountryhouse.co.uk

Entry 392   Map 10

Suffolk

Church House

A short hop from riverside Woodbridge and musical Snape Maltings, between a conservation churchyard and a history-rich field, is something different and unusual: a customised house of gentle colours and textures, home to an architect and a designer. From the hand-carved oak porch to the lovely wildlife garden, there's a feeling of warmth and delight. Under the eaves: two jewel-bright and comfortable bedrooms full of books and fresh flowers. In the kitchen: a big farmhouse table laid for breakfasts with homemade bread (locally ground flour from the family farm), granola and marmalade. And, a short walk away, an excellent village pub.

Minimum stay: 2 nights at weekends. Children over 6 welcome.

Rooms	1 twin/double; 1 twin/double with separate bath/shower: £80-£85. Singles £65-£70.
Meals	Pub 1 mile.
Closed	Rarely.

	Sally & Richard Pirkis
	Church House,
	Clopton,
	Woodbridge, IP13 6QB
Tel	+44 (0)1473 735350
Email	sallypirkis@gmail.com
Web	www.churchhousebandbsuffolk.co.uk

Entry 393   Map 10

Suffolk

Willow Tree Cottage

Seductively near RSPB Minsmere, medieval castles and the glorious Heritage coast. The evening sun pours into the back of this contemporary cottage with butter yellow walls; you are on the edge of the village but all is quiet with an orchard behind and a bird-filled garden for tea and cake. No sitting room, but easy chairs in your pretty bedroom face views. Caroline is a good cook and breakfast is delicious (try her kedgeree and homemade jams). Snape Maltings for music, Southwold for the famous pier, Aldeburgh with its shingle beach, boats, fun shops and good places to eat – all are close by. Holly the labrador adds to the charm.

Minimum stay: 2 nights at weekends.

Rooms	1 double: £75-£80. Singles £50-£55.
Meals	Pub/restaurant 1.5 miles.
Closed	Rarely.

	Caroline Youngson
	Willow Tree Cottage,
	3 Belvedere Close, Kelsale,
	Saxmundham, IP17 2RS
Tel	+44 (0)1728 602161
Mobile	+44 (0)7747 624139
Email	cy@willowtreecottage.me.uk
Web	www.willowtreecottage.me.uk

Entry 394   Map 10

Suffolk

Oak Tree Farm

A magnificent ancient oak tree stands guard over this 300-year old Georgian-fronted farmhouse. John and Julian love all things Art Nouveau/Art Deco and their home is filled with pieces from those periods, including china with masses of different patterns; fine books galore too, and peaceful bedrooms with smart white linen. Breakfast is a moveable feast: in the conservatory in summer, or by the fire in the dining room in winter; the bird feeders get moved too so you're kept amused while you tuck in! You can wander the five-acre garden and meadows, pretty Yoxford village has antique shops to browse, and Snape Maltings is a hop.

Minimum stay: 2 nights at weekends. Children over 5 welcome.

Rooms	3 twin/doubles: £90.
	Singles £60.
Meals	Pubs/restaurants 5-minute walk.
Closed	Rarely.

Julian Lock & John McMinn
Oak Tree Farm,
Little Street, Yoxford,
Saxmundham, IP17 3JN
Tel   +44 (0)1728 668651
Mobile   +44 (0)7969 459261
Email   oaktreefarmyoxford@gmail.com
Web   www.oaktreefarmyoxford.co.uk

Entry 395   Map 10

Suffolk

Trustans Barn

Ancient oak beams have been carefully kept in this smart Suffolk barn conversion. It's a family affair here: friendly sisters Sally and Rosie give you contemporary bedrooms with artistic touches, king-sized beds, sleek bathrooms and drench showers. Breakfast is served at two scrubbed pine tables in the airy slate-floored breakfast room; a big blackboard lists tasty choices – everything from home-laid eggs and local sausages to home-grown tomatoes and muesli. Masses to do nearby: Snape Maltings music, wonderful old churches, summer festivals, the Heritage Coast… A great place for a peaceful holiday with a group of friends.

Minimum stay: 2 nights in high season.

Rooms	5 doubles, 1 twin/double: £95–£120.
Meals	Pubs less than a mile away.
Closed	Christmas.

Sally Prime
Trustans Barn,
Westleton Road,
Darsham,
Saxmundham, IP17 3BP
Tel   +44 (0)1728 668684
Email   sallyandrosie@trustansbarn.co.uk
Web   www.trustansbarn.co.uk

Entry 396   Map 10

Suffolk

Church Farmhouse

This Elizabethan farmhouse is by the ancient thatched church in a little hamlet close to Southwold. Minsmere RSPB bird sanctuary, Snape Maltings and the coast are nearby for lovely days out. Sarah, characterful, well-travelled and entertaining, is also an excellent cook, so breakfast will be a treat with bowls of fruit, Suffolk bacon and free-range eggs; occasional candle-lit dinners are worth staying in for, too. Bedrooms have supremely comfy beds well-dressed in pure cotton. Although there is no sitting room, you can enjoy tea and cake and linger in the garden, there are flowers in every room and books galore.

Children over 12 welcome.

Rooms	1 double, 1 twin/double; 1 double with separate bath: £95–£110. Singles £65–£80.
Meals	Dinner £28. Pubs/restaurants within 4 miles.
Closed	Christmas.

Sarah Lentaigne
Church Farmhouse,
Uggeshall, Southwold, NR34 8BD

Tel	+44 (0)1502 578532
Mobile	+44 (0)7748 801418
Email	sarahlentaigne@btinternet.com
Web	www.churchfarmhousesuffolk.co.uk

Entry 397   Map 10

Suffolk

Camomile Cottage

Aly and Tim's 16th-century longhouse is a feast of old beams, kilims, antiques and art. They give you homemade cake on arrival; relax in the garden or the guest lounge, kick off your shoes and enjoy a glass of wine by the log fire. Beamed bedrooms have period furnishings, goose down duvets, luxury linen, flowers and handmade chocolates; bathrooms have Molton Brown toiletries. Aly will also bring you tea in bed! Breakfast is in the garden room: cornbread toast, eggs from the hens, croissants and all sorts of cooked choices. Eye is an attractive old market town; Southwold, Bury St Edmunds and Snape Maltings are all close.

Minimum stay: 2 nights at weekends.

Rooms	2 doubles: £99–£110. Singles £85.
Meals	Pubs/restaurants 0.5 miles.
Closed	Rarely.

Aly Kahane
Camomile Cottage,
Brome Avenue,
Eye, IP23 7HW

Tel	+44 (0)1379 873528
Email	aly@camomilecottage.co.uk
Web	www.camomilecottage.co.uk

Entry 398   Map 10

Suffolk

Bulls Hall

Half a mile from the village of Occold – a B&B of character and peace. The house is 16th-century and listed, the lovely grounds – lawns, meadow, summerhouse and ponds – teem with wildlife. Warm, friendly Angela welcomes you to a cosy, traditional, unspoiled home: low doorways, a big inglenook, a deep new mattress on a vintage iron bed, books, guides, games and delightfully uneven brick floors. There's a long parquet'd double off the dining room, a staircase to a lofty family suite, and a beautiful breakfast to wake up to: Suffolk black bacon, homemade jams, eggs from the hens. Visit the Broads, stroll to the pub.

Minimum stay: 2 nights on bank holidays.

Rooms	1 double: £80–£90. 1 suite for 4 with separate bath: £170–£190. Singles £80.
Meals	Pub/restaurant 0.5 miles.
Closed	Rarely.

Angela Hall
Bulls Hall,
Bulls Hall Road,
Occold,
Eye, IP23 7PH
Tel   +44 (0)1379 678683
Email   angela.hall53@gmail.com

Entry 399   Map 10

Surrey

Swallow Barn

A converted squash court, coach house and stables, once belonging to next-door's manor, have become a home of old-fashioned charm. Full of family memories, and run very well by Joan, this B&B is excellently placed for Windsor, Wisley, Brooklands and Hampton Court; close to both airports too. Lovely trees in the garden, fields and woods beyond, a paddock and a swimming pool... total tranquillity, and you can walk to the pub. None of the bedrooms is huge but the beds are firm, the garden views are pretty and the downstairs double has its own sitting room. Breakfasts are both generous and scrumptious.

Children over 8 welcome.

Rooms	1 double with sitting room; 1 twin with separate shower: £90–£100. Apple Store – 1 twin: £90–£100. Singles £55.
Meals	Pub/restaurant 0.75 miles.
Closed	Rarely.

Joan Carey
Swallow Barn,
Milford Green, Chobham,
Woking, GU24 8AU
Tel   +44 (0)1276 856030
Mobile   +44 (0)7768 972904
Email   info@swallow-barn.co.uk
Web   www.swallow-barn.co.uk

Entry 400   Map 4

Surrey

Broadway Barn

If you love art, gardening and good food, you'll love Mindi and her brilliant conversion of a pretty brick Regency barn on Ripley High Street. You sleep in comfortable bedrooms styled with creativity: a painting from a Parisian laundrette, ceramic lamps with bird motifs, leather chests as tables. You relax in a long, light, mirrored conservatory with glazed terrace doors, and are free to wander around the newly planted walled garden. You breakfast deliciously on local eggs and home-baked treats... Minutes from Guildford and Wisley's RHS garden, the village has a Michelin-starred restaurant, cafés and pubs.

Surrey

South Lodge

The beautiful Surrey Hills surround this smart home overlooking the village green. Paul and Joanna's house gets the sun all day and has a country chic feel. They look after you well, and give you tea and cake on arrival, three cosy, pretty bedrooms in the eaves and locally sourced and homemade treats at breakfast. Joanna's catering business is run from the house so there are always people coming and going – this is a fun place to stay with a lovely friendly feel. Hop next door for a tasty supper at The Grumpy Mole (popular so you need to book). Near Dorking, and handy for Gatwick, too – it's a 15-minute drive.

Rooms	4 doubles: £110. Singles £110.
Meals	Restaurant next door.
Closed	Rarely.

Rooms	2 doubles; 1 twin with separate bath: £100-£115. Singles £95.
Meals	Evening meal with wine from £35. Pub next door.
Closed	Christmas.

Mindi McLean
Broadway Barn,
High Street, Ripley,
Woking, GU23 6AQ

Tel	+44 (0)1483 223200
Email	mindi@broadwaybarn.com
Web	www.broadwaybarn.com

Joanna Rowlands
South Lodge,
Brockham Green, Brockham,
Betchworth, RH3 7JS

Tel	+44 (0)1737 843883
Email	bookings@brockhambandb.com
Web	www.brockhambandb.com

Surrey

Surrey

Blackbrook House

Arriving at this elegant Victorian home surrounded by immaculate lawn, woodland, paddocks and a swing hanging from a huge conifer, you immediately want to explore. Emma and Rae are easy-going, and want you to unwind and feel at home. Bedrooms are spacious and smart with floral fabrics, deep pocket sprung mattresses and good linen; bathrooms are tip-top. Breakfast is a delicious spread: free-range eggs from next door, local bacon and sausages, freshly squeezed apple juice from the orchard. Admire the rose garden, enjoy a game of tennis, head out into the Surrey Hills. Return to a snug sitting room with TV and lots of books. Bliss.

The Dovecote at Greenaway

An enchanting cottage in an idyllic corner of Chiddingfold. People return time and again – for the house (1545), the garden blooming with flowers, vegetables, hens and dovecote, the glowing interiors, and Sheila and John. The sitting room is inviting with rich colours, flowers, beams and a roaring log fire; the turning oak staircase leads to bedrooms that are cosy and sumptuous at the same time, and bathrooms with deep roll top tubs and a pretty armchair. Breakfast is a spread with homemade bread and home-grown tomatoes. Gorgeous countryside, walks on the Greensand Way... who would guess London and the airports were so close?

Rooms	1 double: £95–£100.
	1 suite for 2: £105–£115.
	Singles from £60.
Meals	Pub 0.5 miles.
Closed	Christmas & New Year.

Rooms	1 double; 1 double, 1 twin sharing
	bath: £100–£125.
	Singles £100.
Meals	Pubs 300 yds.
Closed	Rarely.

	Emma & Rae Burdon
	Blackbrook House,
	Blackbrook, Dorking, RH5 4DS
Tel	+44 (0)1306 888898
Mobile	+44 (0)7880 723512
Email	blackbrookbb@btinternet.com
Web	www.surreybandb.co.uk

	Sheila & John Marsh
	The Dovecote at Greenaway,
	Pickhurst Road,
	Chiddingfold, GU8 4TS
Tel	+44 (0)1428 682920
Email	info@bedandbreakfastchiddingfold.co.uk
Web	www.bedandbreakfastchiddingfold.co.uk

Entry 403   Map 4

Entry 404   Map 4

Surrey

The Venison House

Drive through Surrey parkland grazed by rare breed cattle to reach this bijou hideaway. The circular cottage topped with a terracotta turret is quite unlike any other B&B you're likely to visit. It's set into a corner of Alison's lovely walled garden, with oval windows overlooking the park. Step through the sage green door into a country-chic bedroom with monogrammed pillows and crisp linen. Along a corridor leading to the sparkling shower room, there's a double-fronted cupboard concealing an immaculate kitchen. Alison provides homemade bread, marmalade, bacon, tomatoes and eggs, so guests can make a delicious, DIY breakfast in bed.

Rooms	1 double with separate bathroom & kitchenette: £120–£150.
Meals	Pubs/restaurants 2 miles.
Closed	Rarely.

	Alison Bird
	The Venison House,
	Garden Cottage, Park Hatch,
	Loxhill, Godalming, GU8 4BL
Tel	+44 (0)1483 200410
Mobile	+44 (0)7768 745765
Email	agmbird@gmail.com

Entry 405   Map 4

Sussex

Lordington House

Croquet on the lawn in summer, big log fires and woolly jumpers in winter, brilliant food all year round. On a sunny slope of the Ems Valley, life ticks by peacefully as it has always done... The house is vast and impressive, a lime avenue links the much-loved garden with the AONB beyond and friendly guard dog Shep looks on. The 17th-century staircase is a glory, the décor is engagingly old-fashioned: Edwardian beds with firm mattresses and floral covers, carpeted Sixties-style bathrooms, toile wallpaper on wardrobe doors. A privilege to stay in a house of this age and character!

Pets by arrangement.

Rooms	1 double; 1 twin/double with separate bath/shower; 1 double sharing bath/shower with single: £115–£145. 1 single sharing bath/shower with double: £57–£72.
Meals	Packed lunch from £6. Pub 1 mile.
Closed	Rarely.

	Mr & Mrs Hamilton
	Lordington House,
	Lordington,
	Chichester, PO18 9DX
Tel	+44 (0)1243 375862
Email	hamiltonjanda@btinternet.com

Entry 406   Map 4

Sussex

Crows Hall Farm

The Renwicks are tremendous hosts. Their wonderful flagstone-halled farmhouse in the South Downs National Park is great for walking and cycling and close to Goodwood. Amanda's style is simple and cottagey, but never twee. She's gone for moss green walls, open brickwork and a classically dressed, big handmade bed in the main room; the second room has fantastic views of the walled garden and beyond. In between, the beamed bathroom is fab and fun, with flamingos, freestanding bath and shower (all yours, or shared with your own party). Breakfasts are local, flexible feasts on the terrace or in the quirky rustic kitchen. Marvellous!

Rooms are reached by their own staircase with private access.

Rooms	2 doubles sharing separate bathroom (let to same party only): £110–£150.
Meals	Pubs 2.5 miles.
Closed	Rarely.

	Amanda Renwick
	Crows Hall Farm,
	Chilgrove Road,
	Lavant,
	Chichester, PO18 9HP
Mobile	+44 (0)7801 296192
Email	amanda@crowshall.com

Entry 407   Map 4

Sussex

Seabeach House

Sitting sleepily behind its white gate this pretty stone cottage is surrounded by the Sussex Downs National Park. Throughout Francesca's friendly home her love of folk art, rich oils, antiques and hand-painted pieces adds zest. Comfy cottagey bedrooms are on the ground floor; wake to local sausages and eggs, garden tomatoes, homemade jams with croissants and brioche. Francesca loves cooking, and dinner, with home-grown veg, is good too. Explore garden and fields, admire wide views from a pretty terrace and chat to Popeye the dog. There's art, theatre and sailing in Chichester, the castle in Arundel, and events galore at Goodwood.

Rooms	Annexe: 1 double, 1 twin sharing bath (let to same party only): £95–£150.
Meals	Dinner, 3 courses, £25. BYO. Pub 1 mile.
Closed	Rarely.

	Francesca Emmet
	Seabeach House,
	Selhurst Park, Halnaker,
	Chichester, PO18 0LX
Tel	+44 (0)1243 537944
Email	francescaemmet@hotmail.co.uk
Web	www.bandbatseabeachhouse.co.uk

Entry 408   Map 4

Sussex

The Old Manor House

Wild flowers in jugs, old wooden floors and beams, pretty cottagey curtains: Judy's manor house near Chichester has bags of character and she is friendly and kind. Originally constructed round a big central fireplace, the rooms are all refreshingly simple allowing features to shine. Sunny bedrooms up steep stairs have seagrass flooring, limed furniture, gentle colours and warm bathrooms. Enjoy delicious breakfasts by the wood-burner in the dining room: fresh fruit smoothies and an organic full English. Great for horse racing, castle visiting, sailing, theatre and festivals; fantastic walks on the South Downs, too. Lovely.

Rooms	2 doubles: £95.
Meals	Pub/restaurant 500 yds.
Closed	Christmas.

Judy Wolstenholme
The Old Manor House,
Westergate Street, Westergate,
Chichester, PO20 3QZ

Tel	+44 (0)1243 544489
Email	judy@veryoldmanorhouse.com
Web	www.veryoldmanorhouse.com

Entry 409   Map 4

Sussex

Rother Cottage

Katherine is engaging and creative and her house has an informal, lived-in feel. Find an eclectic mix of furniture, vases overflowing with garden flowers, beams galore, a winter wood fire and a sunny open-plan dining/sitting room where you have breakfast. Up the steep, crooked stair to your own part of the house: a simple bedroom with a hand-sewn Indian throw on a comfy bed; the bathroom is basic and back downstairs. The colourful garden has views over the South Downs. Goodwood racecourse is close, Glyndebourne an hour; it's a fabulous area for rambling, cycling, visiting Sussex villages, and there are heaps of pubs for supper.

Minimum stay: 2 nights.

Rooms	1 double with separate bath: £85.
	1 single: £70.
Meals	Pubs/restaurants 3 miles.
Closed	Christmas, New Year & Easter.

Katherine Wyld
Rother Cottage,
245 Ambersham Green,
Midhurst, GU29 0BX

Tel	+44 (0)1798 861365
Mobile	+44 (0)7984 427762
Email	cusackcouture@yahoo.co.uk

Entry 410   Map 4

Sussex

Weston House

Come for Goodwood races and seasonal festivals galore – summer, music and literary. Return to comfortable bedrooms with armchairs, Portmeirion china and spotless en suite bathrooms; the sunny room at the back looks out over pretty garden, fields and the South Downs beyond (you're on the main road but it's surprisingly quiet). Cherry gives you breakfast at a long polished table by the fire in the lovely beamed dining room, or out on the stone terrace if it's summery. You're close to the theatre and sailing in Chichester and the castle in Arundel, Petworth is teeming with antique shops, and you can walk to the pub for a good supper.

Rooms	2 twin/doubles: £90–£100.
Meals	Pubs/restaurants 2-minute walk.
Closed	Christmas & New Year.

Cherry Corben
Weston House,
Tillington,
Petworth, GU28 0RA
Tel   +44 (0)1798 344556
Email   westonhousebookings@btinternet.com
Web   www.westonhousetillington.co.uk

Entry 411   Map 4

Sussex

The Hyde Granary

A 1,000-acre estate, where roe deer roam and the odd buzzard circles above. The granary stands at the end of a one-mile drive, alongside a coach house and clock tower, in the shadow of the big house. Airy interiors are just the ticket: timber frames, exposed walls, beams in the dining room and a drying room for walkers. Bedrooms are uncluttered and have a country feel: one has a claw-foot bath, the other is in the eaves. Margot, a homeopath, can realign your back after a long journey, and does super breakfasts. There's a small garden for sundowners in summer, you can walk to the village and Gatwick is close.

Rooms	1 double; 1 double with separate bath/shower: £90. Singles £65. Extra bed/sofabed available £15–£30 per person per night.
Meals	Pub 1.7 miles.
Closed	Christmas & New Year.

Margot Barton
The Hyde Granary,
The Hyde, London Road, Handcross,
Haywards Heath, RH17 6EZ
Tel   +44 (0)1444 401930
Email   margot@thehydegranary.com
Web   www.thehydegranary.com

Entry 412   Map 4

Sussex

The Jointure Studios

A thriving village with an arty heritage. In the centre is your apartment above a lovely big gallery/hall – with piano and wood-burning stove. Find a happy mix of antique and new, a quiet comfy bedroom with leafy views and a cosy sitting room with a kitchen area. Shirley leaves you homemade cakes and breakfast things, and each morning brings over a tray of fruits, croissants, local artisan bread and eggs for you to cook how you wish. The Ditchling Museum of Art + Craft is inspiring, South Downs National Park is your stomping ground, Brighton and Glyndebourne are close. Return and rustle up supper, or stroll down the road to a good pub.

Minimum stay: 2 nights at weekends.

Rooms	1 twin/double (apartment with sitting room and kitchen): £100-£120. Singles £100.
Meals	Pubs/restaurants 1-minute walk.
Closed	Rarely.

Shirley Crowther
The Jointure Studios,
11 South Street,
Ditchling, BN6 8UQ

Tel   +44 (0)1273 841244
Email   thejointurestudios@gmail.com
Web   www.jointurestudiosbandb.co.uk

Entry 413   Map 4

Sussex

Old Whyly

Breakfast in a light-filled, chinoiserie dining room – there's an effortless elegance to this manor house, once home to one of King Charles's Cavaliers. Bedrooms are atmospheric, one in French style. The treats continue outside with a beautiful flower garden annually replenished with 5,000 tulips, a lake and orchard, a swimming pool and a tennis court – fabulous. Dine under the pergola in summer: food is a passion and Sarah's menus are adventurous with a modern slant. Glyndebourne is close so make a party of it and take a divine 'pink' hamper, with blankets or a table and chairs included. Sheer bliss.

Rooms	2 twin/doubles; 1 double with separate shower, 1 twin/double with separate bath: £98-£145. Singles by arrangement.
Meals	Dinner, 3 courses, £35. Hampers £38. Pub/restaurant 0.5 miles.
Closed	Rarely.

Sarah Burgoyne
Old Whyly,
London Road,
East Hoathly, BN8 6EL

Tel   +44 (0)1825 840216
Email   stay@oldwhyly.co.uk
Web   www.oldwhyly.co.uk

Entry 414   Map 5

Sussex

The Flint Barns

An extraordinarily beautiful setting in the South Downs with views all the way to the sea... this pioneering English vineyard (take a tour and discover the story) is an unusual place to stay. Find huge style with a homely feel thanks to cheery Ade. More poshtel than hostel, there are chunky doors, reclaimed oak, bedrooms with luxurious mattresses and small sparkling shower rooms. A fabulous communal sitting room has a roaring wood-burner and books; breakfast (and dinner if you want) is at long tables in the lofty dining room: lovingly cooked and local. Spill onto the courtyard for barbecues, walk straight onto the South Downs Way.

Minimum stay: 2 nights.

Rooms	3 doubles: £110. 1 family room for 3: £140-£180. 1 bunk room for 2, 1 bunk room for 5 (dorm room with 5 singles), 1 bunk room for 4, 3 bunk rooms for 8 (en suite plus extra shower rooms): £80-£280.
Meals	Dinner, 2 courses, £20. Pubs 2-3 miles.
Closed	During picking & pruning season: mid-January to mid-February; end of September to end of October.

Adrian Lamb
The Flint Barns,
Rathfinny Wine Estate, Alfriston,
Polegate, BN26 5TU

Tel	+44 (0)1323 874030
Email	flintbarns@rathfinnyestate.com
Web	www.flintbarns.com

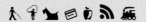

Entry 415   Map 5

Sussex

Ocklynge Manor

On top of a peaceful hill, a short stroll from Eastbourne, find tip-top B&B in an 18th-century house with an interesting history – ask Wendy! Now it is her home, and you will be treated to home-baked bread, delicious tea time cakes and scrummy jams – on fine days you can take it outside. Creamy carpeted, bright and sunny bedrooms, all with views over the lovely walled garden, create a mood of relaxed indulgence and are full of thoughtful touches: dressing gowns, DVDs, your own fridge. Breakfasts are superb: this is a very spoiling, nurturing place.

Please see owner's website for availability.

Rooms	1 twin; 1 double with separate shower: £100-£120. 1 suite for 3: £120-£130. Singles £60-£110.
Meals	Pub 5-minute walk.
Closed	Rarely.

Wendy Dugdill
Ocklynge Manor,
Mill Road, Eastbourne, BN21 2PG

Tel	+44 (0)1323 734121
Mobile	+44 (0)7979 627172
Email	ocklyngemanor@hotmail.com
Web	www.ocklyngemanor.co.uk/availability_22.html

Entry 416   Map 5

Sussex

Netherwood Lodge

The scent of fresh flowers and a smattering of chintz over calm uncluttered interiors will please you. Engaging Margaret is a mine of local knowledge and offers you peaceful, cosy, ground-floor bedrooms beautifully dressed with wool carpets, designer interlined curtains, luxurious bed linens and gloriously comfortable beds. Enjoy an award-winning breakfast overlooking the garden (it's stunning); all is homemade or locally sourced. Then set off to discover this beautiful corner of East Sussex – ideal for walking, visiting National Trust houses and gardens and, of course, Glyndebourne.

Sussex

Thimbles

Enter the characterful hallway of this higgledy-piggledy house and fall under the spell of its charm. Imagine family antiques, pictures, plates, just-picked flowers and duvets as soft as a cloud: a timeless elegance, a fresh country style. Feast your eyes on the garden, six gentle acres that rise to fantastic views… a hammock, 89 varieties of roses, humming honey bees, a lake with an island (for barbecues!), a long lazy swing. Breakfasts and suppers are a dream: eggs from the hens, bacon from the pigs, jams from a jewel of a kitchen garden. Vicki, her family and Lottie the Irish terrier are the icing on the cake.

Rooms	1 twin; 1 double with separate bath: £100-£125. Singles from £80.	Rooms	1 suite for 2: £90. 1 single sharing bathroom with family (extra bed available): £65. Singles £65. Extra bed/sofabed available £30 per person per night.
Meals	Pub/restaurant 0.75 miles.	Meals	Dinner, 1-3 courses, £12.50-£21.50. Lunch £12.50. Pub 1 mile.
Closed	Rarely.	Closed	Rarely.

	Margaret Clarke		**Vicki Wood**
	Netherwood Lodge,		Thimbles,
	Muddles Green,		New Pond Hill, Cross in Hand,
	Chiddingly, Lewes, BN8 6HS		Heathfield, TN21 0NB
Tel	+44 (0)1825 872512	Tel	+44 (0)1435 860745
Email	netherwoodlodge@hotmail.com	Mobile	+44 (0)7960 588447
Web	www.netherwoodlodge.co.uk	Email	vicki.simonwood@btinternet.com
		Web	www.thimblesbedandbreakfast.co.uk

Entry 417   Map 5

Entry 418   Map 5

Sussex

King John's Lodge

Deep in the High Weald, down a maze of country lanes, is an enchanting 1650s house in eight acres of heaven: Jill's pride and joy. Inside: oak beams, stone fireplaces, big sofas, and a Jacobean dining room with leaded glass windows, fine setting for a perfect English breakfast. Wing chairs, floral fabrics, dressers with china bowls: the country-house feel extends to the comfortable, carpeted bedrooms. Discover Sissinghurst, Great Dixter, Rye... return to sweeping lawns, wild gardens, ancient apple trees, a woodland walk (spot Titania and Oberon) and a delightful nursery and tea room run by Jill's son.

Minimum stay: 2 nights at weekends & in high season. Broadband unreliable: please ring if you don't get a reply straightaway.

Rooms	2 doubles, 1 twin: £95–£105.
	1 family room for 3: £130–£150
	Singles from £75.
Meals	Dinner, 3 courses, £30 (minimum 4).
	Pubs/restaurants 2.5 miles.
Closed	Rarely.

Jill Cunningham
King John's Lodge,
Sheepstreet Lane,
Etchingham, TN19 7AZ
Tel   +44 (0)1580 819232
Email   kingjohnslodge@aol.com
Web   www.kingjohnslodge.com

Entry 419   Map 5

Sussex

Appletree Cottage

An enviable position facing south for this old hung-tile farmer's house, covered in roses, jasmine and wisteria; views are over farmland towards the coast at Fairlight Glen. Jane will treat you to tea and cake when you arrive – either before a warming fire in the drawing room, or in the garden in summer. Bedrooms are sunny, spacious, quiet and traditional, with gorgeous garden views. Breakfast well on juice from their own apples, homemade jams and marmalade, local bacon and sausages. Perfect for walkers with a footpath at the front gate; birdwatchers will be happy too, and you are near the steam railway at Bodiam.

Minimum stay: 2 nights at weekends May-Sept. Children over 8 welcome.

Rooms	1 twin/double; 2 doubles, sharing
	bath (let to same party only):
	£85–£90.
	1 single with separate bath: £55–£60.
Meals	Pub/restaurant 0.5 miles.
Closed	Rarely.

Jane & Hugh Willing
Appletree Cottage,
Beacon Lane, Staplecross,
Robertsbridge, TN32 5QP
Tel   +44 (0)1580 831724
Mobile   +44 (0)7914 658861
Email   appletree.cottage@hotmail.co.uk
Web   www.appletreecottage.co

Entry 420   Map 5

The Cloudesley

One mile from the sea, a remarkable house full of beautiful things. Shahriar – photographer, holistic therapist, Chelsea gold-medal winner – has created an artistic bolthole: books, African masks, an honesty bar, chic bedrooms and two sitting rooms that double as art galleries. You are looked after with great kindness. Shahriar has a couple of treatment rooms where, in cahoots with local therapists, he offers massage, shiatsu and reiki. You breakfast on exotic fruits, Armagnac omelettes, or the full cooked works; on a bamboo terrace in summer. Don't miss Derek Jarman's cottage at Dungeness or St Clement's for great food.

Minimum stay: 2 nights at weekends. Children over 6 welcome. Whole house available.

Swan House

Effortless style drifts through the beamed rooms of this boutiquey B&B in a 1490s bakery, from a roaring inglenook fireplace to an honesty bar in a mock bookcase – all run by relaxed creative hosts Brendan and Lionel. Bedrooms hold surprises: Elizabethan frescoes, an old pulley for bags of flour, doors with trompe-l'œil, seashell mosaics and handmade soaps. Step out into lively Old Hastings, wander down to see fishing boats tucked in for the night or find an antiques bargain. Seagulls herald the new day: pick a morning paper; breakfast like kings on organic croissants and local kippers (dinners also on request). Unique.

Minimum stay: 2 nights at weekends.

Rooms	3 doubles, 2 twin/doubles: £80–£140. Extra bed £25.
Meals	Pubs/restaurants 5-minute drive.
Closed	Rarely.

Rooms	3 doubles: £120–£150. 1 suite for 4: £115–£145
Meals	Restaurants 2-minute walk.
Closed	Christmas.

	Shahriar Mazandi
	The Cloudesley,
	7 Cloudesley Road,
	St Leonards-on-Sea, TN37 6JN
Mobile	+44 (0)7507 000148
Email	s.mazandi@gmail.com
Web	www.thecloudesley.co.uk

	Brendan McDonagh
	Swan House,
	1 Hill Street,
	Hastings, TN34 3HU
Tel	+44 (0)1424 430014
Email	res@swanhousehastings.co.uk
Web	www.swanhousehastings.co.uk

Warwickshire

Little Bridge Cottage

Your own snug contemporary bolthole. The open-plan living space has a washed oak floor, patchwork armchair, doors to a patio, and a nifty kitchen area. Hop upstairs to a sunny bedroom; shower rooms (wet room down, en suite up) are smart. Karen gives you home-baked cookies, and a breakfast of homemade granola, smoked salmon or full English – brought through from the main house. Walk, cycle, have yoga arranged; Birmingham is a few minutes by train. A Sami hut adds to the fun: book it as an extra sitting room, for children to sleep in, and to cook supper over the fire – Karen brings a basket of salad, Aga potatoes and marinated steaks… wonderful!

Hut where you can cook your own supper; space for 2 children to sleep.

Rooms	1 triple with single sofabed: £125. Extra bed/sofabed available £25 per person per night.
Meals	Hut supper £25 (DIY). Pubs/restaurants 3 miles.
Closed	Occasionally & Christmas.

	Karen Morris
	Little Bridge Cottage,
	Lea Marston,
	Sutton Coldfield, B76 0BN
Tel	+44 (0)1675 470020
Mobile	+44 (0)7411 433791
Email	littlebridgecottage@gmail.com
Web	www.littlebridgecottage.co.uk

Entry 423   Map 8

Warwickshire

Park Farm House

Fronted by a circular drive, the warm red-brick farmhouse is listed and old – it dates from 1655. Linda is friendly and welcoming, a genuine B&B pro, giving you an immaculate guest sitting room filled with pretty family pieces. The bedrooms sport comfortable mattresses, mahogany or brass beds, blankets on request, bathrobes, flowers and magazines; bathrooms are traditional but spotless. A haven of rest from the motorway (morning hum only) this is in the heart of a working farm yet hugely convenient for Birmingham, Warwick, Stratford and Coventry. You may get their own beef at dinner and the vegetables are home-grown.

Rooms	1 double, 1 twin: £79-£82. Singles from £48.
Meals	Dinner, 3 courses, from £25. Supper £19. Pub/restaurant 1.5 miles.
Closed	Rarely.

	Linda Grindal
	Park Farm House,
	Spring Road,
	Barnacle, Shilton,
	Coventry, CV7 9LG
Tel	+44 (0)2476 612628
Web	www.parkfarmguesthouse.co.uk

Entry 424   Map 8

Warwickshire

Shrewley Pools Farm

A charming, eccentric home and fabulous for families, with space to play and animals to see: sheep, bantams and pigs. A fragrant, romantic garden with a blossoming orchard and a fascinating house (1640), all low ceilings, aged floors and steep stairs. Timbered passages lead to large, pretty, sunny bedrooms (all with electric blankets) with leaded windows and polished wooden floors and a family room with everything needed for a baby. In a farmhouse dining room Cathy serves sausages, bacon, and eggs from the farm, can do gluten-free breakfasts and is happy to do teas for children. Buy a day ticket and fish in the lake.

Rooms	1 twin: £65.
	1 family room for 4 (cot available): £110.
	Singles £55–£65.
	Extra bed/sofabed available £20–£30
	per person per night.
Meals	Packed lunch £5. Child's high tea £5.
	Pub/restaurant 1.5 miles.
Closed	Christmas.

	Cathy Dodd
	Shrewley Pools Farm,
	Five Ways Road, Haseley,
	Warwick, CV35 7HB
Tel	+44 (0)1926 484315
Mobile	+44 (0)7818 280681
Email	cathydodd@hotmail.co.uk
Web	www.shrewleypoolsfarm.co.uk

Entry 425   Map 8

Warwickshire

Austons Down

A fine modern country house with splendid views of the rural Vale of Arden. Your hosts are generous and chatty and look after you well. Their comfortable and relaxed family home has an elegant, light-filled sitting room complete with antiques, fabulous marquetry and open fire; bedrooms are fresh and traditional, bathrooms immaculate. Breakfast on homemade bread, compotes, a continental spread or full English. Admire Jacob sheep on the farm, relax in the terraced gardens. Plenty to visit nearby too: Warwick Castle, Stratford, National Trust properties, classic car museums… and the Monarch's Way is on the doorstep.

Minimum stay: 2 nights at weekends.

Rooms	1 double, 2 twin/doubles: £90–£160.
	Singles £60–£140.
	Extra bed/sofabed available £15–£25
	per person per night.
Meals	Pubs/restaurants 5-minute drive.
Closed	Rarely.

	Lucy Horner
	Austons Down,
	Saddlebow Lane,
	Claverdon, CV35 8PQ
Tel	+44 (0)1926 842068
Mobile	+44 (0)7767 657352
Email	lmh@austonsdown.com
Web	www.austonsdown.com

Entry 426   Map 8

Warwickshire

Marston House

A generous feel pervades this lovely family home; Kim's big friendly kitchen is the hub of the house. She and John are easy-going and kind and there's no standing on ceremony. Feel welcomed with tea on arrival, delicious breakfasts, oodles of interesting facts about what to do in the area. The house, with solar electricity, is big and sunny; old rugs cover parquet floors, soft sofas tumble with cushions, sash windows look onto the smart garden packed with birds and borders. Bedrooms are roomy, traditional and supremely comfortable. A special, peaceful place with a big heart, great walks from the door and Silverstone a short hop.

Rooms	1 twin/double with separate bath; 1 twin/double with separate shower: £95-£110. Singles £80.
Meals	Supper, 3 courses from £30. Dinner £35 (min. 4). Pub 5-minute walk.
Closed	Rarely.

Kim & John Mahon
Marston House,
Byfield Road, Priors Marston,
Southam, CV47 7RP

Tel	+44 (0)1327 260297
Mobile	+44 (0)7813 831028
Email	kim@mahonand.co.uk
Web	www.ivabestbandb.co.uk

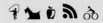

Entry 427   Map 8

Warwickshire

Sequoia House

A riverside stroll along the old tramway path brings you to the centre of Stratford. Step into the handsome hallway of this impeccable Victorian house to find high ceilings, deep bays, generous landings and a homely sitting room. The Evanses downsized from the hotel they used to run here, and are happy to treat just a few guests: trouser presses (yes!) and piles of towels mingle with fine old furniture in immaculate bedrooms; two have Swan Theatre views. Hotel touches, a lovely warm welcome, Jean's cake on arrival and homemade preserves at breakfast. Park off road – or leave the car at home.

Rooms	4 doubles: £125. Singles £85.
Meals	Pub/restaurant 100 yds.
Closed	Christmas & New Year.

Jean & Philip Evans
Sequoia House,
51 Shipston Road,
Stratford-upon-Avon, CV37 7LN

Tel	+44 (0)1789 268852
Mobile	+44 (0)7833 727914
Email	info@sequoia-house.co.uk
Web	www.sequoia-house.co.uk

Entry 428   Map 8

Cross o' th' Hill Farm

Stratford is a 12-minute walk by footpath across a field, and from the veranda you can see the church where Shakespeare is buried. The farm predates medieval Stratford with later additions to the house in 1860, though it has an earlier Georgian feel. All is chic, spacious and full of light with deco chandeliers, floor to ceiling sash windows, large uncluttered bedrooms and contemporary bathrooms. Wake to bird song, play the baby grand piano, enjoy croquet on the lawn and picnic in the gardens and orchards. Decima grew up here; she and David are charming hosts and passionate about art and architecture.

Minimum stay: 2 nights at weekends.

Grove Farm

Down quiet lanes to the house that Charlie was born in — her young family are the third generation to live here. Bright bedrooms up in the eaves have oak beams, gingham armchairs and comfy beds; small bathrooms, recently revamped. Hop down for homelaid eggs, homemade bread, sausages, bacon and black pudding from down the road — outside when the sun shines, or by the fire in the dining room. Children will love it: dogs, rabbits, hens all happy to have a pat, a swing, log cabin, dens and Flappy the cockerel too. Roses and gangs of cheerful hollyhocks dot the gardens, you can roam the woodland and owls hoot you to sleep. Charming.

Rooms	2 doubles; 1 double with separate bath/shower: £110. Singles £70.
Meals	Pubs/restaurants 15-minute walk.
Closed	Christmas & New Year.

Rooms	1 double: £85-£90. 1 family room for 4: £100-£160. Singles £50.
Meals	Pubs/restaurants 1.5 miles.
Closed	Rarely.

	Decima Noble
	Cross o' th' Hill Farm,
	Clifford Lane,
	Stratford-upon-Avon, CV37 8HP
Tel	+44 (0)1789 204738
Mobile	+44 (0)7973 971067
Email	decimanoble@hotmail.com
Web	www.cross-o-th-hill-farm.com

	Charlie Coldicott
	Grove Farm,
	Stratford Road,
	Ettington,
	Stratford-upon-Avon, CV37 7NX
Mobile	+44 (0)7774 776682
Email	grovefarmbb@btconnect.com

Warwickshire

Stamford Hall

Soft hills and lines of poplars bring you to the high, pretty red-brick Georgian house with a smart hornbeam hedge. James, whose art decorates the walls, and Alice look after you impeccably but without fuss. You have a generous sitting room overlooking the garden, with gleaming furniture, early estate and garden etchings, and pastel blue sofas. Peaceful bedrooms are on the second floor and both have charm: soft wool tartan rugs on comfy beds, calming colours, attractive fabrics, restful outlooks. Wake to delicious breakfast and Alice's full English; walk it off in open countryside or head for Stratford.

Rooms	1 double, 1 twin: £85. Singles £60.
Meals	Pub 1 mile.
Closed	Christmas & occasionally.

James & Alice Kerr
Stamford Hall,
Fosse Way, Ettington,
Stratford-upon-Avon, CV37 7PA

Tel   +44 (0)1789 740239
Email   stamfordhall@gmail.com
Web   www.stamfordhall.co.uk

Entry 431   Map 8

Warwickshire

Salford Farm House

Beautiful within, handsome without. Thanks to subtle colours, oak beams and lovely old pieces, Jane has achieved a seductive combination of comfort and style. A flagstoned hallway and an old rocking horse, ticking clocks, beeswax, fresh flowers: this house is well-loved. Jane was a ballet dancer, green-fingered Richard is MD of nearby Hillers, an award-winning fruit farm, café and shop – you may expect meat and game from the Ragley Estate and delicious fruits in season. Bedrooms have a soft, warm elegance and flat-screen TVs, bathrooms are spotless and welcoming, views are to garden or fields. Wholly delightful.

Rooms	2 twin/doubles: £100. Singles £75.
Meals	Dinner £30. Restaurant 2.5 miles.
Closed	Rarely.

Jane & Richard Beach
Salford Farm House,
Salford Priors, Evesham, WR11 8XN

Tel   +44 (0)1386 870000
Mobile +44 (0)7798 820713
Email   salfordfarmhouse@aol.com
Web   www.salfordfarmhouse.co.uk

Entry 432   Map 8

Warwickshire

The Old Manor House

An attractive 16th-century manor house with peaceful landscaped gardens sweeping down to the river Stour. The beamed double has oak furniture and a big bathroom; the fresh twin rooms (one in a private wing) are simply lovely. There is a large and elegant drawing and dining room for visitors to share, with antiques, contemporary art and an open fire. Jane prepares first-class breakfasts, and in warm weather you can have tea on the terrace: enjoy the pots of tulips in spring, old scented roses in summer, the meadow land beyond. A comfortable, lived-in family house with Stratford and the theatre close by. Guests love it here.

Children over 7 welcome. Dog fee: £12.50 per night.

Rooms	1 double, 2 twin/doubles, each with separate bath: £90–£110. Singles £50–£65.
Meals	Supper £20. Dinner, 3 courses, from £25. Restaurants nearby.
Closed	Rarely.

Jane Pusey
The Old Manor House,
Halford,
Shipston-on-Stour, CV36 5BT

Tel	+44 (0)1789 740264
Mobile	+44 (0)7786 467916
Email	info@oldmanor-halford.fsnet.co.uk
Web	www.oldmanor-halford.co.uk

Entry 433   Map 8

Wiltshire

Duchy Rag House

Fable has it that King Charles owed his tailor a lot of money so Duchy of Lancaster land was given in payment for the debt... and the house got its name. It's a home with character: antiques, vases of lilies, portraits, a damask sofa by a wood-burner; best boutique rooms have sumptuous beds, robes, TV, WiFi and a tea tray with rather good home-baked flapjacks. Tuck into Wootton Bassett bangers and bacon with homemade bread in the morning; if you need to scoot early Richard and Karen can send you off with a 'breakfast to go' filled roll. Terraces with pots of agapanthus are perfect for a sundowner after a day in the Cotswolds.

Rooms	1 double; 1 double, 1 twin sharing bathroom (let to same party only): £65–£95. As a family suite (1 double, 1 twin sharing bath): £150.
Meals	Pubs/restaurants 1 mile.
Closed	Christmas.

Karen & Richard Alcock
Duchy Rag House,
Leigh,
Swindon, SN6 6RQ

Tel	+44 (0)1666 861136
Email	rickalcock@live.com
Web	www.duchyraghouse.co.uk

Entry 434   Map 3

Wiltshire

Bullocks Horn Cottage

Up a country lane is this hidden-away house which the delightful Legges have turned into a haven of peace. Liz loves fabrics and flowers and mixes them with flair, Colin has painted a mural for the conservatory, bright with plants and wicker sofa. Sunny bedrooms are traditional and colourful with lovely views; the sitting room has a log fire, fine antiques, big comfy sofas, and the garden is so special it's appeared in magazines. Home-grown organic veg and herbs and local seasonal food make an appearance at dinner which, on balmy nights, you may eat under the arbour, covered in climbing roses and jasmine.

Children over 10 welcome.

Rooms	1 twin; 1 twin/double with separate shower: £95. Singles £62.50.
Meals	Dinner £25-£30. BYO. Pub 1.5 miles.
Closed	Christmas.

Colin & Liz Legge
Bullocks Horn Cottage,
Charlton,
Malmesbury, SN16 9DZ

Tel   +44 (0)1666 577600
Email   bullockshorn@clara.co.uk
Web   www.bullockshorn.co.uk

Entry 435   Map 3

Wiltshire

Carriers Farm

The stylishly converted dairies behind the main house are surrounded by acres of peaceful, organic pasture. Old milk churns act as planters, and you step in to delightful bedrooms 'Hare', 'Pheasant' or 'Fox'. Find restful whites with oak floors, pretty pine pieces, feather pillows and tip-top linen. Wake for delicious breakfast choices served in the sunny garden room: smoked salmon and cream cheese, homemade breads and jams, local ham and sausages, eggs from the hens. Fiona is friendly and helpful, and it's a treat to stay. Westonbirt Arboretum and Highgrove are close, and you can walk over the fields to supper at the pub.

Rooms	3 doubles: £85-£110. Singles £68.
Meals	Pubs within walking distance.
Closed	Rarely.

Fiona Butterfield
Carriers Farm,
Luckington Road, Sherston,
Malmesbury, SN16 0QA

Tel   +44 (0)1666 841445
Email   carriersfarm@btinternet.com
Web   www.carriersfarm.co.uk

Entry 436   Map 3

Wiltshire

Bridges Court

You're in the heart of the village with its small shop, friendly pub and the Melvilles' lovely 18th-century farmhouse. They haven't lived here long but it's so homely you'd never tell. Dogs wander, horses whinny, there's a beautiful garden with a Kiftsgate rose and a swimming pool for sunny days. On the second floor, off a corridor filled with paintings, are three florally inspired bedrooms: comfortable, bright and spacious with views to the village green. Breakfast leisurely on all things local at the long table in a dining room filled with silver and china. And there's a pleasant guests' sitting room to relax in.

Rooms	1 double, 1 twin; 1 double with separate bath: £90. Singles £65. Discounts available for 3+ nights, excluding Badminton weekend.
Meals	Pub in village.
Closed	Rarely.

	Fiona Melville
	Bridges Court,
	Luckington, SN14 6NT
Tel	+44 (0)1666 840215
Mobile	+44 (0)7711 816839
Email	fionamelville2003@yahoo.co.uk
Web	www.bridgescourt.co.uk

Entry 437   Map 3

Wiltshire

Manor Farm

Farmyard heaven in the Cotswolds. A 17th-century manor farmhouse in 550 arable acres; horses in the paddock, dozing dogs in the yard, tumbling blooms outside the door and a perfectly tended village, with duck pond, a short walk. Beautiful bedrooms are softly lit, with muted colours, plump goose down pillows and the crispest linen. Breakfast in front of the fire is a banquet of delights, tea among the roses is a treat, thanks to charming, welcoming Victoria; she will arrange a table for dinner at the pub too. This is the postcard England of dreams, with Castle Combe, Lacock, grand walking and gardens to visit.

Over 12s welcome.

Rooms	2 doubles (1 with shower & bath, 1 with shower); 1 twin with separate bath: £90-£100. Singles £50.
Meals	Pub 1 mile.
Closed	Rarely.

	Victoria Lippiatt-Onslow
	Manor Farm,
	Alderton, Chippenham, SN14 6NL
Tel	+44 (0)1666 840271
Mobile	+44 (0)7721 415824
Email	victoria.lippiatt@btinternet.com
Web	www.themanorfarm.co.uk

Entry 438   Map 3

Wiltshire

Dauntsey Park House

Be awed by history here. Parts of the house – like the grand dining room where you breakfast – date from Elizabethan times; the stunning summer drawing room is Edwardian. Both rooms are yours to use. Emma and her Italian husband have four young children and a flair for matching new with old: a striking glass chandelier sets off the sturdy oak table beneath; a turbine keeps the house in hot water. Up a wide staircase, two wallpapered bedrooms with views to the river are huge and comfortable with a self-indulgent feel (one has a thunderbox loo!). St James the Great church with its 14th-century doom board is in the garden. Lovely.

Rooms	1 double, 1 twin: £110–£120.
	Singles £90.
Meals	Pubs/restaurants in village.
Closed	November – February.

Emma Amati
Dauntsey Park House,
Dauntsey,
Chippenham, SN15 4HT
Tel   +44 (0)1249 721777
Email   enquiries@dauntseyparkhouse.co.uk
Web   www.dauntseyparkhouse.co.uk

Entry 439   Map 3

Wiltshire

Manor Farm

A sleepy village and a charming Queen Anne house with a *petit château* feel... The beautiful walled garden has groomed lawns, orchard, wildflower meadow and wandering hens and ducks. Inside is as lovely. Clare is an artist and runs a gallery and courses in the studio; her art along with family portraits and photos give the house a friendly, welcoming feel. The eclectically furnished drawing room, shared among guests, has a wood fire; pannelled, elegant bedrooms have garden views and comfortable beds topped with fine cotton and feather pillows. Wake for scrumptious, all-organic breakfasts, served by the big cosy Aga in the kitchen.

Min stay: 2 nights at weekends. Pets by arrangement.

Rooms	2 doubles, 1 twin: £100.
	1 single: £75. Singles £75.
Meals	Pub 3-minute walk.
Closed	Rarely.

Clare Inskip
Manor Farm,
Little Somerford, Malmesbury,
Chippenham, SN15 5JW
Tel   +44 (0)1666 822140
Mobile   +44 (0)7970 892344
Email   clareinskip@gmail.com
Web   clareinskip.com/rooms/

Entry 440   Map 3

Wiltshire

Fisherman's House

Swing off the village road to find the prettiest 1810 house, and vivacious Heather who has filled her home with fresh garden flowers, good art and a real eye for design and colour. You'll be welcomed in the large sitting room with lots of plumped up sofas and a roaring fire on chilly days; in summer you'll want tea in the fecund garden which swoops down to the river – a huge draw for birds, maybe even a kingfisher. Bedrooms have pretty wallpapers, fresh ginghams and chintzes, interesting books, impeccable bathrooms. Wake to freshly-squeezed orange juice, toothsome scrambled eggs, all the other gubbins and homemade marmalade. Lovely!

Rooms	1 double;1 twin with separate bath: £45-£90. 1 single: £45.
Meals	Pubs/restaurants 4-minute walk.
Closed	Rarely.

Heather Coulter
Fisherman's House,
Mildenhall, Marlborough, SN8 2LZ

Tel	+44 (0)1672 515390
Mobile	+44 (0)7785 225363
Email	heathercoulter610@btinternet.com
Web	www.fishermanshouse.co.uk

Entry 441   Map 3

Wiltshire

Scarwood

A honeysuckle-clad house looking down the river Kennet valley. Mike and Louise's home has a friendly vibe; he speaks French and they have stories to tell of their travels. Discover walls of books, a tribal rug on a chair, kilims, African pieces, a magnificent gold-framed patriarchal portrait above a wood-burner. Bedrooms have art, flowers and fine linen; one has a charming old Indian banister as the bedhead. Breakfast is in the sunny, open-plan kitchen: honey from the farm next door, local Ramsbury sausages. Savernake Forest is on the doorstep – heaven for walking and foraging; Marlborough has an annual jazz festival; Avebury stone circle is nearby.

Rooms	1 double; 1 twin/double with separate bathroom: £70-£80. Singles £55-£65.
Meals	Pubs/restaurants 2.5 miles.
Closed	Christmas.

Louise McNeilage
Scarwood,
Mildenhall, Marlborough, SN8 2NG

Tel	+44 (0)1672 515707
Mobile	+44 (0)7867 977761
Email	louisedeb@hotmail.co.uk
Web	www.scarwood.co.uk

Entry 442   Map 3

Wiltshire

Westcourt Farm

A medieval, Grade II* cruck truss hall house... beautifully restored by Rozzie and Jonny and snoozing amid wildflower meadows, hedgerows, ponds and geese. Delightful people, they love to cook and can spoil you rotten. Rooms are well decorated, crisp yet traditional, the country furniture is charming and the architecture fascinating. Bedrooms have comfortable beds and fine linen, bathrooms are spot-on; there's a lovely light drawing room and a barn for meetings and parties too. Encircled by footpaths and fields, Westcourt is the oldest house in a perfect village, two minutes from a rather good pub.

Rooms	1 double, 1 twin: £85. Singles £50.
Meals	Pub/restaurant in village.
Closed	Rarely.

	Jonny & Rozzie Buxton Westcourt Farm, Shalbourne, Marlborough, SN8 3QE
Tel	+44 (0)1672 871399
Email	rozzieb@btinternet.com
Web	www.westcourtfarm.com

Entry 443   Map 3

Wiltshire

Rushall Manor

A gorgeous country house – and Caroline is a treat of a host. The dining room shines with glass, antiques and family portraits; a particularly impressive admiral gazes benignly down as you tuck into breakfast: local eggs and sausages, and jams from the orchard. The harmonious sitting room has comfy sofas, books and games; pretty bedrooms have perfect mattresses and linen (and, from one, fantastic views up to Salisbury Plain); bathrooms come with cast-iron baths, scented soaps and lashings of hot water. Stonehenge and Salisbury are nearby, walks are good, and Caroline holds the village fête in her delightful garden.

Rooms	1 twin; 1 double, 1 twin, both with separate bath: £65-£100. Singles £65.
Meals	Dinner £30. Pubs 1 mile.
Closed	Rarely.

	Caroline Larken Rushall Manor, Rushall, Pewsey, SN9 6EG
Tel	+44 (0)1980 630301
Email	bandb@rushallmanor.com
Web	www.rushallmanor.com

Entry 444   Map 3

Wiltshire

Wiltshire

Oaklands

A spacious townhouse, south-facing garden, two dear dogs and lovely old Silver Cross pram sitting under the stairs. No wonder this delightful, 1880s house has been in the family forever. It was the first house in Warminster to have a bathroom; these have multiplied since and it's a comfortable home filled with fine antiques and attractive furnishings. Andrew and Carolyn, relaxed and charming, serve delicious breakfasts in the large conservatory. Bedrooms are inviting: beds are topped with fine linen, and you have views over churchyard, lawns and trees; bathrooms sparkle – one has a big walk-in shower. Restaurants are a stroll.

Deverill End

Colourful gardens surround this comfortable house, and fantastic views of the Wiltshire downs, Wylye valley and a tall steeple stretch as far as the eye can see. Sim and Joy are well-travelled and friendly; their sunny sitting room, warmed by a wood-burner, is full of books, art and African treasures. Comfortable bedrooms are all downstairs: soft colours, posies of flowers, little shower rooms. In the kitchen or dining room is where you feast on a breakfast of eggs and fruits from the garden, homemade jams and home-grown tomatoes in season – they used to grow 300 acres of them in Africa! Bath and Salisbury are an easy hop.

Children over 10 welcome.

Rooms	1 double; 1 double, 1 twin/double sharing bath (let to same party only): £75-£90. Singles £55.
Meals	Pub/restaurant 0.5 miles.
Closed	Christmas & occasionally.

Rooms	2 doubles, 1 twin: £80. Singles £60-£80.
Meals	Pub 5-minute walk.
Closed	Rarely.

Carolyn & Andrew Lewis
Oaklands,
88 Boreham Road,
Warminster, BA12 9JW

Tel	+44 (0)1985 300564
Mobile	+44 (0)7702 587533
Email	apl1944@yahoo.co.uk
Web	www.stayatoaklands.co.uk

Joy Greathead
Deverill End,
Deverill Road, Sutton Veny,
Warminster, BA12 7BY

Tel	+44 (0)1985 840356
Email	deverillend@gmail.com
Web	www.deverillend.co.uk

Wiltshire

The Mill House

In a tranquil village next to the river is a house surrounded by water meadows and wilderness garden. Roses ramble, marsh orchids bloom and butterflies shimmer. This 12-acre labour of love is the creation of ever-charming Diana and her son Michael. Their home, the time-worn 18th-century miller's house, is packed with country clutter – porcelain, foxes' brushes, ancestral photographs above the fire – while bedrooms are quaint, flowery and old-fashioned with firm comfy beds. Breakfasts are served at small tables in the pretty dining room. Diana has lived here for many many years, and has been doing B&B for at least 30 of them!

Please phone to enquire rather than email. Children over 6 welcome.

Rooms	3 doubles: £100–£140.
	1 family room for 4: £100–£140.
	Singles from £70.
Meals	Pub 5-minute walk.
Closed	Rarely.

Michael Mertens
The Mill House,
Berwick St James,
Salisbury, SP3 4TS

Tel	+44 (0)1722 790331 (and fax)
Email	m.mertens@btinternet.com
Web	www.millhouse.org.uk

Wiltshire

The Garden Cottage

You'll love the Woodford Valley and this thatched cottage at the edge of the village. It has long views, stacks of character and traditionally decorated rooms: a ground floor twin with roll top bath and two cosy doubles upstairs that share a bathroom. Fabrics are flowered, headboards upholstered, mattresses top quality. Or choose to snuggle up by the wood-burner in a charming shepherd's hut and sleep out under the stars – one has a king-sized bed. Breakfast in the handsome kitchen, or pretty garden, on Annie's homemade soda bread and good things local. Sit out by the roses, honeysuckle and an ancient mulberry; head off to Avebury and Stonehenge.

Cash or cheque accepted. Arrivals before 4pm.

Rooms	2 doubles sharing bathroom (let to same party only); 1 twin with separate bathroom: £90.
	1 shepherd's hut for 2 with shower, sink and loo: £90.
Meals	Pub 0.5 miles.
Closed	Occasionally.

Annie Arkwright
The Garden Cottage,
Upper Woodford,
Salisbury, SP4 6PA

| Tel | +44 (0)1722 782447 |
| Email | annie747@btinternet.com |

Wiltshire

The White Cottage

In the Woodford valley is a white thatched cottage, pretty as a picture and surrounded by fields. Steve has farmed here all his life and Fiona looks after you beautifully. The cosy guest suite is reached via an outside oak stair, the double room with leafy views and the single with a big day bed. Bedding is delicious, décor is restful, the bathroom shines. Breakfast is a feast: local sausages, Fiona's granola and marmalade, eggs from the free-ranging chickens. There's a shepherd's hut too if you fancy sleeping under the stars. Walk to Stonehenge, cycle to Salisbury; the coast is close and three nearby pubs serve home-cooked food.

Wiltshire

Dowtys

A beautifully converted Victorian dairy farm with fabulous views over the Nadder valley. Peaceful, private, stylish bedrooms, one on the ground floor, have original beams, antiques and supremely comfy Vi-Spring beds; bathrooms are perfect. The sunny guest sitting room has a contemporary feel too, with its wood-burner and sliding doors to the well-tended garden. Enjoy a delicious breakfast in the old milking parlour, now the dining room, or on the terrace, sit beneath the espaliered limes in the lovely garden, dip into the National Trust woods. Footpaths start from the gate and your charming hosts will help you with all your plans.

Rooms	1 suite for 3 with separate bathroom: £80-£95. Extra single room available £15 (let to same party only). 1 shepherd's hut: £75. Extra floor mattress available in shepherd's hut (for up to 12s) £10.
Meals	Continental breakfast for shepherd's hut guests. Pubs/restaurants 10-minute walk.
Closed	Rarely.

	Fiona Langdon The White Cottage, Salterton, Salisbury, SP4 6AN
Tel	+44 (0)1722 782431
Mobile	+44 (0)7968 314171
Email	flangdon@btconnect.com

Rooms	1 double with sitting room; 1 twin with separate bath/shower: £78-£95. 1 double with separate bath/shower (with 2nd triple bedroom only available as a family suite sharing bathroom): £78-£95. Singles from £60.
Meals	Packed lunch from £7. Pub 0.25 miles.
Closed	Rarely.

	Di & Willi Verdon-Smith Dowtys, Dowtys Lane, Dinton, Salisbury, SP3 5ES
Tel	+44 (0)1722 716886
Email	dowtys.bb@gmail.com
Web	www.dowtysbedandbreakfast.co.uk

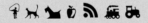

Entry 449   Map 3

Entry 450   Map 3

Worcestershire

Huntlands Farm

Deep in the rural shires Lucy and Stephen run delightful B&B on a working farm (sheep, cattle, pigs). They've lovingly coaxed this 15th-century house back to life: huge rooms, two with four-posters, are deeply comfortable with patterned rugs on wide floorboards, reclaimed wardrobes and views over the orchard or farm. You get roll top tubs to wallow in, fluffy towels and local soaps. Breakfast in the convivial dining room on eggs from the hens, sausages from the pigs and homemade preserves. There's dinner too, roasts and stews or traditional Caribbean fare. The Malvern showground is nearby.

Min. stay: 2 nights. Children over 10 welcome.

Rooms	2 doubles, 1 twin/double: £80–£100.
	1 suite for 2: £95–£100.
	1 family room for 4 with sofabed
	& separate bathroom
	(price for 2 adults & 2 children
	under 10): £70–£85.
Meals	Dinner, 3 courses, £24.50.
	Pubs/restaurants 0.5 miles.
Closed	Rarely.

	Lucy Brodie
	Huntlands Farm,
	Gaines Road, Whitbourne,
	Worcester, WR6 5RD
Tel	+44 (0)1886 821955
Mobile	+44 (0)7828 286360
Email	lucy@huntlandsfarm.co.uk
Web	www.huntlandsfarm.co.uk

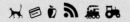

Worcestershire

South House Alpacas

If it's the good life you're after then look no further. This handsome Georgian house looks out over not only a beautiful walled garden complete with ancient mulberry tree but rows of neat vegetables, trellised vines and an orchard with a growing herd of alpacas. Guests stay on the first floor of the old coach house and the softly carpeted, beamed rooms are light and spacious with wooden furniture and gorgeous beds; shower with organic soap whilst gazing out on your Andean neighbours! Your charming hosts are passionate about their animals and their little slice of England – this is the most civilised self-sufficiency project imaginable.

Rooms	2 doubles: £110–£120.
Meals	Supper £15.
	Dinner, 2-3 courses, £25–£35.
	Pub 1 mile.
Closed	Rarely.

	Amanda Dartnell
	South House Alpacas,
	Main Street, South Littleton,
	Evesham, WR11 8TJ
Tel	+44 (0)1386 830848
Email	amandadartnell@icloud.com
Web	www.southhouse.co.uk

Old Country Farm & The Lighthouse

Ella's passion for this tranquil place – and conservation of its wildlife – is infectious. She's keen on home-grown and local food too so breakfast is delicious. Dating from the 1400s, the farm is a delightful rambling medley: russet stone and colour-washed brick, huge convivial round table by the Aga, rugs on polished floors. The sitting room has wood-burner, piano and books, and you sleep soundly in pretty, cottagey bedrooms: lovely linen, garden flowers. In winter you stay in The Lighthouse, down the lane: an inspired green-oak retreat with soaring beams, snug library, comfy downstairs bedrooms and roses in the garden. Magical.

The Birches

Thoughtful Katharine is attentive; Edward puts you at ease humming a jolly tune. Come and go as you please from this self-contained annexe, spotless and contemporary. French windows lead to a pretty terrace, then to a charming garden opening to fields and views of the Malverns. Though the house is easily accessible, the tranquillity is sublime; plenty of spots to sit and ponder the view back to the timber-framed house. Hens pottering on the lawn lay eggs for breakfast, served – in your room – with local bacon and sausages, and bread from Ledbury's baker. Wander further for abundant leafy walks and lovely Regency Malvern.

Rooms	1 double; 1 double with separate bath; 1 double with separate shower: £65–£90. Singles £35–£55.
Meals	Pubs/restaurants 3 miles.
Closed	Rarely.

Rooms	Annexe – 1 double: £80. Singles £60.
Meals	Pub/restaurant 0.3 miles.
Closed	Rarely.

Ella Grace Quincy
Old Country Farm & The Lighthouse,
Mathon,
Malvern, WR13 5PS

Tel	+44 (0)1886 880867
Email	ella@oldcountryhouse.co.uk
Web	www.oldcountryhouse.co.uk

Katharine Litchfield
The Birches,
Birts Street, Birtsmorton,
Malvern, WR13 6AW

Tel	+44 (0)1684 833821
Mobile	+44 (0)7875 458441
Email	katharine-thebirches@hotmail.co.uk
Web	www.the-birchesbedandbreakfast.co.uk

Sunnybank

A Victorian gentleman's residence just a short walk up the hill from the centre of bustling *Last of the Summer Wine* Holmfirth, still with its working Picturedrome cinema (touring bands too), arts and folk festivals, restaurants and shops. Attentive hosts look after you when the Whites are away. Peaceful bedrooms have a mix of contemporary, Art Nouveau and Art Deco pieces, caramel cream velvets and silks, spoiling bathrooms and lovely valley or garden views. A full choice Yorkshire breakfast will set you up for a lazy stroll round the charming gardens, or a brisk yomp through rural bliss.

Minimum stay: 2 nights at weekends. Children over 12 welcome.

Thurst House Farm

This solid Pennine farmhouse, its stone mullion windows denoting 17th-century origins, is English to the core. Your warm, gracious hosts give guests a cosy and carpeted sitting room with an open fire in winter; bedrooms are equally generous, with inviting brass beds, lovely antique linen and fresh flowers. Outside: clucking hens, two friendly sheep and a hammock in a garden with beautiful views. Tuck into homemade bread, marmalade and jams at breakfast, and good traditional English dinners, too – just the thing for walkers who've trekked the Calderdale or the Pennine Way.

Children over 8 welcome.

Rooms	2 doubles, 1 twin/double (extra single bed): £68-£115. Singles £58-£105.
Meals	Afternoon tea, with sandwiches, on request. Packed lunch £12. Pubs/restaurants 500 yds.
Closed	Rarely.

Rooms	1 double, 1 family room for 4: £80. Singles by arrangement.
Meals	Dinner, 4 courses, £25. BYO. Packed lunch £5. Restaurants within 0.5 miles.
Closed	Christmas & New Year.

Peter & Anne White
Sunnybank,
78 Upperthong Lane,
Holmfirth, HD9 3BQ
Tel   +44 (0)1484 684065
Email   info@sunnybankguesthouse.co.uk
Web   www.sunnybankguesthouse.co.uk

David & Judith Marriott
Thurst House Farm,
Soyland, Ripponden,
Sowerby Bridge, HX6 4NN
Tel   +44 (0)1422 822820
Mobile   +44 (0)7759 619043
Email   judith@thursthousefarm.co.uk
Web   www.thursthousefarm.co.uk

Entry 455   Map 12

Entry 456   Map 12

Yorkshire

Ponden Hall

A house brimming with atmosphere and said to be the inspiration for *Wuthering Heights*. Julie's knowledge of the history is impressive and she offers tours of her fascinating home. Arrive for tea and home-baked cake and soak up the mullion windows, huge flagstones, period pieces and original paintings. Bedrooms have just the right balance of luxury and individuality: an amazing box bed, rocking horse, raftered ceilings – and log stoves in two. A full Yorkshire breakfast is served in the magnificent main hall. Walk the Pennine Way, hop on a steam train at Keighley; Haworth is close too – for all things Brontë and independent shops.

Rooms	2 doubles: £85-£175.
	1 family room for 4: £145.
Meals	Pubs/restaurants 10-minute walk.
Closed	24-30 December.

Julie Akhurst
Ponden Hall,
Ponden Lane, Stanbury, Haworth,
Keighley, BD22 0HR
Tel   +44 (0)1535 648608
Email   stay@ponden.force9.co.uk
Web   www.ponden-hall.co.uk

Entry 457   Map 12

Yorkshire

Ponden House

Bump your way up the farm track to Brenda's sturdy house, high on the Pennine Way. The spring water makes wonderful tea, the ginger scones are delicious and the house hums with interest and artistic touches. Comfy sofas are jollied up with throws, there are homespun rugs and hangings, paintings, plants and a piano. Feed the hens, plonk your boots by the Aga, chat with your lovely hostess as she turns out fab home cooking; food is a passion. Bedrooms are exuberant, comfortable and cosy, it's great for walkers and there's a hot tub under the stars (bookable by groups in advance). Good value with a relaxed, homely feel.

Rooms	2 doubles; 1 twin with separate
	bath (occasionally sharing
	bathroom with family): £80-£85.
	Singles £50.
Meals	Dinner, 3 courses, £18. BYO.
	Packed lunch £6.
	Pub/restaurant 1 mile.
Closed	Rarely.

Brenda Taylor
Ponden House,
Stanbury,
Haworth, BD22 0HR
Tel   +44 (0)1535 644154
Email   brenda.taylor@pondenhouse.co.uk
Web   www.pondenhouse.co.uk

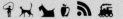

Entry 458   Map 12

Yorkshire

Cold Cotes

Sue and Mark give you relaxation, delicious breakfasts and a dollop of contemporary chic in their 1890s farmhouse on the edge of the Yorkshire Dales. There's a sitting room with stacks of books, squashy sofas, maps, and a separate library for those who want to escape in a book. Smart bedrooms have sitting areas with garden views; those in the barn are just as swish and comfortable. Outside find a beautiful woodland walk, impressive sweeping borders and a cobblestone walk along a stream. The fruit and veg garden provides abundant produce; a little lawned area is surrounded by cherry trees and has a perfect seating area.

Minimum stay: 2 nights.

Rooms	3 twin/doubles: £85.
	4 suites for 2 (twin/double): £99.
	Singles £75.
Meals	Cold platters and snacks available.
	Pub/restaurant 2 miles.
Closed	Mid-December to end of February.

Sue & Mark
Cold Cotes,
Felliscliffe, Harrogate, HG3 2LW
Tel   +44 (0)1423 770937
Mobile   +44 (0)7970 713334
Email   info@coldcotes.com
Web   www.coldcotes.com

Entry 459   Map 14

Yorkshire

Sophie's

A pretty village of old stone houses with a river running through, a wide main street, an ancient church... and Sophie's coffee shop and deli right in the middle. Comfortable, light and spotless bedrooms are above; the top floor one has a balcony for admiring wide views over fields. Step downstairs for breakfast in the friendly coffee shop, where you sit on Lloyd Loom chairs, or squishy sofas in front of the wood stove; tuck into local produce, granola and excellent coffee as you watch the world go by. There's a peaceful sun-trap garden at the back, Harrogate is a short drive and the Yorkshire Dales wait to be explored.

Minimum stay: 2 nights.

Rooms	1 double, 1 twin: £85–£110.
Meals	Pub/restaurant 4 miles.
Closed	Rarely.

Sophie Jacob
Sophie's,
High Street, Hampsthwaite,
Harrogate, HG3 2ET
Tel   +44 (0)1423 779219
Email   sophie@thecoffeeshop2010.co.uk
Web   www.sophiesbedandbreakfast.co.uk

Entry 460   Map 14

Yorkshire

Lane House

Pam and art restorer Richard are chatty and friendly – they love having guests, and are happy to advise on trips. Their converted barn has an artistic vibe throughout. The big, attractive open-plan living space has a galleried landing above; airy bedrooms have soaring beams, striking light fittings, colourful throws; bathrooms are smart. Pam likes to cook so you're in for a treat: tuck in to local produce, eggs from the hens, homemade granola, breads and jams; delicious, perhaps Lebanese or Moroccan, dishes for dinner too. The 50 acres are yours to wander: farmland, woods, a beck – and there's a four-mile Heritage Trail to Bentham.

Minimum stay: 2 nights at weekends.

Rooms	2 doubles: £85–£95.
Meals	Dinner £15. BYO.
	Pubs/restaurants 0.5 miles.
Closed	Christmas.

Pam Zahler
Lane House,
Fowgill, High Bentham,
Lancaster, LA2 7AH
Tel   +44 (0)15242 61998
Email   pamzahler@hotmail.com
Web   www.lanehouseandcottage.co.uk

Entry 461   Map 12

Yorkshire

Ellerbeck House

Walk from the door of this beautifully restored country house, or head west to the Lakes, east to the Dales, north to Scotland. Period rooms display exquisite antiques and Harriet's artistic touch: sofas and curtains in dark pink and cream, Persian rugs on shiny oak floors, marble fireplaces, stained glass in the stairwell, huge sash windows overlooking the lawn. One window holds the breakfast table – full Cumbrian, at flexible times. Outside, a courtyard for sitting out with the birds and the breeze. It's all so pretty, as is this bucolic – yet accessible – spot near Kirkby Lonsdale, Settle, and Kendal of Mint Cake fame.

Rooms	1 double: £90.
	Singles £45–£55.
Meals	Pubs/restaurants 2 miles.
Closed	Rarely.

Harriet Sharp
Ellerbeck House,
Westhouse, Ingleton,
Carnforth, LA6 3NH
Tel   +44 (0)15242 41872
Email   harrietnsharp@gmail.com
Web   www.ellerbeckhouse.co.uk

Entry 462   Map 12

Yorkshire

Low Mill

Off the village green this handsome historic mill in the Dales keeps many of its original features. The huge beamed guest sitting room has a roaring fire, and the old waterwheel is working! Friendly relaxed Neil and Jane have restored their home, then filled it with interesting art, quirky sculpture, flowers and vintage gems. Bedrooms have tip-top linen and luxurious throws; bathrooms are fabulous. Eat well at separate tables on all things local and home-grown: bacon, pancakes, homemade bread; and for dinner, perhaps Yorkshire ham or herby lamb. The pretty riverside garden is perfect for chilling with a glass of wine.

Children over 11 welcome.

Rooms	2 doubles: £105-£170.
	1 suite for 2: £90-£160.
	Singles £78-£170.
Meals	Dinner, 2-3 courses, £20-£25.
	Pubs 5-minute drive.
Closed	Rarely.

Neil McNair
Low Mill,
Bainbridge,
Leyburn, DL8 3EF
Tel   +44 (0)1969 650553
Email   lowmillguesthouse@gmail.com
Web   www.lowmillguesthouse.co.uk

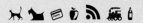

Entry 463   Map 12

Yorkshire

Stow House

Past ancient stone walls and fields of lambs you reach sleepy Aysgarth and this dignified rectory. Step inside to find – Shoreditch pizzazz! Sarah and Phil have swapped the world of London advertising for a dream house in the Dales; she does cocktails, he does breakfasts and their take on Victoriana is inspiring. Floors, banisters and sash windows have been restored, stairs carpeted in plush red, sofas covered in zinging velvet. Bathrooms are wow, bedrooms are soothing and the papier mâché hare's head above the bar says it all. A stroll down the hill are the Aysgarth Falls, beloved of Ruskin, Wordsworth and Turner.

Minimum stay: 2 nights at weekends.

Rooms	6 doubles: £110-£175.
	1 family room for 3: £110-£175.
	Extra bed/sofabed available £10-£20
	per person per night.
Meals	Pubs/restaurants 5-minute walk.
Closed	January & occasionally.

Sarah & Phil Bucknall
Stow House,
Aysgarth,
Leyburn, DL8 3SR
Tel   +44 (0)1969 663635
Email   info@stowhouse.co.uk
Web   www.stowhouse.co.uk

Entry 464   Map 12

Yorkshire

The Grange

Through glorious Dales to the pretty village green, where you have a wing of this attractive, old stone house to yourselves. Step into an airy space with original oak beams, comfy sofa, Persian rug and books. Antique and contemporary pieces blend, the bed is clad in pure cotton, the simple shower room has fluffy towels, and there's a kitchen area for rustling up snacks. Your hosts are delightful: Sam has his cabinet making business in the outbuildings; Georgina (professional cook) brings over locally sourced breakfasts and hearty suppers: eggs from the hens, homemade marmalade, smoked salmon… lasagne, crumbles. A friendly place.

Minimum stay: 2 nights at weekends.

Rooms	1 double with sitting and kitchen area: £80. Singles £70.
Meals	Dinner, 2-3 courses, £30-£40. Light supper £15. Restaurant 75 yds.
Closed	Rarely.

Georgina Anderson
The Grange,
East Witton,
Leyburn, DL8 4SL
Mobile +44 (0)7957 144467
Email georgina@thegrangebedandbreakfast.co.uk
Web www.thegrangebedandbreakfast.co.uk

Entry 465   Map 12

Yorkshire

Low Sutton

Judi and Steve care tremendously for their guests, and are passionate about Yorkshire. Their smallholding is a gem of sustainability and peace. Wood fires in the vast dining/sitting room and cosy snug burn fuel from their own copse; insulation and underfloor heating keep the homely rooms comfy; one of the sparkling bathrooms is solar-heated; undyed wool yarn is produced from the Ryeland sheep. There are dogs, chickens and six acres to explore; your horse is welcome too. Judi is a keen cook: expect good Aga dinners with veg from the garden, local produce and homemade jams for breakfast. Castles, markets, gardens – all in easy reach.

Rooms	2 doubles: £85. Singles £70.
Meals	Packed lunch £7. Dinner, 2-3 courses, £25-£30. Pub/restaurant 1.5 miles.
Closed	Rarely.

Judi Smith
Low Sutton,
Masham, Ripon, HG4 4PB
Tel +44 (0)1765 688565
Mobile +44 (0)7821 600521
Email info@lowsutton.co.uk
Web www.lowsutton.co.uk

Entry 466   Map 12

Yorkshire

Firs Farm

The landscape is rural and rolling, the lanes are narrow and quiet, and Healey is pretty-as-a-picture: mellow York stone, smart gardens and immaculate paintwork on every house. Richard and Sarah, relaxed and genial, offer homemade cakes and coffee when you arrive and the cosy feel of their home makes you feel instantly at ease. Enjoy a sitting room with an open fire and fabulous fabrics, fresh and cottagey bedrooms with spotted upholstered windows seats, and vases of flowers in every corner. There are great views from the lovely walled garden, acres to roam, wonderful walking, and tip-top towns to visit all around.

Children over 10 welcome.

Rooms	1 double; 1 twin/double with separate bath/shower: £75-£90. Singles £65.
Meals	Packed lunch £7. Pubs/restaurants 1 mile.
Closed	Christmas & New Year.

	Richard & Sarah Townsend
	Firs Farm,
	Healey,
	Ripon, HG4 4LH
Tel	+44 (0)1765 688910
Email	sarah@firsfarmbandb.co.uk
Web	www.firsfarmbandb.co.uk

Entry 467   Map 12

Yorkshire

Laverton Hall

The hall is a beauty, even on a dull day, and the village is a dream. Half an hour from Harrogate find space, beauty, history (it's 400 years old), three walled gardens and comfort in great measure: beloved antiques, a rocking horse in the hall, feather pillows, thick white towels, and sumptuous breakfasts followed by delightful Rachel's Cordon Bleu dinner – delicious rack of lamb a favourite. The sunny guest sitting room is elegant and charming, the cream and white twin and the snug little single have long views to the river. The area is rich with abbeys and great houses, and then there are the glorious Dales to be explored.

Rooms	1 twin/double: £95. 1 single: £60.
Meals	Dinner, 3 courses, £30. Pubs/restaurants 2 miles.
Closed	Christmas.

	Rachel Wilson
	Laverton Hall,
	Laverton, Ripon, HG4 3SX
Tel	+44 (0)1765 650274
Mobile	+44 (0)7711 086385
Email	rachel.k.wilson@hotmail.co.uk
Web	www.lavertonhall.co.uk

Entry 468   Map 12

Yorkshire

Lawrence House

In an immaculate estate village, a classically elegant house run with faultless precision by John and Harriet – former wine importer and interior decorator. The house is listed and Georgian, the garden is formal, flagged and herbaceous, the position – by the back gate to Fountains Abbey and Studley Royal – is glorious. Enjoy linen sofas, books, heirlooms and log fire in the drawing room just for guests, and the promise of a very good dinner. Bedrooms and bathrooms are in a private wing, light, well-proportioned, full of special touches, with the largest at the front.

Rooms	1 twin/double, 1 twin: £120. Singles £80.
Meals	Dinner £30. Pub/restaurant 1 mile.
Closed	Christmas & New Year.

	John & Harriet Highley Lawrence House, Studley Roger, Ripon, HG4 3AY
Tel	+44 (0)1765 600947
Email	john@lawrence-house.co.uk
Web	www.lawrence-house.co.uk

Entry 469   Map 12

Yorkshire

Mallard Grange

Perfect farmhouse B&B. Hens, cats, sheepdogs wander the garden, an ancient apple tree leans against the wall, guests unwind and feel part of the family. Enter the rambling, deep-shuttered 16th-century farmhouse, cosy with well-loved family pieces, and feel at peace with the world. Breakfast is generous – homemade muffins, poached pears with cinnamon, a sizzling full Monty. A winding steep stair leads to big, friendly bedrooms, two cheerful others await in the converted 18th-century smithy, and Maggie's enthusiasm for this glorious area is as genuine as her love of doing B&B. It's a gem!

Over 12s welcome.

Rooms	2 twin/doubles: £85-£110. Old Blacksmith's Shop & Carthouse – 2 twin/doubles on ground floor: £85-£110. Singles £80.
Meals	Pubs/restaurants 10-minute drive.
Closed	Christmas & New Year.

	Maggie Johnson Mallard Grange, Aldfield, Ripon, HG4 3BE
Tel	+44 (0)1765 620242
Mobile	+44 (0)7720 295918
Email	maggie@mallardgrange.co.uk
Web	www.mallardgrange.co.uk

Entry 470   Map 12

Yorkshire

Carlton House

Quietly tucked into a corner of the sedate green, a short stride from the pub, lies a stylishly renovated 18th-century farmhouse. The old wash house, tractor shed and stable have become airy, chic, characterful rooms with beams and fabulous bathrooms. In summer, pull up a chair in a pretty yard with hanging baskets or find a tranquil spot in the charmingly secret garden. The dining room with open fire is a delight, so linger over a breakfast of delicious local produce, then set off for market towns, dales and moors. There's a big-hearted family feel here – Denise's oat and raisin crunchies and soda bread are to die for! Lovely.

Rooms	Outbuildings – 2 doubles, 1 twin/double: £68-£85. Singles £55.
Meals	Pub/restaurant 2-minute walk.
Closed	Rarely.

	Denise & David Mason
	Carlton House,
	Sandhutton,
	Thirsk, YO7 4RW
Tel	+44 (0)1845 587381
Email	info@carltonbarns.co.uk
Web	www.carltonbarns.co.uk

Entry 471   Map 12

Yorkshire

Patrick Brompton Hall

A stately, Queen Anne beauty of a place, in glorious Wensleydale. Sweep up, glide through the entrance hall and upstairs to your private quarters where classic country house styling calmly meets the 21st century. There's a perfect parkland view from the most comfortable of beds, and the smart bathroom has a big bath and lashings of hot water. Continental breakfast on pretty china is served in the dining room. Charles and Emma are friendly and know the area well; enjoy their parkland walk from the door, find plenty of good pubs and historic houses nearby, and market towns Bedale and Richmond are a short drive. Come home to a soak in the hot tub.

Minimum stay: 2 nights.

Rooms	1 double: £120.
Meals	Continental breakfast. Restaurant 2 miles. Tearoom 1.5 miles.
Closed	Rarely.

	Emma & Charles Ropner
	Patrick Brompton Hall,
	Bedale, DL8 1JL
Mobile	+44 (0)7780 470900
Email	info@dalesendcottages.co.uk
Web	www.dalesendcottages.co.uk

Entry 472   Map 12

Yorkshire

Manor House

It's the handsomest house in the village. Annie – warm, intelligent, fun – invites you in to spacious interiors elegantly painted, artfully cluttered. Tall shuttered windows and a big open fire, candles in sconces and heaps of flowers, wool carpets and charming fabrics: a genuinely relaxing family home. Bedrooms are a treat, one with green views on two sides and a bathroom with a French country feel; fittings are vintage but spotless. Breakfast is good too with eggs from the hens and local chipolatas and bacon. Stride the Dales, discover Georgian Richmond, a hop away; return to a delicious simple supper, with veg from the garden.

Rooms	1 double; 1 twin/double with separate bath: £95-£100. Singles £80.
Meals	Supper, 2 courses, £25-£30. BYO. Pubs 1 mile.
Closed	Christmas.

Annabel Burchnall
Manor House,
Middle Street,
Gayles,
Richmond, DL11 7JF
Tel   +44 (0)1833 621578
Email   annieburchnall@hotmail.com

Entry 473   Map 12

Yorkshire

No 54

No. 54 is in the middle of a peaceful row of attractive terraced houses a few minutes walk from the centre of town. Step inside to find a great mix of antique, vintage and quirky pieces, flagged floors, rugs and open wood fires. The inviting, supremely comfortable bedrooms are in a single-storey extension overlooking a secluded courtyard full of shrubs, climbers and pretty flowers; bathrooms are sparkling. Lizzie is warm and friendly and her home baking and breakfasts are delicious. The walking is good too, and on sunny days the back doors are thrown open onto the patio and garden – lovely! This is a happy welcoming place.

Children over 11 welcome.

Rooms	2 doubles, 1 twin: £70-£130. Singles £70-£85.
Meals	Restaurants 10-minute walk.
Closed	Christmas & New Year.

Lizzie Rohan
No 54,
Bondgate,
Helmsley, YO62 5EZ
Tel   +44 (0)1439 771533
Email   lizzie@no54.co.uk
Web   www.no54.co.uk

Entry 474   Map 13

Helmsley Garden Cottage & Railway Carriage

Your own stone cottage with hydrangeas at the door – perfect! Tucked behind Louise's house and antique shop, it looks on to a sunny patch of garden and is filled with gorgeous furniture, old beams and warm charm. The dining room is cosy with comfy armchairs, tea-making things and homemade treats; there's a little table for tasty meals too – Louise brings it all to you. Upstairs find your pretty bedroom under the eaves. Or you can choose to stay in the amazing vintage carriage under an apple tree – children love it! A short walk to cafés and Helmsley Castle; return, settle with a book on an elegant antique sofa and feel completely at home.

Please see owners' website for availability calendar. Self-catering option in Railway Carriage.

Rooms	1 double with private dining & sitting rooms: £140. Carriage – 1 double with sitting area, 1 bunk room: £140. Extra bed/sofabed available £10 per person per night.
Meals	Dinner from £10 per person. Extra breakfasts £10 per person. Pubs/restaurants 1-minute walk.
Closed	Rarely.

Louise Craig
Helmsley Garden Cottage &
Railway Carriage,
1 Bondgate, Helmsley,
York, YO62 5BW
Tel   +44 (0)1439 771864
Email louise.craig@aol.co.uk
Web   www.helmsley-gardencottage.co.uk

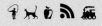

Entry 475   Map 13

Byland Abbey Inn

Lovers of history will be in heaven here – from two of the bedrooms you overlook the ruins of the medieval Abbey; stones from which were used to build this former inn, now a B&B where you have your independence. Karen meets and greets, and brings you a super Yorkshire breakfast, but other than that you are left to your own devices. Wander the pretty gardens, stroll the Hambleton hills, return to sumptuous bedrooms with tweedy touches, grand furniture and enormous bathrooms with roll-tops. It's a half-hour stroll to pretty Coxwold for a pub supper, or hop in the car to York for a plethora of restaurants.

Rooms	1 double, 1 twin/double: £110–£140. 1 suite for 3 (sofabed available): £175. Flowers, chocolates, champagne and other treats by arrangement.
Meals	Restaurants 1.5 miles.
Closed	Rarely.

Karen Pinchon
Byland Abbey Inn,
Byland Abbey, Coxwold,
Helmsley, YO61 4BD
Tel   +44 (0)1347 868204
Email abbey.inn@english-heritage.org.uk
Web   www.english-heritage.org.uk/visit/
       places/byland-abbey/inn/

Entry 476   Map 12

Yorkshire

Shallowdale House

Phillip and Anton have a true affection for their guests so you will be treated royally. Sumptuous bedrooms dazzle in yellows, blues and limes, acres of curtains frame wide views over the Howardian Hills, bathrooms are immaculate. You breakfast on the absolute best: fresh fruit compotes, dry-cured bacon or Whitby kippers, homemade rolls and marmalade. Admire the amazing garden, then walk off in any direction straight from the house. Return to a cosily elegant drawing room with a fire in winter, and an enticing library. Dinner is a real treat — coffee and chocolates before you crawl up to bed? Bliss.

Min. stay: 2 nights at weekends. Over 12s welcome.

Rooms	2 twin/doubles; 1 double with separate bath/shower: £120-£155. Singles £100-£125.
Meals	Dinner, 4 courses, £39.50. Pub 0.5 miles.
Closed	Christmas & New Year.

	Anton van der Horst & Phillip Gill
	Shallowdale House,
	West End,
	Ampleforth, YO62 4DY
Tel	+44 (0)1439 788325
Email	stay@shallowdalehouse.co.uk
Web	www.shallowdalehouse.co.uk

Entry 477   Map 12

Yorkshire

Cundall Lodge Farm

Ancient chestnuts, crunchy drive, sheep grazing, hens free-ranging. This four-square Georgian farmhouse could be straight out of Central Casting. Smart, traditional rooms have damask sofas, comfy armchairs, bright wallpapers and views to Sutton Bank's White Horse or the river Swale – and tea and oven-fresh cakes welcome you. Spotless bedrooms are inviting: pretty fabrics, antiques, flowers, Roberts radios. This is a working farm and the breakfast table groans with eggs from the hens, homemade jams and local bacon. The garden and river walks guarantee peace, and David and Caroline are generous and delightful.

Over 14s welcome.

Rooms	1 double, 2 twin/doubles: £85-£100.
Meals	Packed lunch £7. Pubs/restaurants 2 miles.
Closed	Christmas & February.

	Caroline Barker
	Cundall Lodge Farm,
	Cundall, York, YO61 2RN
Tel	+44 (0)1423 360203
Mobile	+44 (0)7773 494260
Email	enquiries@cundall-lodgefarm.co.uk
Web	www.cundall-lodgefarm.co.uk

Entry 478   Map 12

Yorkshire

The Mount House

A dollop of stylish fun in the rolling Howardian Hills (AONB), Nick and Kathryn's redesigned village house is light, airy and filled with gorgeous things – good antiques, heaps of photographs, splashy modern art and flowers. The ground-floor twin with white cast-iron beds has its own cosy book-filled sitting room; the sunny upstairs double has views across roof tops to open countryside. Continental breakfasts are a treat, in the garden if it's fine, and Kathryn – an excellent cook – will spoil you at dinner too if you wish. Discover Castle Howard, Nunnington Hall, old market towns and great walking on the doorstep; only 20 minutes from York too.

Min. stay: 2 nights at weekends & in high season.

Rooms	1 double, 1 twin with sitting room; 1 double with separate bath: £90–£140. Singles £75–£100.
Meals	Continental breakfast. Dinner, 3-4 courses, £30-£40. BYO. Pub/restaurant 200 yds.
Closed	Rarely.

Kathryn Hill
The Mount House,
Terrington, York, YO60 6QB

Tel	+44 (0)1653 648206
Mobile	+44 (0)7780 536937
Email	mount.house@clayfox.co.uk
Web	www.howardianhillsbandb.co.uk

Entry 479   Map 13

Yorkshire

Corner Farm

Tea and home-baked cakes on arrival: you get a lovely welcome here! This peaceful farmhouse is so well insulated it's snug and warm even on the coldest day. With York so close and stunning estates nearby, this is a cosy nest from which to explore the area – or just the village pub. Bathrooms are swish and bedrooms are light, fresh and comfortable: cast-iron beds, fine sheets, cute satin cushions. Much-loved Dexters graze on six acres – Tim and Sharon are aiming for self-sufficiency – and apples from the orchard are pressed for your breakfast juice, flexibly served and with lots of choice, including home-laid eggs.

Rooms	1 double, 1 twin: £80–£95. Singles £55–£65.
Meals	Packed lunch £4. Pub 100 yds.
Closed	Rarely.

Sharon Stevens
Corner Farm,
Low Catton, York, YO41 1EA

Tel	+44 (0)1759 373911
Mobile	+44 (0)7711 440796
Email	cornerfarmyork@gmail.com
Web	www.cornerfarmyork.co.uk

Entry 480   Map 13

Yorkshire

Dowthorpe Hall

Caroline is lovely, cooking is her passion and she trawls the county for the best; fish and seafood from Hornsea, Dexter beef, game from the local shoot; her fruits and veg are home-grown. All is served in a sumptuous Georgian dining room by flickering candlelight, after which you retire to a comfortable drawing room; this is a marvellously elegant, and happy, house. Sleep peacefully on a luxurious mattress, wake to the aroma of bacon, sausages, eggs and home-baked bread. There are acres of gorgeous garden to roam – orchards, pathways, potager and pond – and a trio of historic houses to visit.

Rooms	1 twin/double; 1 double with separate bathroom: £90–£110. Singles £70.
Meals	Dinner £25. Pubs 0.25–5 miles.
Closed	Rarely.

John & Caroline Holtby
Dowthorpe Hall,
Skirlaugh, Hull, HU11 5AE
Tel   +44 (0)1964 562235
Email   john.holtby@farming.co.uk
Web   www.dowthorpehall.com

Entry 481   Map 13

Yorkshire

Village Farm

Tucked behind houses and shops, this was once the village farm with land stretching to the coast. Now the one-storey buildings overlooking a courtyard are large bedrooms in gorgeous colours with luxurious touches. Chrysta, who moved from London, is living her dream and looks after you well: baths are deep, beds crisply comfortable, heating is underfoot. Delicious breakfasts are served at wooden tables in a cheerful light room with a contemporary feel; dinner is candlelit and locally sourced. Stride the cliffs, watch birds at Flamborough Head or make for Spurn Point – remote and lovely.

Rooms	1 double, 1 twin/double: £80. 1 family room for 4: £80–£95. Singles £60.
Meals	Dinner, 2–3 courses, £18–£22. Pubs/restaurants within 20 yds.
Closed	Rarely.

Chrysta Newman
Village Farm,
Back Street, Skipsea,
Driffield, YO25 8SW
Tel   +44 (0)1262 468479
Email   info@villagefarmskipsea.co.uk
Web   www.villagefarmskipsea.co.uk

Entry 482   Map 13

Yorkshire

Yorkshire

The Wold Cottage

Drive through mature trees, and a proper entrance with signs, to a listed Georgian manor house in 300 glorious acres; tea awaits in the guest sitting room. The graceful dining room has heartlifting views across the landscaped gardens, and there are many original features: fan-lights, high ceilings, broad staircases. Bedrooms are sumptuous, traditional, with lots of thoughtful extras: chocolates, biscuits, monogrammed waffle robes. You are warmed by straw bale heating, and the food is local and delicious. An award-winning breakfast sets you up for a day of discovery: visit RSPB Bempton Cliffs, and the Wolds that have inspired David Hockney.

Min. stay: 2 nights at weekends & in high season.

Dale Farm

Huge skies as you drive along the open road to Dale Farm... the sea is just over the brow. Nifty inside too: bedrooms and bathrooms sparkle in whites and beach blues; mattresses are luxurious and handmade (the double is snugly in the attic); lots of books in the sitting room. Paul is a keen cook so breakfast is a varied feast: home-grown tomatoes, salmon from a local smokehouse, full English, and more! Peaceful woodland surrounds you; the logs fuel the biomass boiler and fires. Ramble and find Paul's metal sculptures and a fire-pit in the woods, croquet on the lawn, a beach down the road with a café... lovely.

Rooms	2 doubles, 2 twins: £100–£130. Barn – 1 double: £100–£130. Barn – 1 family room for 4: £100–£160. Singles £60–£75.
Meals	Supper £28. Wine from £15.
Closed	Rarely.

Rooms	1 double, 1 twin; 1 triple with separate bathroom: £90. 3 cabins for 2 (bathroom & wc in house 50yds; short breaks available at £60 per night): £350 per week. Singles £70. Extra bed/sofabed available £20 per person per night.
Meals	Pubs/restaurants 2 miles.
Closed	Rarely.

	Derek & Katrina Gray The Wold Cottage, Wold Newton, Driffield, YO25 3HL
Tel	+44 (0)1262 470696
Mobile	+44 (0)7811 203336
Email	katrina@woldcottage.com
Web	www.woldcottage.com

	Elizabeth Halliday Dale Farm, Bartindale Road, Hunmanby, Filey, YO14 0JD
Tel	+44 (0)1723 890175
Mobile	+44 (0)7751 674706
Email	elizabethhalliday1@gmail.com
Web	www.dalefarmholidays.co.uk

Entry 483   Map 13

Entry 484   Map 13

Yorkshire

The Farmhouse

Chris and Clare own and run a Swiss ski chalet and their traditional farmhouse has that vibe: friendly, communal, open-house. Find glowing lamps, Persian rugs, open fires and squashy sofas. Sleep well in good beds: airy Garden Room, Pigeon Loft with double-ended bath, sleekly simple Potting Shed tucked in the garden. Breakfast is in the yellow ochre dining room: homemade everything, Whitby kippers, copious coffee. The garden has views over heathered hills; you're in the heart of the North York Moors with hikes and bike trails galore; Whitby and the coast are close. Return for a four-course dinner – a sociable affair with local produce.

Min. stay: 2 nights. Over 16s welcome.

Yorkshire

Thorpe Hall

Arrive and listen: nothing, bar the wind in the trees and the odd seagull. The eye gathers glimmering sea and mighty headland, the final edge of the moors... are there still smugglers? This old listed house smells of polish and flowers, the drawing room breathes history. Angelique is a delight and has furnished it all, including TV-free bedrooms (one downstairs), with an eclectic mix of old and new; wonky walls and creaky floors add to the atmospheric feel. She's hung contemporary art on ancient walls and made a veg patch with young Phoebe. David helps out with simple breakfast when he's not globetrotting. The very opposite of stuffy.

Rooms	1 double: £110-£120. 1 suite for 2: £120-£130. 1 annexe for 2 with kitchen: £132-£142. Singles £80-£100.
Meals	Dinner £25-£45, Friday & Saturday (rest of week by arrangement). Pubs/restaurants 10-minute walk.
Closed	January – March.

Rooms	3 doubles, 1 twin; 3 doubles sharing separate bath & shower rooms: £70-£90. Singles £70-£80. Extra bed/sofabed available £15 per person per night.
Meals	Pub within 0.25 miles.
Closed	Usually Christmas & January.

Chris & Clare Carr
The Farmhouse,
Orchard Farm,
Orchard Lane, Goathland,
Whitby, YO22 5JX
Tel   +44 (0)1947 896391
Email   enquiries@thefarmhouseyorkshire.co.uk

Angelique Russell
Thorpe Hall,
Middlewood Lane, Fylingthorpe,
Whitby, YO22 4TT
Tel   +44 (0)1947 880667
Email   thorpehall@gmail.com
Web   www.thorpe-hall.co.uk

Entry 485   Map 13

Entry 486   Map 13

Yorkshire

20 St Hilda's Terrace

Little back lanes, an old gate, a secret walled garden and a large bay-windowed Georgian house. You're bang in the heart of Whitby yet the feel is very peaceful with airy rooms, flowers, botanical fabrics, elegant antiques, original art – and a Blüthner piano to play. Your pretty bedroom is reached up a graceful staircase; find high ceilings, a plump bed and views through sash windows. Your breakfast is continental and you can have it in the drawing room, the garden on fine days, or in bed if you're feeling lazy. Stroll to the beach for wild walks, explore the Yorkshire Moors or the shops in town – returning will be a pleasure.

Rooms	1 double with separate bath/shower: £80.
Meals	Continental breakfast. Pubs/restaurants 0.3 miles.
Closed	Rarely.

Pip Baines
20 St Hilda's Terrace,
Whitby, YO21 3AE
Tel   +44 (0)1947 602435
Email   marylouisa@talktalk.net

Entry 487   Map 13

Yorkshire

Union Place

A listed Adam Georgian townhouse – elegance epitomised. Lofty well-proportioned rooms with polished floors and cornices and fireplaces intact are delightfully dotted with sophisticated, quirky *objets*: bead-and-embroidery lampshades and chandeliers, bone china, a small mirrored Indian ceramic child's dress – and your urbane host Richard's accomplished paintings. Bedrooms, one painted duck egg blue, one green with floral wallpaper, are beautiful, with lots of lace and fine linen; the claw-foot roll top in the shared bathroom cuts a dash. Breakfast is unbeatable... then it's off to explore the North Yorkshire Moors. Superb.

Cloakroom available for guests.

Rooms	2 doubles sharing bath (extra wc available): £75–£85.
Meals	Pubs/restaurants within walking distance.
Closed	Christmas.

Richard & Jane Pottas
Union Place,
9 Upgang Lane, Whitby, YO21 3DT
Tel   +44 (0)1947 605501
Email   pottas1@btinternet.com
Web   www.unionplacewhitby.co.uk

Entry 488   Map 13

Channel Islands

Photo: Alec Studerus

Guernsey

Seabreeze

Maggie's house – the most southern on Guernsey – comes with enormous sea views: Herm and Sark glistening in the water under a vast sky, framed by a pretty front garden. The breakfast terrace is hard to beat. Find sofas in the conservatory, entertaining stories from Maggie and Francis, fabulous walks, a beach for picnics. The house started life as HQ for French pilots in WWI; these days warm, rustic interiors make for a great island base. It's not grand, just very welcoming with rooms that hit the spot: bathrobes, super showers, fresh flowers. Use the bikes (or hire locally) then spin up the lane to a top island restaurant. Brilliant.

Self-catering available in studio.

Rooms	2 twin/doubles: £75–£110. 1 studio for 2 with kitchenette: £125. Singles £50–£85.
Meals	Pubs/restaurants 500 yds & 0.5 miles.
Closed	14 December to February.

	Maggie Talbot-Cull Seabreeze, La Moye Lane, Route de Jerbourg, St Martin, GY4 6BN
Tel	+44 (0)1481 237929
Email	seabreeze-guernsey@mail.com
Web	www.guernseybandb.com

Entry 489   Map 4

Scotland

Aberdeenshire

Lynturk Home Farm

The stunning drawing room, with pier-glass mirror, baby grand and enveloping sofas, is reason enough to come; the food, served in a candlelit deep-sage dining room, is delicious too, with produce from the farm. A home full of life where you're treated as friends – your hosts are delightful, helped along by a very personable Jack Russell. It's peaceful, too, on the Aberdeenshire Castle Trail. The handsome farmhouse has been in the family since 1762 and you can roam the rolling 300 acres. Inside: flowers, polished furniture, Persian rugs, family portraits and supremely comfortable bedrooms with fine linen. "A blissful haven," says a guest.

Rooms	1 double, 2 twin/doubles: £100. Singles £60.
Meals	Dinner, 4 courses, £30. Pub 1 mile.
Closed	Rarely.

John & Veronica Evans-Freke
Lynturk Home Farm,
Alford, AB33 8HU
Tel	+44 (0)1975 562504
Mobile	+44 (0)7773 389793
Email	lynturk@hotmail.com

Entry 490   Map 19

Angus

Newtonmill House

The house and grounds are in perfect order; the owners are warm, charming and discreet. This is a little-known part of Scotland, with glens and gardens to discover; fishing villages, golf courses and deserted beaches, too. Return to a cup of tea in the sitting room or summerhouse, a wander in the lovely walled garden, and a marvellous supper of local produce; Rose grows interesting varieties of potato and her hens' eggs make a great hollandaise! Upstairs are crisp sheets, soft blankets, feather pillows, flowers, homemade fruit cake and warm sparkling bathrooms with thick towels. Let this home envelop you in its warm embrace.

Dogs by arrangement.

Rooms	1 twin; 1 double with separate bath: £100-£120. Singles £70-£75.
Meals	Dinner, £30-£36. BYO. Packed lunch £10. Pub 3 miles.
Closed	Christmas.

Rose & Stephen Rickman
Newtonmill House,
Brechin, DD9 7PZ
Tel	+44 (0)1356 622533
Mobile	+44 (0)7793 169482
Email	rrickman@srickman.co.uk
Web	www.newtonmillhouse.co.uk

Entry 491   Map 19

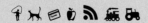

Angus

Nether Finlarg

John's farmhouse is a mile up the track, well-signposted off the Dundee-Aberdeen road. Fitting harmoniously into the landscape it comes with 400 acres and a lovely big garden rich in wildlife. Inside is an open-plan living area, friendly and bright, with a mish-mash of furniture including a fine antique dresser, and a sitting room with a log fire just for guests. The twin is en suite and the double is cosy, with a big sash window and a delightful view. John's breakfasts, Scottish or continental, set you up for the day so head for the hills or Dundee, a fantastic city full of history. Dinner? Choose little Glamis (six miles) or bustling Forfar.

Rooms	1 twin; 1 double with separate bath: £70-£85.
Meals	Pubs/restaurants 5 miles.
Closed	Christmas & New Year.

John Rymer,
Nether Finlarg,
Forfar, DD8 1XQ
Tel   +44 (0)1307 820250
Email   john@rymermail.com

Entry 492   Map 19

Argyll & Bute

Meall Mo Chridhe

Caring owners, exquisite food and a welcome sight amid the savage beauty of Britain's most westerly village. The warm ochre walls of this listed Georgian manse peep through wooded gardens across the Sound to Mull. Rooms are beautiful – French antiques, a wood stove, roll top baths – but it's the food that draws most to this far-flung spot. What David magics from his 45-acre smallholding (a bit of everything that grows, grunts, bleats or quacks) Stella transforms into feasts. Dine on spiced mackerel, minted lamb, hazelnut meringue; and duck eggs at breakfast. A gem buried in spectacular, wild walking country.

Rooms	5 doubles: £80-£150. Singles £50-£90.
Meals	Dinner, 2 courses with coffee, £28. Pub 0.25 miles.
Closed	Easter to end of October.

Stella & David Cash
Meall Mo Chridhe,
Kilchoan, Acharacle, PH36 4LH
Tel   +44 (0)1972 510238
Mobile +44 (0)7730 100639
Email   enquiries@westcoastscotland.co.uk
Web   www.westcoastscotland.co.uk

Entry 493   Map 17

Argyll & Bute

Callachally House

By the small fishing river at the mouth of the Glen, settled into its own wooded grounds, is a big Scottish farmhouse (once a drovers' inn) where on a still summer night you hear the lapping of the sea. A fine, traditional, cultured place, it's been in Ian's family since time began and overflows with colour and character. Bedrooms share bathrooms and each is a gem: old polished floors topped with bright rugs, chalky blue walls hung with paintings; you might hear sheepdogs barking at night. Wake to a fine breakfast (Ian loves to cook), head off down winding roads with views of islands and mountains, return to sprawling armchairs by the log fire.

Rooms	3 doubles sharing 2 bathrooms (adjoining twin available): £90. Singles £70.
Meals	Restaurants 2 miles away.
Closed	December – March.

Ian Mazur
Callachally House,
Glenforsa, Aros,
Isle of Mull, PA72 6JN
Email   ianmazur@icloud.com
Web   www.largeholidayhousemull.co.uk

Entry 494   Map 17

Argyll & Bute

Ardtorna

Come for perfect comfort and uninterrupted views of loch and mountain. These thoughtful, professional hosts are happy to share their new, open-plan, eco-friendly house where contemporary Scandinavian and Art Deco styles are cleverly blended with homely warmth. Sink into a bedroom with a wall of glass for those views; each has a wet room or spa bath with Molton Brown treats. Flowers and jauntily coloured coffee pots decorate the oak table in the stunning dining room, and food is home-baked and delicious. Argyll brims with historic sites and walks; return to watch the sun go down over the Morvern hills. Fabulous.

Rooms	4 twin/doubles: £99-£200. Singles £99.
Meals	Pub/restaurant 3 miles.
Closed	Rarely.

Karen O'Byrne
Ardtorna,
Mill Farm, Barcaldine,
Oban, PA37 1SE
Tel   +44 (0)1631 720125
Mobile   +44 (0)7867 785524
Email   info@ardtorna.co.uk
Web   www.ardtorna.co.uk

Entry 495   Map 17

Melfort House

A truly seductive combination of a wild landscape of ancient woods and hidden glens with rivers that tumble to a blue sea and a big, beautiful house with views straight down the loch. The whole place glows with polished antiques, oak floors, exquisite fabrics, prints and paintings. And Yvonne and Matthew are brilliant at looking after you – whether you're super-active, or not – their fabulous Scottish food's a treat. Bedrooms have soft plaids, superb views and handmade chocolates; bathrooms have huge towels and locally made soaps. Sally forth with boots or bikes, return to a dram by the log fire. Don't book too short a stay!

Rooms	2 twin/doubles: £95–£130.
	1 suite for 2: £95–£125.
	Singles from £70. Sofabed £15.
Meals	Dinner, 3 courses, from £32.
	Packed lunch £10.
	Pub/restaurant 400 yds.
Closed	Rarely.

Yvonne & Matthew Anderson
Melfort House,
Kilmelford, Oban, PA34 4XD
Tel	+44 (0)1852 200326
Mobile	+44 (0)7795 438106
Email	relax@melforthouse.co.uk
Web	www.melforthouse.co.uk

Entry 496   Map 14

Glenmore

A pleasingly idiosyncratic traditional country house with no need to stand on ceremony. Built in the 1800s but with 1930s additions setting the style, find solid oak doors and floors, red-pine panelling, Art Deco pieces and a unique carved staircase. Alasdair's family has been here for 150 years and many family antiques remain. One of the huge bedrooms can be arranged as a suite to include a single room and a sofabed; bath and basins are chunky 30s style with chrome plumbing. From the organic garden and the house there are magnificent views of Loch Melfort with its bobbing boats; you're free to come and go as you please.

Rooms	1 double with separate
	bath/shower: £85–£100.
	1 family room for 5: £95–£170.
	Singles £50–£65.
Meals	Pub 0.5 miles, restaurant 1.5 miles.
Closed	Christmas & New Year.

Melissa & Alasdair Oatts
Glenmore,
Kilmelford, Oban, PA34 4XA
Tel	+44 (0)1852 200314
Mobile	+44 (0)7786 340468
Email	oatts@glenmore22.fsnet.co.uk
Web	www.glenmorecountryhouse.co.uk

Entry 497   Map 17

Argyll & Bute

Achanduin Cottage

Sara's restoration of this old crofthouse is just right. The feel is restful, comfortable, understated. Everything's well chosen: rustic and reclaimed pieces, interesting art, colourful rugs. The bright east suite has its own sitting room with wood-burner; the west room has a fine mahogany bed, old farmhouse desk and a grand roll top bath in its bookish bathroom. All this set back in yachty Ardfern, sitting pretty on its Highland Loch... Perfect for Highland lovers – Donald's an outdoors guide – for lovers of art, good food and conversation – Sara's an inspired cook; both have a keen sense of place and sustainability.

Rooms	1 double: £75.
	1 suite for 2: £90
Meals	Pub 200 yds.
Closed	Rarely.

	Sara Wallace
	Achanduin Cottage,
	Ardfern,
	Lochgilphead, PA31 8QN
Tel	+44 (0)1852 500708
Email	sara@achanduincottage.co.uk
Web	www.achanduincottage.com

Entry 498   Map 14

Ayrshire

Alton Albany Farm

Discover Ayrshire... pine forests, hills and wild beauty. Alasdair and Andrea (sculptor and garden photographer) are generous hosts who love having you to stay – your visit starts with tea, coffee and cake. There's an arty vibe with their work on display; the dining room brims with garden books and games; large bedrooms have cosy lamps and more books. Big breakfasts by a log fire are a treat, perhaps with haggis, garden fruit, homemade bread. Rich in wildlife and orchids the garden has a rambling charm, the salmon-filled river Stinchar runs past and dogs are welcome – resident Clover and Daisy are friendly. Great fish restaurant nearby.

Min. stay: 2 nights at weekends & in high season.

Rooms	1 double; 1 double, 1 twin sharing
	bath (let to same party only): £85.
	Singles £50.
Meals	Pubs/restaurants 10-12 miles.
Closed	Rarely.

	Andrea & Alasdair Currie
	Alton Albany Farm,
	Barr, Girvan, KA26 0TL
Tel	+44 (0)1465 861148
Mobile	+44 (0)7881 908764
Email	alasdair@gardenexposures.co.uk
Web	www.altonalbanyfarm.com

Entry 499   Map 14

Chlenry Farmhouse

Handsome in its glen; a traditional family farmhouse full of old-fashioned comfort with charming, well-travelled owners and friendly dogs. In peaceful bedrooms with leafy views, solid antiques jostle with photos, flowers, bowls of fruit, and magazines on country matters. There are capacious bath tubs, robes – and suppers for walkers: the Southern Upland Way passes nearby. Breakfasts are properly fortifying and evening meals can be simple or elaborate, often with game or fresh salmon. Convenient for ferries to Belfast and Larne; Galloway gardens and golf courses are close too – return to a snug sitting room with an open fire.

Rooms	1 double, 1 twin sharing bath; 1 twin/double with separate bath: £90. Singles £50.
Meals	Supper £20. Dinner, 4 courses, £40. Packed lunch £6. Pub 1.5 miles.
Closed	Christmas, New Year, February & occasionally.

David & Ginny Wolsley Brinton
Chlenry Farmhouse,
Castle Kennedy, Stranraer, DG9 8SL
Tel   +44 (0)1776 705316
Mobile   +44 (0)7704 205003
Email   wolseleybrinton@aol.com
Web   www.chlenryfarmhouse.com

Entry 500   Map 14

Chipperkyle

This beautiful Scottish-Georgian family home has not a hint of formality, and the sociable Dicksons put you at your ease. Your sitting and dining rooms connect through a large arch; find gloriously comfy sofas, family pictures, rugs on wooden floors, masses of books and a constant log fire. Upstairs: good linen, striped walls, armchairs and windows with views – this wonderful house just gets better and better. There are 200 acres, dogs, cats, donkeys and hens – children can collect the eggs and go on tractor rides. The countryside is magnificent, beaches fabulous and this is a classified dark sky area. A house full of flowers and warmth.

Min. stay: 2 nights at weekends & in high season

Rooms	1 double (cot available); 1 twin with separate bath/shower: £110. Discounts for children.
Meals	Occasional dinner from £20 (available for groups). Pub 3 miles.
Closed	Rarely.

Willie Dickson
Chipperkyle,
Kirkpatrick Durham,
Castle Douglas, DG7 3EY
Tel   +44 (0)1556 650223
Mobile   +44 (0)7917 610008
Email   willie@chipperkyle.co.uk
Web   www.chipperkyle.co.uk

Entry 501   Map 11

Dumfries & Galloway

Three Glens

Getting here is just part of the adventure – up a steep track to an environmentally friendly build with 360 degree views. Emerging from the stone dyke that breaks the hill, the house is surrounded by sheep and a rolling landscape. Your host will welcome you in, make you feel at home and feed you well: a full Scottish breakfast, a sumptuous dinner, and everything (just about) sourced from the farm. Head off on stunning walks, visit castles – or simply stay put and relax. Sheep horns for hooks, an Austrian *kachelöfen*, a wall of windows that swish open. Luxurious en suite bedrooms await downstairs. Stop, unwind and feel your heart soar.

Minimum stay: 2 nights at weekends.

Rooms	2 doubles, 2 twins: £150.
Meals	Dinner, 3 courses with wine, £35.
	Pubs/restaurants 20-minute walk.
Closed	Rarely.

Neil & Mary Gourlay
Three Glens,
Moniaive, Thornhill, DG3 4EG

Mobile	+44 (0)7525 808 859
Email	info@3glens.com
Web	www.3glens.com

Entry 502   Map 15

Dumfries & Galloway

Holmhill Country House

Among the rolling hills of Dumfries and Galloway, by the banks of the Nith, is a hidden gem of a Georgian country house. It was a favourite of philosopher Thomas Carlyle, who had his own pipe-smoking spot in the marvellously colourful garden. There are seven acres to explore, utter tranquillity, stunning views of the Keir Hills and excellent fishing. Rosie and Stewart love sharing their family home with guests, and can treat you to breakfast, and possibly dinner, by the fire in the graceful dining room. Masses of space everywhere, each room deftly combining rustic virtue with modern savoir-faire.

Pets by arrangement.

Rooms	2 twin/doubles: £110.
	Singles £80.
Meals	Pubs/restaurants 0.5 miles.
Closed	Christmas & New Year.

Rosie Lee
Holmhill Country House,
Thornhill, DG3 4AB

Tel	+44 (0)1848 332239
Email	holmhillbooking@gmail.com
Web	www.holmhillthornhill.co.uk

Entry 503   Map 15

Dumfries & Galloway

Byreburnfoot House

Tucked away up a gravelled drive overlooking the banks of the salmon-rich Esk, this pretty Victorian forester's house combines traditional charm with modern comforts. Find an elegant and rural decor, with airy rooms, wooden floors and antique pieces – grandfather clock, writing desk, chandeliers. Beds are big, the linen is trimmed and views are sublime. Warm hosts Bill and Lorraine are keenly green-fingered: their 1.5 acres of orchards, flower-fringed lawns and organic kitchen garden are productive – and their cooking is delicious! Bill is happy to arrange salmon and trout fishing. Stay a few days and become part of it all.

Rooms	2 doubles; 1 twin/double with separate bath: £100–£110. Singles £70.
Meals	Dinner, 3 courses, £30. Packed lunch from £7.50. Pub/restaurant 5 miles.
Closed	Rarely.

Bill & Loraine Frew
Byreburnfoot House,
Canonbie, DG14 0XB

Tel	+44 (0)1387 371209
Mobile	+44 (0)7764 194901
Email	enquiries@byreburnfoot.co.uk
Web	www.byreburnfoot.co.uk

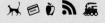

Entry 504   Map 15

Dumfries & Galloway

White Hill

Fresh air, huge gardens and stacks of Scottish charm. The aged paint exterior is forgotten once you're inside this treasure-trove of history and heritage. The Bell-Irvings are natural hosts; twenty generations of their family have lived here and worn the floorboards dancing. Throw logs on the fire, ramble round the azalea'd gardens or explore the woods, fish the river, and dine opulently under the gaze of portraits of their 'rellies'. Breakfast is a delightfully hearty affair. A very special chance to share a real ancestral home in the Scottish borders with a kind, funny, lovely couple (and their very friendly springer spaniel).

Rooms	2 twins: £98. Singles £54.
Meals	Dinner £30. Pubs/restaurants 4 miles.
Closed	Rarely.

Robin & Janet Bell-Irving
White Hill,
Ecclefechan, Lockerbie, DG11 1AL

Tel	+44 (0)1576 510206
Email	johnbi@talktalk.net
Web	www.aboutscotland.com/south/whitehill.html

Entry 505   Map 15

Dumfries & Galloway

The Waterside Rooms

Prepare to be given a thorough looking after! Generous spirited Nic and Julie gave up their day jobs, travelled around Europe in a camper van and ended up here, dipping their toes in the Solway Firth. Birdwatchers will swoon, burnt out city folk will find balm, independence seekers will adore their own entrance to a neat-as-a-pin suite: peaceful colours soothe in a comfy sitting room, well-dressed bedroom and sparkling shower room; your own fridge too. Breakfast on a feast of local produce and homemade breads and preserves in the colourful main house, sit in the pretty garden with its watery views, walk, cycle, sail. Blissful.

Rooms	1 suite for 2 with sitting room: £95. Extra bed/sofabed available £12 per person per night.
Meals	Pub/restaurant 3 miles.
Closed	Rarely.

Nic & Julie Pearse
The Waterside Rooms,
Dornock Brow House, Dornock,
Eastriggs, Annan, DG12 6SX
Tel   +44 (0)1461 40232
Email   enquiries@thewatersiderooms.co.uk
Web   www.thewatersiderooms.co.uk

Edinburgh

Geraldsplace

Elegant Georgian New Town… so splendid and handsome it's a World Heritage Site. Welcoming, enthusiastic, charming Gerald runs a B&B on one of its finest streets. His patio basement apartment is full of character, comfort and colour. Bedrooms have cosiness, warmth, fine fabrics, excellent art… and special extras: DVDs and a book swop shelf, a laptop with fast broadband, a tea tray, a decanter of single malt whisky; bathrooms are newly done. Breakfast is a feast and mostly organic. There's a private garden opposite, an incredibly convenient location and, of course, Gerald, your brilliantly well-informed, up-to-the-minute host.

Minimum stay: 3 nights.

Rooms	2 twin/doubles: £99–£129. Singles £74–£104. Extra bed/sofabed available £30 per person per night.
Meals	Restaurants within 3-minute walk.
Closed	Rarely.

Gerald Della-Porta
Geraldsplace,
21b Abercromby Place, EH3 6QE
Tel   +44 (0)131 558 7017
Mobile +44 (0)7766 016840
Email   gerald11@geraldsplace.com
Web   www.geraldsplace.com

Edinburgh

10 London Street

A Roman X marks this special spot: a beautiful Georgian terraced house in Edinburgh's world heritage New Town, home to descendants of Scots author John Gibson Lockhart. Step into a family home of period elegance and charming informality: accept a dram by the fire in the sash-windowed drawing room, relax at the dining table over a leisurely continental breakfast. Sleep undisturbed in 'Beauregard', with its lovely views and paintings; or 'Gibson' with its off-courtyard privacy and self-catering option. The best of Edinburgh is a stroll away, the new tram service from the airport is an easy glide into town.

Rooms	2 doubles (1 with self-catering option): £160.
Meals	Continental breakfast. Pub/restaurant 500 yds.
Closed	Rarely.

Pippa Lockhart
10 London Street,
EH3 6NA
Tel +44 (0)131 556 0737
Email pippalockhart@gmail.com
Web www.londonstreetaccommodation.co.uk

Entry 508   Map 15

Edinburgh

14 Hart Street

The brightly lit Georgian house has a smart front of polished brass and glossy paint. The warm raspberry hall is lined with art, and the graceful dining room is just as inviting: decanters on the sideboard, period furniture, glowing lamps, and a welcoming home-baked something. Fresh bright bedrooms are elegant and comfortable with whisky and wine on a tray and smart, sparkling bathrooms. Wake for breakfast at a beautifully polished table, with plenty of coffee, newspapers and chat; James and Angela are easy to talk to and love having guests to stay. Perfect for a peaceful city break, and Princes Street is a five-minute walk.

Rooms	2 doubles, 1 twin/double: £90-£150.
Meals	Restaurants 10-minute walk.
Closed	Rarely.

James & Angela Wilson
14 Hart Street,
EH1 3RN
Tel +44 (0)131 557 6826
Mobile +44 (0)7795 203414
Email hartst.edin@virgin.net
Web www.14hartst.com

Entry 509   Map 15

Edinburgh

Two Hillside Crescent

Leave your worries behind as you enter this exquisitely restored Georgian townhouse. All is peaceful, spacious and light, with an upbeat contemporary feel. Bedrooms are on the first and second floors: imagine sleek modern furniture, big beds, superb mattresses, clouds of goose down, crisp linen, and immaculate bathrooms with organic toiletries and lashings of hot water. Over a superb breakfast your charming hosts will help you get the most out of your stay. Calton Hill is across the road for the best views of the city, and you're a stroll from the start of the Royal Mile. Wonderful.

Rooms	5 twin/doubles: £125–£165. Singles from £95.
Meals	Pubs/restaurants across the road.
Closed	Rarely.

Elaine Adams
Two Hillside Crescent,
EH7 5DY
Tel   +44 (0)131 556 4871
Email   info@twohillsidecrescent.com
Web   www.twohillsidecrescent.com

Entry 510   Map 15

Edinburgh

2 Cambridge Street (The Dynamite Club)

A mischievous humour, tinged with historical and cultural references, alerts you to the specialness of this place, a ground-floor B&B in the lee of Edinburgh Castle, in the heart of theatre land. Find fin-de-siècle Scotland, with darkly striking colours on walls, antiques aplenty, and a captivating attention to detail. There are interactive art installations that sing and play, a line of old theatre seats up on the wall, photos and 'objets' serving startling and original purposes. Erlend and Hélène are delightful and free-spirited; Erlend, a quietly spoken (but don't be fooled) Shetlander, serves a breakfast to remember.

Rooms	2 doubles: £95–£140. Singles £90–£110.
Meals	Pubs/restaurants 1-minute walk.
Closed	Christmas.

Erlend & Hélène Clouston
2 Cambridge Street
(The Dynamite Club),
EH1 2DY
Tel   +44 (0)131 478 0005
Email   erlendc@blueyonder.co.uk
Web   www.wwwonderful.net

Entry 511   Map 15

Edinburgh

11 Belford Place

Guests love Sue's modern townhouse, quietly tucked away in a private road above the Water of Leith yet a short distance from the city. From the wooden-floored entrance a picture-lined staircase winds upward. Handsome bedrooms display china cups and floral spreads; dazzling bathrooms have Molton Brown goodies. Wake for Stornoway black pudding, kedgeree, homemade jams and delicious ginger compote at the gleaming table. Owls sometimes hoot in the pretty sloping garden, there's an outside luggage store, parking is free and art galleries and Murrayfield Stadium are nearby.

Min. stay: 2 nights in Aug. Children over 12 welcome.

Rooms	2 twin/doubles: £70–£120.
Meals	Restaurants 10-minute walk.
Closed	Christmas.

	Susan Kinross
	11 Belford Place,
	EH4 3DH
Tel	+44 (0)131 332 9704
Mobile	+44 (0)7712 836399
Email	suekinross@blueyonder.co.uk

Entry 512   Map 15

Edinburgh

12 Belford Terrace

Leafy trees, a secluded garden, a stone wall and, beyond, a quiet riverside stroll. On the doorstep of the Modern Art and Dean galleries with Edinburgh's theatres and restaurants just a 15-minute walk, this Victorian end terrace, beside Leith Water, oozes an easy-going elegance, helped by Carolyn's laid-back but competent manner. Garden level bedrooms have their own entrance and are big and creamy with stripy fabrics, antiques, sofas and huge windows. (The single has a Boy's Own charm.) Carolyn spoils with crisp linen, books and biscuits and a delicious, full-works breakfast. After a day in town, relax on the sunny terrace.

Rooms	1 double, 1 twin/double: £80–£120.
	1 single with separate shower:
	£40–£55.
Meals	Pub/restaurants 10-minute walk.
Closed	Christmas.

	Carolyn Crabbie
	12 Belford Terrace,
	EH4 3DQ
Tel	+44 (0)131 332 2413
Email	carolyncrabbie@blueyonder.co.uk

Entry 513   Map 15

Millers64

Who could fail to relax here after a busy day? The bedrooms are comfortable and contemporary, the hosts are knowledgeable and friendly, and the breakfasts are stupendous (jam and marmalade courtesy of Louise and Shona's mum), served gourmet style at the big table. This elegant terraced villa is reached via Leith Walk, a wide busy thoroughfare that gets you to Edinburgh's hub in 20 minutes on foot; Leith's waterfront is an easy half mile. Victorian stained glass and cornices mix with a serene eastern theme (note the stylish pewter sinks from Thailand) and the quietest room is at the back.

Minimum stay: 3 nights in high season.

Wallace's Arthouse Scotland

The apartment door swings open to a world of white walls, smooth floors, modern art, acoustic jazz, and smiling Wallace with a glass of wine – well worth the three-storey climb up this old Assembly Rooms building. Your host – New York fashion designer and arts enthusiast, Glasgow-born, not shy – has created a bright, minimalist space sprinkled with humour and casual sophistication. Bedrooms capture light and exude his inimitable style; the kitchen's narrow bar is perfect for a light breakfast. Leith is Edinburgh's earthy side with its docks and noisy street life, but fine restaurants abound and the centre is close. Memorable.

Rooms	1 double: £110–£140.
	1 suite for 2: £120–£160.
	Singles from £80.
Meals	Pubs/restaurants 0.5 miles.
Closed	Rarely.

Rooms	2 doubles: £110.
	Singles £95.
	Extra bed/sofabed available
	£40–£45 per person per night.
Meals	Pubs/restaurants 10 yds.
Closed	Christmas Eve & Christmas Day.

	Louise Clelland
	Millers64,
	64 Pilrig Street, EH6 5AS
Tel	+44 (0)131 454 3666
Email	louise@millers64.com
Web	www.millers64.com

	Wallace Shaw
	Wallace's Arthouse Scotland,
	41-4 Constitution Street, EH6 7BG
Tel	+44 (0)131 538 3320
Mobile	+44 (0)7941 343714
Email	cawallaceshaw@mac.com
Web	www.wallacesarthousescotland.com

Fife

Greenlaw House

With superb views towards the Lomond Hills, Debbie's bright, warm converted farm steading will please you the moment you step in. There's a interesting blend of antiques and fascinating modern art throughout. The oak-floored sitting room has Afghan rugs, sofas by a log-burner, books, a grand piano; catch the summer sun on the decked area. Bedrooms have posies of garden flowers and views over the beautiful stone-walled garden; the upstairs one is more lived-in. Debbie loves to cook: smoked salmon, homemade granola and jams, porridge with cream. Falkland Palace, hunting haunt of the Stuart kings, is close, and the walks are wonderful.

Rooms	1 double; 1 double, 1 twin sharing bath (let to same party only): £80-£90. Singles £50. Extra bed/sofabed available £15 per person per night.
Meals	Dinner £25-£30. Restaurants 15-minute drive.
Closed	Christmas & New Year.

Debbie Butler
Greenlaw House,
Braeside, Collessie,
Cupar, KY15 7UX
Tel   +44 (0)1337 810413
Email   butlerjackson@googlemail.com
Web   www.greenlawhouse.com

🐦 🐱 🐕 👶 📶 🚂

Entry 516   Map 15

Fife

Kinkell

An avenue of beech trees patrolled by guinea fowl, Hebridean sheep and Highland cows leads to the house. If the sea views and salty smack of St Andrews Bay air don't get you, step inside and have your senses tickled. Your hosts are wonderful and offer you a glass of something on arrival; the elegant drawing room has two open fires, rosy sofas, a grand piano – gorgeous. Bedrooms and bathrooms are immaculate and sunny. Sandy and Frippy are great cooks and make full use of local produce. Gaze on the sea from the garden, head down to the beach, walk the wild coast. A friendly, comfortable family home.

Online booking available.

Rooms	3 twin/doubles: £100. Singles £60.
Meals	Dinner £30. Restaurants 2 miles.
Closed	Rarely.

Sandy & Frippy Fyfe
Kinkell,
St Andrews, KY16 8PN
Tel   +44 (0)1334 472003
Mobile   +44 (0)7836 746043
Email   fyfe@kinkell.com
Web   www.kinkell.com/house

🐦 🐱 🐕 📖 👶 📶 🚂

Entry 517   Map 16

Glasgow

64 Partickhill Road

Be greeted by three free-range hens and Gertie the terrier on arrival at this relaxed family home. It's the bustling West End but the road is peaceful and there's a lovely big garden. Caroline and Hugh are lovers of the arts: the house is full of pictures, vintage finds and books. There are wood floors, rugs, a fire in the comfy sitting room and your bedroom is bright and spacious. Tuck into a delicious breakfast, in the conservatory, of good croissants, organic bacon and sausages, homemade bread and jams. Easy for the underground, trendy cafés and delis, museums, theatres and the university. A city treat.

Rooms	1 double (extra twin available): £80-£90.
Meals	Packed lunch available. Pubs/restaurant 0.25 miles.
Closed	Occasionally.

Caroline Anderson
64 Partickhill Road,
G11 5NB
Tel   +44 (0)141 339 1946
Mobile   +44 (0)7962 144509
Email   carolineanderson64@gmail.com

Entry 518   Map 15

Highland

St Callan's Manse

Fun, laughter and conversation flow in this warm and happy home. You share it with prints, paintings, antiques, sofas, amazing memorabilia, two dogs, four ducks, 10 hens and 1,200 teddy bears of every size and origin. Snug bedrooms have pretty fabrics, old armoires, flower-patterned sheets and tartan blankets; your sleep will be sound. Caroline cooks majestic breakfasts and dinners; Robert, a fund of knowledgeable anecdotes, can arrange just about anything. Their Highland hospitality knows no bounds! All this in incomparable surroundings: 60 acres of land plus glens, forests, buzzards, deer and the odd golden eagle. A gem.

Rooms	1 double with separate bath, 1 double with separate shower: £90. Singles £65.
Meals	Dinner, 2-4 courses, £20-£35. BYO. Pub/restaurant in village 1.5 miles.
Closed	March & occasionally.

Robert & Caroline Mills
St Callan's Manse,
Rogart, IV28 3XE
Tel   +44 (0)1408 641363
Email   caroline@rogartsnuff.me.uk
Web   www.spanglefish.com/ stcallansmanse

Entry 519   Map 21

Highland

The Peatcutter's Croft

Some say there's more beauty in a mile on the west coast than in the rest of the world put together – vast skies, soaring mountains, shimmering water, barely a soul in sight. Pauline and Seori left London to give their family the freedom to roam. Now they have a colourful cast of companions: sheep, hens, ducks, rabbits – all live here. In the adjoining byre: country simplicity, a Norwegian wood-burner, colour, texture and style. Sea eagles patrol the skies, porpoises bask in the loch, red deer come to eat the garden. This, coupled with Pauline's home cooking, makes it very hard to leave. Dogs and children are very welcome.

Rooms	1 apartment for 2, with mezzanine for 2 children: £70–£100. Singles from £45.
Meals	Dinner, 3 courses, £30. BYO. Pub/restaurant 30 miles.
Closed	Christmas.

Seori & Pauline Burnett
The Peatcutter's Croft,
Croft 12, Badrallach, Dundonnell,
Garve, Ullapool, IV23 2QP

Tel	+44 (0)1854 633797
Email	info@peatcutterscroft.com
Web	www.peatcutterscroft.com

Entry 520   Map 17

Highland

Wemyss House

The peace is palpable, the setting overlooking the Cromarty Firth is stunning. Take an early morning stroll and spot buzzards, pheasants, rabbits and roe deer. The deceptively spacious house with sweeping maple floors is flooded with light and fabulous views, big bedrooms are warmly decorated with Highland rugs and tweeds, there's Christine's grand piano in the living room, Stuart's handcrafted furniture at every turn, and a sweet dog called Bella. Aga breakfasts include homemade bread, preserves and eggs from happy hens; Christine and Stuart are wonderful hosts.

Rooms	2 doubles, 1 twin/double: £115–£120.
Meals	Restaurants 15-minute drive.
Closed	November – March.

Christine Asher & Stuart Clifford
Wemyss House,
Bayfield, Tain, IV19 1QW

Tel	+44 (0)1862 851212
Mobile	+44 (0)7759 484709
Email	stay@wemysshouse.com
Web	www.wemysshouse.com

Entry 521   Map 18

Knockbain House

This is a well-loved farm, its environmental credentials supreme, and David and Denise are warm and interesting. A beautiful setting, too: landscaped gardens, a 700-acre farm (cows, lambs, barley) and rolling countryside stretching to Cromarty Firth. A grandfather clock ticks away time to relax, by floor-to-ceiling windows and a wood-burner in the antiques-filled sitting room; over a breakfast of local and home-grown produce; with a drink on the pond-side terrace; in bedrooms with fresh bathrooms and stunning views. David can advise on great walks, and has made maps of the farm's footpaths. Revel in the glorious unspoilt nature.

Babes in arms & over 10s welcome.

Craigiewood

The best of both worlds: Highland remoteness (red kites, wild goats) and Inverness just four miles away. The landscape surrounding this elegant cottage exudes a sense of ancient mystery… woodpeckers, deer, glorious roses all round. Araminta is a delightful host and her home has a lovely family feel; bedrooms are old-fashioned and cosy; the drawing room is snug with stove and books. Gavin almost built the house single-handed, planting a glorious garden here, and many throughout Scotland – his special touch remains. Meander up through rowan trees to a view point, sit and enjoy the peace. Inverewe, Attadale and Cawdor – all on the doorstep.

Rooms	1 double, 1 twin: £70-£95. Singles £45-£70.		Rooms	2 twins: £80-£90. Singles £40-£50.
Meals	Dinner from £25. Pubs/restaurants 1 mile.		Meals	Pub 2 miles.
Closed	Christmas & New Year.		Closed	Christmas & New Year.

David & Denise Lockett
Knockbain House,
Dingwall, IV15 9TJ

Tel	+44 (0)1349 862476
Mobile	+44 (0)7736 629838
Email	davidlockett@avnet.co.uk
Web	www.knockbainhouse.co.uk

Araminta Dallmeyer
Craigiewood,
North Kessock, Inverness, IV1 3XG

Tel	+44 (0)1463 731628
Mobile	+44 (0)7831 733699
Email	2minty@craigiewood.co.uk
Web	www.craigiewood.co.uk

Entry 522   Map 18

Entry 523   Map 18

Highland

The Old Ferryman's House

This 200-year-old former ferryman's house is small, homely and well lived-in. Mountain views, the river Spey close by and a garden with a tray of tea and homemade treats… Plants tumble from whisky barrels and pots and there are woodpeckers and otters to spy. The sitting room is cosy with the wood-burner and brimming with books. Elizabeth, a keen traveller who has lived in the Sudan, cooks delicious, imaginative meals: eggs from her hens, homemade bread and preserves, heather honey and sometimes herbs and veg from the garden. There's no TV – no need here: it's an unmatched spot for explorers and nature lovers. Good value too.

Rooms	1 double, 1 twin/double sharing 1 bath and 2 wcs with single: £75. 1 single: £38.
Meals	Dinner, 3 courses, £25. BYO. Packed lunch £7.50.
Closed	Occasionally in winter.

Elizabeth Matthews
The Old Ferryman's House,
Boat of Garten, PH24 3BY
Tel   +44 (0)1479 831370

Entry 524   Map 18

Highland

The Grange

A Victorian townhouse with its toes in the country: the mountain hovers above, the loch shimmers below and the garden slopes steeply to great banks of rhododendrons. Bedrooms, the one in the turret with a sumptuous bathroom, are large, luscious, warm and inviting: crushed velvet, beautiful blankets, immaculate linen – all ooze panache. Expect decanters of sherry, innovative decor, a Louis XV bed and a superb suite with contemporary touches. Elegant breakfasts are served at mahogany tables with linen napkins; Joan's warm vivacity and love of B&B means guests keep coming back. And just a 10-minute walk into town.

Rooms	2 doubles: £130-£140. 1 suite for 2: £130-£145.
Meals	Restaurants 12-minute walk.
Closed	Mid-November to March.

Joan & John Campbell
The Grange,
Grange Road,
Fort William, PH33 6JF
Tel   +44 (0)1397 705516
Email   info@thegrange-scotland.co.uk
Web   www.thegrange-scotland.co.uk

Entry 525   Map 17

Highland

Aurora

The perfect spot for walkers and climbers (single-track roads, lochs, rivers and mountains) and the perfect B&B for groups: three smart, uncluttered bedrooms have flexible sleeping arrangements and spick and span shower rooms. The guest sitting room is light and airy with binoculars, books to borrow, maps and a small fridge for your wine – stay put for glorious sunsets and views to Harris. Breakfast time abounds with good seasonal food; breads, yoghurt and jams are all homemade, and you eat round a big table. There's a drying room and bike storage, but those wanting to relax will love it here too.

Minimum stay: 2 nights.

Rooms	2 doubles: £78–£90.
	1 triple: £120–£135.
	Singles £68–£80.
Meals	Packed lunch £6.
	Pub/restaurant within 0.5 miles.
Closed	November – March.

Ann Barton
Aurora,
Shieldaig,
Torridon, IV54 8XN

Tel	+44 (0)1520 755246
Email	info@aurora-bedandbreakfast.co.uk
Web	www.aurora-bedandbreakfast.co.uk

Isle of Skye

The Cottage Stein

John and Fiona are warm and welcoming – you'll feel at home straight away. They've renovated their 200-year-old crofter's cottage with love and contemporary style, the views from bedrooms and guest sitting room are astonishing and a short walk takes you to the edge of the loch. Wake to breakfast in the cosy dining room – continental and cooked options, including full Scottish and lighter and sweeter choices, are all served with John's delicious homemade bread. Heaps to do nearby: boat trips, art galleries, Dunvegan castle and great walks. Supper is easy: it's a stroll to Skye's oldest inn and a fabulous restaurant – both right on the water.

Minimum stay: 2 nights in high season. Children over 12 welcome.

Rooms	1 double, 1 twin/double: £110–£125.
	Singles £85–£100.
Meals	Pubs/restaurants 1-minute walk.
Closed	Rarely.

John & Fiona Middleton
The Cottage Stein,
Stein, Waternish, IV55 8GA

Tel	+44 (0)1470 592734
Mobile	+44 (0)7742 193901
Email	stay@thecottagestein.co.uk
Web	www.thecottagestein.co.uk

Lanarkshire

The Lint Mill

Rolling hills, fields of sheep and a babbling stream surround this perfectly peaceful converted mill. Deborah and Colin escaped city life to create a smallholding full of flowers, beehives, vegetables, funky sheep, pigs, chickens with fancy houses and horses with a dressage paddock. The light, roomy wing has a separate entrance and private garden, a spiral staircase, its own sitting room and a big wood-burner. Unwind, walk in the countryside, enjoy the fruits (and scones) of their labour, get creative in their artists' studio or pop to excitement in Edinburgh or Glasgow. Foodies will be treated to all manner of local delights.

Please see owners' website for availability calendar.

Rooms	1 double with sitting room & conservatory: £90-£105. Singles £60. Extra bed/sofabed available £60 per person per night.
Meals	Dinner, 2-4 courses, £20-£30. Supper £10. Platter for 2, £15. Restaurants 2 miles.
Closed	Rarely.

	Colin & Deborah Richardson-Webb The Lint Mill, Carnwath, Lanark, ML11 8LY
Tel	+44 (0)1555 840042
Mobile	+44 (0)7966 164742
Email	info@thelintmill.co.uk
Web	www.thelintmill.co.uk

Lanarkshire

Cormiston Farm

Wend your way through the soft hills of the Clyde Valley to a Georgian farmhouse in 26 acres of farmland and mature garden. Richard's a keen cook and produce from the walled garden – including delicious eggs from the quails – takes centre stage. Wonderful to retire to quiet, spacious rooms with bucolic views, stunning beds and rich fabrics; characterful Art Deco bathrooms, too. Tuck nippers up in bunks, then slip back for a snifter in front of the log fire in the sitting room. It's home from home, and licensed, too! There's untamed landscape to explore – and the children will love the friendly alpacas.

Rooms	2 doubles, each with separate bath: £86-£108. Singles £65-£81. Extra bunk room available.
Meals	Dinner, 4 courses, £25-£30. Supper, 2 courses, £20. Pub 2 miles.
Closed	Rarely.

	Richard Philipps Cormiston Farm, Cormiston Road, Biggar, ML12 6NS
Tel	+44 (0)1899 221507
Email	info@cormistonfarm.com
Web	www.cormistonfarm.com

Midlothian

Crookston House

Scots Baronial grandeur complete with turrets, balustrades, ancestral portraits and impressive entrance... yet a family home with life and warmth. Engaging hosts welcome you with tea and a homemade something. A splendid staircase leads to huge traditional bedrooms with antiques, art and cosy gowns. Watch the wild birds tucking in as you breakfast too, on home-laid eggs and local treats. The 47 acres have swathes of snowdrops in spring and colour all year. Georgina and Malcolm know the area well; heaps to do: river Tweed fishing, walks, mountain bike trails. Return to a toasty, red sitting room with comfy sofas, log fire and lots of interesting books.

Children over 4 welcome. Pets by arrangement.

Rooms	1 double, 1 twin; 1 double with separate shower: £95–£135.
Meals	Pubs/restaurants 11 miles.
Closed	Rarely.

Georgina Leslie
Crookston House,
Heriot, EH38 5YS
Tel   +44 (0)1875 835661
Email   georgina@crookstonhouse.com
Web   www.crookstonhouse.com

Moray

Westfield House

Sweep up the drive to the grand home of an illustrious family: Macleans have lived here since 1862, and there are 500 peaceful acres of farmland. Inside: polished furniture and burnished antiques, a tartan-carpeted hall, an oak stair hung with ancestral oils. Veronica cooks sublimely; dinner is served at a long candelabra'd table, with vegetables from the vegetable garden. A winter fire crackles in the guest sitting room, old-fashioned bedrooms are inviting (plump pillows, fine linen, books, lovely views), the peace is deep. The coast is close and the walking is splendid; a historic house in a perfect setting and Veronica is charming.

Rooms	1 twin; 1 twin with separate bath & shower: £100. 1 single with separate bath: £50. Extra bed/sofabed available £20 per person per night.
Meals	Supper, 2 courses, £20. Dinner, 3 courses, £25. Pub 3 miles.
Closed	Rarely.

Veronica Maclean
Westfield House,
Elgin, IV30 8XL
Tel   +44 (0)1343 547308
Email   veronica.maclean@yahoo.co.uk
Web   www.westfieldhouseelgin.co.uk

Perth & Kinross

Beinn Bhracaigh

Excellent views stretch out from this Victorian villa. All the bedrooms are in relaxing creams, with duck-egg blues in throws and subtly patterned cushions propped like toast in a toast rack; TVs and fine Scottish soaps complete the Perthshire picture. Friendly hosts give you a continental breakfast in your room or a full Scottish and good coffee at separate tables in the dining room. Great fun and conviviality can be had in the evening when guests take over the honesty bar with its many wines and more than 50 whiskies. Amble to Pitlochry Theatre; discover an area rich with castles, fishing, white water rafting and walks.

Minimum stay: 2 nights at weekends. Children over 8 welcome.

Rooms	8 doubles, 3 twin/doubles: £69-£102. 1 suite for 2: £89-£129. Singles from £49.
Meals	14 pubs/restaurants within 10-minute walk.
Closed	Rarely.

James & Kirsty Watts
Beinn Bhracaigh,
14 Higher Oakfield,
Pitlochry, PH16 5HT
Tel   +44 (0)1796 470355
Email   info@beinnbhracaigh.com
Web   www.beinnbhracaigh.com

Entry 532   Map 15+18

Perth & Kinross

Cuil an Duin

Rhododendrons form a brilliant guard of honour to escort you to the front door, and you arrive to tea and scones in the drawing room. Admire mountain views, head off into woodland, roam the gardens, chat to the horses – the 20 acres are stunning. Inside is just as good: elegant rooms, Persian rugs, modern art, flowers, a gleaming Bechstein; sunny bedrooms are luxuriously comforting. Happy hens foraging in the fields lay your breakfast eggs, artisan shops provide the trimmings. Sally and David are charming, Flora the Labrador and Chloe the cat stay behind the kitchen door until given the all clear, and there are outdoor pursuits galore.

Min. stay: 2 nights at weekends & in high season.

Rooms	1 double, 1 twin/double; 1 double with separate bath: £115-£145. Singles £100-£1
Meals	Pubs/restaurant 1.5 miles.
Closed	Rarely.

Sally Keay & David Royce
Cuil an Duin,
Ballinluig,
Pitlochry, PH9 0NN
Tel   +44 (0)1796 482807
Email   enquiries@cuil-an-duin.com
Web   www.cuil-an-duin.com

Entry 533   Map 15+18

Perth & Kinross

Perth & Kinross

Essendy House

Down a tree-lined drive blazing with colour, Tess and John's charming country house is surrounded by lochs, castles and serenity. Inside is cosy and comfortable with wood fires, flowers, porcelain, Tess's striking murals and trompe l'oeil and an unusual collection of family artefacts. Traditional bedrooms have antiques, good linen, silk or floral touches and views of Dunsinane Hill. Enjoy hearty breakfasts and suppers in the huge dining room or under the vines in the conservatory; the terrace is heaven in summer. There's lots to do: visit cathedral and theatre, walk in Macbeth's Birnam Wood, play golf, ski, fish and admire swooping ospreys.

Mackeanston House

They grow their own organic fruit and vegetables in the walled garden, make their own preserves, bake their own bread. Likeable and energetic – Fiona a wine buff and talented cook, Colin a tri-lingual guide – your hosts are hospitable people whose 1690 farmhouse combines informality and luxury in peaceful, central Scotland. Light-filled bedrooms have pretty fabrics, fine antiques, TVs and homemade cake. Roomy bathrooms have robes and a radio; one has a double shower (with a seat if you wish it). Dine by the log fire in the dining room, or in the conservatory with views to Stirling Castle.

Rooms	1 double, 1 twin: £110. Singles £55.		Rooms	1 double, 1 twin/double: £100–£110. Singles £65. Extra bed/sofabed available £30 per person per night.
Meals	Packed lunch £5. Supper, 2 courses, £25. Pub/restaurant 2 miles.		Meals	Dinner, 3-4 courses, £33–£36. Pub 1 mile.
Closed	Christmas & New Year; February/March.		Closed	Rarely.

John Monteith
Essendy House,
Blairgowrie, PH10 6QY

Tel	+44 (0)1250 884260
Mobile	+44 (0)7841 121538
Email	johnmonteith@hotmail.com
Web	www.essendy.org

Fiona & Colin Graham
Mackeanston House,
Doune, Stirling, FK16 6AX

Tel	+44 (0)1786 850213
Mobile	+44 (0)7921 143018
Email	info@mackeanstonhouse.co.uk
Web	www.mackeanstonhouse.co.uk

Entry 534   Map 15+18

Entry 535   Map 15

Perth & Kinross

Old Kippenross

What a setting! Old Kippenross rests in 150 peaceful acres of gorgeous park and woodland overlooking the river Allan – spot red squirrels and deer, herons, dippers and otters. The 15th-century house has a Georgian addition and an air of elegance and great courtesy, with its rustic white-vaulted basement, and dining and sitting rooms strewn with soft sofas and Persian rugs. Sash-windowed bedrooms are deeply comfortable, warm bathrooms are stuffed with towels. Susan and Patrick (an expert on birds of prey) are welcoming, the food is good and there's a croquet lawn in the walled garden.

Children over 10 welcome. Dogs by arrangement only.

Rooms	1 double, 1 twin/double (adjoining single room, let to same party only): £108-£112. Singles £69-£71.
Meals	Dinner £30. BYO. Pub 1.5 miles.
Closed	Rarely.

Susan & Patrick Stirling-Aird
Old Kippenross,
Kippenross,
Dunblane, FK15 0LQ
Tel   +44 (0)1786 824048
Email   kippenross@hotmail.com
Web   www.oldkippenross.co.uk

Entry 536   Map 15

Scottish Borders

Eastfield House

Throw back the duvet and revel in the view from your room across the fields to the Cheviot Hills. Full breakfasts are served at the mahogany dining table. Bilingual French-Belgian Francis loves to cook and also produces sumptuous dinners, while florist Camilla fills the house with fragrant displays. Walk, cycle, fish (local guest permits available), discover castles, abbeys and glorious beaches less than an hour away. Slump in front of the fire, read a book in the conservatory, then retire to elegant rooms with comfy beds, chequered headboards and pretty fabrics. Bathrooms are sparkling, fresh and hung with eye-catching pictures.

Well behaved children & pets welcome.

Rooms	1 double; 1 double with separate bath: £85-£95.
Meals	Dinner £10-£50. Pubs/restaurants 5-minute drive.
Closed	Rarely.

Francis & Camilla Raeymaekers
Eastfield House,
Greenlaw, TD10 6YJ
Tel   +44 (0)1361 810750
Mobile   +44 (0)7788 560326
Email   raeymaekers@aol.com

Entry 537   Map 15

Fauhope House

Near to Melrose Abbey and the glorious St Cuthbert's Walk, this solid 1890s house is immersed in bucolic bliss. Views soar to the Eildon Hills through wide windows with squashy seats; all is luxurious, elegant, fire-lit and serene with an eclectic mix of art. Bedrooms are warm with deeply coloured walls, pale tartan blankets and soft velvet and linen; bathrooms are modern and pristine. Breakfast is served with smiles at a flower-laden table and overlooking those purple hills. A short walk through the blooming garden and over a footbridge takes you to the interesting town of Melrose, with shops, restaurants and its own theatre.

Whitehouse Country House

A proud avenue of trees leads to Angela and Roger's handsome 19th-century country house in the heart of the Scottish Borders. They have been welcoming guests for over 20 years providing comfort, relaxation and great hospitality. Enjoy log fires and deep armchairs in the elegant dining and drawing rooms, traditional bedrooms with the most comfortable beds and glorious views from every room. Angela's cooking is heavenly and she uses wild salmon, game and the finest in-season local produce. Explore historic Border towns, cycle the Tweed Cycleway, walk St Cuthbert's Way – your hosts know the area well and are happy to advise.

Pets by arrangement.

Rooms	3 twin/doubles: £130–£145. Singles £98.
Meals	Pub/restaurant 0.5 miles.
Closed	Rarely.

Rooms	1 double, 2 twins: £120–£140. Singles £80–£90. Extra bed/sofabed £25–£35 per person per night.
Meals	Dinner £22–£29. Supper tray £10. Packed lunch £7. Pub 3 miles.
Closed	Rarely.

	Ian & Sheila Robson Fauhope House, Gattonside, Melrose, TD6 9LU
Tel	+44 (0)1896 823184
Mobile	+44 (0)7816 346768
Email	info@fauhopehouse.com
Web	www.fauhopehouse.com

	Angela & Roger Tyrer Whitehouse Country House, St Boswells, Melrose, TD6 0ED
Tel	+44 (0)1573 460343
Mobile	+44 (0)7877 800582
Email	stay@whitehousecountryhouse.com
Web	www.whitehousecountryhouse.com

Scottish Borders

Singdean

Remote, high up, rugged and off-grid. You have your own entrance to a smart-and-soulful suite in this glorious Border cottage, where you'll be toasty warm and comfortable. Find an enormous double bed, delicious linen, exposed stonework, reclaimed wood cladding and thick fabrics. Take a deep breath out, light the candles, laze in the hot tub and look up at the stars... romantics will be thrilled to bits. Fresh, ski-style breakfasts are brought to you by welcoming hosts Christa and Del and awe-inspiring walks and wildlife are on your doorstep. Peruse the shop for a quirky souvenir, or venture down to Hawick for the cashmere.

Rooms	1 suite for 2: £145.
Meals	Packed lunch included by prior arrangement (voluntary contribution to the Landscaping fund). Pub 6 miles.
Closed	Rarely.

Christa & Del Dobson
Singdean,
Newcastleton, TD9 0SP
Tel   +44 (0)1450 860622
Email   info@alppine.co.uk
Web   www.alppine.co.uk

Entry 540   Map 16

Stirling

Cardross

Dodge the lazy sheep on the long drive to arrive (eventually!) at a sweep of gravel and lovely old Cardross in a gorgeous setting. Bang on the enormous ancient door and either Archie or Nicola (plus labradors and lively Jack Russells) will usher you in. And what a delight it is; come here for a blast of Scottish history! Traditional big bedrooms have airiness, long views, antiques, wooden shutters, towelling robes and good linen; one bathroom has a cast-iron period bath. The drawing room is vast, the house is filled with warm character, the Orr Ewings can tell you all the history.

Over 14s welcome.

Rooms	1 twin; 1 twin with separate bath: £110–£120. Singles £70–£75.
Meals	Occasional dinner £35. Pubs/restaurants 3-6 miles.
Closed	Christmas & New Year.

Sir Archie & Lady Orr Ewing
Cardross,
Port of Menteith,
Kippen, FK8 3JY
Tel   +44 (0)1877 385223
Email   enquiries@cardrossestate.com
Web   www.cardrossestate.com

Entry 541   Map 15

Stirling

Duchray Castle

Warm friendly Frances has thought of everything: a furnished terrace by the round tower, logs ablaze in the Great Hall, sofas, books, magazines, DVDs, and Arran Aromatics by the bath. Deep in the Trossachs National Park, at the end of the long forest track, you arrive in the clearing and there is the castle – simple, beautiful and steeped in five centuries of history. Inside all is deliciously cosy. Bedrooms are relaxing (the grandest with a log-burner), bathrooms are sleek, there are spiral stone stairs, sweeping wood floors, gilded mirrors, and breakfasts of the finest local produce. Stay a long weekend – or more.

Minimum stay: 2 nights.

Rooms	2 doubles, 1 twin, 1 four-poster: £105–£185. Singles £75–£105.
Meals	Pubs/restaurants 2.5 miles.
Closed	Rarely.

Frances Bigwood
Duchray Castle,
Duchray Road, Aberfoyle, FK8 3XL
Tel   +44 (0)1877 389333
Email   frances@duchraycastle.com
Web   www.duchraycastle.com

Entry 542   Map 15

Stirling

Powis House

A sprawling 18th-century mansion with the volcanic Ochil Hills as a stunning backdrop and a colourful entrance hall of antlers and stuffed animals. Country style bedrooms invite with polished old floors, tartan throws, garden views and original bathrooms. You have a huge dining room with warming wood-burner, a guest lounge on the first floor, a sunny stone-flagged patio with places to sit and acres of estate with a woodland walk to explore. Colin and Jane are caring and interesting; Colin is a keen cook and has ghost stories galore to share. Historical Stirling is close: castle, university, festival and more.

Rooms	2 doubles, 1 twin: £100. Singles £65.
Meals	Pub/restaurant 3 miles.
Closed	November – February.

Jane & Colin Kilgour
Powis House,
FK9 5PS
Tel   +44 (0)1786 460231
Email   info@powishouse.co.uk
Web   www.powishouse.co.uk

Entry 543   Map 15

Pairc an t-Srath

Richard and Lena's lovely home overlooks the beach at Borve – another absurdly beautiful Harris view. Inside, smart simplicity abounds: wooden floors, white walls, a peat fire, colourful art. Airy bedrooms fit the mood perfectly: trim carpets, chunky wood beds, Harris tweed throws, excellent shower rooms (there's a bathroom, too, if you want a soak). Richard crofts, Lena cooks, perhaps homemade soup, venison casserole, wet chocolate cake with raspberries. Views from the dining room tumble down hill, so expect to linger over breakfast. You'll spot otters in the loch, while the standing stones at Callanish are unmissable.

Rooms	2 doubles, 1 twin: £104–£108.
	1 single: £52–£54. Singles £54.
Meals	Dinner, 3 courses, £37.
	Restaurant 3 miles, pub 7 miles.
Closed	Christmas & New Year.

Lena & Richard MacLennan
Pairc an t-Srath,
Borve, Isle of Harris, HS3 3HT

Tel	+44 (0)1859 550386
Email	info@paircant-srath.co.uk
Web	www.paircant-srath.co.uk

Entry 544   Map 20

Wales

Caerphilly

Carmarthenshire

Gellihaf House

A handsome house bordered by stone walls, horse chestnuts and ancient oaks. Ann and Les have elegantly restored all, keeping heaps of original features; find oak floors, stained glass, heritage colours, eclectic period furniture, a wood fire and a galleried landing for curling up with a book. Inviting bedrooms have feather duvets, smart phone docking stations, coffee; bathrooms are drench-shower smart. Breakfast, local and generous, comes with Welsh cakes and homemade bread. Castles galore, the Brecon Beacons and Cardiff are all close – return to an acre of pretty garden with quirky summerhouse and sitting spots for views and sunshine.

A non-refundable deposit of 25% of the total price is charged on stays of 3 nights or more.

Mount Pleasant Farm

Wake to circling red kites with a breathtaking backdrop of the Black Mountain. Every room has wonderful views, and Sue and Nick are warm and delightful hosts. Food is a passion here and you'll enjoy homemade bread and jams, deep yellow eggs, organic veg and local lamb and pork; vegetarians are spoiled too – Sue is a brilliant cook. After dinner there's snooker, a log fire, a cosy sofa; then a seriously comfy bed in a room with a lovely country-house feel. There are excellent walks in the valley, fly fishing on the Towy, Llyn y Fan Fach in Brecon Beacons National Park; Aberglasney and the Botanic Gardens are nearby too.

Over 12s welcome.

Rooms	2 doubles, 1 twin/double: £85. 10% off if you pay in advance (non-refundable).
Meals	Pub 100 yds.
Closed	23 December to 31 January.

Rooms	1 twin/double; 1 twin/double, 1 twin sharing bath (let to same party only): £70-£75.
Meals	Dinner, 3 courses with wine, £20. Pub/restaurant 3 miles.
Closed	Christmas.

Ann Morgan
Gellihaf House,
Gellihaf,
Blackwood, NP12 2QE
Tel +44 (0)1443 268494
Email hello@gellihafhouse.com
Web www.gellihafhouse.com

Sue & Nick Thompson
Mount Pleasant Farm,
Llanwrda, SA19 8AN
Tel +44 (0)1550 777537
Email nick@rivarevival.co.uk

Carmarthenshire

The Glynhir Estate

This fine old house on a Huguenot estate stands on the western edge of the Black Mountain. Outside: a waterfall, a two-acre kitchen garden, a brigade of chickens, and peacocks that patrol the grounds with panache. Inside, the house has spurned the urge to take itself too seriously and remains decidedly lived in. Find William Morris wallpaper in the dining room, lemon trees in the conservatory and old cabinets stuffed with interesting things in the sitting room. Country-house bedrooms fit the mood perfectly: smart and comfortable with excellent bathrooms. You can ride, walk, fish or visit Aberglasney Garden – just ask Katy.

Rooms	3 doubles: £80.
	1 family room for 3
	(suitable for 2 adults and 1-2
	children under 12): £100.
	Singles £50.
Meals	Dinner from £19.50.
	Pubs/restaurants 2 miles.
Closed	November – March.

Katy Jenkins
The Glynhir Estate,
Glynhir Road, Llandybie,
Ammanford, SA18 2TD

Tel	+44 (0)1269 850438
Mobile	+44 (0)7810 864458
Email	enquiries@theglynhirestate.com
Web	www.theglynhirestate.com

Carmarthenshire

Sarnau Mansion

Listed and Georgian, this handsome house has 16 acres of grounds complete with pond, well-tended walled garden and woodland with nesting red kites. Bedrooms are calm and traditionally furnished with heritage colours, art poster prints and green views; big bathrooms have plenty of hot water. The oak-floored sitting room with leather Chesterfields has French windows leading onto the rhododendron lawn, the guest dining room has separate tables, and there's home cooking from Cynthia. A peaceful place from which to explore beaches, castles and more – 15 minutes from the National Botanic Garden of Wales.

Children over 5 welcome.

Rooms	2 doubles, 1 twin; 1 double with
	separate bath: £80-£95.
	Singles £50-£60.
Meals	Pub 1 mile.
Closed	Rarely.

Cynthia & David Fernihough
Sarnau Mansion,
Llysonnen Road, Bancyfelin,
Carmarthen, SA33 5DZ

Tel	+44 (0)1267 211404
Email	d.fernihough@btinternet.com
Web	www.sarnaumansion.co.uk

Broniwan

The Jacobs began farming organically here in the 70s and concentrate now on their kitchen garden – meals celebrate their success. Their cosy ivy-clad home is quietly, colourfully stylish, with books, watercolours and good local art; the attractive guest bedroom has a traditional Welsh bedspread and views to the Preseli hills. There are acres to roam and the meadow garden's pond brims with life. Carole is passionate about history and literature and can advise on days out: try the Museum of Quilts in Lampeter, or Aberglasney, an hour's drive. Do linger; this is such a rich spot.

Minimum stay: 2 nights.

Ffynnon Fendigaid

Arrive through rolling countryside – birdsong and breeze the only sound; within moments you will be sprawled on a leather sofa admiring modern art and wondering how a little bit of Milan arrived here along with Huw and homemade cake. A place to come and pootle, with no rush; you can stay all day to stroll the fern-fringed paths through the acres of wild garden to a lake and a grand bench, or opt for hearty walking. Your bed is big, the colours are soft, the bathrooms are spotless and the food is local – try all the Welsh cheeses. Wide beaches are close by, red kites and buzzards soar above you. Pulchritudinous.

Rooms	1 double: £80-£90. Singles £45.
Meals	Dinner £25-£30. BYO. Restaurants 7-8 miles.
Closed	Rarely.

Rooms	2 doubles: £78-£80. Singles £48-£50.
Meals	Dinner, 2-3 courses, £20-£22. Pub 1 mile.
Closed	Rarely.

Carole & Allen Jacobs
Broniwan,
Rhydlewis,
Llandysul, SA44 5PF
Tel +44 (0)1239 851261
Email broniwan@btinternet.com
Web www.broniwan.weebly.com

Huw Davies
Ffynnon Fendigaid,
Rhydlewis, Llandysul, SA44 5SR
Tel +44 (0)1239 851361
Mobile +44 (0)7974 135262
Email ffynnonf@btinternet.com
Web www.ffynnonf.co.uk

Conwy

Pengwern Country House (Snowdonia)

The steeply wooded Conwy valley snakes down to this stone and slate property set back from the road in Snowdonia National Park, and the walks are wonderful. Inside has an upbeat traditional feel: a large sitting room with tall bay windows and pictures by the Betws-y-Coed artists who once lived here. Settle with a book by the wood-burner; Gwawr and Ian are naturally friendly and treat guests as friends. Bedrooms have rough plastered walls, colourful fabrics and super bathrooms; one comes with a double-ended roll top tub and views of Lledr Valley. Breakfast on fruits, herb rösti, soda bread – superb.

Minimum stay: 2 nights.

Rooms	1 double, 1 twin/double, 1 four-poster: £72-£84. Singles from £62.
Meals	Packed lunch £5.50. Pubs/restaurants within 1.5 miles.
Closed	Christmas & New Year.

	Gwawr & Ian Mowatt
	Pengwern Country House ,
	Allt Dinas,
	Betws-y-Coed, LL24 0HF
Tel	+44 (0)1690 710480
Email	gwawr.pengwern@btopenworld.com
Web	www.snowdoniaaccommodation.co.uk

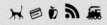

Entry 551   Map 7

Denbighshire

Plas Efenechtyd Cottage

Efenechtyd means 'place of the monks' but there's nothing spartan about Dave and Marilyn's handsome brick farmhouse. Breakfasts of local sausages, eggs from their hens, salmon fishcakes with mushrooms and homemade bread are served at a polished table in the dining room with exotic wall hangings from Vietnam and Laos. Light bedrooms have an uncluttered feel, excellent mattresses and good linen; bathrooms are warm as toast. In the pretty cottage garden: a summerhouse and Marilyn's beehive. Motor to Ruthin, with its windy streets and interesting shops, or strike out for Offa's Dyke with a packed lunch; this is stunning countryside.

Rooms	1 double, 1 twin/double: £75. Singles £55.
Meals	Packed lunch £6. Pub 1.6 miles.
Closed	Rarely.

	Dave Jones & Marilyn Jeffery
	Plas Efenechtyd Cottage,
	Efenechtyd, Ruthin, LL15 2LP
Tel	+44 (0)1824 704008
Mobile	+44 (0)7540 501009
Email	info@plas-efenechtyd-cottage.co.uk
Web	www.plas-efenechtyd-cottage.co.uk

Entry 552   Map 7

Plas Penucha

Swing back in time with polished parquet, tidy beams, a huge Elizabethan panelled lounge with books, leather sofas and open fire – a cosy spot for Nest's dogs and for tea in winter. Plas Penucha – 'the big house on the highest point in the parish' – has been in the family for 500 years. Airy, old-fashioned bedrooms have long views across the garden to Offa's Dyke and one has a shower in the corner. The L-shaped dining room has a genuine Arts & Crafts interior; outside, rhododendrons and a rock garden flourish. There are views to the Clywdian Hills and beyond is St Asaph, with the smallest medieval cathedral in the country.

Gladstone's Library

If this glorious, unusual, historic and stunning place fails you as a retreat, then look deep within yourself. You have 250,000 books, silence, space, convivial company if you need it, Theatre Clwyd and Chester but 15 minutes away. Eucharist is held every weekday, delicious local food is there for you in the bistro, an open fire and sofas in the Gladstone room. The staff are lovely, the mood sheer old-fashioned decency. It is a Roberts radio, rather than TV, place. Bedrooms are warm, simple and unpretentious. Come for as long as you need to recover from this mad world. It will, for all adults, feel like a privilege.

Reception 8.30am–5pm. Check in from 2pm, check out 10am; you are welcome to use the facilities and library once you have checked out. If arriving after 5pm please do let us know in advance.

Rooms	1 double, 1 twin: £76. Singles £38.
Meals	Dinner £19. Packed lunch £5. Pub/restaurant 2-3 miles.
Closed	Rarely.

Rooms	14 doubles, 3 twins: £90-£95. 7 singles: £63-£73. Hairdryers, Roberts Radio and Wi-Fi in all rooms.
Meals	Restaurant on site. Breakfast 8am–9am Mon–Fri; 8.30am–9.30am Sat & Sun. Lunch 12 noon–2pm. Dinner 6.45pm–7.15pm.
Closed	Christmas & New Year.

	Nest Price Plas Penucha, Pen y Cefn Road, Caerwys, Mold, CH7 5BH
Tel	+44 (0)1352 720210
Email	nest@plaspenucha.co.uk
Web	www.plaspenucha.co.uk

	Gladstone's Library Church Lane, Hawarden, Deeside, CH5 3DF
Tel	+44 (0)1244 532350
Email	enquiries@gladlib.org
Web	www.gladstoneslibrary.org/ accommodation/

Gwynedd

Y Goeden Eirin

A little gem tucked between the sea and the mountains, an education in Welsh culture, and a great place to explore wild Snowdonia, the Llyn peninsula and the dramatic Yr Eifl mountain. Inside presents a cosy picture: Welsh-language and English books share the shelves, paintings by contemporary Welsh artists enliven the walls, an arty 70s décor mingles with sturdy Welsh oak in the bedrooms – the one in the house the best – and all bathrooms are super. Wonderful food is served alongside the Bechstein in the beamed dining room – the welcoming, thoughtful Eluned has created an unusually delightful space.

Rooms	1 double, 2 twin/doubles (Sea and Mountain Rooms, shower only): £80-£90. Singles £60-£70.
Meals	Packed lunch £12. Pub/restaurant 0.75 miles.
Closed	Christmas, New Year & occasionally.

Eluned Rowlands
Y Goeden Eirin,
Dolydd, Caernarfon, LL54 7EF
Tel   +44 (0)1286 830942
Email   eluned.rowlands@tiscali.co.uk
Web   www.ygoedeneirin.co.uk

Entry 555   Map 6

Gwynedd

Coes Faen Lodge

Effortless simplicity is the key to this new spa B&B. A glass and rock entrance, a hallway suffused with light: this Victorian lodge on the edge of Mawddach Estuary has been stunningly, meticulously revived. Bedrooms are cocoons of sleek opulence, bathrooms are rich in slate and stone, and detailing is sublime: mood lighting, hands-free technology, pearlescent tiles that reflect the light. Choose a sauna smelling of cedar or a rooftop hot tub and terrace... Richard and Sara have Welsh roots and love both place and landscape. Acres of woodland garden await behind; breakfasts and dinners are original and exquisite.

Minimum stay: 2 nights at weekends.

Rooms	6 doubles: £115-£215.
Meals	Dinner from £35. Pubs/restaurants 0.5 miles.
Closed	Rarely.

Richard & Sara Parry-Jones
Coes Faen Lodge,
Coes Faen, Abermaw, LL42 1TE
Tel   +44 (0)1341 281632
Email   richard@coesfaen.com
Web   www.coesfaen.co.uk

Entry 556   Map 7

Gwynedd

The Slate Shed at Graig Wen

Sarah and conservationist John spent months travelling in a camper looking for their own special place and found this lovely old Welsh slate cutting mill… captivated by acres of wild woods and stunning views. You'll feel at ease as soon as you step into their eclectic modern home with its reclaimed slate and wood, cosy wood-burners, books, games, snug bedrooms (one downstairs) and superb bathrooms. Breakfast communally on local eggs and sausages, honey from the mountainside, homemade bread and granola. Hike or bike the Mawddach Trail, climb Cadair Idris, wonder at the views… and John's chocolate brownies.

Minimum stay: 2 nights at weekends & in high season. Children over 10 welcome.

Rooms	4 doubles, 1 twin/double: £80-£130. Singles £65.
Meals	Packed lunch £6.50. Pub 5 miles.
Closed	Rarely.

Sarah Heyworth
The Slate Shed at Graig Wen,
Arthog, LL39 1YP
Tel   +44 (0)1341 250482
Email hello@graigwen.co.uk
Web   www.slateshed.co.uk

Entry 557   Map 7

Monmouthshire

Myrtle Cottage

Boldly tackle the steep road up for a slice of heaven in Llandogo. You're in the heart of Ed and Tori's home, and along with little Elsie, George, Alicia and Amelia, they make terrific hosts. The sunny bedroom has French windows leading to the garden, and lovely wide views across the Wye Valley. Tori bakes fabulous breads, cakes and waffles and breakfasts in the family kitchen are scrumptious. Hike up and down the river, visit the pub at Brockweir, drop in for a beer at Ed's brewery – we recommend Humpty's Fuddle! On the first Saturday of the month you can enjoy a delicious stone-baked pizza at the brewery too.

Please note, the bendy road up the hill and the driveway farm track are steep, and may not be suitable for all vehicles, especially in winter!

Rooms	1 double sharing bath with family (extra bed for children available): £70. Singles £50.
Meals	Monthly pizza evenings at Brewery. Picnics & lunches £7.50-£25. Pubs/restaurants 3 miles.
Closed	Rarely.

Edward & Tori Biggs
Myrtle Cottage,
Llandogo,
Monmouth, NP25 4TP
Mobile +44 (0)7824 663550
Email   meadowfarm1@aol.com

Entry 558   Map 7

Monmouthshire

Upper Red House

Head down the lane into deepest Monmouthshire and the meadows, orchards and woodland of Teona's organic farm. There are six ponds and miles of bushy hedges; bees, ponies, peafowl and wild flowers flourish. The 17th-century house, restored from dereliction, has lovely views, flagstones and oak, limewashed walls and a magical feel. Up steep stairs are rustic bedrooms with beams, lots of books, no TV; the attic rooms get the best views of all. Bathrooms are simple, one has a huge old roll top tub. After a good vegetarian breakfast at the long kitchen table take a farm tour, explore Offa's Dyke or the Wye Valley – and enjoy the silence.

Children over 8 welcome.

Rooms	2 doubles: £80-£95.
	2 singles sharing bath with 1 double
	(let to same party only): £35-£45.
Meals	Vegetarian packed lunch £6.
	Pubs/restaurants 3.5 miles.
Closed	Rarely.

Teona Dorrien-Smith
Upper Red House,
Llanfihangel-Ystern-Llewern,
Monmouth, NP25 5HL
Tel   +44 (0)1600 780501
Email upperredhouse@mac.com
Web   www.upperredhouse.co.uk

Monmouthshire

Penpergwm Lodge

A rambling Edwardian house… Margot and Maud, resident pug and terrier, make a characterful welcoming party and you step into a warmly painted hall with old rugs on wooden boards. Simon and Catriona give you tea and biscuits in a sunny, lived-in sitting room: heaps of books, family bits and pieces, squashy sofa by the fire. Breakfast is served here, or round the long table in the dining room. Bedrooms are time-worn trad with embroidered covers and chintz; bathrooms are a skip across the landing. Enjoy the beautiful garden with parterre, potager, orchard and brick follies, bring a jumper in winter and don't mind the worn corners… a charming home.

Rooms	2 twins, each with separate bath: £75.
	Singles £45.
Meals	Pub 2 miles.
Closed	Rarely.

Catriona Boyle
Penpergwm Lodge,
Penpergwm,
Abergavenny, NP7 9AS
Tel   +44 (0)1873 840208
Email boyle@penpergwm.co.uk
Web   www.penplants.com

Pembrokeshire

Pembrokeshire Farm B&B

Down a beautiful lane flanked by moss-covered walls, two miles from Narberth, is an old fortified longhouse in 25 rolling acres – pristine, peaceful and cosy. Here live three dogs, three donkeys, cats, hens and friendly hosts Rayner and Carol. There's a real fire and books aplenty, equine paintings and fantastic art, and big gorgeous gardens with croquet, a lake and a boat to mess about in. The décor is traditional, the bed linen immaculate, the bathrooms are spanking new and the views to the Preseli Hills gorgeous. Narbeth's restaurants are good but Carol's cooking is fabulous.

Over 12s welcome. Pets by arrangement.

Rooms	1 double; 1 double with separate bath: £95-£100.
Meals	Dinner, 3 courses, from £30. Pubs/restaurants 2 miles.
Closed	Rarely.

Rayner & Carol Peett
Pembrokeshire Farm B&B,
Caermaenau Fawr,
Clynderwen, SA66 7HB
Tel   +44 (0)1834 860338
Mobile   +44 (0)7796 615332
Email   info@pembrokeshirefarmbandb.co.uk
Web   www.pembrokeshirefarmbandb.co.uk

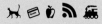

Entry 561   Map 6

Pembrokeshire

Cresselly House

Imagine staying at the Georgian mansion of an old country friend – that's what it's like to stay at Cresselly. Step into a sunny square hall with a sweeping stair and the ancestors on the walls. Beeswax and lavender scent the air, cosy bedrooms are as grandly traditional as can be, new bathrooms sparkle and views swoop over the park. For breakfast or dinner (if requested) you can seat yourself at the fine Georgian mahogany dining table, gleaming from many decades of polishing. The walking and riding are glorious, and there's impressive stabling for your horse: this is the heartland of the South Pembrokeshire Hunt.

Over 16s welcome.

Rooms	3 doubles, 1 twin: £120-£180.
Meals	Dinner, 2 courses, £25-£55. Pub 1 mile.
Closed	Rarely.

Hugh Harrison-Allen
Cresselly House,
Cresselly,
Kilgetty, SA68 0SP
Tel   +44 (0)1646 651992
Email   info@cresselly.com
Web   www.cresselly.com

Entry 562   Map 6

Pembrokeshire

Knowles Farm

The Cleddau estuary winds its way around this organic farm – its lush grasses feed the cows that produce milk for the renowned Rachel's yogurt. Your hosts love the land, are committed to its conservation and let you come and go as you please; picnic in the garden, wander the bluebell woods, discover a pond; dogs like it too. You have your own entrance to old-fashioned, lived-in pretty bedrooms with comfy beds, simple bathrooms, glorious views and an eclectic selection of books to browse. Breakfast and supper are fully organic or very local: delicious! If Gini is busy with the farm there are terrific river pubs that serve dinner.

Rooms	2 doubles; 1 twin with separate bath: £78-£95. Singles £50-£55.
Meals	Supper from £12. Dinner, 4 courses, £22, (not in school holidays). Packed lunch £6. Pub 1.5 miles, restaurant 3 miles.
Closed	Rarely.

Virginia Lort Phillips
Knowles Farm,
Lawrenny, SA68 0PX
Tel   +44 (0)1834 891221
Mobile +44 (0)7815 208772
Email   ginilp@lawrenny.org.uk
Web   www.lawrenny.org.uk

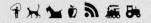

Entry 563   Map 6

Pembrokeshire

Awelon

Wonderful views of Manorbier beach from this whitewashed family house. Katherine's home has a relaxed, natural feel with Scandinavian furniture, wide French windows and plenty of books and games. She gives you cosy bedrooms with Welsh blankets, white linen and sparkling shower rooms; tea trays too with homemade cake. Breakfast is at a polished round table looking over the Pembrokeshire Coast Path: homemade muesli, award-winning bacon, vegetarian choices... most locally sourced and all delicious. Enjoy an evening drink on the terrace with the beautifully-designed garden beyond – then a stroll to the popular village pub for supper.

Rooms	1 double; 1 twin with separate bath/shower: £75-£85. Singles £45-£60.
Meals	Pubs/restaurants 5-minute walk.
Closed	November – February.

Katherine Henderson Bowen
Awelon,
Pembroke Road,
Manorbier, Tenby, SA70 7SX
Tel   +44 (0)1834 871587
Email   katherine@manorbierbedandbreakfast.co.uk
Web   www.manorbierbedandbreakfast.co.uk

Entry 564   Map 6

Pembrokeshire

Pembrokeshire

Penfro

This is fun – idiosyncratic and a tad theatrical, rather than conventional and uniformly stylish. The Lappins' home is an impressive Georgian affair, formerly a ballet school. Judith is warm and friendly; her taste – she's also a WW1 expert – is eclectic verging on the wacky and she minds that guests are comfortable and well-fed. You eat communally at the scrubbed table in the flagged Aga kitchen: tasty dinners, homemade jams and good coffee at breakfast. The garden is big and beautiful so enjoy its conversational terrace. And discuss which of the three very characterful bedrooms will suit you best, plumbing and all!

Minimum stay: 2 nights at weekends in summer and bank holidays.

Hayston

Bantams, guinea fowl and dogs wander around this rambling Pembrokeshire farmhouse. Nicky and Johnny's country house has an informal vibe; rooms have a comfortable, faded grandeur and the beautiful garden has a sunny terrace, formal pond, orchard and veg patch. Up a wide staircase to a pretty bedroom with leafy views; there's an extra room for friends or family too. Find a deep-red beamed dining room/library with books, vases of flowers and big log fire. Breakfast is a relaxed affair – tuck into just-laid eggs and local produce and take your time. Castles, surfing championships, Lily Ponds at Bosherston, glorious sandy beaches… wonderful.

Pets by prior arrangement.

Rooms	1 double; 1 double, 1 twin, both with separate bath: £75-£95. Singles £60-£85. Extra bed/sofabed available £10-£15 per person per night.
Meals	Packed lunch from £8. Owners can cater for gluten free diets at no extra cost. Pub 250 yds.
Closed	Rarely.

Rooms	1 twin/double with separate bath: £100. Extra room available. Singles £70.
Meals	Pubs/restaurants 3 miles. Simple suppers available if without transport.
Closed	Christmas.

Judith Lappin
Penfro,
111 Main Street,
Pembroke, SA71 4DB

Tel	+44 (0)1646 682753
Mobile	+44 (0)7763 856181
Email	info@penfro.co.uk
Web	www.penfro.co.uk

Nicola Rogers
Hayston,
Merrion,
Pembroke, SA71 5EA

Tel	+44 (0)1646 661462
Email	haystonhouse@btinternet.com
Web	www.haystonfarmhouse.co.uk

Entry 565   Map 6

Entry 566   Map 6

Pembrokeshire

Cefn-y-Dre Country House

Geoff and Gaye want your stay to go without a hitch, and they're proud of the rich history of their house. Solid, handsome and 500 years old, Cefn-y-Dre is on the fringe of the Pembrokeshire Coast National Park with views to the Preseli Hills. The sitting room is set aside for guests, notable for its striking red chairs used during Prince Charles' investiture in 1969 – quite a talking point! Geoff is a great cook who takes pleasure in using local produce and home-grown veg from the large garden; not so long ago he trained at Ballymaloe. St David's, with its ancient cathedral, is nearby, as are some of Britain's finest beaches.

Rooms	1 double, 1 twin/double; 1 double with separate bath/shower: £89-£109. Singles £70-£79.
Meals	Dinner, 3 courses, £26.50. Pubs/restaurants 2 miles.
Closed	Rarely.

Gaye Williams & Geoff Stickler
Cefn-y-Dre Country House,
Fishguard, SA65 9QS
Tel +44 (0)1348 875663
Email welcome@cefnydre.co.uk
Web www.cefnydre.co.uk

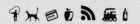

Entry 567 Map 6

Pembrokeshire

Pentower

Curl up with a cat and watch the ferries – or sometimes a porpoise – coasting to Ireland; French windows open onto the terrace and a glorious vista. Mary and Tony are warm and interesting hosts; their turreted 1898 house has an easy-going atmosphere, quarry tiled floors, decorative fireplaces and an impressive staircase. Spotless bedrooms are light and airy, with large showers; the Tower Room has the views. Wake for a very good full English (or Welsh) breakfast in the tiled dining/sitting room – tuck in while admiring the panoramic view over a bay full of boats. Fishguard is a short stroll, and the stunning coastal path is nearby.

Rooms	1 double, 1 twin/double: £85-£90. Singles £55.
Meals	Packed lunch £5. Pubs/restaurants 500 yds.
Closed	Occasionally.

**Tony Jacobs
& Mary Geraldine Casey**
Pentower,
Tower Hill, Fishguard, SA65 9LA
Tel +44 (0)1348 874462
Email sales@pentower.co.uk
Web www.pentower.co.uk

Entry 568 Map 6

Pembrokeshire

Argoed

Steeped in local history, 1600s Argoed is Daniel's family home. Pictures of changes over the years cover the walls, and he has stories galore about this fascinating house. He and Jemma are relaxed and generous – tea and cake will be waiting for you; continental breakfasts are organic and hearty. The big bedroom has calm natural colours; goose down pillows and Welsh blankets keep you snug; your sitting room has vintage wallpapers, wood-burner, comfy red sofas and views across wildflower meadows. Take a boat trip around Ramsey Island, visit St Davids Cathedral and great beaches; Newport is crammed with independent shops and good pubs.

Children under 3 welcome.

Rooms	1 double with separate bathroom: £90.
Meals	Continental breakfast. Pubs/restaurants 1.5 miles.
Closed	Occasionally.

	Daniel & Jemma Slade-Davies
	Argoed,
	Newport, SA41 3XG
Tel	+44 (0)1239 820768
Email	daniel_davies@icloud.com
Web	www.argoed.info

Entry 569   Map 6

Pembrokeshire

The Old Vicarage

A breath of fresh air close to the beautiful Pembrokeshire Coastal Path. Energetic young owners have completely redecorated their new home and it feels bright, uncluttered, easy-going. Welsh blankets, Edwardian tiling, glass and fireplaces blend their charm with stripped boards, simple blinds, painted and bistro-style furniture. Chalkboards tell you what's for breakfast, and supper – Meg's a good cook and sources as locally as possible. Beds are wide and deep, views are peacefully green. Walk to Newport or St Dogmaels, catch the Poppit Rocket back and watch the sun set over the distant sea. The old vicar would surely approve!

Rooms	4 doubles: £85. Singles £75. Extra bed/sofabed available £25 per person per night.
Meals	Dinner £10-£20. Pubs/restaurants 3.5 miles.
Closed	Rarely.

	Megan van Soest
	The Old Vicarage,
	Moylegrove, Cardigan, SA43 3BN
Tel	+44 (0)1239 881711
Email	stay@theoldvicbedandbreakfast.co.uk
Web	www.oldvicaragemoylegrove.co.uk

Entry 570   Map 6

Powys

Ty'r Chanter

Warmth, colour, children and activity: this house is huge fun. Tiggy welcomes you like family; help collect eggs, feed the lambs, drop your shoes by the fire. The farmhouse and barn are stylishly relaxed; deep sofas, tartan throws, heaps of books, long convivial table; views to the Brecon Beacons and Black Mountains are inspiring. Bedrooms are soft, simple sanctuaries with Jo Malone bathroom treats. The children's room zings with murals; toys, kids' sitting room, sandpit – it's child heaven. Walk, fish, canoe, book-browse in Hay or stroll the estate. Homemade cakes and whisky to help yourself to: fine hospitality and Tiggy is wonderful.

Powys

The Old Store House

Unbend here with books, chattering birds, and charming Peter. This is an unconventional, untidy B&B and won't suit the uptight (or anyone who hates clutter and cobwebs), but curious souls will adore the amiable chaos and deep generosity. Downstairs are a sunny, ramshackle, conservatory overlooking the garden and canal, and an equally messy sitting room with a wood-burner, sofas and a piano –- no TV. Bedrooms are large and cosy, with more books, soft goose down, armchairs and bathrooms with views. Breakfast is hearty, perhaps eaten with chickens clucking at your feet. Walk into the hills from the back door.

Rooms	3 doubles: £100.
	1 twin (children's room with separate
	bath/shower): £20 per child.
	Singles £55. Children £20.
Meals	Packed lunch £8.
	Pub 1 mile.
Closed	Christmas.

Rooms	3 doubles, 1 twin: £80.
	Singles £40.
Meals	Packed lunch £4.
	Pub/restaurant 0.75 miles.
Closed	Rarely.

Tiggy Pettifer
Ty'r Chanter,
Gliffaes, Crickhowell, NP8 1RL
Tel   +44 (0)1874 731144
Mobile   +44 (0)7802 387004
Email   tiggy@tyrchanter.com
Web   www.tyrchanter.com

Peter Evans
The Old Store House,
Llanfrynach,
Brecon, LD3 7LJ
Tel   +44 (0)1874 665499
Email   oldstorehouse@btconnect.com
Web   www.theoldstorehouse.co.uk

Entry 571   Map 7

Entry 572   Map 7

Ty Newydd

They live on the canal and own a canoe: hire it for the day and pootle down to the pub, or walk your socks off in the Brecon Beacons. Friendly, generous Rachel and Sid swapped London for Llanfrynach and have breathed new life into the old farmhouse and outbuildings. Bedrooms are ultra comfy (those at the top with vaulted beams), bathrooms are spotless, views are gorgeous. The Taff Trail meets the tow path at the bottom of the garden, there's a tip-top boot dryer for when you get back, and you wake to feasts of local and Fair Trade produce, brought to small tables with a lovely big smile.

Minimum stay: 2 nights (Fri-Sun in high season).

Hafod Y Garreg

A unique opportunity to stay in the oldest house in Wales — a fascinating, 1402 cruck-framed hall house, built for Henry IV as a hunting lodge. Informal Annie and John have filled it with a charming mix of Venetian mirrors, Indian rugs, pewter plates, rich fabrics and oak pieces. Dine by candlelight in the romantic dining room — all sorts of delicious dishes; tuck into a big breakfast in the sweet conservatory. Bedrooms are luxuriously comfortable with embroidered linen, quirky lamps, nifty bathrooms. Reach this relaxed retreat by a bumpy track up across gated fields crowded with chickens, cats… a peaceful, special place.

Rooms	3 doubles, 1 twin/double: £75. Singles £55. Extra bed/sofabed available £15 per person per night.
Meals	Pubs/restaurants 2 miles.
Closed	Rarely.

Rooms	2 doubles: £92. Singles £90.
Meals	Dinner, 3 courses, £27. BYO. Pubs/restaurants 2.5 miles.
Closed	Christmas.

Rachel Griffiths
Ty Newydd,
Llanfrynach,
Brecon, LD3 7LJ
Tel   +44 (0)1874 665797
Email   info@tynewyddholidays.com
Web   www.tynewyddholidays.com

Annie & John McKay
Hafod Y Garreg,
Erwood,
Builth Wells, LD2 3TQ
Tel   +44 (0)1982 560400
Email   john-annie@hafod-y.wanadoo.co.uk
Web   www.hafodygarreg.co.uk

Powys

Rhedyn

Come here if you need to remember how to relax. Such an unassuming, little place, but with real character and soul: great comfort too. Find exposed walls in the bedrooms, funky lighting, pocket sprung mattresses, lovely books to read, and calm colours; bathrooms are modern and delightfully quirky. But the real stars of this show are Muiread and Ciaran: warm, enthusiastic and engaging, with a passion for good local food and a desire for more self-sufficiency – pigs and bees are planned next. This is a totally tranquil place, with agreeable walks through the Irfon valley, and bog snorkelling too!

Rooms	3 doubles: £95.
	Singles £85.
Meals	Dinner, 3 courses, £28.
	Packed lunch £7.50.
	Pub/restaurant 1 mile.
Closed	Rarely.

Muiread & Ciaran O'Connell
Rhedyn,
Cilmery,
Builth Wells, LD2 3LH

Tel	+44 (0)1982 551944
Email	info@rhedynguesthouse.co.uk
Web	www.rhedynguesthouse.co.uk

Entry 575   Map 7

Powys

The Yat

Come for stunning scenery and a house full of colour. Listed, 15th-century and once the home of the wicked squire Bevan, its ancient flags, beams and spirit remain; charming artist Krystyna has restored and reused, designed stained glass and nurtured beautiful things in every corner. Bedrooms are quaint, bathrooms simple with special touches (white robes, good soaps) and there's space to relax and roam: sitting room, conservatory, snug library with games. Food is almost all organic, breakfasts and suppers scrumptious and local. Krystyna and Derek's garden is wonderful too – a happy mix of formal and wild – and you'll leave this home feeling restored.

Rooms	1 double, 1 twin/double: £85.
Meals	Dinner, 3 courses, £45.
	Pubs/restaurants 4 miles.
Closed	Rarely.

Krystyna Zaremba
The Yat,
Glascwm,
Llandrindod Wells, LD1 5SE

Tel	+44 (0)1982 570339
Email	krystyna.zaremba@theyat.net
Web	www.theyat.net

Entry 576   Map 7

Powys

Powys

The Old Vicarage

A wide hall, deep window sills and expanses of glass have created a light and appealing home. On the edge of the hamlet, this Arts and Crafts house has spectacular views. Pat serves afternoon tea when you arrive, and breakfast is in a snug spot by the wood-burner. Bedrooms are traditional, big and blessed with homemade biscuits, tea trays and flowers; both have views across gardens, woodland and paddocks – there are acres to explore. The veg patch provides for dinner and you can enjoy a sunset drink in the walled garden. Walks are wonderful – Offa's Dyke footpath is close by – and the Hay-on-Wye festival is a 30-minute drive.

The Farm

Lose yourself in the wildlife, from a warm-hearted Welsh Marches B&B. There are just five sheep remaining now (all pets!) and your hosts have hearts of gold. Find fresh flowers on the Welsh dresser, a big dining table with a lovely garden view, breakfasts locally sourced and marmalades, jams and bread homemade. (And special diets easily catered for.) Overlooking the garden – yours to enjoy – are big bedrooms with TVs, clock-radios, tea and coffee making facilities and WiFi; one is on the ground floor in an extension, ideal for the less sprightly. Montgomery and Bishop's Castle, lovely little towns, are a must-see.

Rooms	1 double; 1 twin with separate bath: £90-£105. Singles £55-£65.
Meals	Dinner, 3 course set menu, £28. BYO. Please inform us of any special dietary requirements. Packed lunches available by request. Pub 3 miles.
Closed	Rarely.

Rooms	1 double, 2 twin/doubles: £85-£95. Singles £55.
Meals	Dinner from £25. Pubs/restaurants 2 miles.
Closed	Rarely.

	Patricia Birch The Old Vicarage, Evancoyd, Presteigne, LD8 2PA
Tel	+44 (0)1547 560951
Mobile	+44 (0)7903 859012
Email	pat.birch38@gmail.com
Web	www.oldvicaragebandb-welshborder.co.uk

	Sandra & Alan Jones The Farm, Snead, Montgomery, SY15 6EB
Tel	+44 (0)1588 620281
Email	asj.farmsnead@btconnect.com
Web	www.thefarmsnead.co.uk

Entry 577   Map 7

Entry 578   Map 7

Swansea

Blas Gwyr

Llangennith was once a well-kept secret – now walkers, riders, surfers and beach bunnies of all ages flock. Close to the bustling bay is an extended 1700s cottage with a youthful facelift. All is simple but stylish: bedrooms (two overlooking the road) are modern and matching; bathrooms and wet rooms come with warm floors and fluffy towels. Everything from the bedspread to the breakfast is local: make sure you try the laverbread. After a day at sea, fling wet gear in the drying room and linger over a coffee in the courtyard, or walk to the pub for a sun-kissed pint. Laid-back bliss.

Rooms	1 double, 1 double with sofabed, 1 twin/double, 1 suite for 2-4: £115-£125. Children from £15.
Meals	Packed lunch available. Dinner £27.50-£30 (selected weekends). Pub 150 yds.
Closed	Rarely.

Dafydd James
Blas Gwyr,
Plenty Farm, Llangennith, SA3 1HU
Tel   +44 (0)1792 386472
Mobile   +44 (0)7974 981156
Email   info@blasgwyr.co.uk
Web   www.blasgwyr.co.uk

🚶 🍴 📖 🍎 📶

Entry 579   Map 2

Wrexham

Worthenbury Manor

Welcome to one half of a big country house on the border of Wales and Shropshire. Congenial, generous Ian and Elizabeth look after you wonderfully well. The guest sitting room is warmed by a log fire in winter; the dining room has listed Jacobean panelling. Choose between two comfortable bedrooms, one decorated in Georgian style, one in Jacobean, both with rich drapes, chandeliers, fresh coffee and antique four-posters; luxurious bathrooms have baths big enough for two. Breakfast on the best of local and home produce. There's a pretty wildlife friendly garden to enjoy, the Welsh Marches to explore; Powis Castle and Erddig are nearby.

Rooms	1 four-poster; 1 four-poster with separate bath: £80-£100. Singles £50-£65. Extra bed/sofabed available £20-£30 per person per night.
Meals	Dinner, 3 courses, £30. Supper, 2 courses, £20. BYO. Pub/restaurant 5 miles.
Closed	19 December to 2 January.

Elizabeth & Ian Taylor
Worthenbury Manor,
Worthenbury, LL13 0AW
Tel   +44 (0)1948 770342
Email   enquiries@worthenburymanor.co.uk
Web   www.worthenburymanor.co.uk

🍴 📖 🍎 📶 🚂 🚲

Entry 580   Map 7

Quick reference indices

Wheelchair-accessible
At least one bedroom & bathroom accessible for wheelchair users. Phone for details.

Children of all ages welcome
These owners have told us that they welcome children of all ages. Please note cots and highchairs may not necessarily be available.

Scotland

Wales

Quick reference indices

Quick reference indices

Credit cards accepted
These owners have told us
that they accept credit cards,
most commonly Visa and
MasterCard.

Quick reference indices

Vegetarian meals
These owners provide vegetarian meals on request.

Scotland

Wales

Pets welcome

Please let the owner know if
you want to bring pets.

England

Quick reference indices

Alastair Sawday has been publishing books for over 20 years, finding Special Places to Stay in Britain and abroad. All our properties are inspected by us and are chosen for their charm and individuality. And there are many more to explore on our perennially popular website: www.sawdays.co.uk. You can buy any of our books at a reader discount of 25%* on the RRP.

List of titles:	RRP	Discount price
British Bed & Breakfast	£15.99	£11.99
British Hotels and Inns	£15.99	£11.99
Pubs & Inns of England & Wales	£15.99	£11.99
Dog-friendly Breaks in Britain	£14.99	£11.24
French Bed & Breakfast	£15.99	£11.99
French Châteaux & Hotels	£15.99	£11.99
Italy	£15.99	£11.99

*postage and packaging is added to each order

How to order:
You can order online at: www.sawdays.co.uk/bookshop/
or call: **+44 (0)117 204 7810**

Photo: Upper Buckton, entry 342

Photo: Waterlock House, entry 225

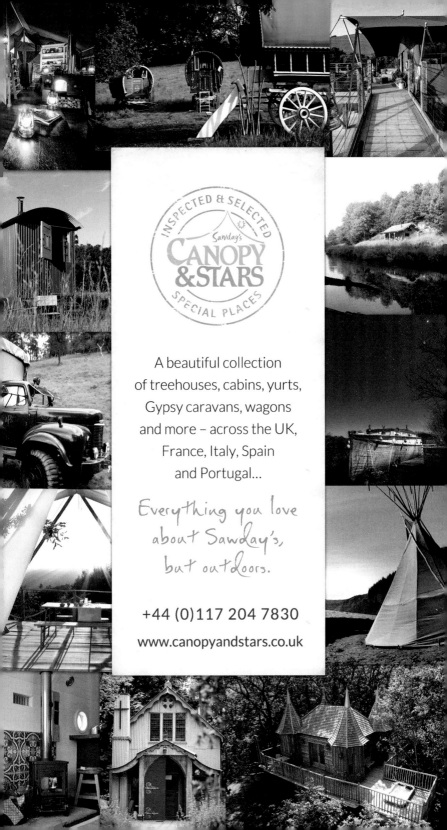

Photo above: 10 London Street, entry 508
Photo overleaf: Uplands House, entry 313

WHY BECOME A MEMBER?

Becoming a part of our 'family' of Special Places is like being awarded a Michelin star. Our stamp of approval will tell guests that you offer a truly special experience and you will benefit from our experience, reputation and support.

A CURATED COLLECTION

Our site presents a relatively small and careful selection of Special Places which helps us to stand out like a brilliantly shining beacon.

INSPECT AND RE-INSPECT

Our inspectors have an eagle-eye for the special, but absolutely no check-lists. They visit every member, see every bedroom and bathroom and, on the lucky days, eat the food.

QUALITY, NOT QUANTITY

We don't pretend (or want) to be in the same business as the sites that handle zillions of bookings a day. Using our name ensures that you attract the right kind of guests for you.

VARIETY

From country-house hotels to city pads and funky fincas to blissful B&Bs, we genuinely delight in the individuality of our Special Places.

LOYALTY

Nearly half of our members have been with us for five years or more. We must be doing something right!

GET IN TOUCH WITH OUR MEMBERSHIP TEAM...

+44 (0)117 204 7810
members@sawdays.co.uk

...OR APPLY ONLINE

sawdays.co.uk/joinus

The friendly crew

Join us

TIME AWAY IS FAR TOO PRECIOUS TO SPEND IN THE WRONG PLACE. THAT'S WHY, BACK IN 1994, WE STARTED SAWDAY'S.

nd still
:table,
stay.

ALASTAIR & TOBY SAWDAY

"Trustworthy, friendly and helpful – with a reputation for offering wonderful places and discerning visitors."

JULIA NAISMITH, HOLLYTREE COTTAGE

"Sawday's. Is there any other?"

SONIA HODGSON, HORRY MILL

1 Powys

Powys

Ty Newydd

2 They live on the canal and own a canoe: hire it for the day and pootle down to the pub, or walk your socks off in the Brecon Beacons. Friendly, generous Rachel and Sid swapped London for Llanfrynach and have breathed new life into the old farmhouse and outbuildings. Bedrooms are ultra comfy (those at the top with vaulted beams), bathrooms are spotless, views are gorgeous. The Taff Trail meets the tow path at the bottom of the garden, there's a tip-top boot dryer for when you get back, and you wake to feasts of local and Fair Trade produce, brought to small tables with a lovely big smile.

Minimum stay: 2 nights (Fri-Sun in high season).

Hafod Y Garreg

A unique opportunity to stay in the oldest house in Wales — a fascinating, 1402 cruck-framed hall house, built for Henry IV as a hunting lodge. Informal Annie and John have filled it with a charming mix of Venetian mirrors, Indian rugs, pewter plates, rich fabrics and oak pieces. Dine by candlelight in the romantic dining room — all sorts of delicious dishes; tuck into a big breakfast in the sweet conservatory. Bedrooms are luxuriously comfortable with embroidered linen, quirky lamps, nifty bathrooms. Reach this relaxed retreat by a bumpy track up across gated fields crowded with chickens, cats… a peaceful, special place.

3 Rooms	3 doubles, 1 twin/double: £75. Singles £55. Extra bed/sofabed available £15 per person per night.	Rooms	2 doubles: £92. Singles £90.
4 Meals	Pubs/restaurants 2 miles.	Meals	Dinner, 3 courses, £27. BYO. Pubs/restaurants 2.5 miles.
5 Closed	Rarely.	Closed	Christmas.

Rachel Griffiths
Ty Newydd,
Llanfrynach,
Brecon, LD3 7LJ
Tel   +44 (0)1874 665797
Email   info@tynewyddholidays.com
Web   www.tynewyddholidays.com

Annie & John McKay
Hafod Y Garreg,
Erwood,
Builth Wells, LD2 3TQ
Tel   +44 (0)1982 560400
Email   john-annie@hafod-y.wanadoo.co.uk
Web   www.hafodygarreg.co.uk

6

7 Entry 573   Map 7

Entry 574   Map 7